Angel Sanctuary

story and art by Kaori Yuki

vol.7

Angel Sanctuary

Vol. 7
Shôjo Edition

STORY AND ART BY KAORI YUKI

Translation/Alexis Kirsch
English Adaptation/Matt Segale
Touch-up & Lettering/James Hudnall
Cover, Graphics & Design/Izumi Evers
Editor/Pancha Diaz

Managing Editor/Annette Roman
Director of Production/Noboru Watanabe
Editorial Director/Alvin Lu
Sr. Director of Acquisitions/Rika Inouye
Vice President of Sales & Marketing/Liza Coppola
Executive Vice President/Hyoe Narita
Publisher/Seiji Horibuchi

Tenshi Kinryou Ku by Kaori Yuki

Printed in Canada.

Published by VIZ, LLC
P.O. Box 77010
San Francisco, CA 94107

Shôjo Edition
10 9 8 7 6 5 4 3 2 1
First printing, March 2005

www.viz.com store.viz.com

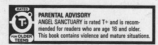

Angel Sanctuary

story and art by **Kaori Yuki**   vol.7

The Story Thus Far

High school boy Setsuna Mudo's life is hellish. He's always been a troublemaker, but his worst sin was falling incestuously in love with his beautiful sister Sara. However, his troubles are preordained—he is the reincarnation of the Lady Alexiel, an angel who rebelled against Heaven and led the demons of Hell in a revolt. Her punishment was to be reborn into tragic life after tragic life. This time, her life is as Setsuna.

Setsuna has only seven days to find his sister Sara in Hell, or his body left behind on Earth will die. However, Sara has gone on to heaven and Setsuna is still in Hell. He learns from the angel Uriel that six days have already passed on Earth. But Uriel does not explain that time runs more slowly in Hell, and that Setsuna actually has less than one day to escape. Enra-ô, the administrator of the Pit where souls await judgment, is the only one who can create an exit from Hell. When Setsuna and his guide Kato get there, Enra-ô tells them that Setsuna's body is already dead.

Meanwhile in Heaven, assassins attempt to kill Rosiel, but a double is murdered instead. Dobiel injects a virus into Rosiel, who turns out to be immune, and Dobiel confesses that Sevothtarte ordered Rosiel's murder.

Contents

THERE ARE SEVEN LAYERS TO THE HOUSE OF HEAVEN AND SEVEN LAYERS TO THE PALACE OF DARKNESS. ABOVE ASSIAH THE EARTH ARE SEVEN LAYERS OF A SPHERE CALLED TENKAI OR SHIKOUTEN, THE HEAVENS WHERE THE SHINING ANGELS LIVE. AT THE TOP IS THE TALL TOWER ETENAMENKI, WHERE A CREATOR CALLED GOD LIVES. THE SEVEN HEAVENS ARE CONNECTED TO THE ADJACENT LANDS BY HOOKS, AND MAINTAIN A PERILOUS BALANCE.

THE SEVEN LAYERS OF LAND THAT LIE BENEATH THE EARTH ARE CALLED HELL, HOME TO THE ANGELS OF DARKNESS. SHEOL IS THE LOWEST LEVEL, WHERE THE RULER OF DARKNESS SITS ON THE THROWN IN HIS HUGE PALACE. THIS RULER IS SAID TO BE LUCIFER

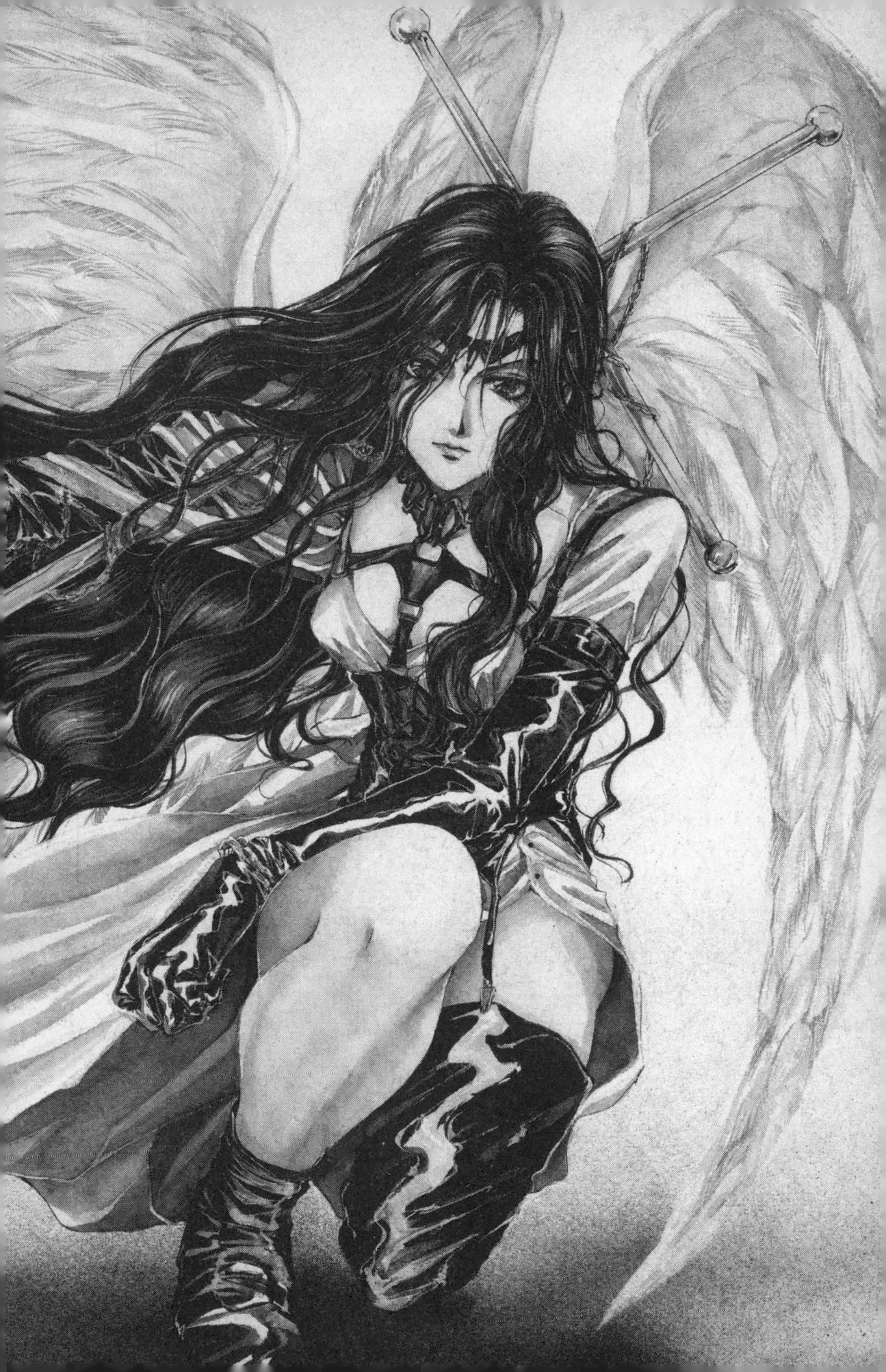

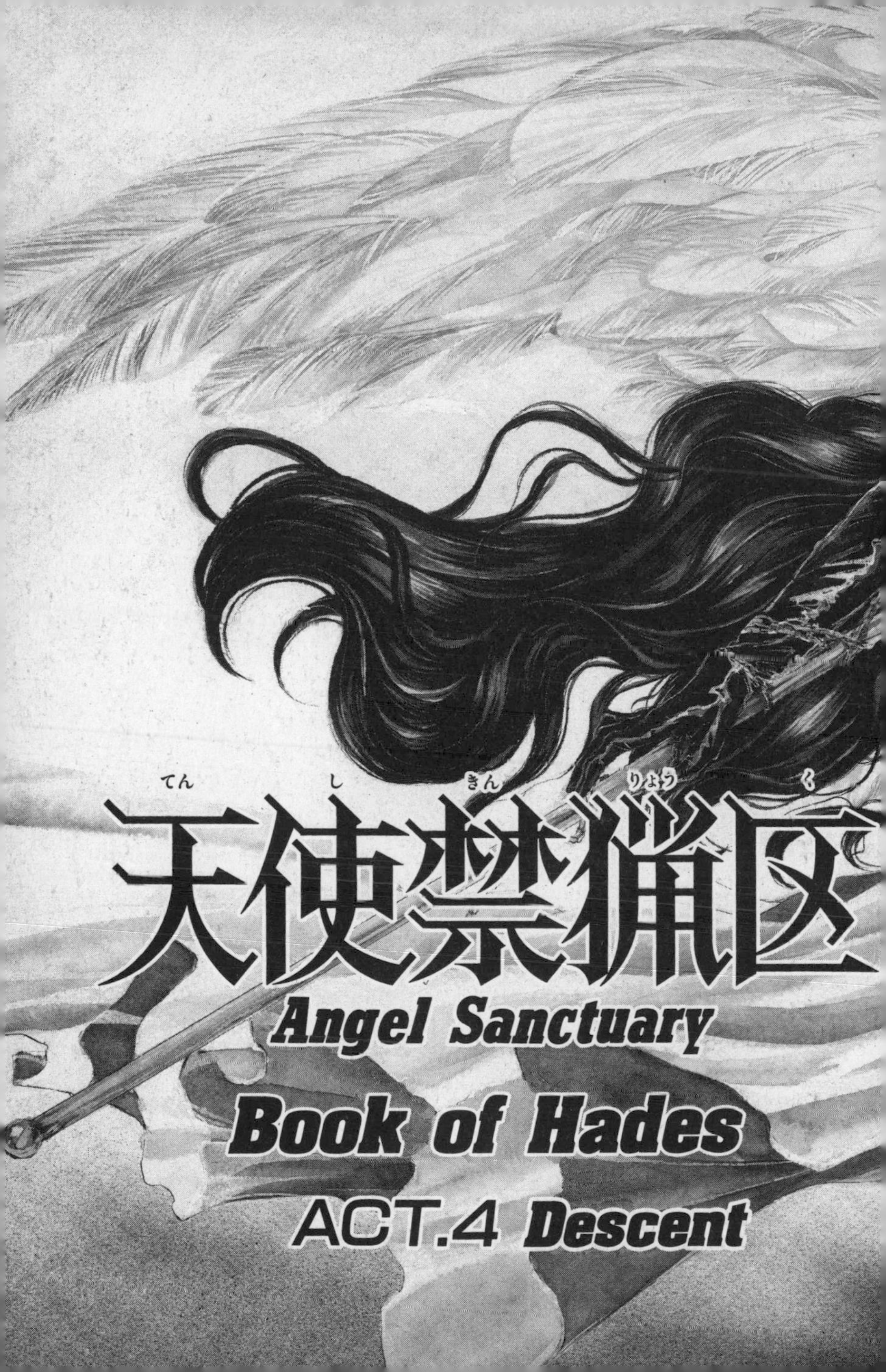
天使禁猟区（てんしきんりょうく）
Angel Sanctuary
Book of Hades
ACT.4 Descent

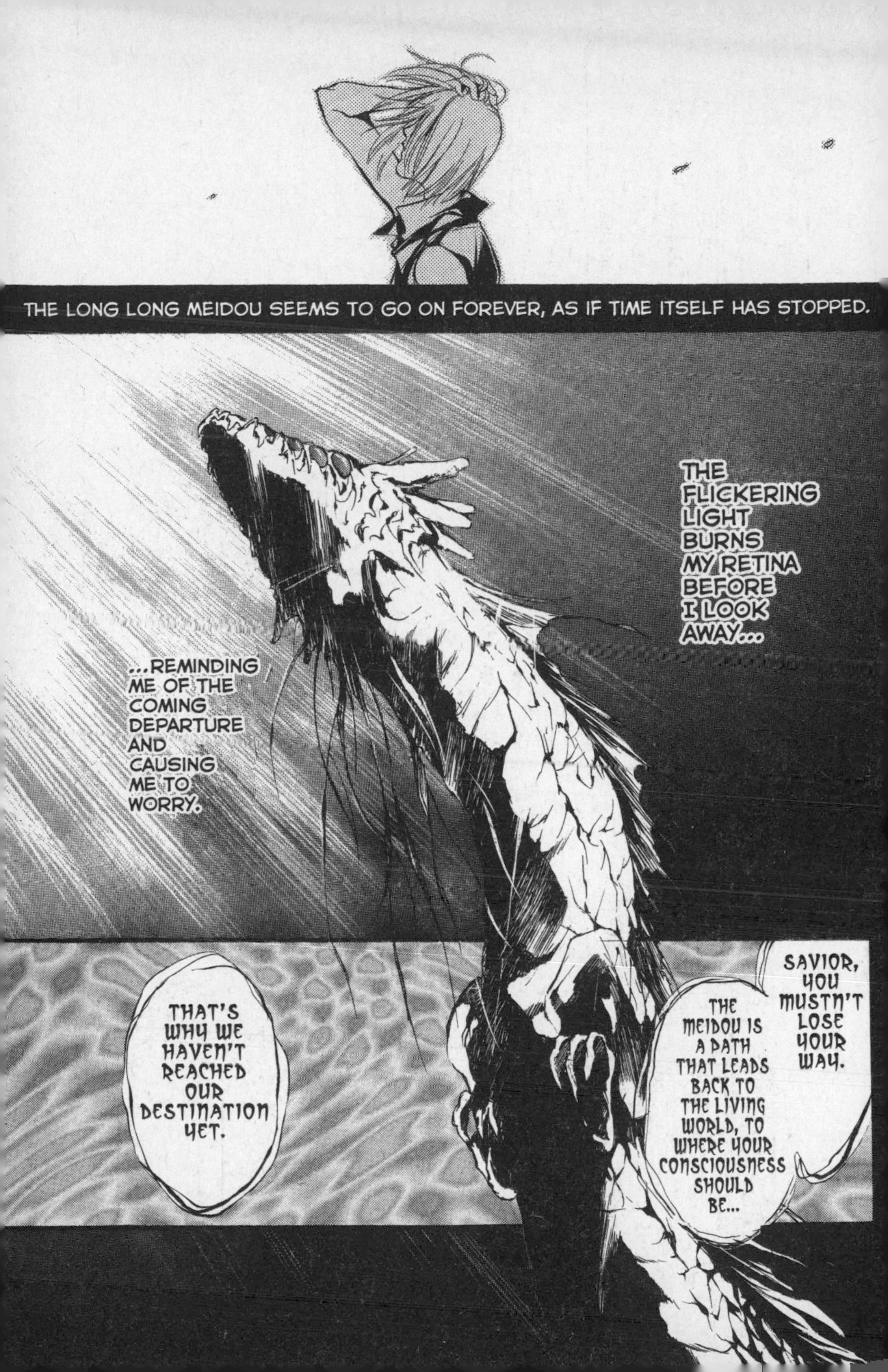
THE LONG LONG MEIDOU SEEMS TO GO ON FOREVER, AS IF TIME ITSELF HAS STOPPED.
THE FLICKERING LIGHT BURNS MY RETINA BEFORE I LOOK AWAY...
...REMINDING ME OF THE COMING DEPARTURE AND CAUSING ME TO WORRY.
SAVIOR, YOU MUSTN'T LOSE YOUR WAY.
THE MEIDOU IS A PATH THAT LEADS BACK TO THE LIVING WORLD, TO WHERE YOUR CONSCIOUSNESS SHOULD BE...
THAT'S WHY WE HAVEN'T REACHED OUR DESTINATION YET.

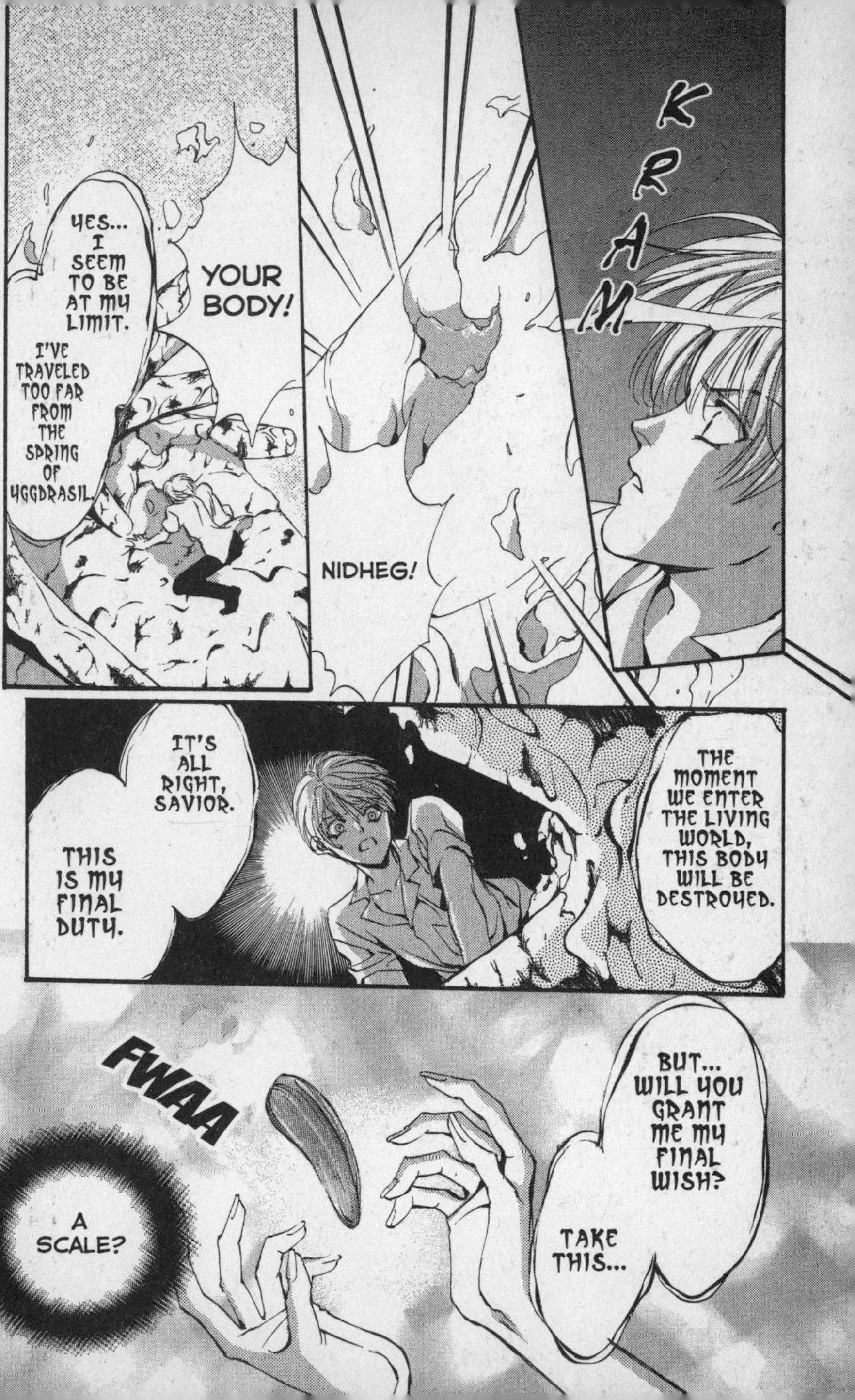
KRAM
NIDHEG!
YOUR BODY!
YES... I SEEM TO BE AT MY LIMIT.
I'VE TRAVELED TOO FAR FROM THE SPRING OF YGGDRASIL.
IT'S ALL RIGHT, SAVIOR.
THE MOMENT WE ENTER THE LIVING WORLD, THIS BODY WILL BE DESTROYED.
THIS IS MY FINAL DUTY.
BUT... WILL YOU GRANT ME MY FINAL WISH?
TAKE THIS...
FWAA
A SCALE?

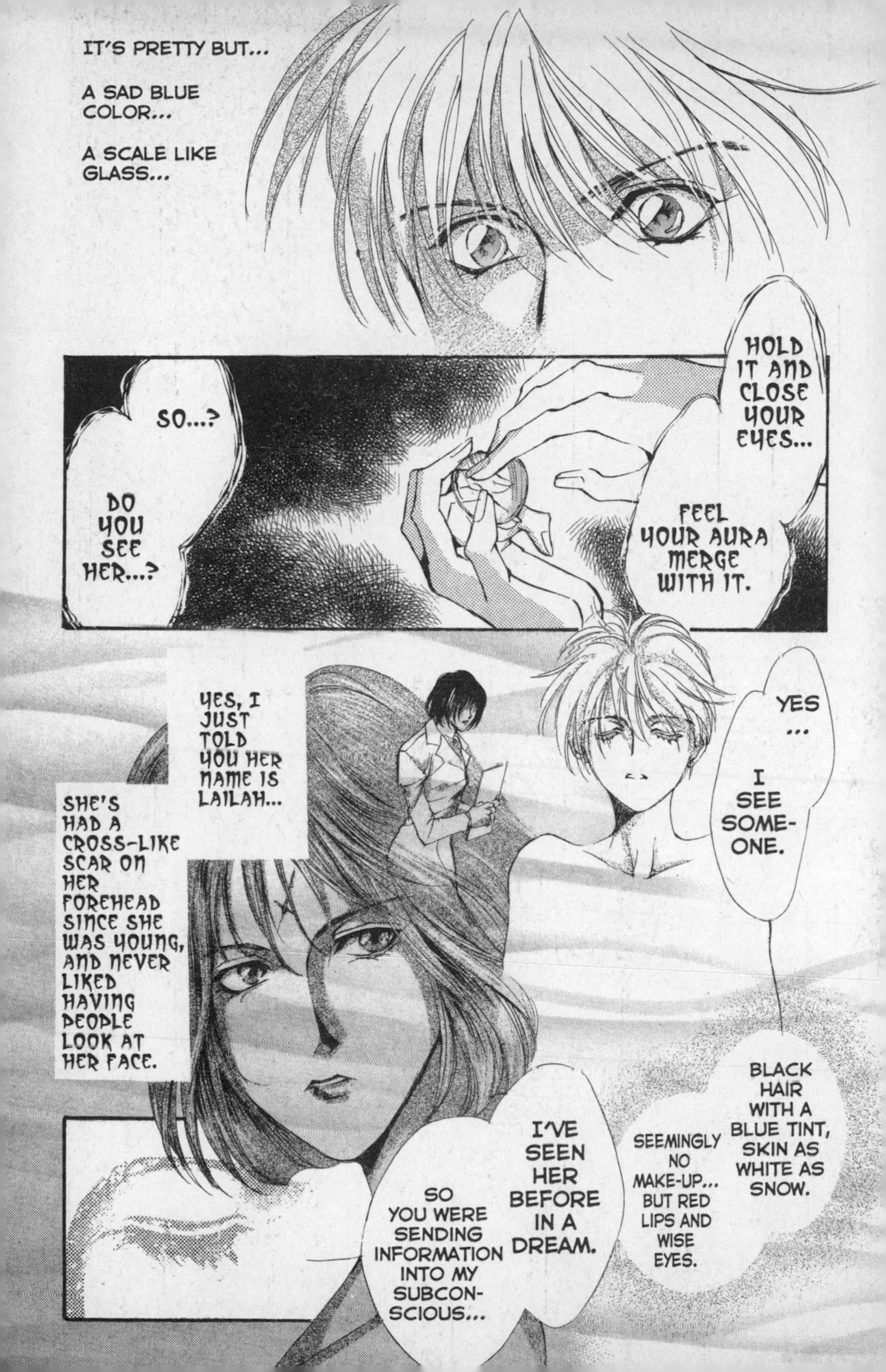
IT'S PRETTY BUT...
A SAD BLUE COLOR...
A SCALE LIKE GLASS...
HOLD IT AND CLOSE YOUR EYES...
FEEL YOUR AURA MERGE WITH IT.
SO...?
DO YOU SEE HER...?
YES ...
I SEE SOME-ONE.
YES, I JUST TOLD YOU HER NAME IS LAILAH...
SHE'S HAD A CROSS-LIKE SCAR ON HER FOREHEAD SINCE SHE WAS YOUNG, AND NEVER LIKED HAVING PEOPLE LOOK AT HER FACE.
BLACK HAIR WITH A BLUE TINT, SKIN AS WHITE AS SNOW.
SEEMINGLY NO MAKE-UP... BUT RED LIPS AND WISE EYES.
I'VE SEEN HER BEFORE IN A DREAM.
SO YOU WERE SENDING INFORMATION INTO MY SUBCON-SCIOUS...

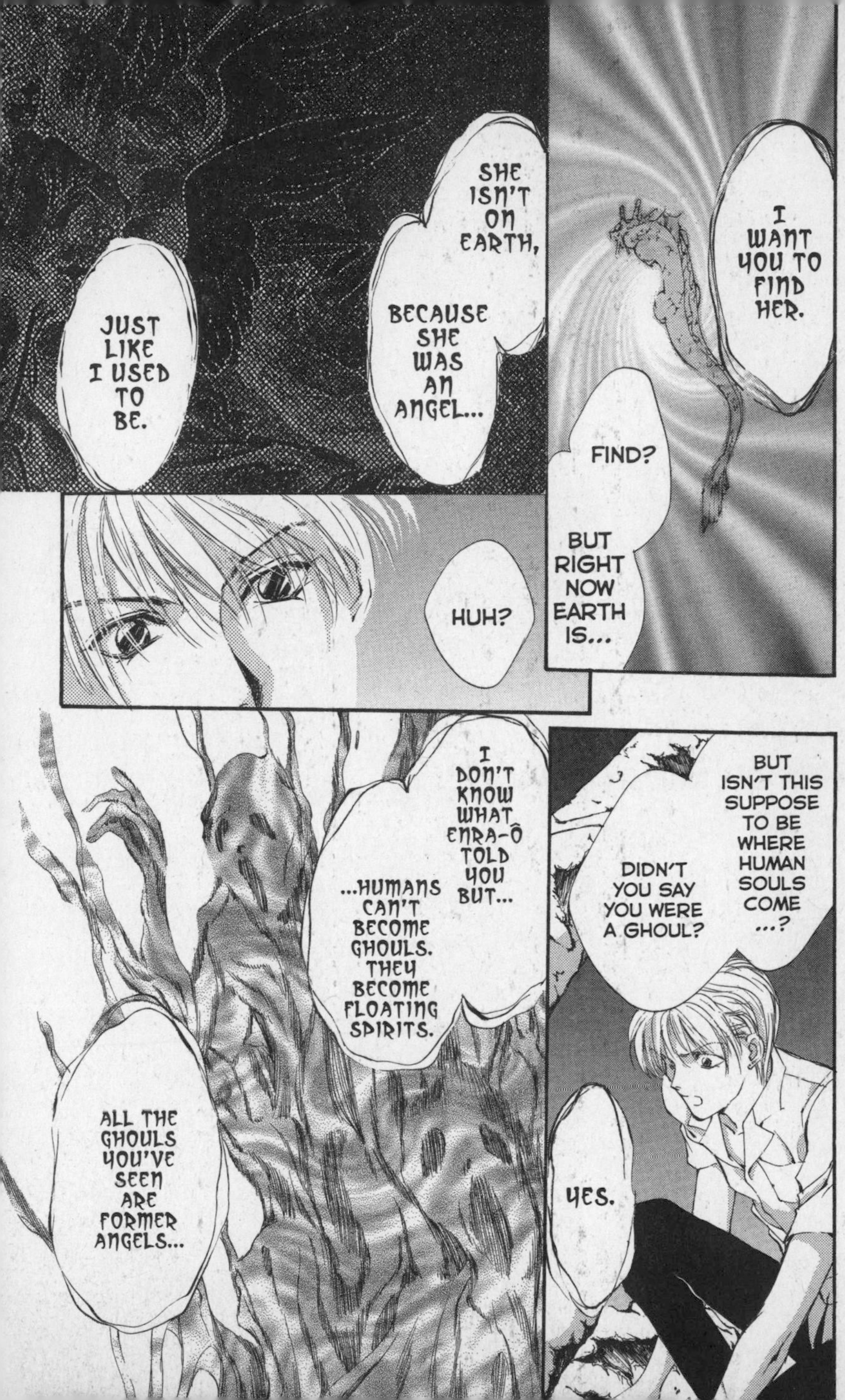
I WANT YOU TO FIND HER.
FIND?
BUT RIGHT NOW EARTH IS...
SHE ISN'T ON EARTH,
BECAUSE SHE WAS AN ANGEL...
JUST LIKE I USED TO BE.
HUH?
BUT ISN'T THIS SUPPOSE TO BE WHERE HUMAN SOULS COME ...?
DIDN'T YOU SAY YOU WERE A GHOUL?
YES.
I DON'T KNOW WHAT ENRA-Ô TOLD YOU BUT...
...HUMANS CAN'T BECOME GHOULS. THEY BECOME FLOATING SPIRITS.
ALL THE GHOULS YOU'VE SEEN ARE FORMER ANGELS...

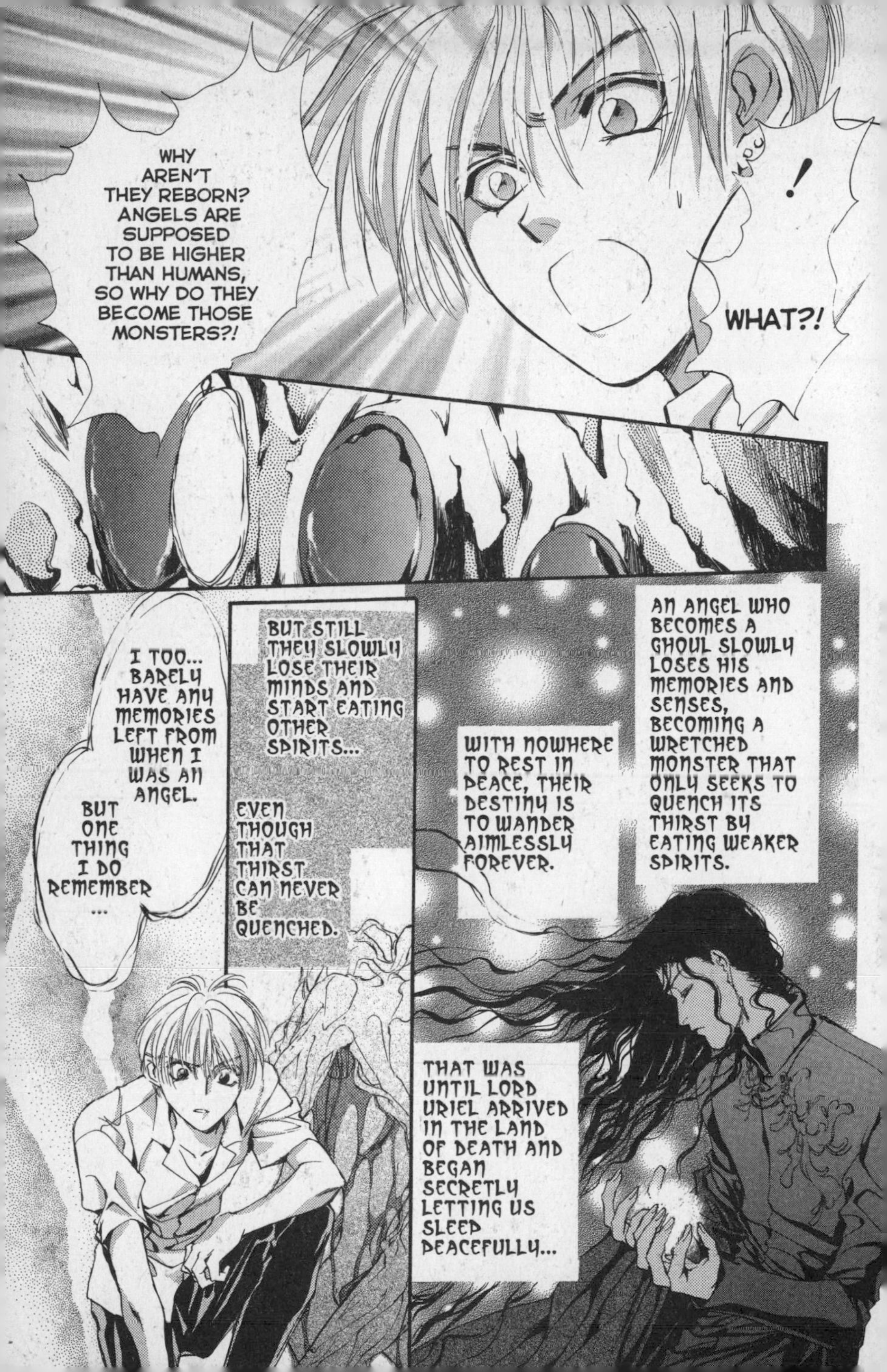
!
WHAT?!
WHY AREN'T THEY REBORN? ANGELS ARE SUPPOSED TO BE HIGHER THAN HUMANS, SO WHY DO THEY BECOME THOSE MONSTERS?!
AN ANGEL WHO BECOMES A GHOUL SLOWLY LOSES HIS MEMORIES AND SENSES, BECOMING A WRETCHED MONSTER THAT ONLY SEEKS TO QUENCH ITS THIRST BY EATING WEAKER SPIRITS.
WITH NOWHERE TO REST IN PEACE, THEIR DESTINY IS TO WANDER AIMLESSLY FOREVER.
BUT STILL THEY SLOWLY LOSE THEIR MINDS AND START EATING OTHER SPIRITS...
EVEN THOUGH THAT THIRST CAN NEVER BE QUENCHED.
THAT WAS UNTIL LORD URIEL ARRIVED IN THE LAND OF DEATH AND BEGAN SECRETLY LETTING US SLEEP PEACEFULLY...
I TOO... BARELY HAVE ANY MEMORIES LEFT FROM WHEN I WAS AN ANGEL.
BUT ONE THING I DO REMEMBER...

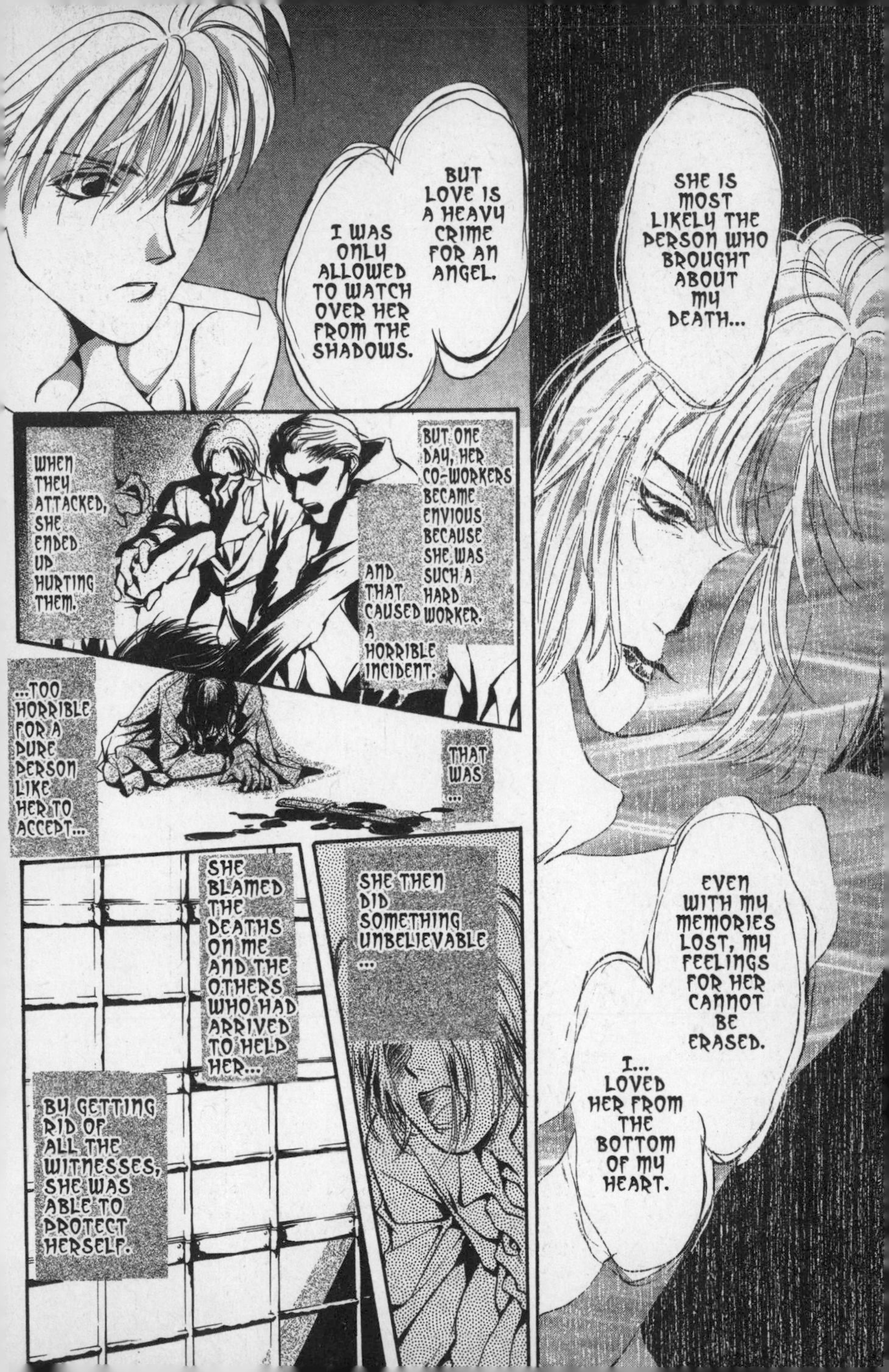
SHE IS MOST LIKELY THE PERSON WHO BROUGHT ABOUT MY DEATH...
EVEN WITH MY MEMORIES LOST, MY FEELINGS FOR HER CANNOT BE ERASED.
I... LOVED HER FROM THE BOTTOM OF MY HEART.
BUT LOVE IS A HEAVY CRIME FOR AN ANGEL.
I WAS ONLY ALLOWED TO WATCH OVER HER FROM THE SHADOWS.
BUT ONE DAY, HER CO-WORKERS BECAME ENVIOUS BECAUSE SHE WAS SUCH A HARD WORKER.
AND THAT CAUSED A HORRIBLE INCIDENT.
WHEN THEY ATTACKED, SHE ENDED UP HURTING THEM.
THAT WAS...
...TOO HORRIBLE FOR A PURE PERSON LIKE HER TO ACCEPT...
SHE THEN DID SOMETHING UNBELIEVABLE...
SHE BLAMED THE DEATHS ON ME AND THE OTHERS WHO HAD ARRIVED TO HELP HER...
BY GETTING RID OF ALL THE WITNESSES, SHE WAS ABLE TO PROTECT HERSELF.

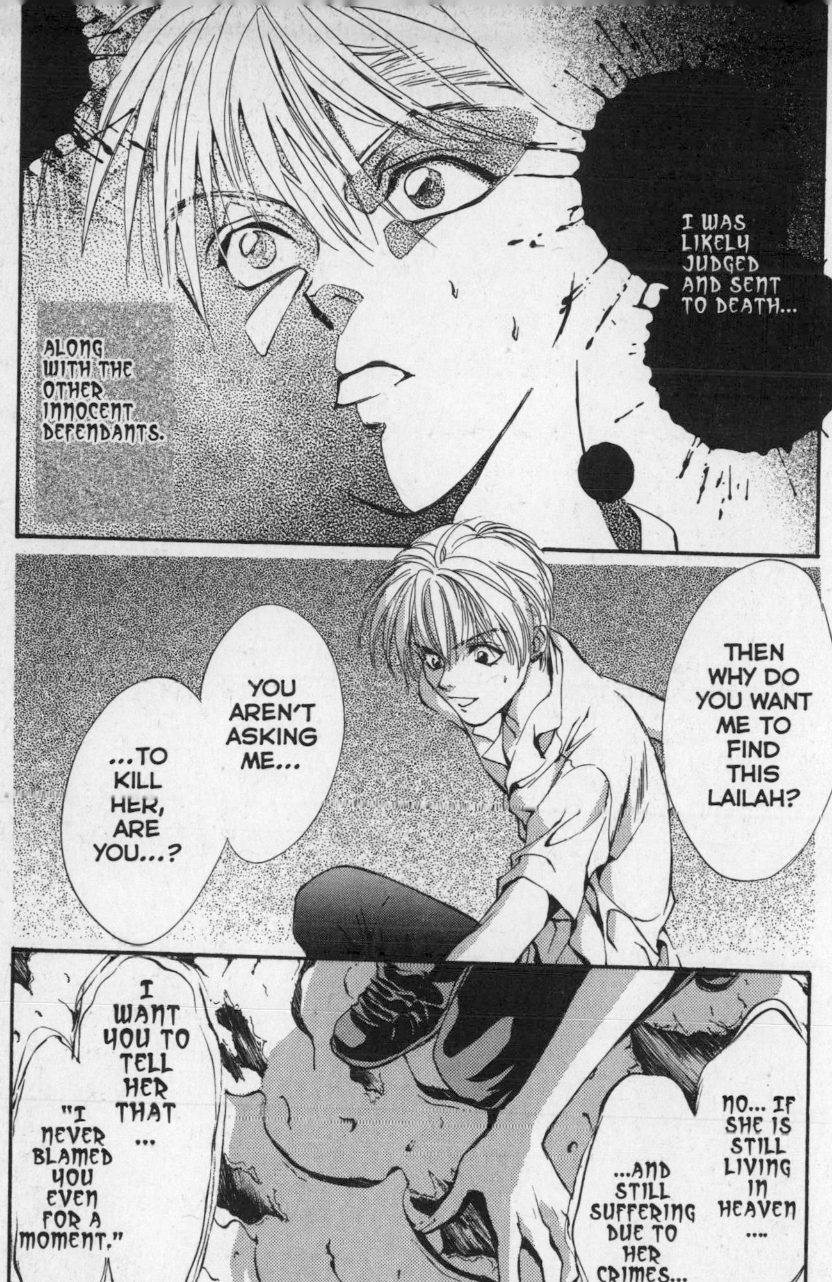
I WAS LIKELY JUDGED AND SENT TO DEATH...
ALONG WITH THE OTHER INNOCENT DEFENDANTS.
THEN WHY DO YOU WANT ME TO FIND THIS LAILAH?
YOU AREN'T ASKING ME...
...TO KILL HER, ARE YOU...?
NO... IF SHE IS STILL LIVING IN HEAVEN ...
...AND STILL SUFFERING DUE TO HER CRIMES...
I WANT YOU TO TELL HER THAT ...
"I NEVER BLAMED YOU EVEN FOR A MOMENT."

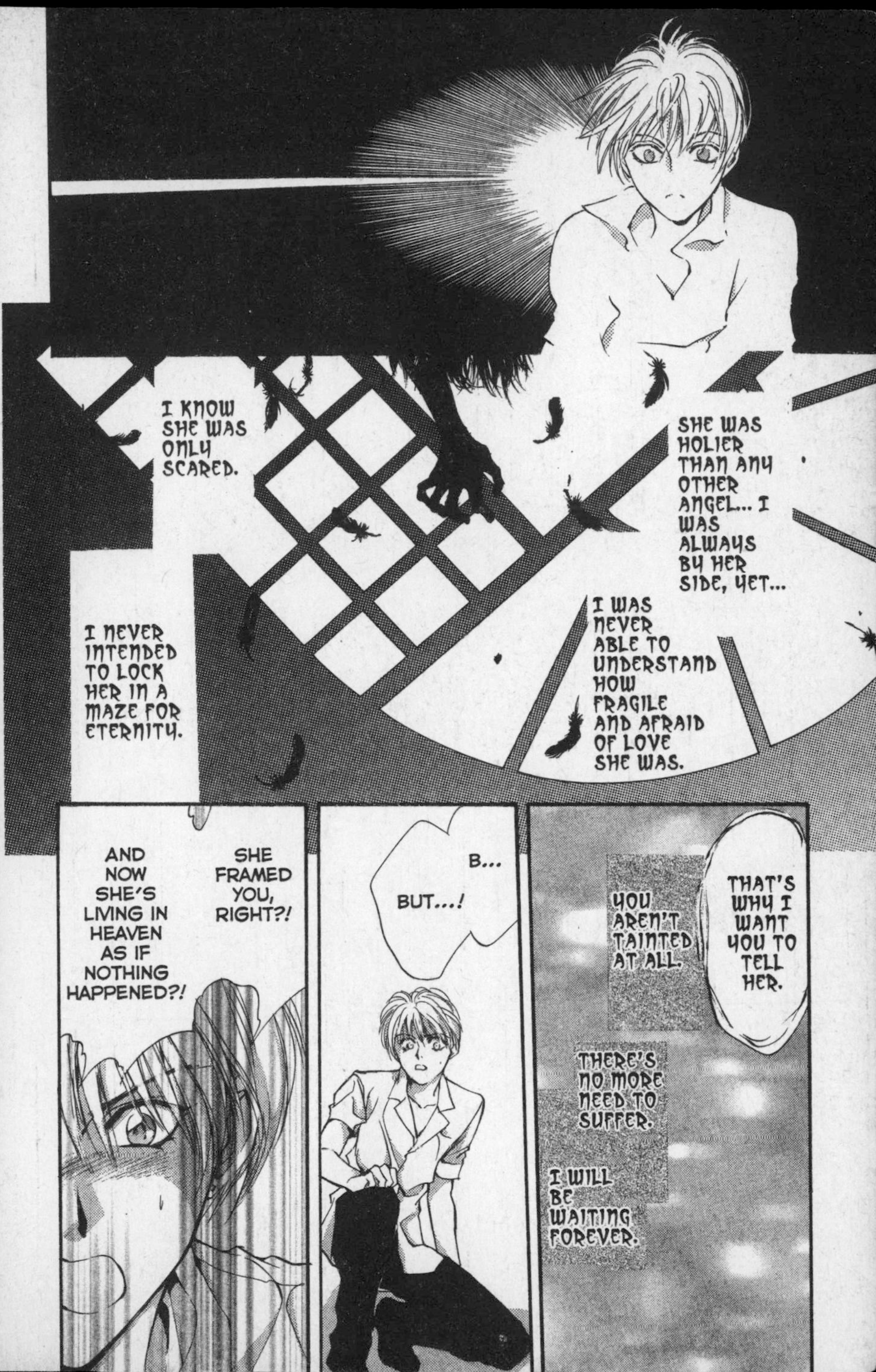
SHE WAS HOLIER THAN ANY OTHER ANGEL... I WAS ALWAYS BY HER SIDE, YET...
I WAS NEVER ABLE TO UNDERSTAND HOW FRAGILE AND AFRAID OF LOVE SHE WAS.
I KNOW SHE WAS ONLY SCARED.
I NEVER INTENDED TO LOCK HER IN A MAZE FOR ETERNITY.
THAT'S WHY I WANT YOU TO TELL HER.
YOU AREN'T TAINTED AT ALL.
THERE'S NO MORE NEED TO SUFFER.
I WILL BE WAITING FOREVER.
B...
BUT...!
SHE FRAMED YOU, RIGHT?!
AND NOW SHE'S LIVING IN HEAVEN AS IF NOTHING HAPPENED?!

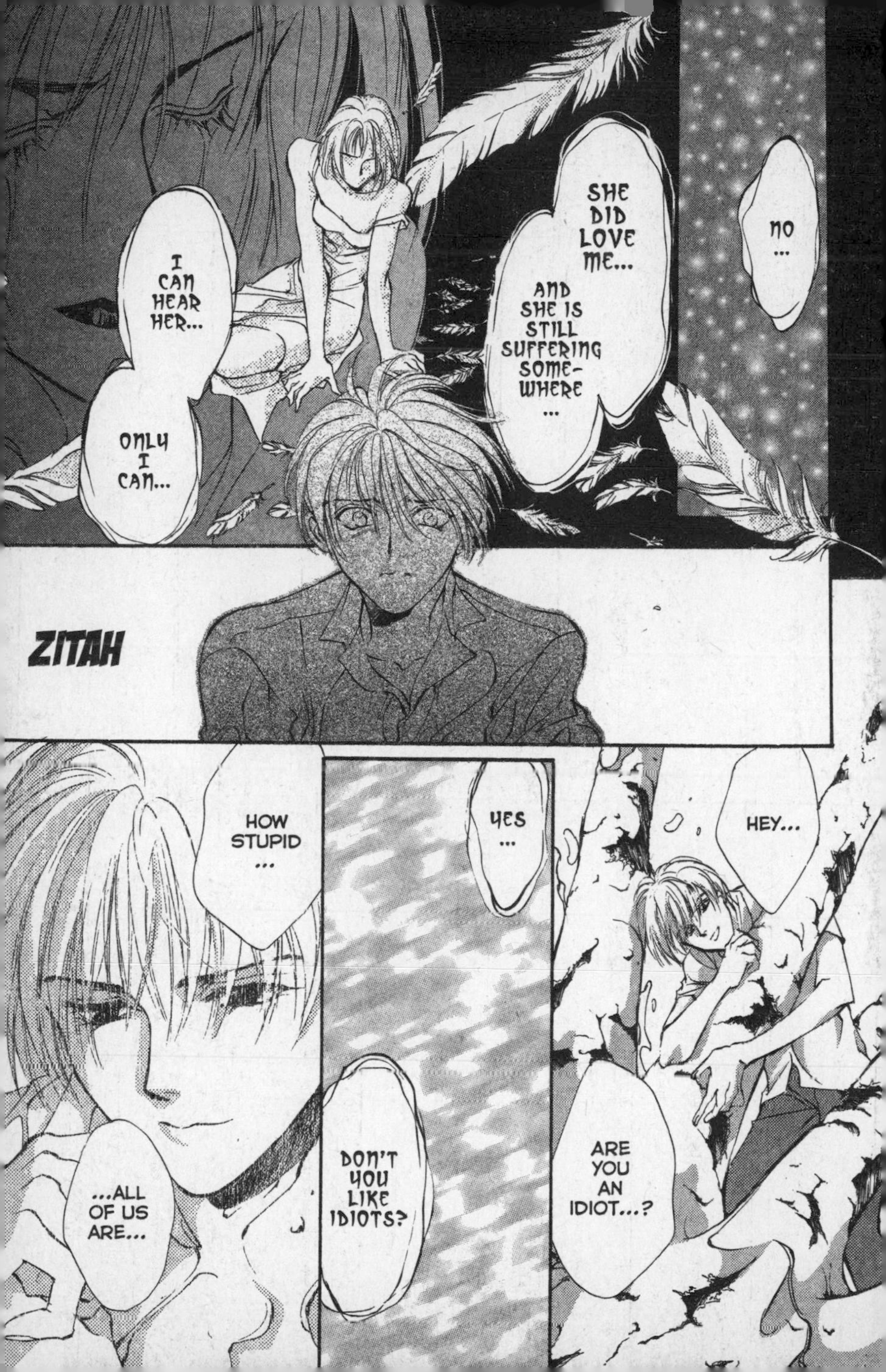
no ...
SHE DID LOVE ME...
AND SHE IS STILL SUFFERING SOME-WHERE ...
I CAN HEAR HER...
ONLY I CAN...
ZITAH
HEY...
ARE YOU AN IDIOT...?
YES ...
DON'T YOU LIKE IDIOTS?
HOW STUPID ...
...ALL OF US ARE...

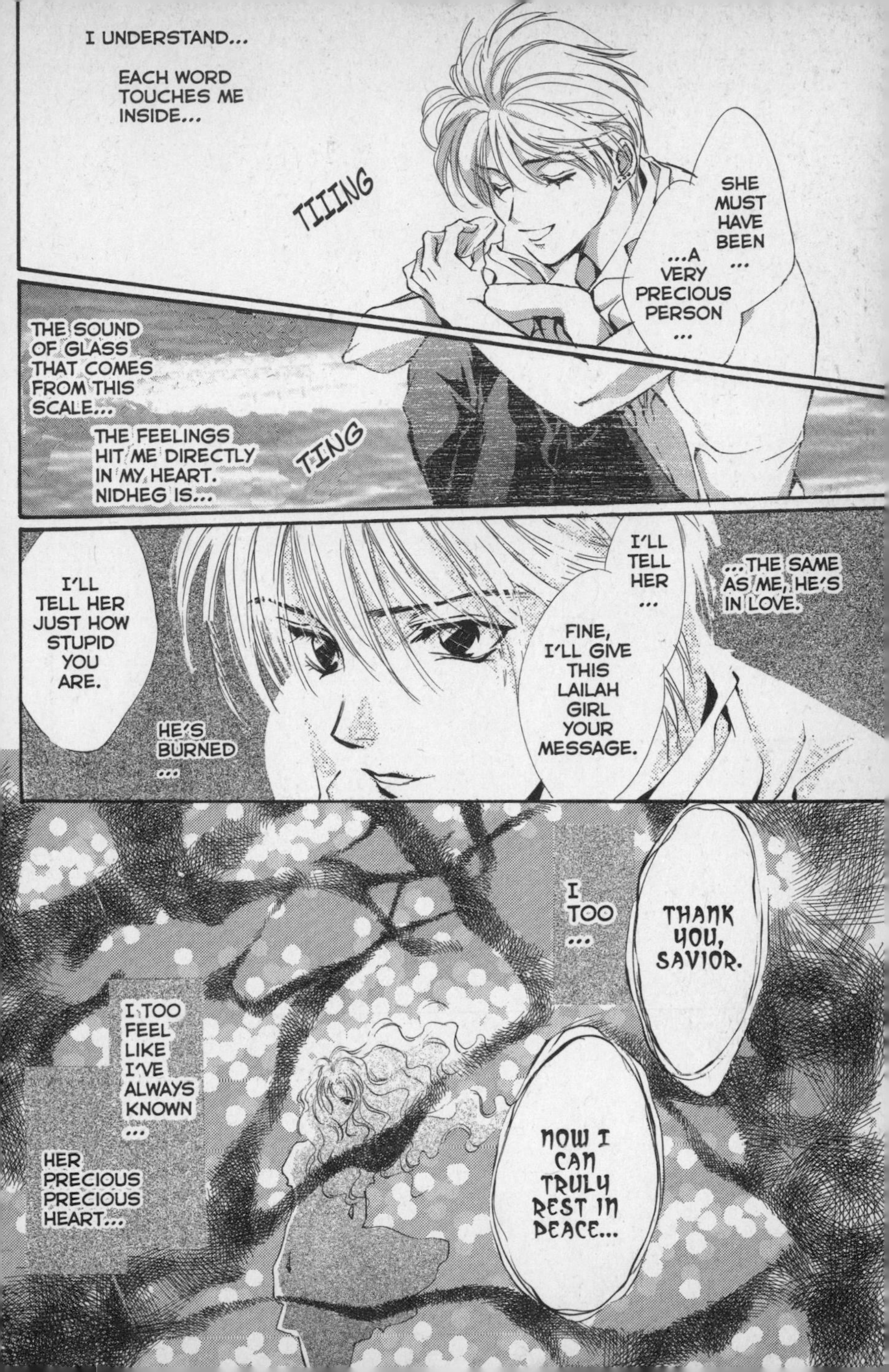
SHE MUST HAVE BEEN ...
...A VERY PRECIOUS PERSON ...
TIIING
I UNDERSTAND...
EACH WORD TOUCHES ME INSIDE...
TING
THE SOUND OF GLASS THAT COMES FROM THIS SCALE...
THE FEELINGS HIT ME DIRECTLY IN MY HEART. NIDHEG IS...
...THE SAME AS ME, HE'S IN LOVE.
I'LL TELL HER ...
FINE, I'LL GIVE THIS LAILAH GIRL YOUR MESSAGE.
I'LL TELL HER JUST HOW STUPID YOU ARE.
HE'S BURNED ...
THANK YOU, SAVIOR.
I TOO ...
NOW I CAN TRULY REST IN PEACE...
I TOO FEEL LIKE I'VE ALWAYS KNOWN ...
HER PRECIOUS PRECIOUS HEART...

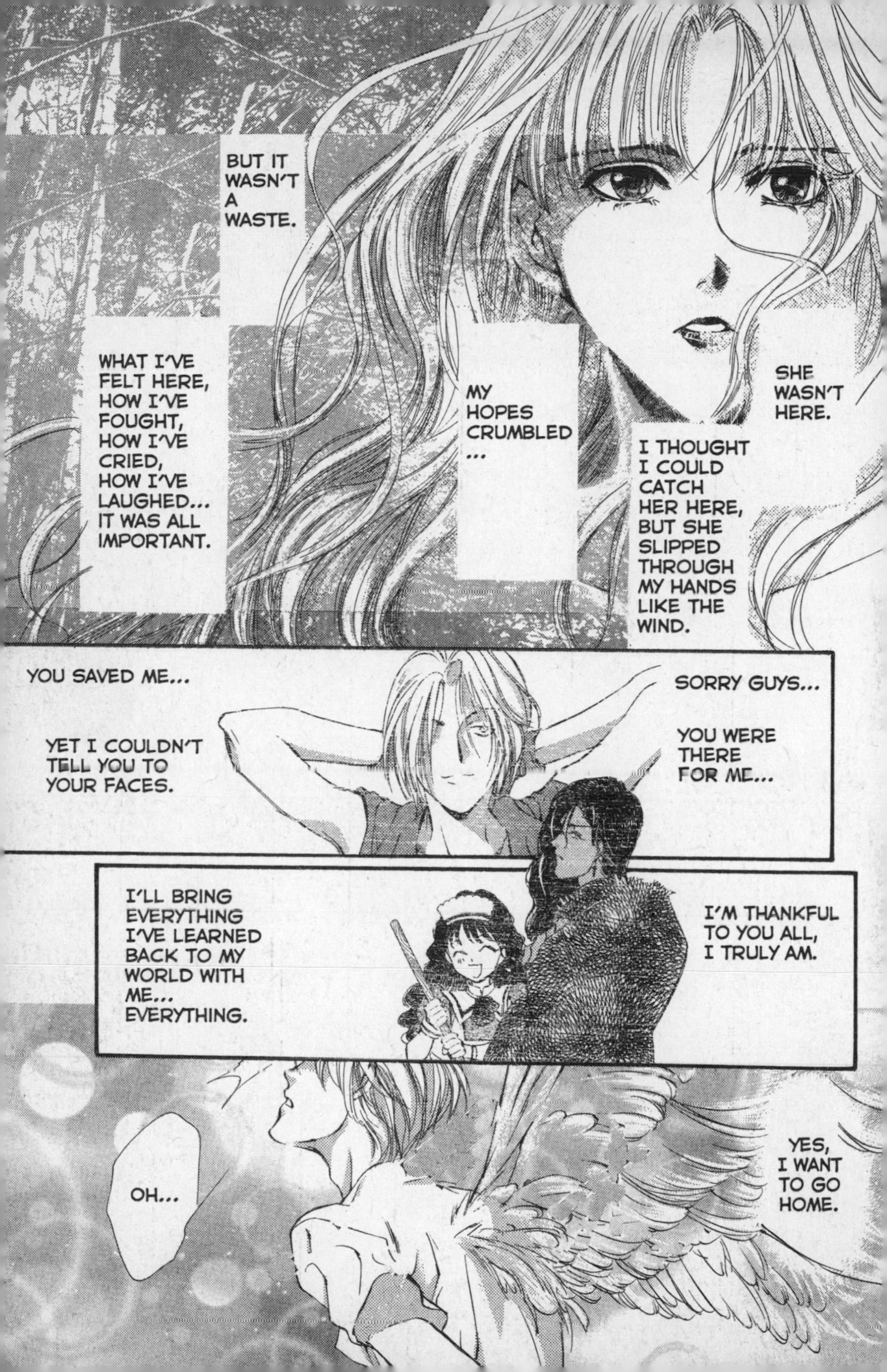
SHE WASN'T HERE.
I THOUGHT I COULD CATCH HER HERE, BUT SHE SLIPPED THROUGH MY HANDS LIKE THE WIND.
MY HOPES CRUMBLED ...
BUT IT WASN'T A WASTE.
WHAT I'VE FELT HERE, HOW I'VE FOUGHT, HOW I'VE CRIED, HOW I'VE LAUGHED... IT WAS ALL IMPORTANT.
SORRY GUYS...
YOU WERE THERE FOR ME...
YOU SAVED ME...
YET I COULDN'T TELL YOU TO YOUR FACES.
I'M THANKFUL TO YOU ALL, I TRULY AM.
I'LL BRING EVERYTHING I'VE LEARNED BACK TO MY WORLD WITH ME... EVERYTHING.
YES, I WANT TO GO HOME.
OH...

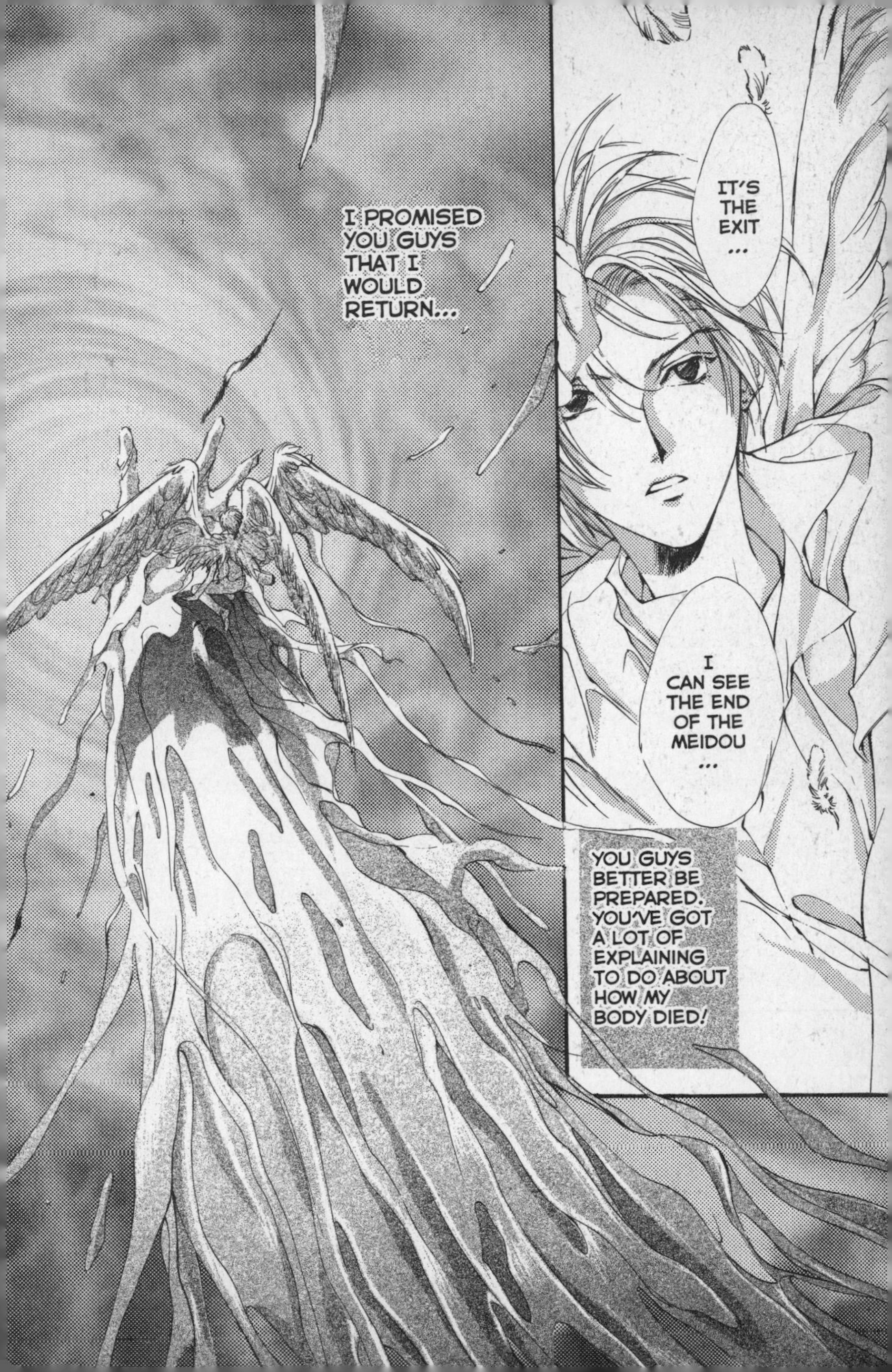
IT'S THE EXIT ...
I CAN SEE THE END OF THE MEIDOU ...
YOU GUYS BETTER BE PREPARED. YOU'VE GOT A LOT OF EXPLAINING TO DO ABOUT HOW MY BODY DIED!
I PROMISED YOU GUYS THAT I WOULD RETURN...

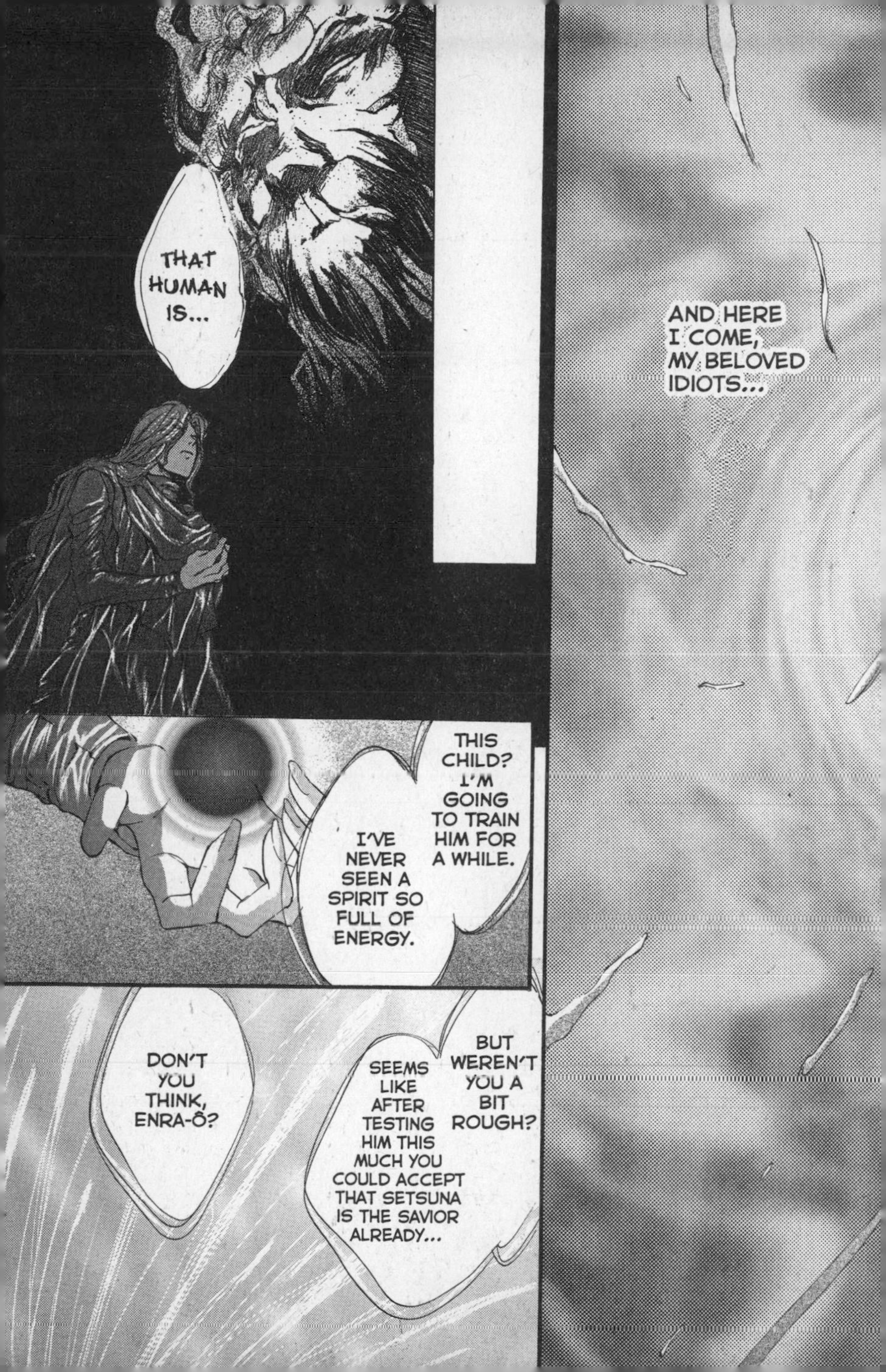
AND HERE I COME, MY BELOVED IDIOTS...
THAT HUMAN IS...
THIS CHILD? I'M GOING TO TRAIN HIM FOR A WHILE.
I'VE NEVER SEEN A SPIRIT SO FULL OF ENERGY.
BUT WEREN'T YOU A BIT ROUGH?
SEEMS LIKE AFTER TESTING HIM THIS MUCH YOU COULD ACCEPT THAT SETSUNA IS THE SAVIOR ALREADY...
DON'T YOU THINK, ENRA-Ō?

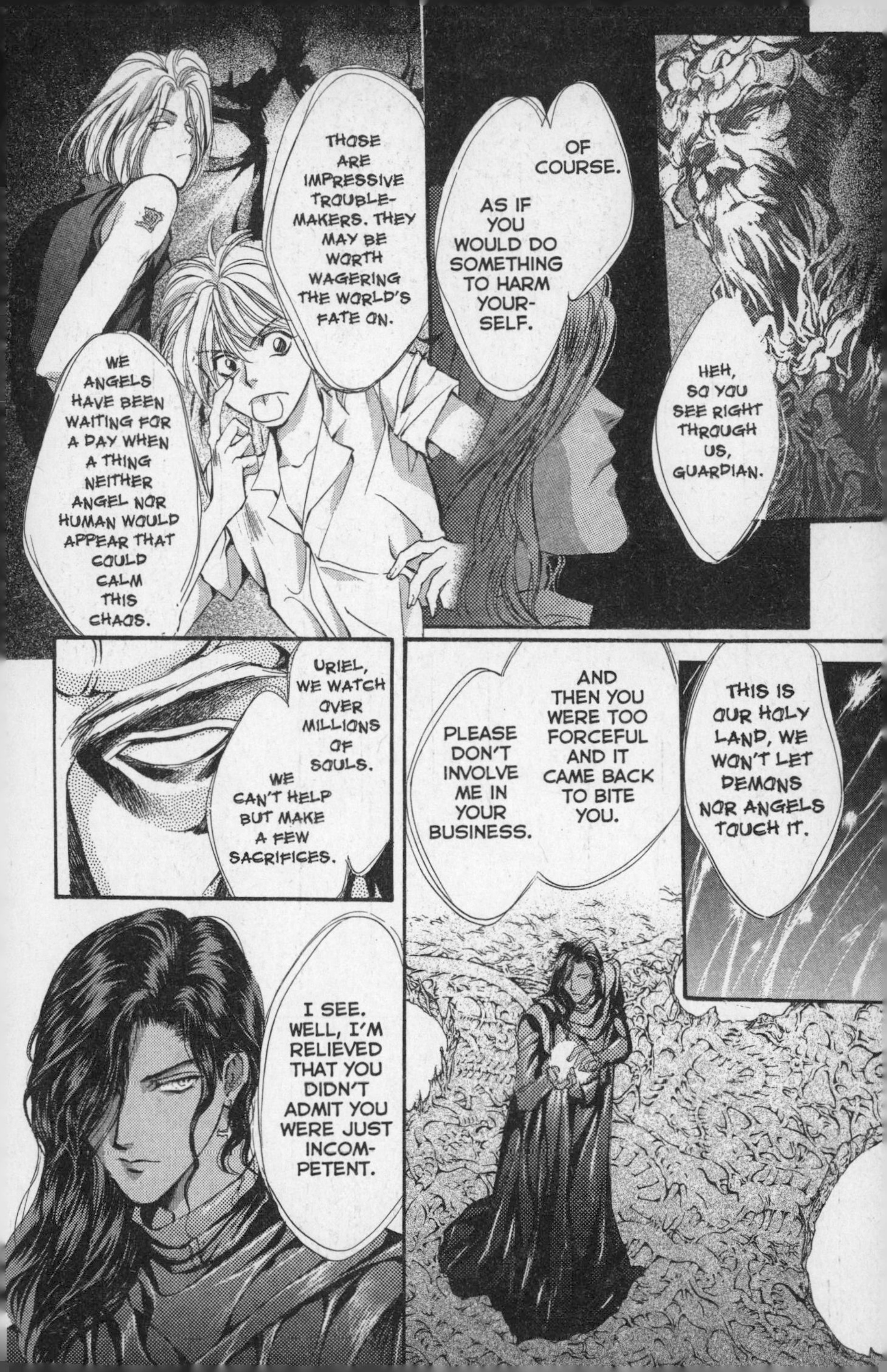

HEH, SO YOU SEE RIGHT THROUGH US, GUARDIAN.
OF COURSE.
AS IF YOU WOULD DO SOMETHING TO HARM YOURSELF.
THOSE ARE IMPRESSIVE TROUBLE-MAKERS. THEY MAY BE WORTH WAGERING THE WORLD'S FATE ON.
WE ANGELS HAVE BEEN WAITING FOR A DAY WHEN A THING NEITHER ANGEL NOR HUMAN WOULD APPEAR THAT COULD CALM THIS CHAOS.
THIS IS OUR HOLY LAND, WE WON'T LET DEMONS NOR ANGELS TOUCH IT.
AND THEN YOU WERE TOO FORCEFUL AND IT CAME BACK TO BITE YOU.
PLEASE DON'T INVOLVE ME IN YOUR BUSINESS.
URIEL, WE WATCH OVER MILLIONS OF SOULS.
WE CAN'T HELP BUT MAKE A FEW SACRIFICES.
I SEE. WELL, I'M RELIEVED THAT YOU DIDN'T ADMIT YOU WERE JUST INCOMPETENT.

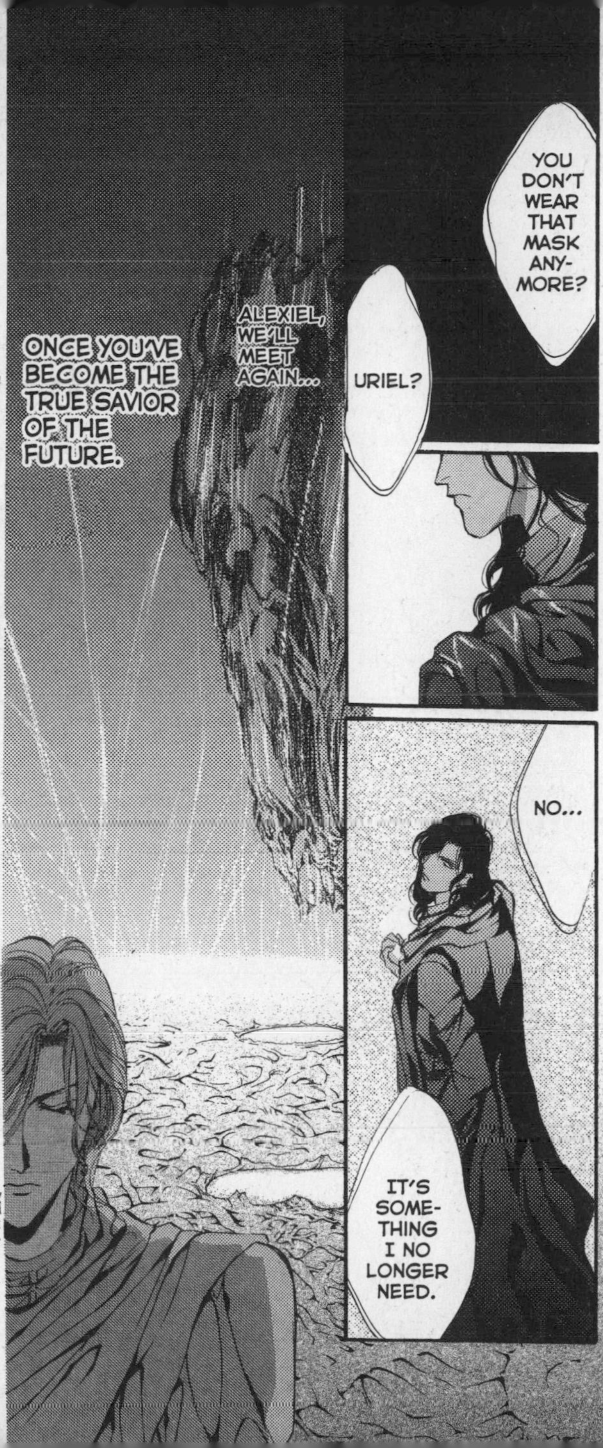
YOU DON'T WEAR THAT MASK ANY-MORE?
URIEL?
NO...
IT'S SOME-THING I NO LONGER NEED.
ALEXIEL, WE'LL MEET AGAIN...
ONCE YOU'VE BECOME THE TRUE SAVIOR OF THE FUTURE.

It's book seven! Lucky seven! Hmm, feels like it's been going for a while... I guess. Well, between the last books my short story collection *Cain* come out, so it's actually been a while since book six. *Cain* has a lot of my really old stuff in it so I was pretty embarrassed when it was released but the cover and logo and stuff were really cool and I liked it. This has nothing to do with anything, but if you look at the book from the side you can see that it is divided into black from the first half and white for the second. It matches the stories, so it's kind of interesting...

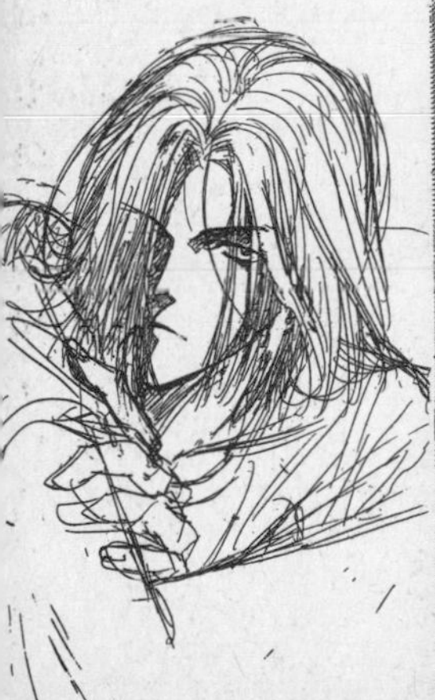

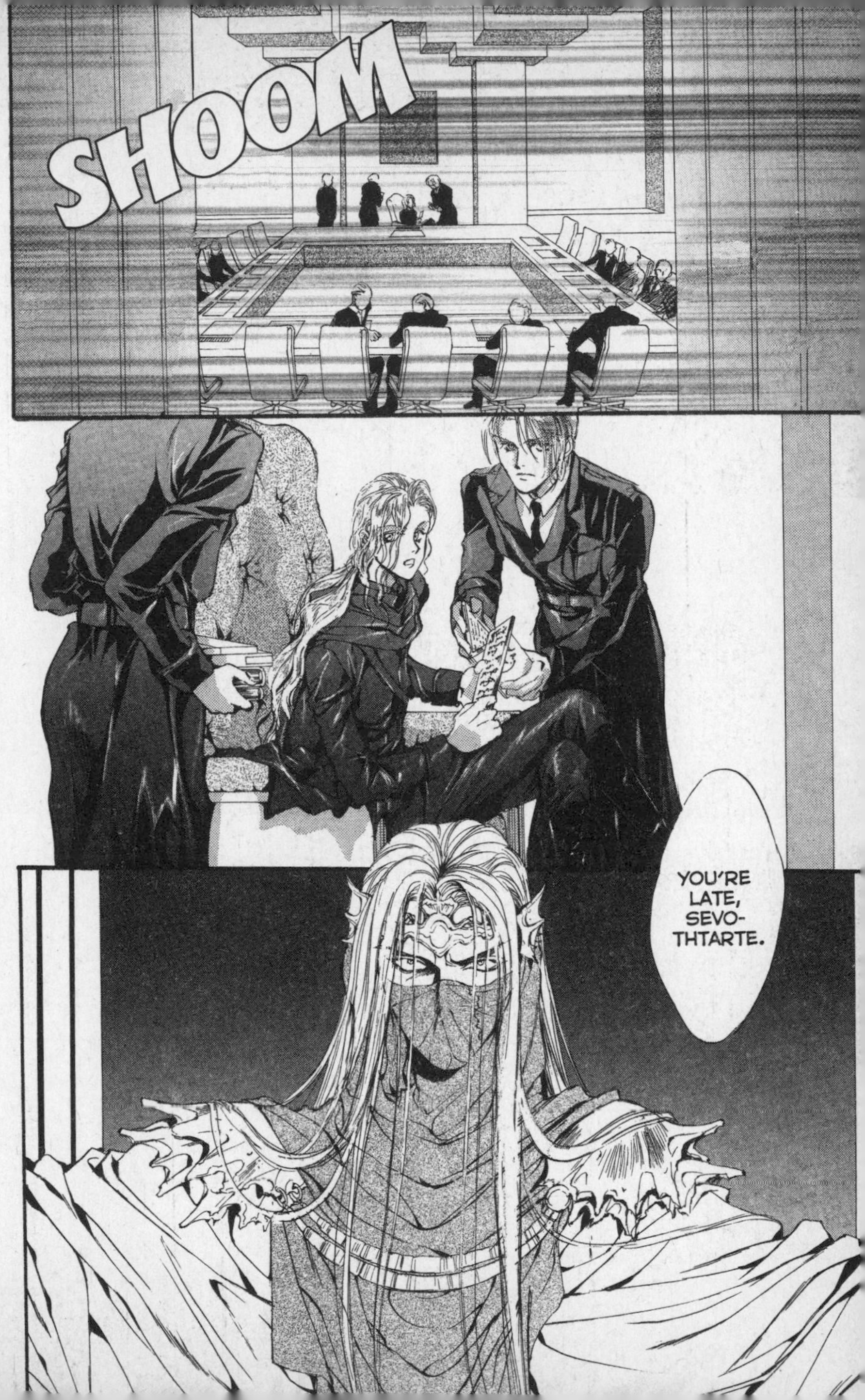
SHOOM
YOU'RE LATE, SEVO-THTARTE.

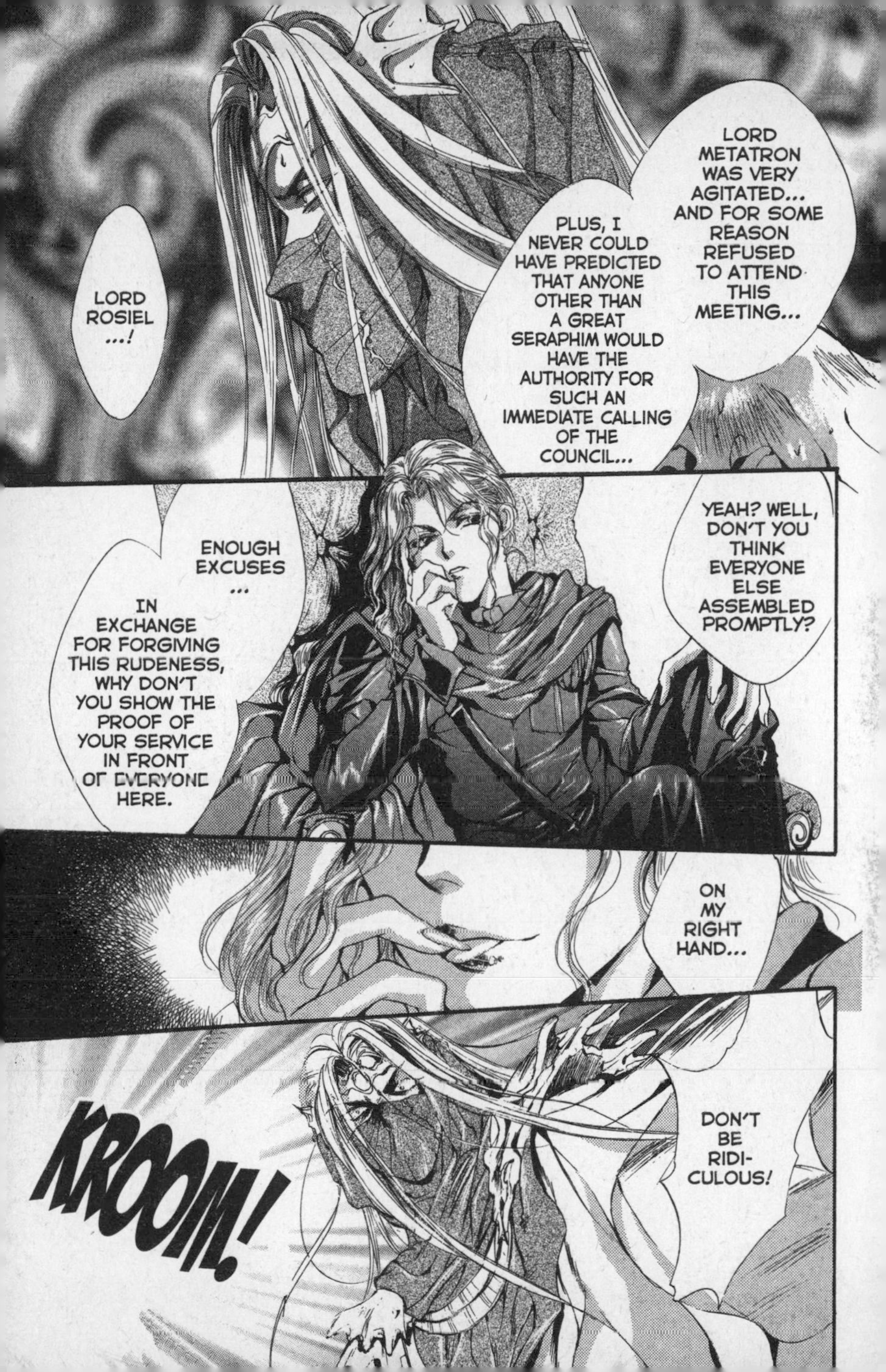
LORD METATRON WAS VERY AGITATED... AND FOR SOME REASON REFUSED TO ATTEND THIS MEETING...
PLUS, I NEVER COULD HAVE PREDICTED THAT ANYONE OTHER THAN A GREAT SERAPHIM WOULD HAVE THE AUTHORITY FOR SUCH AN IMMEDIATE CALLING OF THE COUNCIL...
LORD ROSIEL ...!
YEAH? WELL, DON'T YOU THINK EVERYONE ELSE ASSEMBLED PROMPTLY?
ENOUGH EXCUSES ...
IN EXCHANGE FOR FORGIVING THIS RUDENESS, WHY DON'T YOU SHOW THE PROOF OF YOUR SERVICE IN FRONT OF EVERYONE HERE.
ON MY RIGHT HAND...
DON'T BE RIDI-CULOUS!
KROOM!

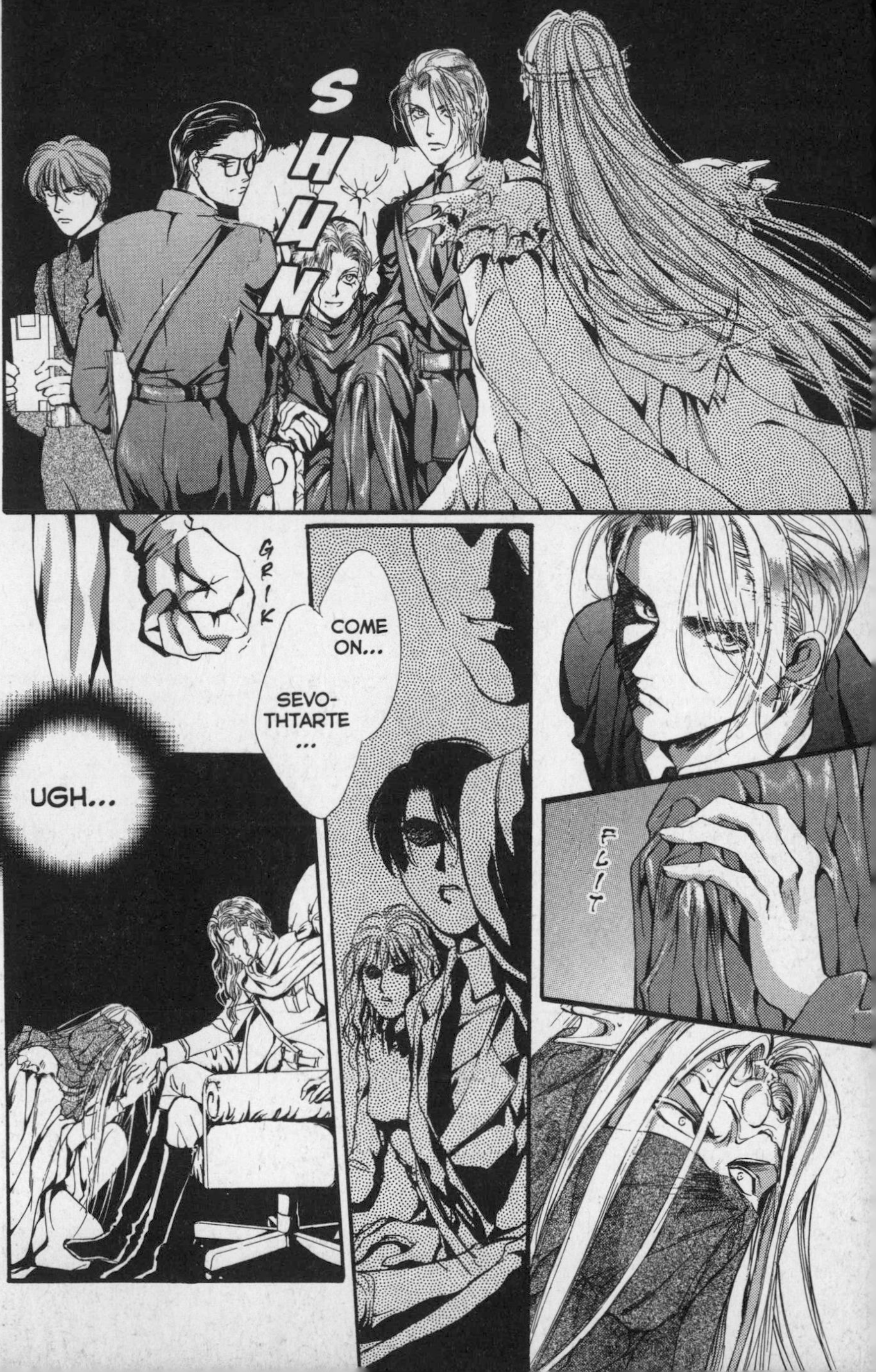
SHUN
FLIT
COME ON...
SEVO-THTARTE...
GRIK
UGH...

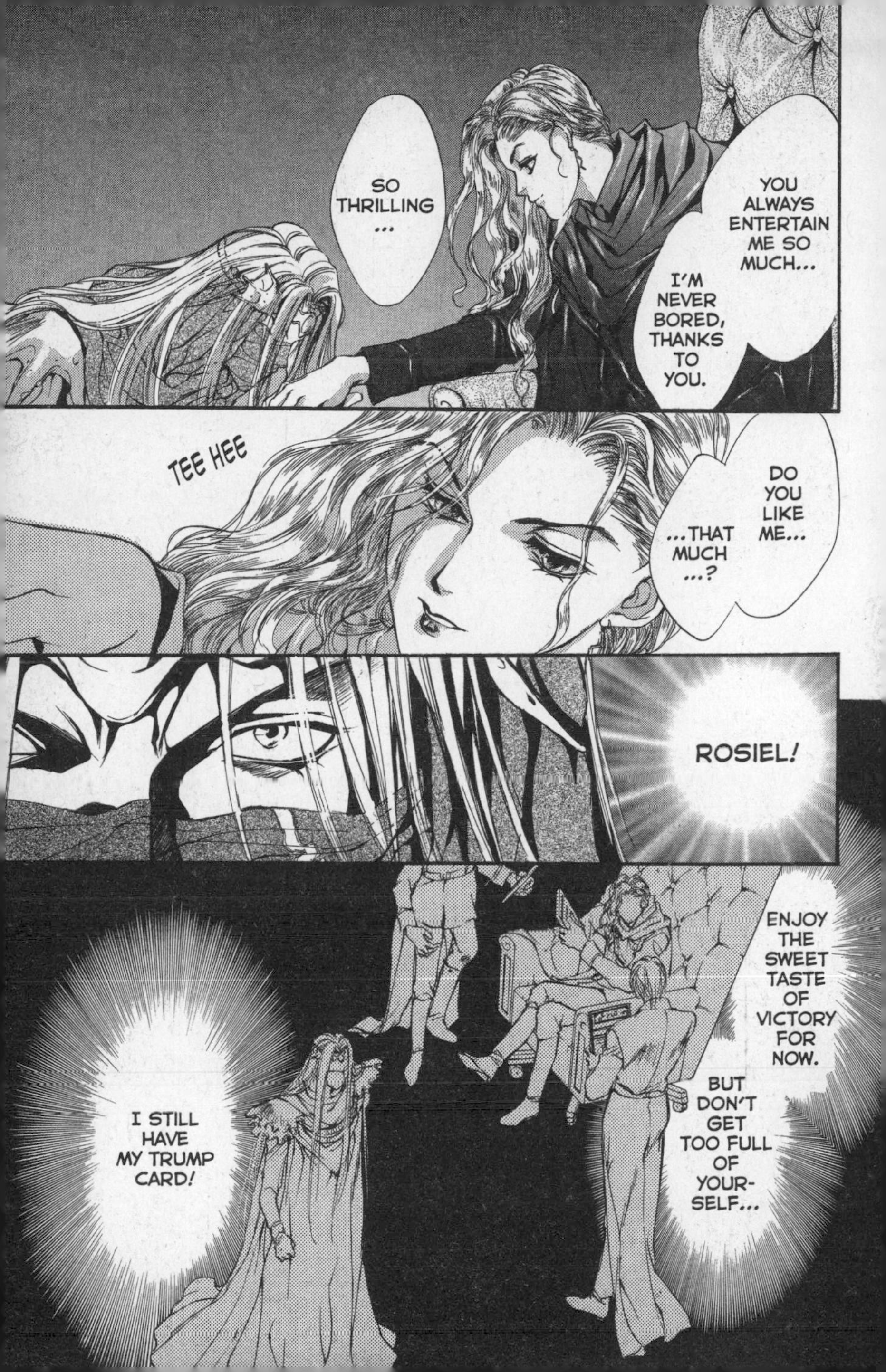
YOU ALWAYS ENTERTAIN ME SO MUCH...
I'M NEVER BORED, THANKS TO YOU.
SO THRILLING ...
DO YOU LIKE ME...
...THAT MUCH ...?
TEE HEE
ROSIEL!
ENJOY THE SWEET TASTE OF VICTORY FOR NOW.
BUT DON'T GET TOO FULL OF YOUR-SELF...
I STILL HAVE MY TRUMP CARD!

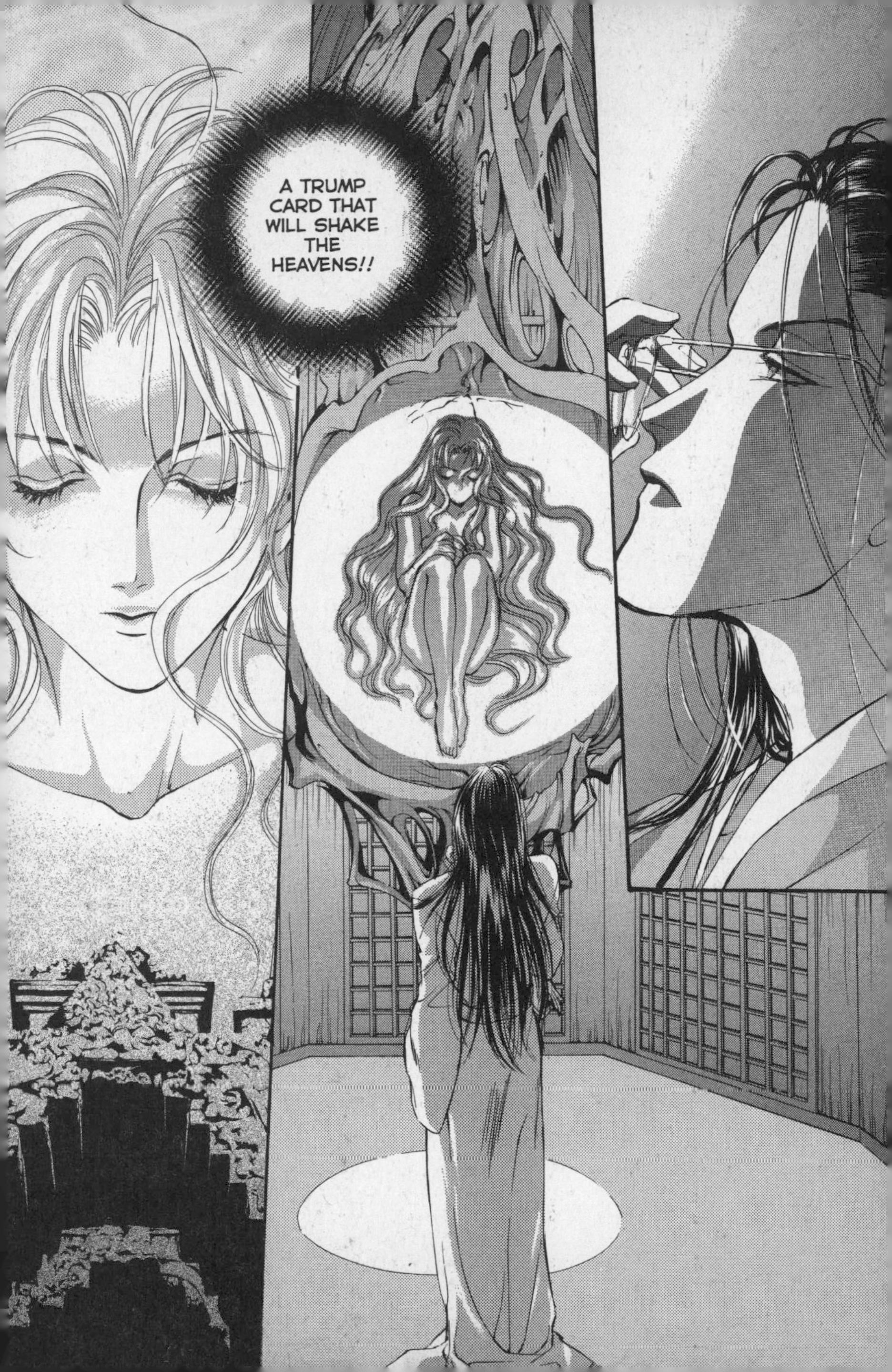
A TRUMP CARD THAT WILL SHAKE THE HEAVENS!!

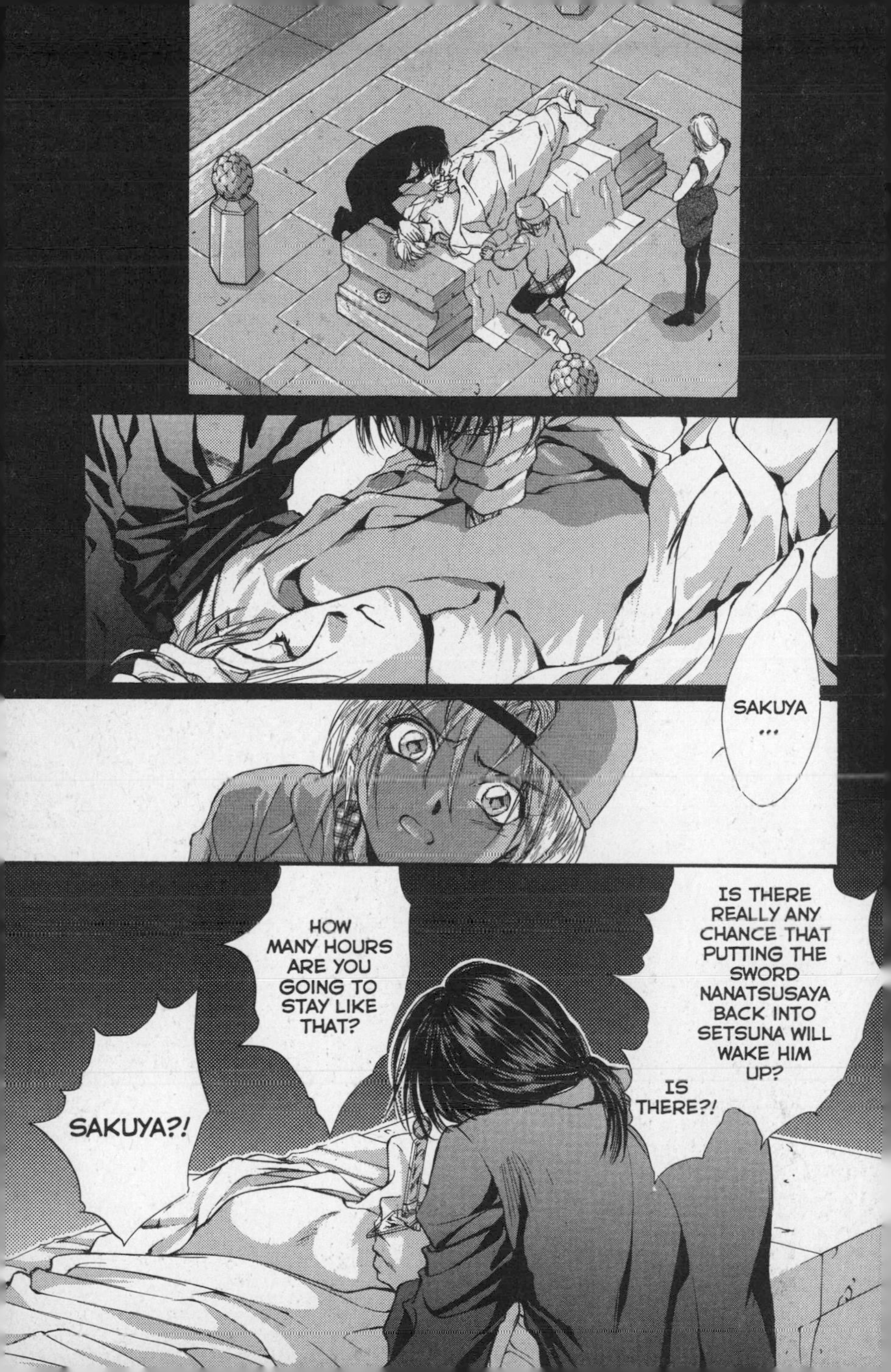
SAKUYA ...
IS THERE REALLY ANY CHANCE THAT PUTTING THE SWORD NANATSUSAYA BACK INTO SETSUNA WILL WAKE HIM UP?
IS THERE?!
HOW MANY HOURS ARE YOU GOING TO STAY LIKE THAT?
SAKUYA?!

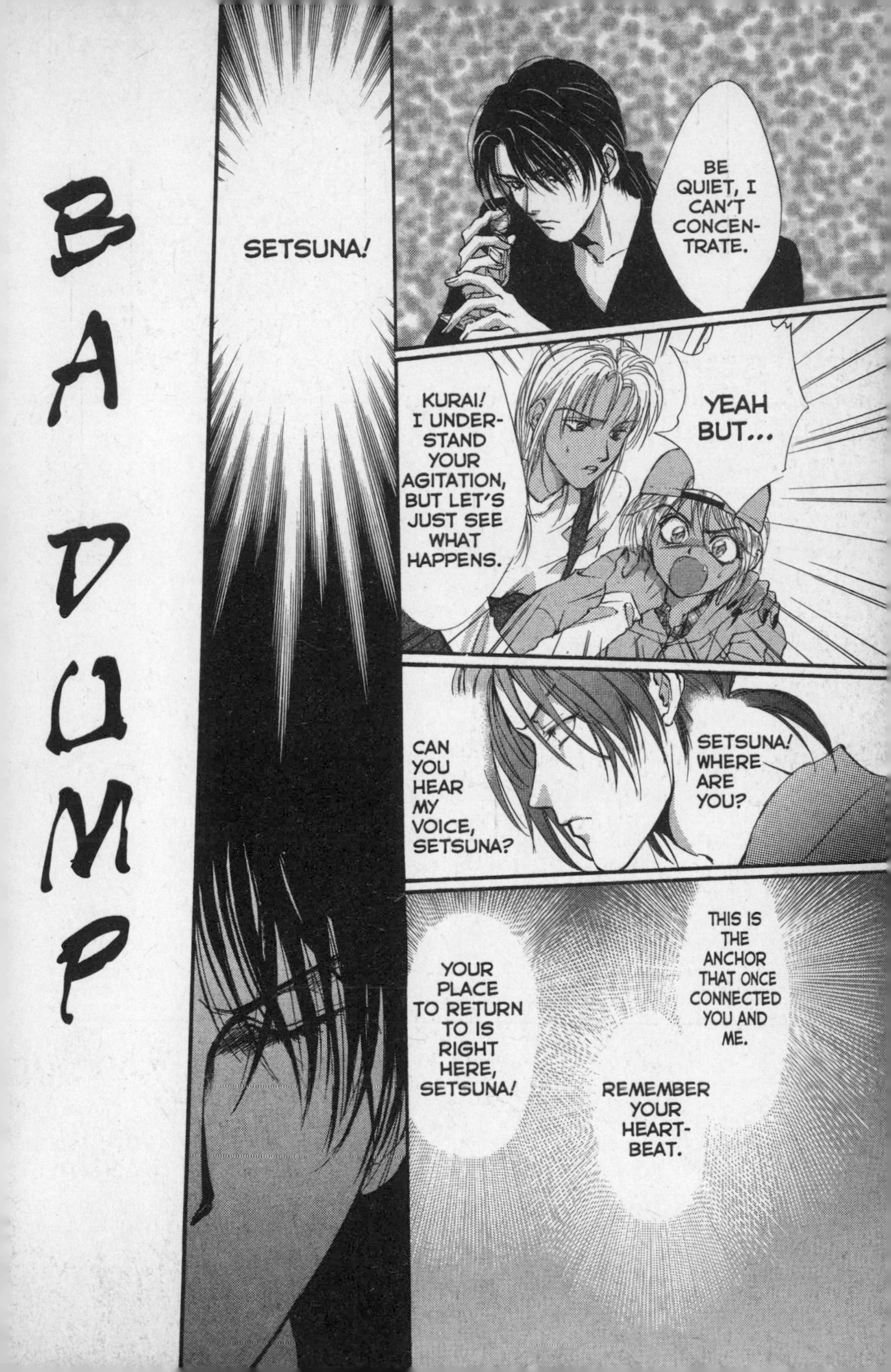
BE QUIET, I CAN'T CONCENTRATE.
YEAH BUT...
KURAI! I UNDERSTAND YOUR AGITATION, BUT LET'S JUST SEE WHAT HAPPENS.
SETSUNA! WHERE ARE YOU?
CAN YOU HEAR MY VOICE, SETSUNA?
THIS IS THE ANCHOR THAT ONCE CONNECTED YOU AND ME.
REMEMBER YOUR HEARTBEAT.
YOUR PLACE TO RETURN TO IS RIGHT HERE, SETSUNA!
SETSUNA!
BADUMP

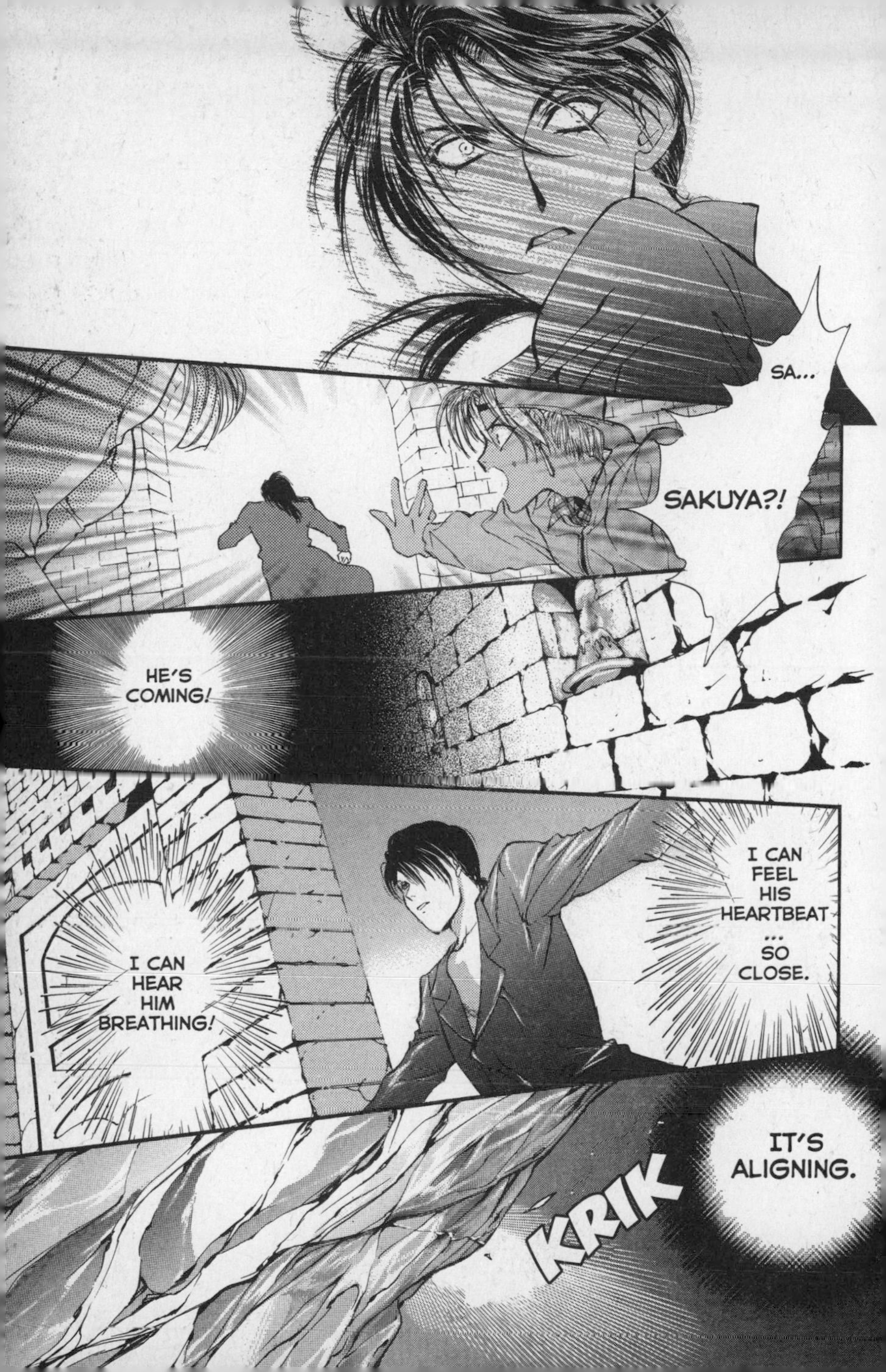
SA...
SAKUYA?!
HE'S COMING!
I CAN FEEL HIS HEARTBEAT ... SO CLOSE.
I CAN HEAR HIM BREATHING!
IT'S ALIGNING.
KRIK

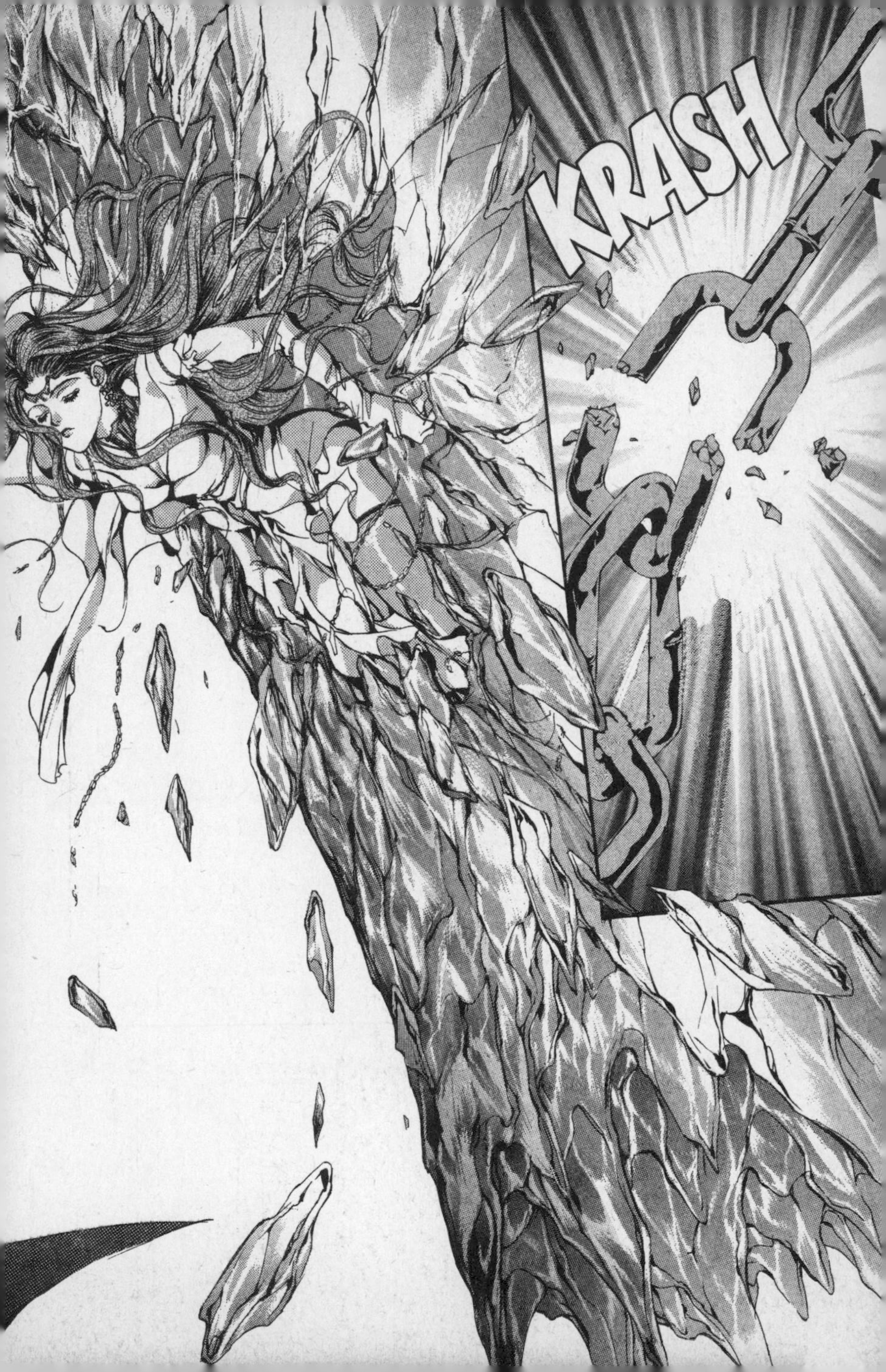
KRASH

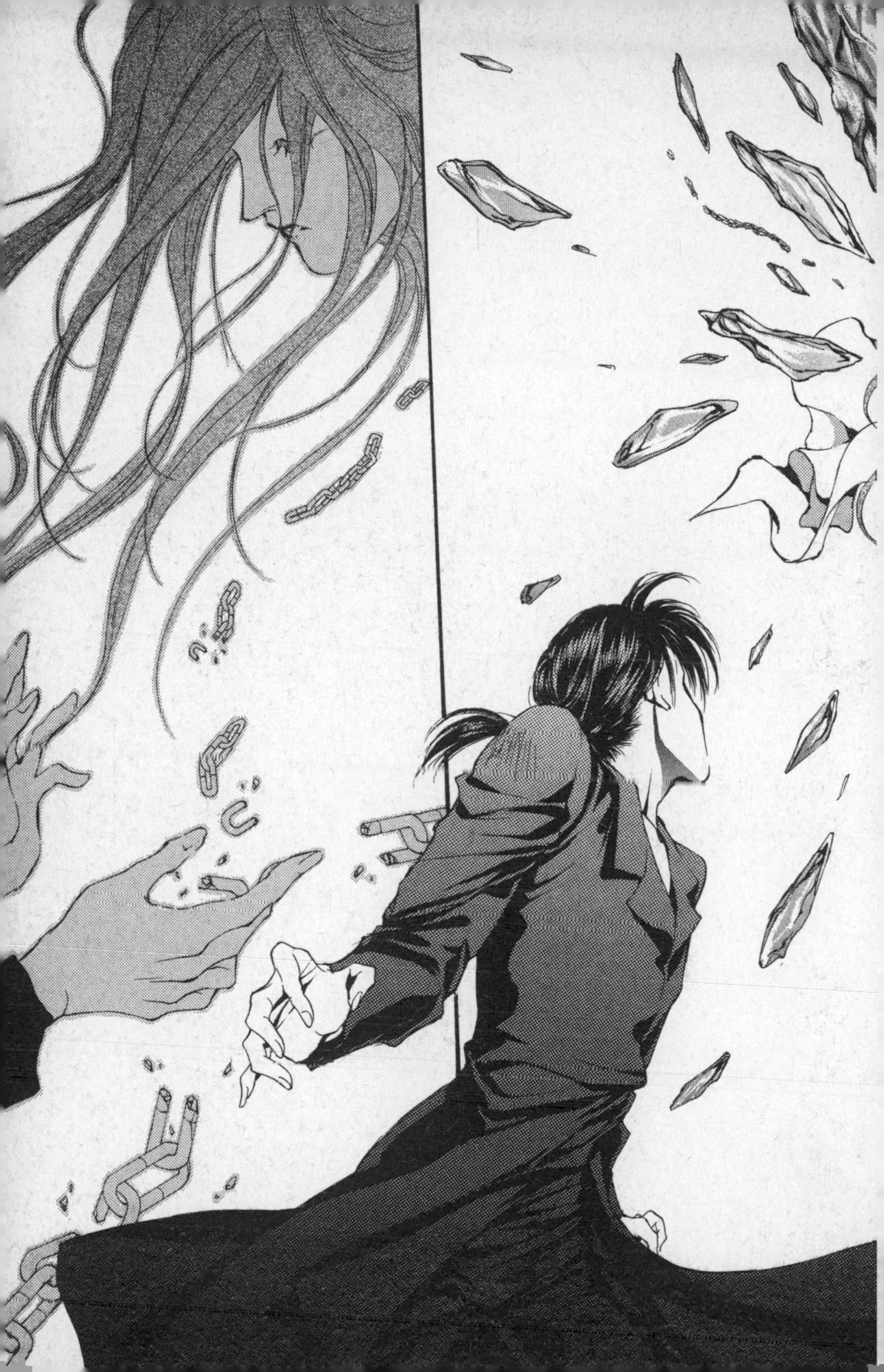

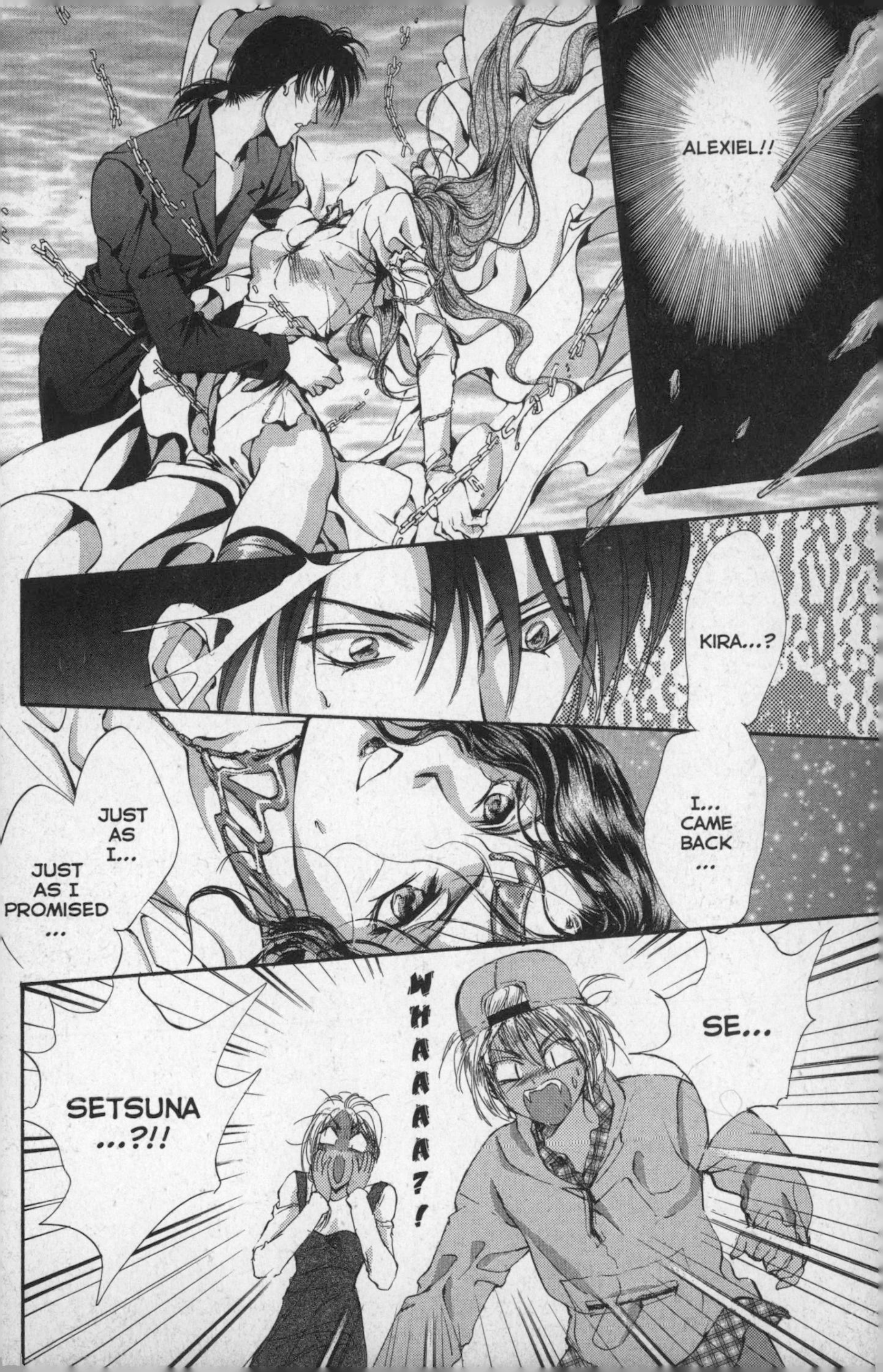
ALEXIEL!!
KIRA...?
I... CAME BACK ...
JUST AS I...
JUST AS I PROMISED ...
SE...
WHAAAAAA?!
SETSUNA ...?!!

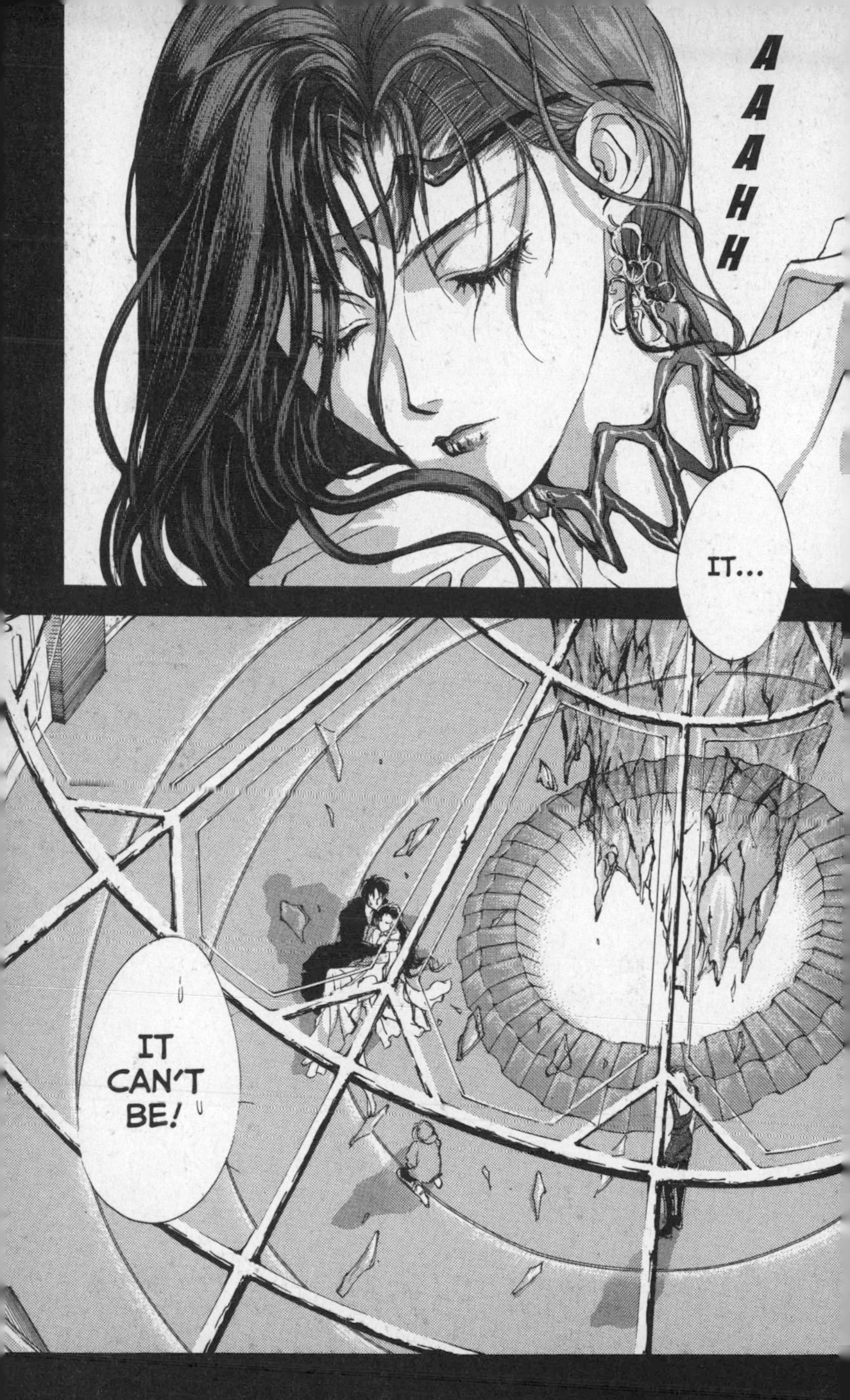
AAAAHH
IT...
IT CAN'T BE!

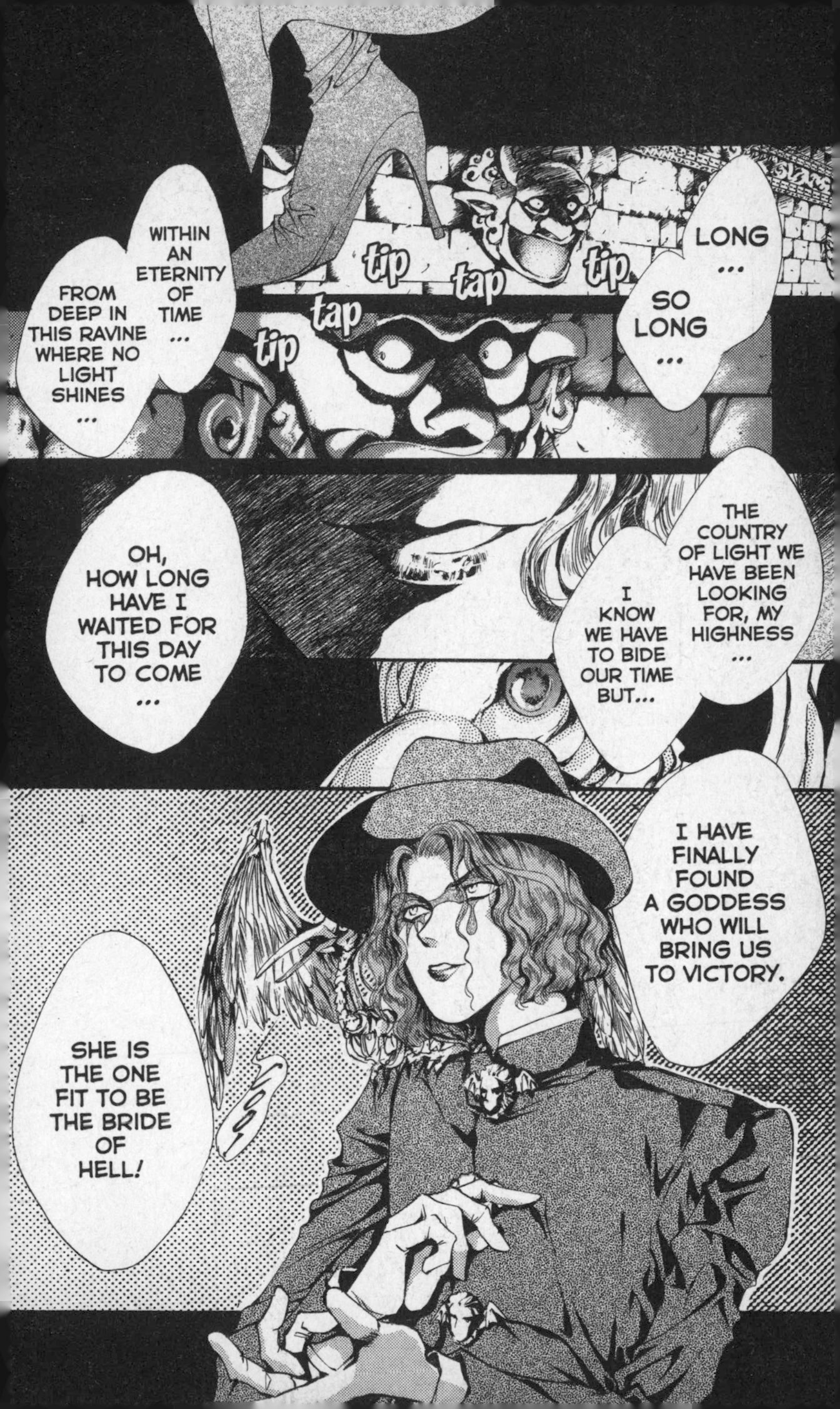

LONG ...
SO LONG ...
tip
tap
tip
tap
tip
WITHIN AN ETERNITY OF TIME ...
FROM DEEP IN THIS RAVINE WHERE NO LIGHT SHINES ...
THE COUNTRY OF LIGHT WE HAVE BEEN LOOKING FOR, MY HIGHNESS ...
I KNOW WE HAVE TO BIDE OUR TIME BUT...
OH, HOW LONG HAVE I WAITED FOR THIS DAY TO COME ...
I HAVE FINALLY FOUND A GODDESS WHO WILL BRING US TO VICTORY.
SHE IS THE ONE FIT TO BE THE BRIDE OF HELL!

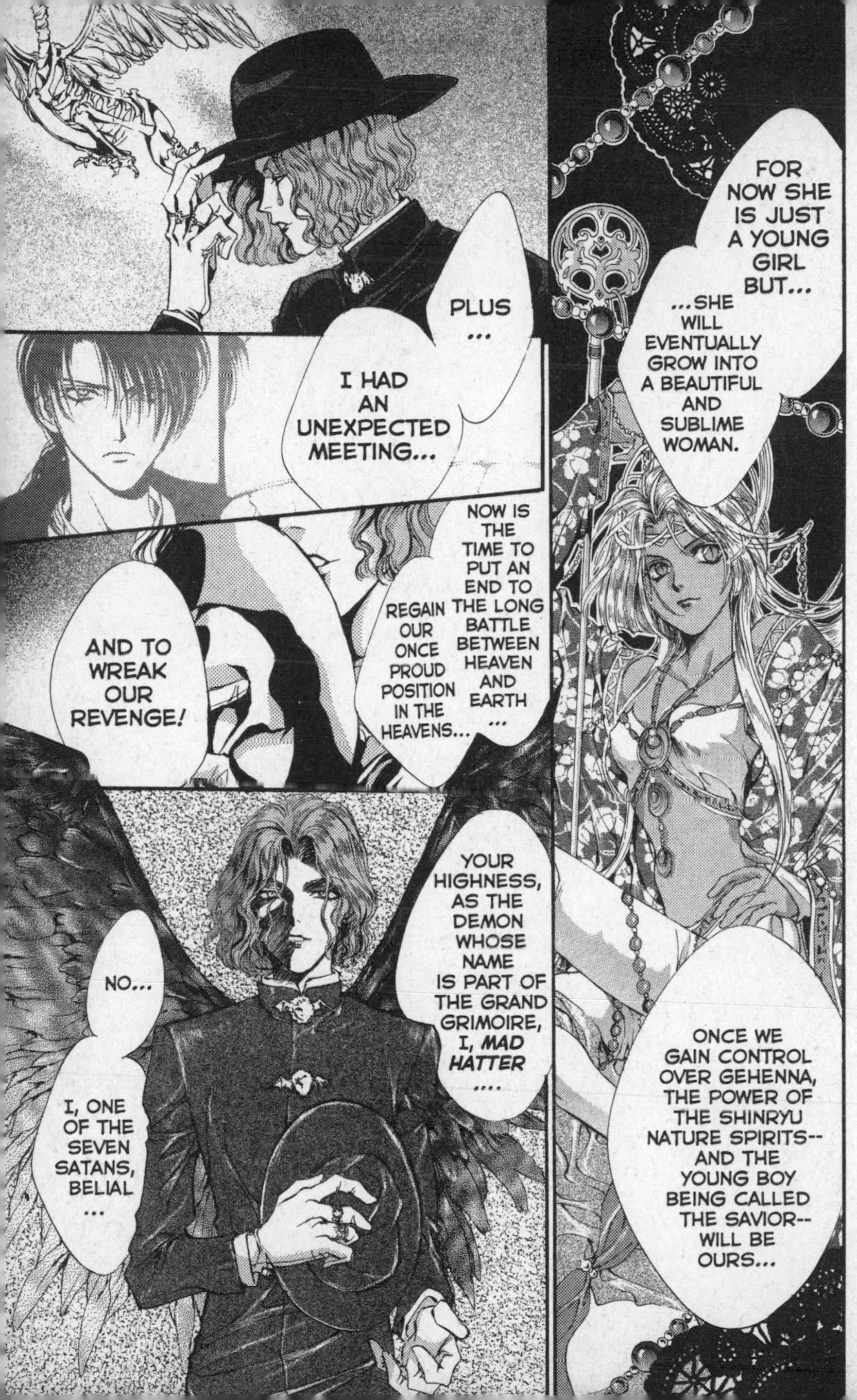
FOR NOW SHE IS JUST A YOUNG GIRL BUT...
...SHE WILL EVENTUALLY GROW INTO A BEAUTIFUL AND SUBLIME WOMAN.
ONCE WE GAIN CONTROL OVER GEHENNA, THE POWER OF THE SHINRYU NATURE SPIRITS--AND THE YOUNG BOY BEING CALLED THE SAVIOR--WILL BE OURS...
PLUS ...
I HAD AN UNEXPECTED MEETING...
NOW IS THE TIME TO PUT AN END TO THE LONG BATTLE BETWEEN HEAVEN AND EARTH ...
REGAIN OUR ONCE PROUD POSITION IN THE HEAVENS...
AND TO WREAK OUR REVENGE!
YOUR HIGHNESS, AS THE DEMON WHOSE NAME IS PART OF THE GRAND GRIMOIRE, I, *MAD HATTER* ....
NO...
I, ONE OF THE SEVEN SATANS, BELIAL ...

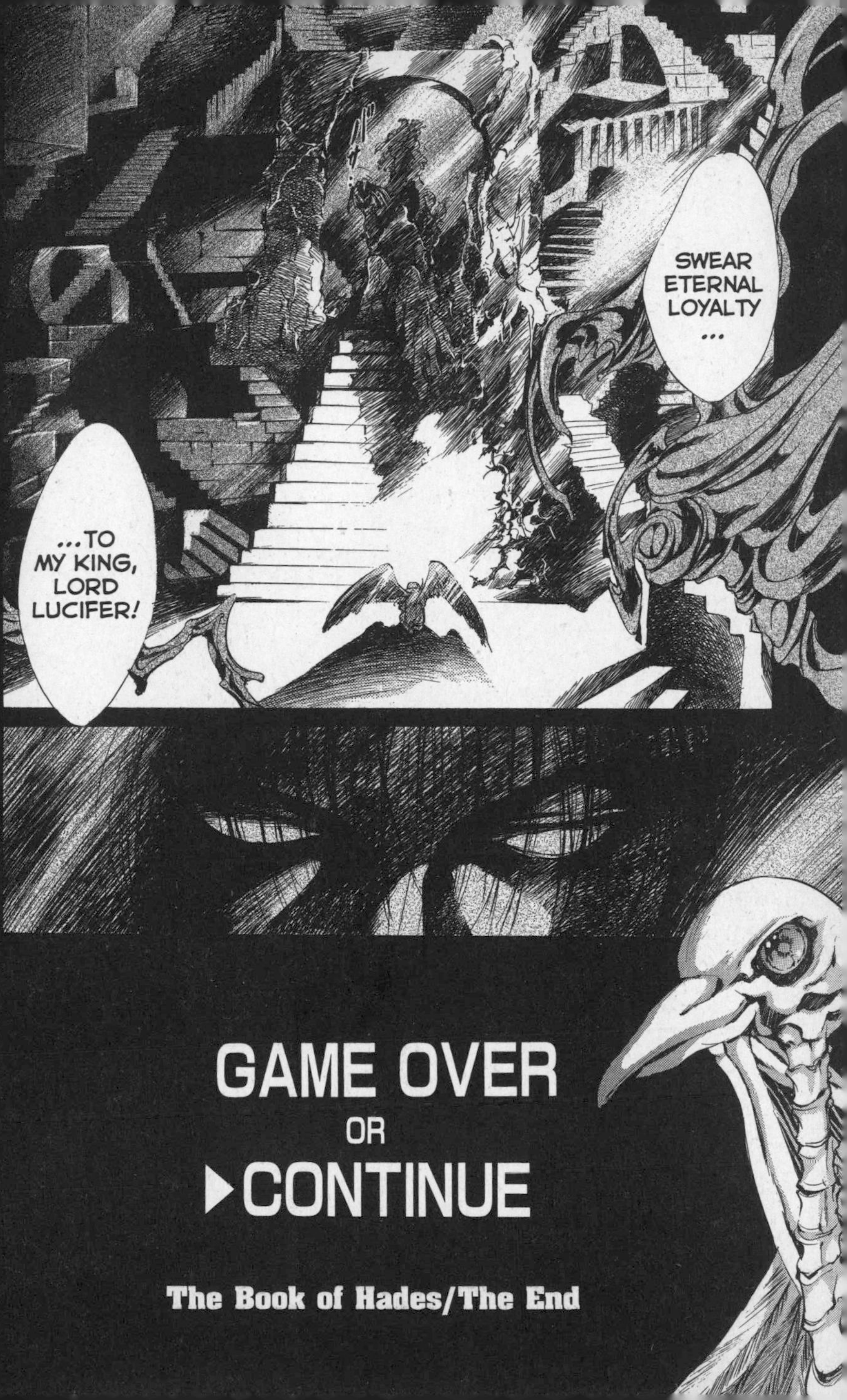
SWEAR ETERNAL LOYALTY ...
...TO MY KING, LORD LUCIFER!
GAME OVER
OR
▶CONTINUE
The Book of Hades/The End

NOW ～～➤ LOADING

Hi, this time I'm so busy that I don't have any time to write a postscript, so I'm bunching up a lot of stuff here. The Hades arc, which lasted longer than I thought, has finally concluded. Phew. Setsuna entering Alexiel's body... I came up with this idea a while ago and didn't think it would take this long to get to it. Anyway, the new saga begins, the Gehenna arc. The story that starts on the next page is... Hmm... Those who read this in the magazine are probably thinking "Don't you mean the Yetzirah arc?" Yes, I know, the currently running arc is actually called that in Hana to Yume magazine. But this is the correct title. There was a mix-up in the magazine due to... me... The actual Yetzirah saga is supposed to come up a little later, but once a few chapters were published we couldn't change it... So that's been corrected for the comic release... Sorry for the mix-up. And as I say this the Yetzirah arc continues in the magazine...

Oh yeah, I got a lot of responses from the last postscript. I'm glad I wrote what I did. I got comments like "I'm going to keep being a big fan!" and "It felt like you had gone so far away but I'm so happy you're back!" and "I'm so impressed with how you love to draw manga." Though I did feel weird reading about how someone is happy that drawing manga comes natural to me. All of your warm letters mean so much to me. And of course, I also love music. Just because I didn't write about it doesn't mean I stopped enjoying it. Oh! I'm out of space! All right, bye bye!

The music recommendations are very helpful, as always. I'm getting a lot of indie band tapes these days. Sometimes I have two or three people sending me the same tape, does that mean that band's about to hit it big? I liked them too.

...supposedly...

we are angels

really COMING SOON!
↓

Oh yeah, Papaya Boing!! ...is what one of my assistants wanted me to write in the comic... Well, it's suppose to be because Alexiel's breasts are so big and bouncy... Does writing that in the comic make Alexiel happy? I don't know... It's a mystery! Right, Q-chan?

天使禁猟区（てんしきんりょうく）

Angel Sanctuary

The Book of Gehenna

ACT.1 The Angel of Fire

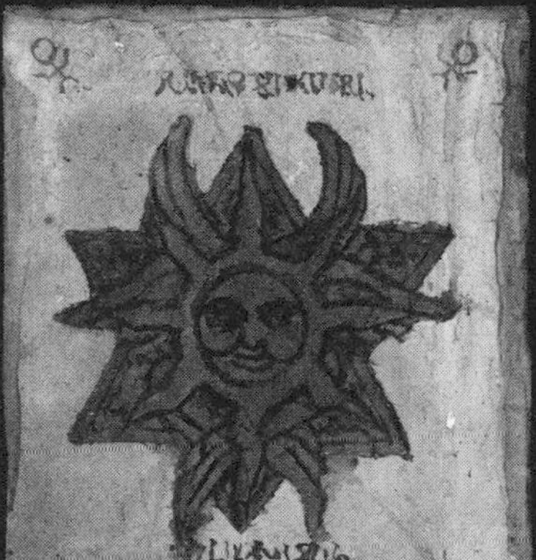

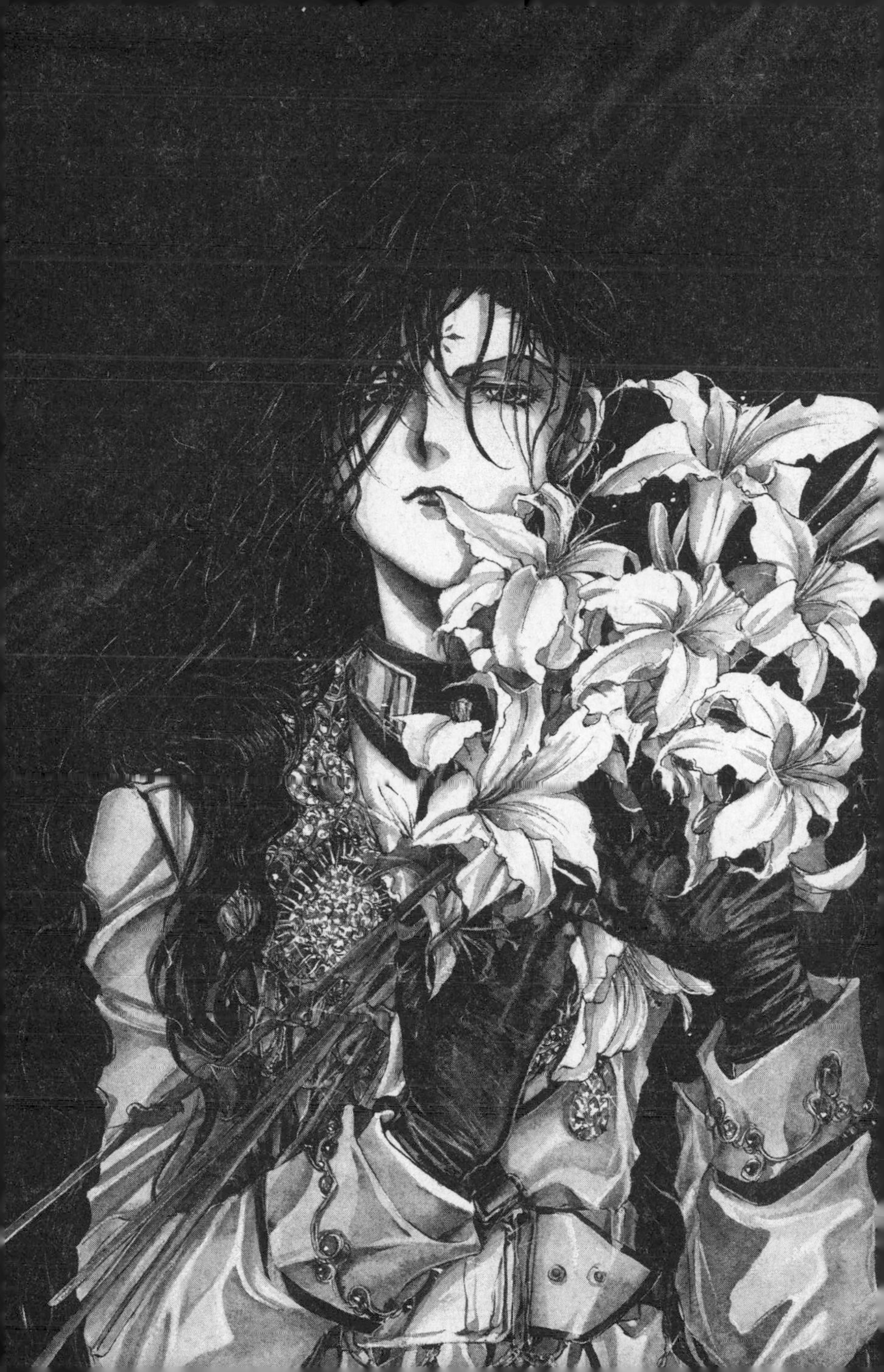

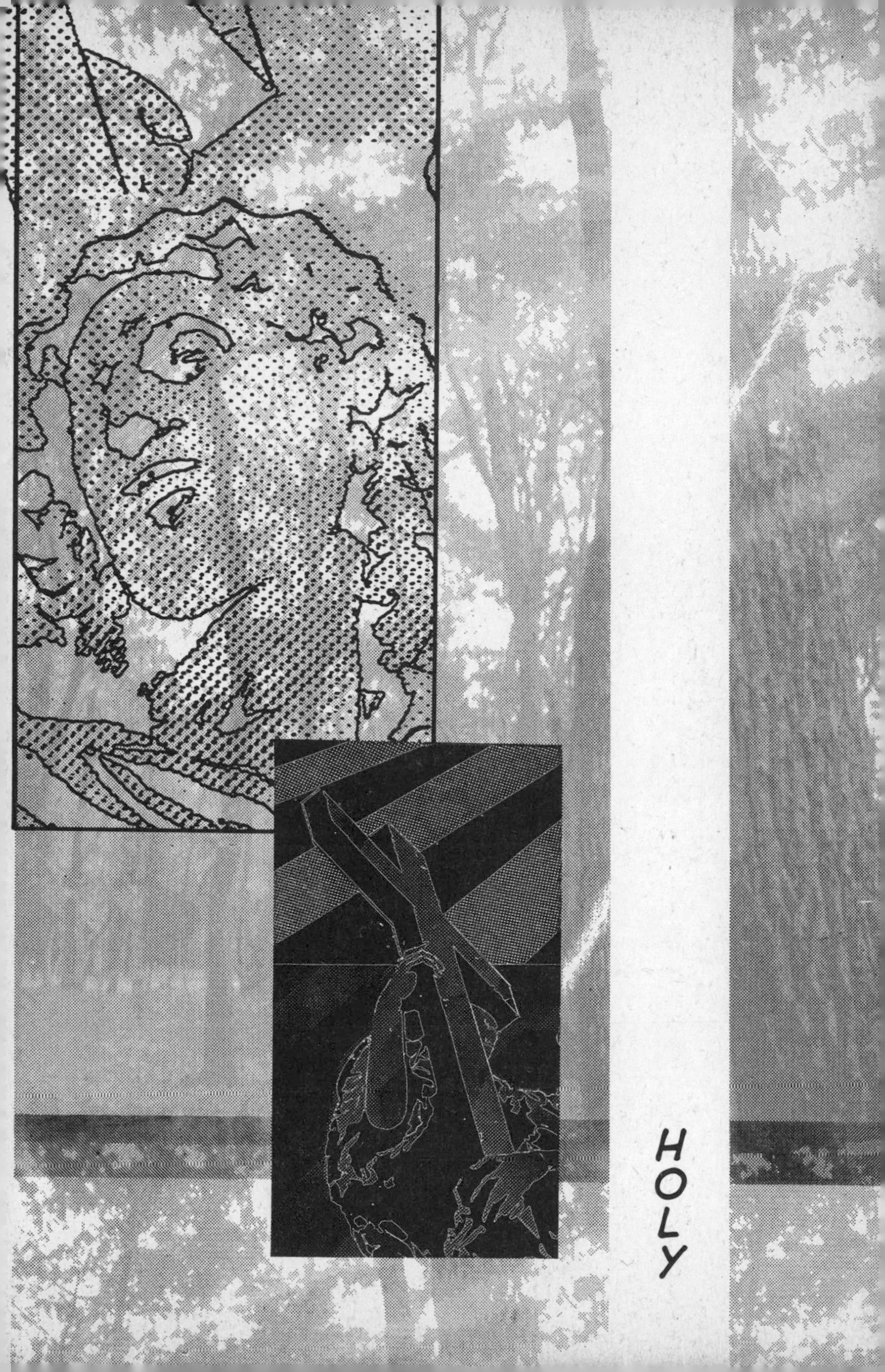
HOLY

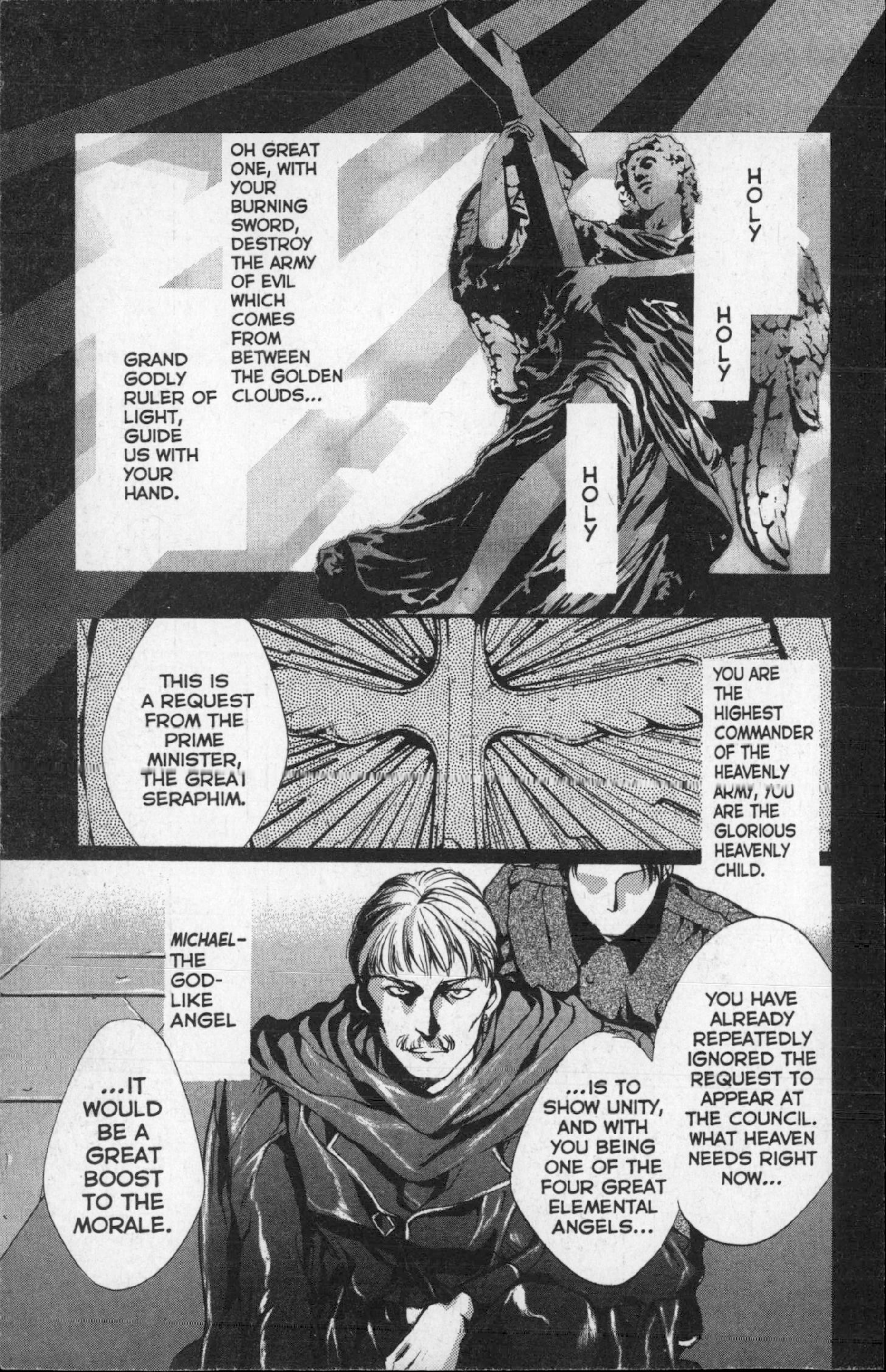
HOLY
HOLY
HOLY
OH GREAT ONE, WITH YOUR BURNING SWORD, DESTROY THE ARMY OF EVIL WHICH COMES FROM BETWEEN THE GOLDEN CLOUDS...
GRAND GODLY RULER OF LIGHT, GUIDE US WITH YOUR HAND.
YOU ARE THE HIGHEST COMMANDER OF THE HEAVENLY ARMY, YOU ARE THE GLORIOUS HEAVENLY CHILD.
THIS IS A REQUEST FROM THE PRIME MINISTER, THE GREAT SERAPHIM.
MICHAEL– THE GOD-LIKE ANGEL
YOU HAVE ALREADY REPEATEDLY IGNORED THE REQUEST TO APPEAR AT THE COUNCIL. WHAT HEAVEN NEEDS RIGHT NOW...
...IS TO SHOW UNITY, AND WITH YOU BEING ONE OF THE FOUR GREAT ELEMENTAL ANGELS...
...IT WOULD BE A GREAT BOOST TO THE MORALE.

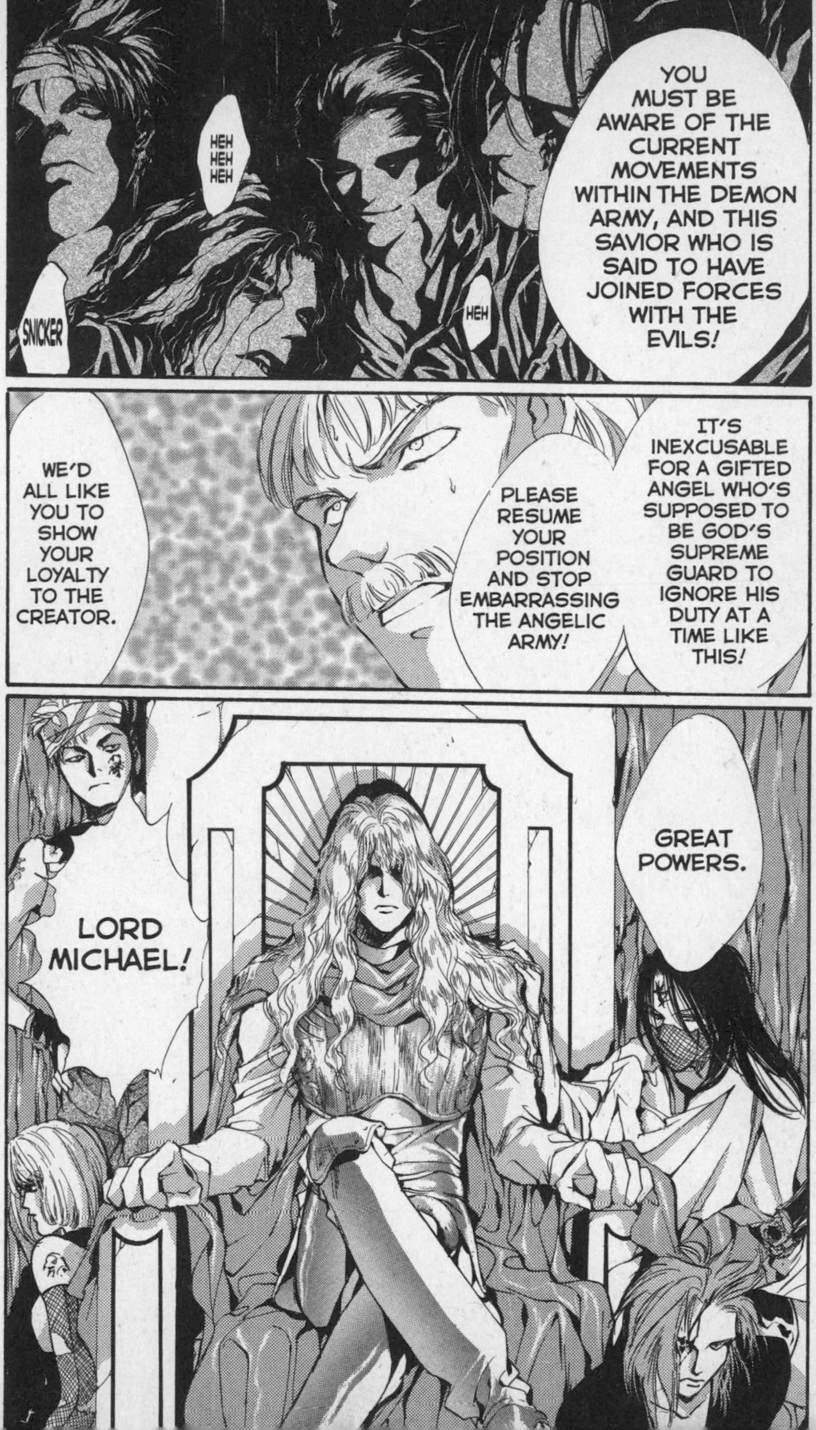
YOU MUST BE AWARE OF THE CURRENT MOVEMENTS WITHIN THE DEMON ARMY, AND THIS SAVIOR WHO IS SAID TO HAVE JOINED FORCES WITH THE EVILS!
HEH HEH HEH
HEH
SNICKER
IT'S INEXCUSABLE FOR A GIFTED ANGEL WHO'S SUPPOSED TO BE GOD'S SUPREME GUARD TO IGNORE HIS DUTY AT A TIME LIKE THIS!
PLEASE RESUME YOUR POSITION AND STOP EMBARRASSING THE ANGELIC ARMY!
WE'D ALL LIKE YOU TO SHOW YOUR LOYALTY TO THE CREATOR.
GREAT POWERS.
LORD MICHAEL!

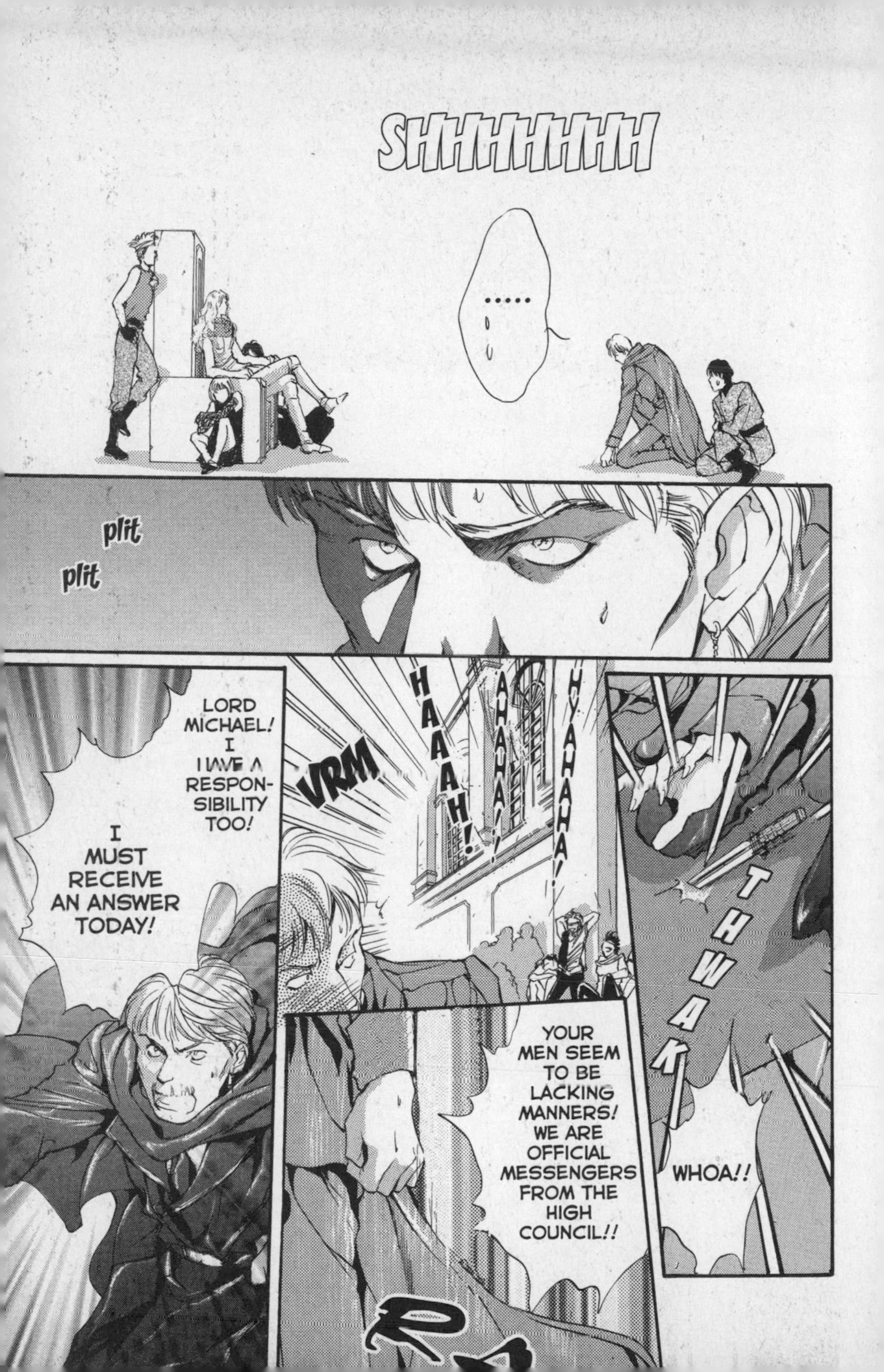
SHHHHHHHHH
.....
plit
plit
THWAK
WHOA!!
HAAAAH!
AHAHA!!
HYAHAHA!!
VRM
YOUR MEN SEEM TO BE LACKING MANNERS! WE ARE OFFICIAL MESSENGERS FROM THE HIGH COUNCIL!!
LORD MICHAEL! I HAVE A RESPONSIBILITY TOO!
I MUST RECEIVE AN ANSWER TODAY!

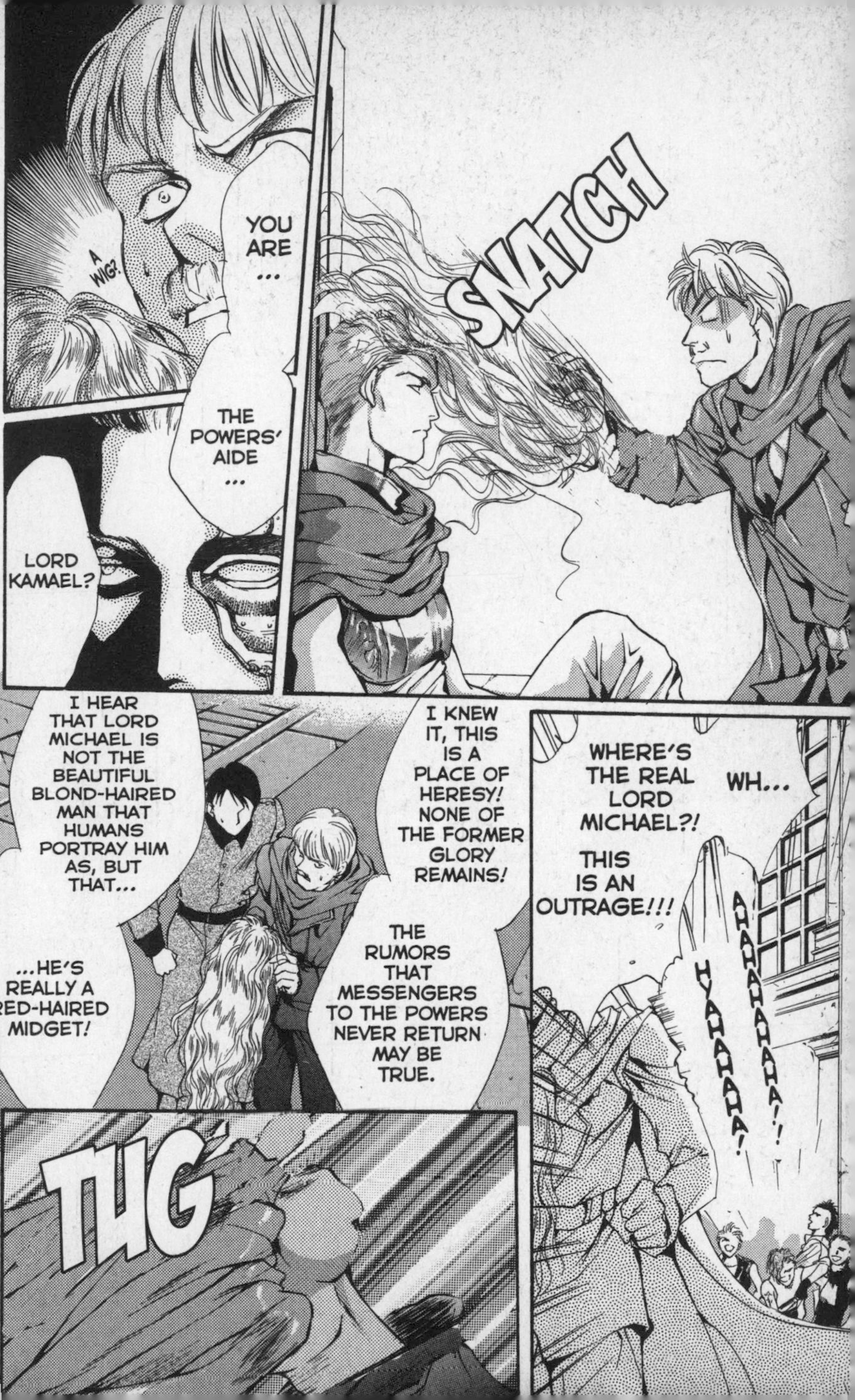
SNATCH
YOU ARE ...
A WIG?
THE POWERS' AIDE ...
LORD KAMAEL?
WH...
WHERE'S THE REAL LORD MICHAEL?!
THIS IS AN OUTRAGE!!!
AHAHAHAHA!!
HYAHAHAHA!
I KNEW IT, THIS IS A PLACE OF HERESY! NONE OF THE FORMER GLORY REMAINS!
THE RUMORS THAT MESSENGERS TO THE POWERS NEVER RETURN MAY BE TRUE.
I HEAR THAT LORD MICHAEL IS NOT THE BEAUTIFUL BLOND-HAIRED MAN THAT HUMANS PORTRAY HIM AS, BUT THAT...
...HE'S REALLY A RED-HAIRED MIDGET!
TUG

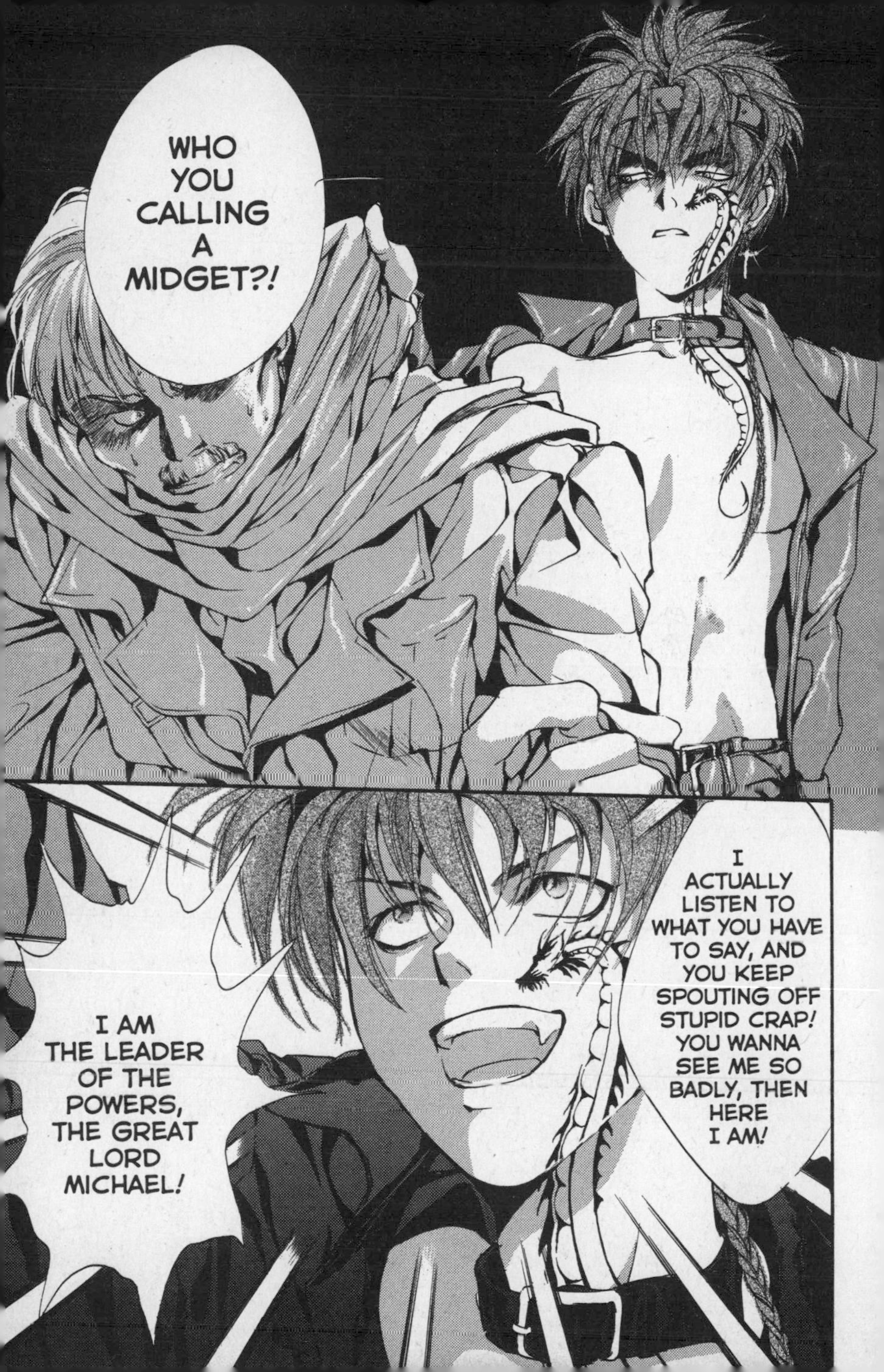
WHO YOU CALLING A MIDGET?!
I ACTUALLY LISTEN TO WHAT YOU HAVE TO SAY, AND YOU KEEP SPOUTING OFF STUPID CRAP! YOU WANNA SEE ME SO BADLY, THEN HERE I AM!
I AM THE LEADER OF THE POWERS, THE GREAT LORD MICHAEL!

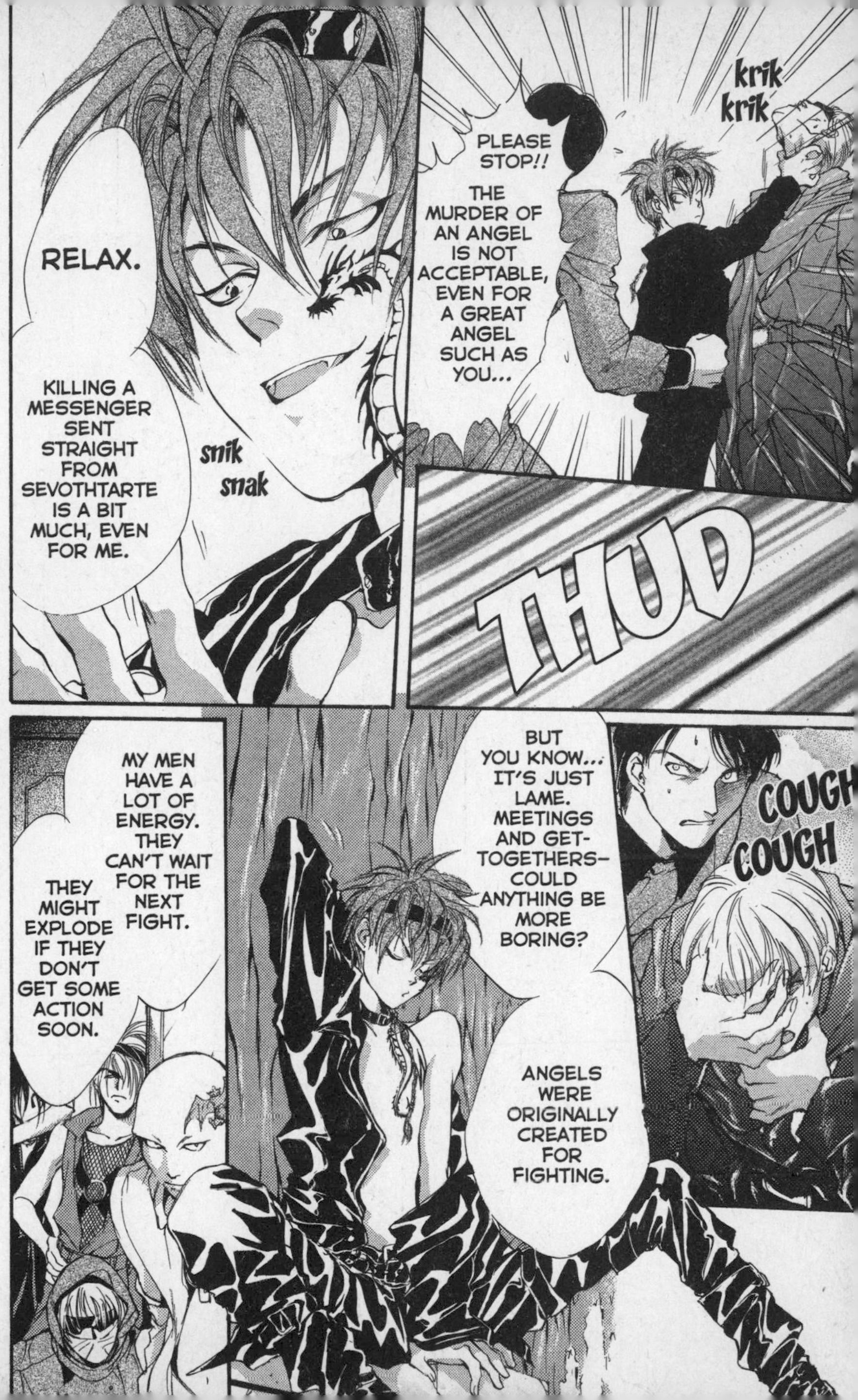
krik krik
PLEASE STOP!!
THE MURDER OF AN ANGEL IS NOT ACCEPTABLE, EVEN FOR A GREAT ANGEL SUCH AS YOU...
THUD
RELAX.
snik snak
KILLING A MESSENGER SENT STRAIGHT FROM SEVOTHTARTE IS A BIT MUCH, EVEN FOR ME.
COUGH COUGH
BUT YOU KNOW... IT'S JUST LAME. MEETINGS AND GET-TOGETHERS—COULD ANYTHING BE MORE BORING?
ANGELS WERE ORIGINALLY CREATED FOR FIGHTING.
MY MEN HAVE A LOT OF ENERGY. THEY CAN'T WAIT FOR THE NEXT FIGHT.
THEY MIGHT EXPLODE IF THEY DON'T GET SOME ACTION SOON.

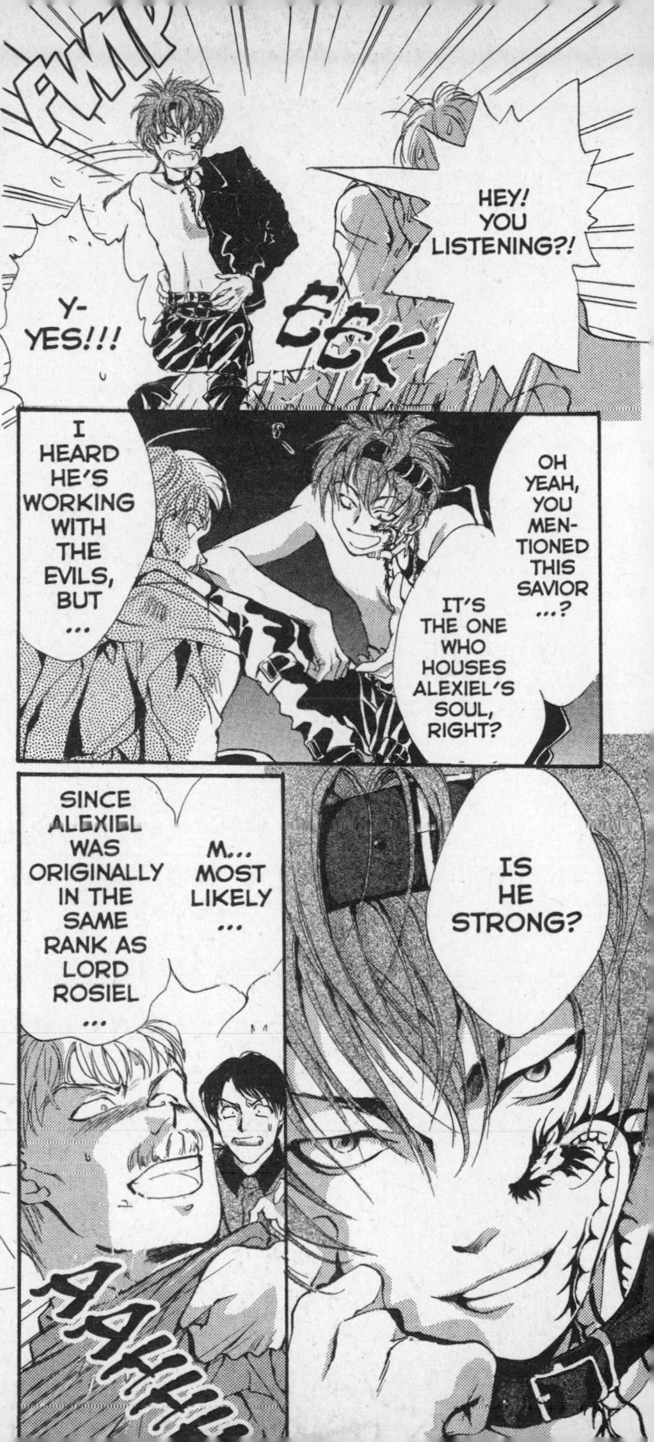
FWIP
HEY! YOU LISTENING?!
EEK
Y- YES!!!
OH YEAH, YOU MEN-TIONED THIS SAVIOR ...?
IT'S THE ONE WHO HOUSES ALEXIEL'S SOUL, RIGHT?
I HEARD HE'S WORKING WITH THE EVILS, BUT ...
IS HE STRONG?
M... MOST LIKELY ...
SINCE ALEXIEL WAS ORIGINALLY IN THE SAME RANK AS LORD ROSIEL ...
AAHH

A S

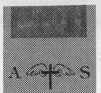

Finally *Michael* has made his appearance! I know lots of people were waiting for this but... I'm surprised he's been so popular! He's not that cute, so I figured he wouldn't be very popular. I guess he just had a big impact with his tattoo and first scene. Anyway, my thinking was to create a Michael that has never been seen before... Since he's the Angel of Fire, I figured that red would be a good color for him and this is what happened... The thing with his twin brother is no big mystery, you can figure it out with a little research.

It's that famous person. If you don't know already, then maybe keeping it that way is best.

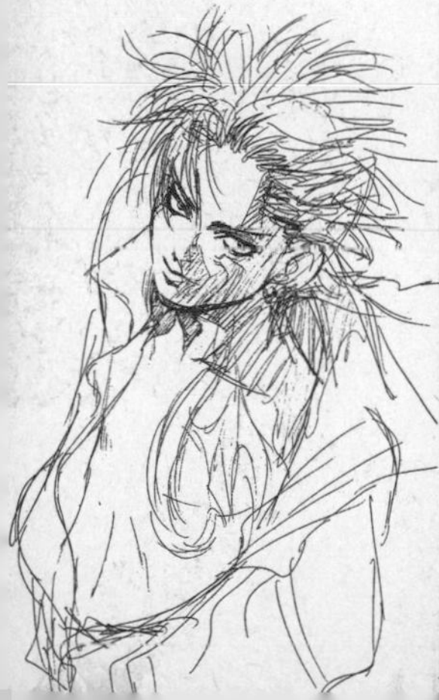

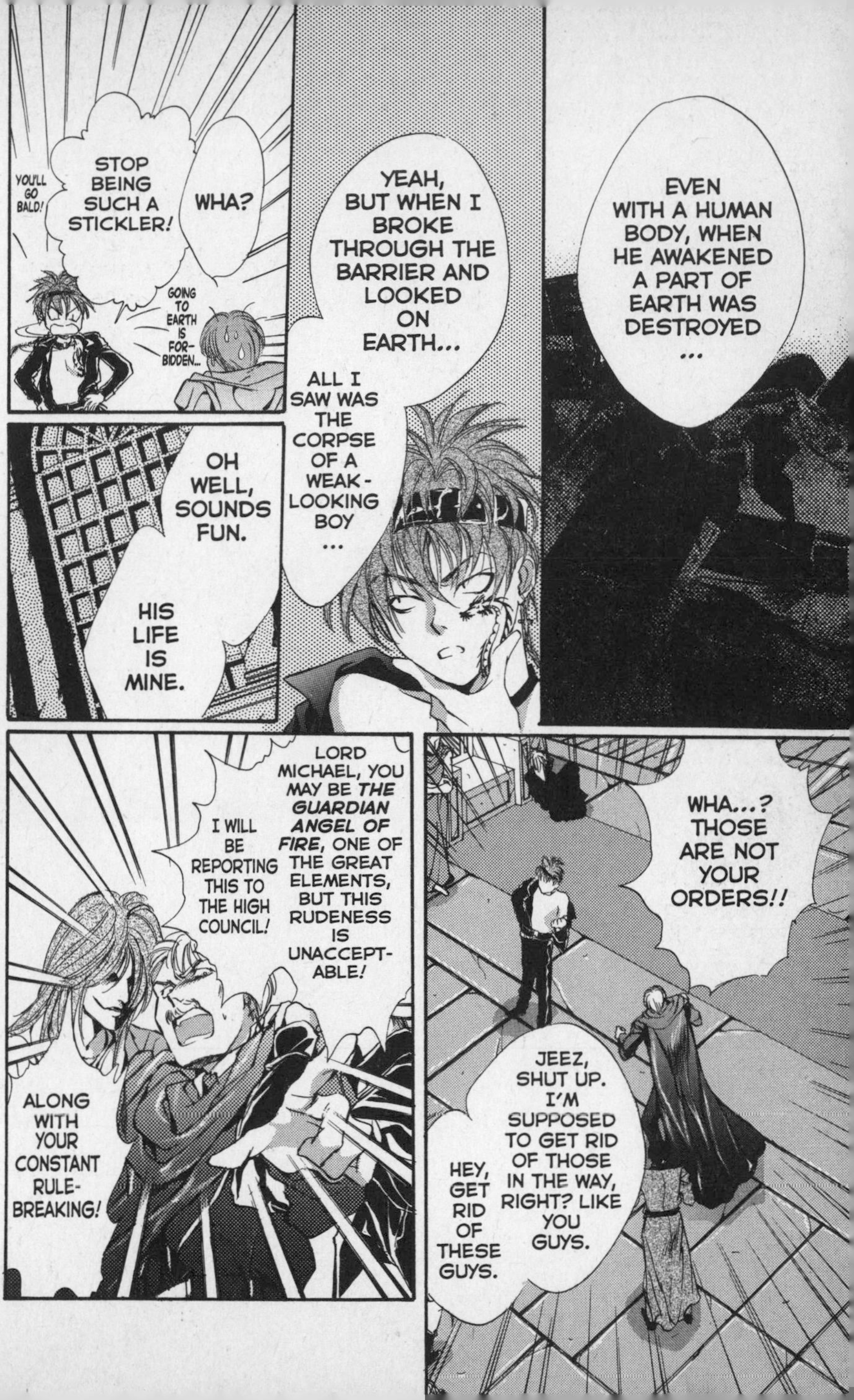
EVEN WITH A HUMAN BODY, WHEN HE AWAKENED A PART OF EARTH WAS DESTROYED ...
YEAH, BUT WHEN I BROKE THROUGH THE BARRIER AND LOOKED ON EARTH...
ALL I SAW WAS THE CORPSE OF A WEAK-LOOKING BOY ...
WHA?
GOING TO EARTH IS FORBIDDEN...
STOP BEING SUCH A STICKLER!
YOU'LL GO BALD!
OH WELL, SOUNDS FUN.
HIS LIFE IS MINE.
WHA...? THOSE ARE NOT YOUR ORDERS!!
JEEZ, SHUT UP. I'M SUPPOSED TO GET RID OF THOSE IN THE WAY, RIGHT? LIKE YOU GUYS.
HEY, GET RID OF THESE GUYS.
LORD MICHAEL, YOU MAY BE *THE GUARDIAN ANGEL OF FIRE*, ONE OF THE GREAT ELEMENTS, BUT THIS RUDENESS IS UNACCEPTABLE!
I WILL BE REPORTING THIS TO THE HIGH COUNCIL!
ALONG WITH YOUR CONSTANT RULE-BREAKING!

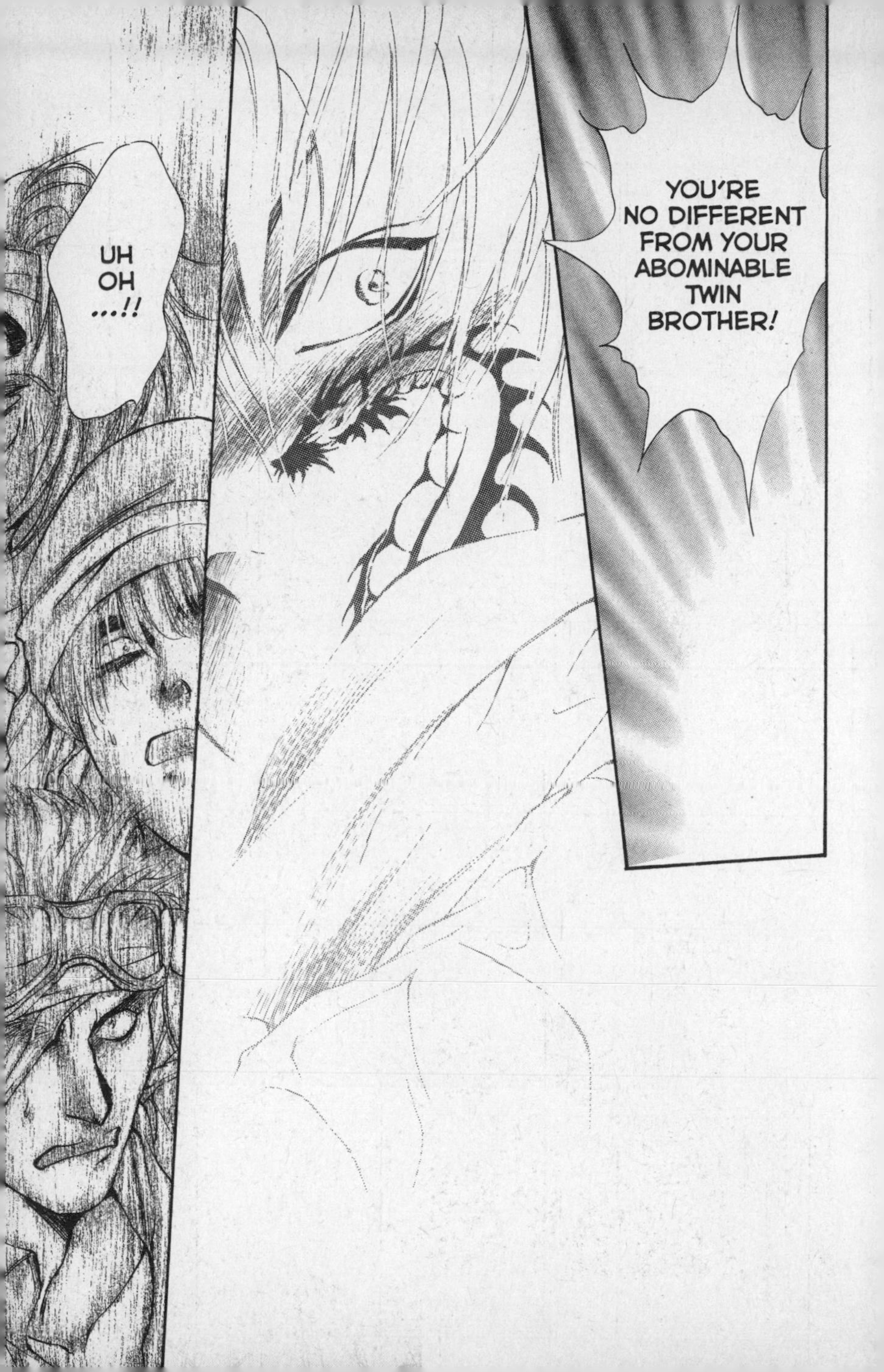
YOU'RE NO DIFFERENT FROM YOUR ABOMINABLE TWIN BROTHER!
UH OH ...!!

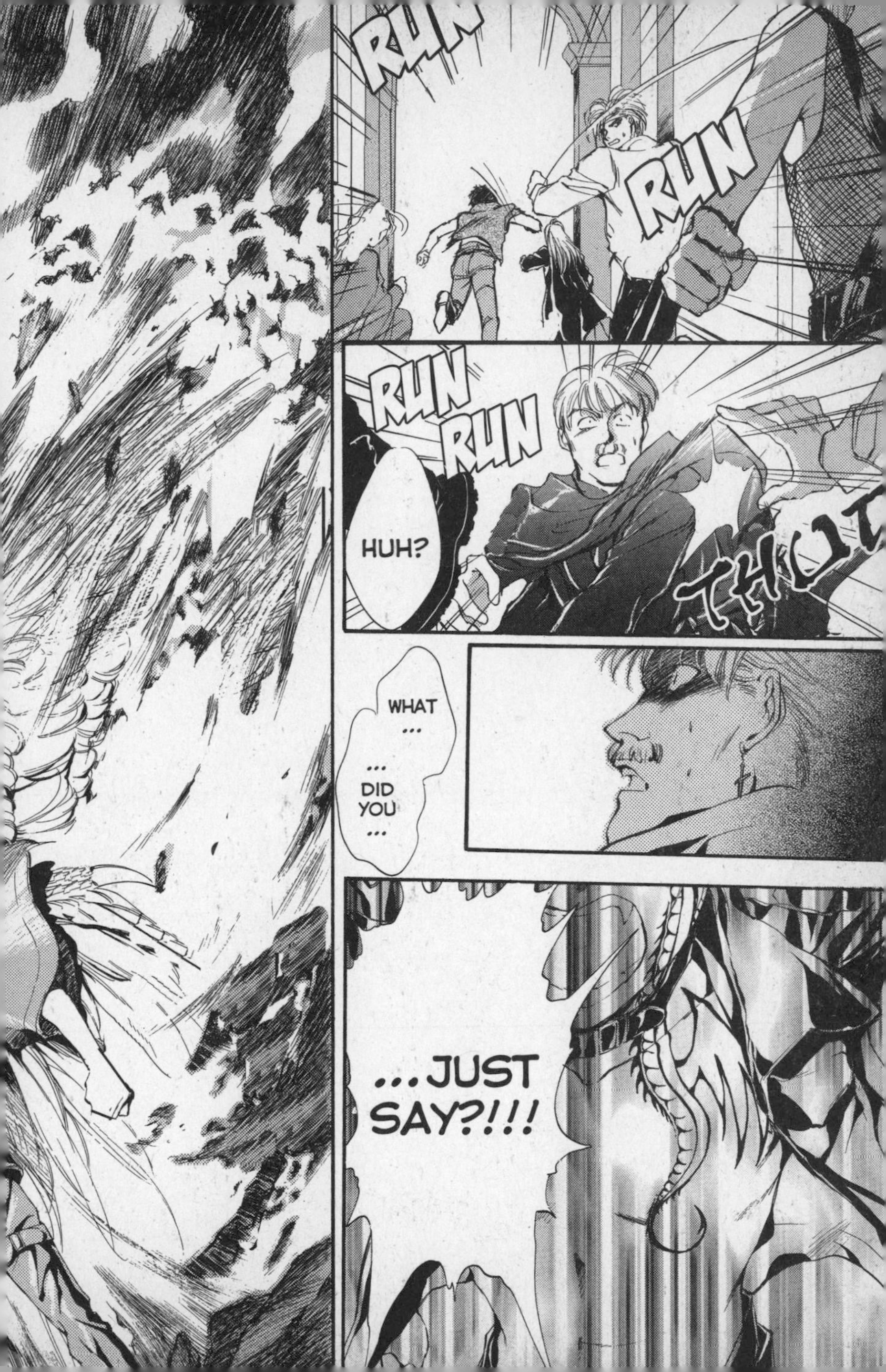
RUN
RUN
RUN RUN
HUH?
THU
WHAT ...
... DID YOU ...
... JUST SAY?!!!

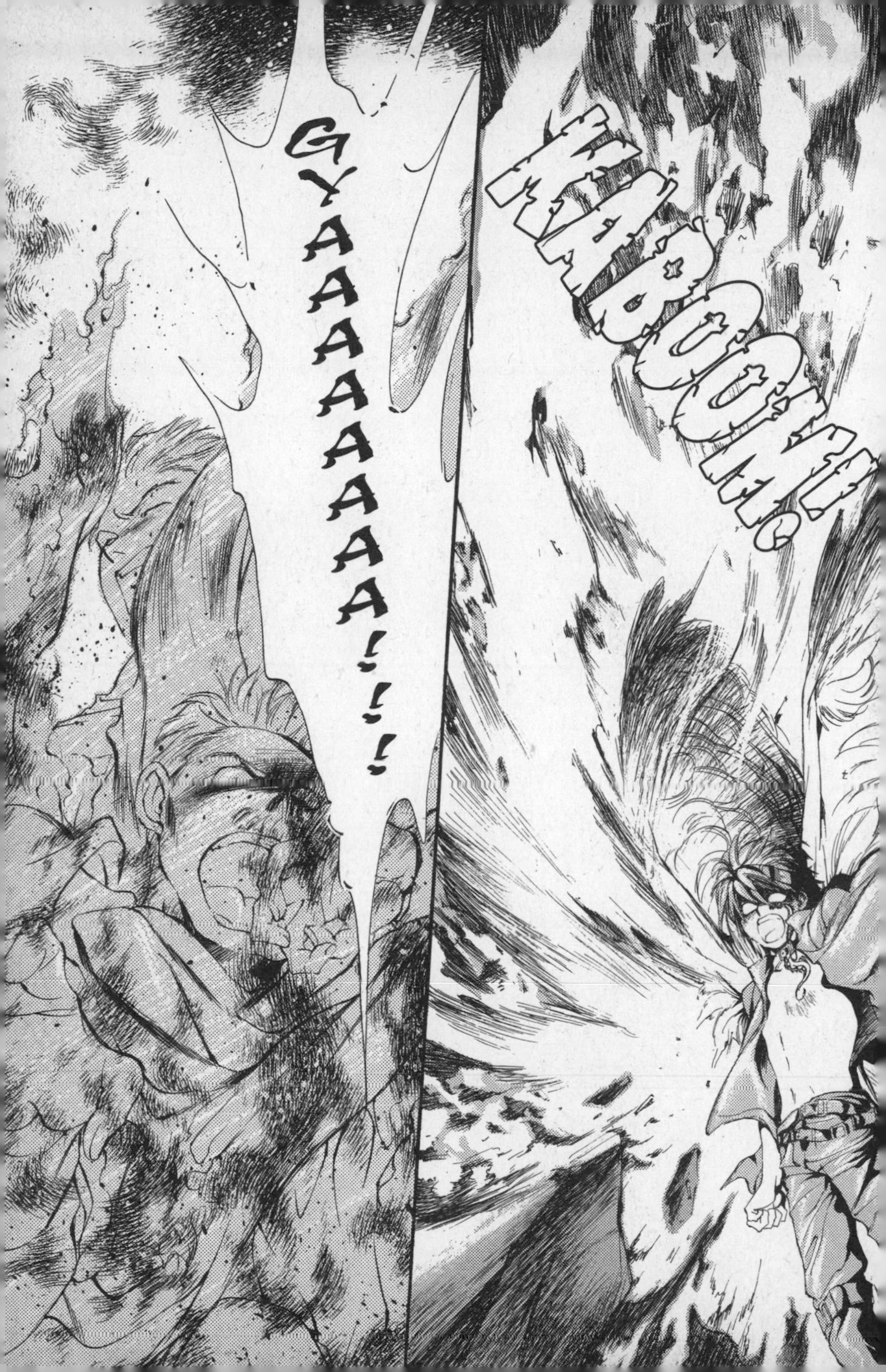
KABOOM!
GYAAAAAAAA!!!

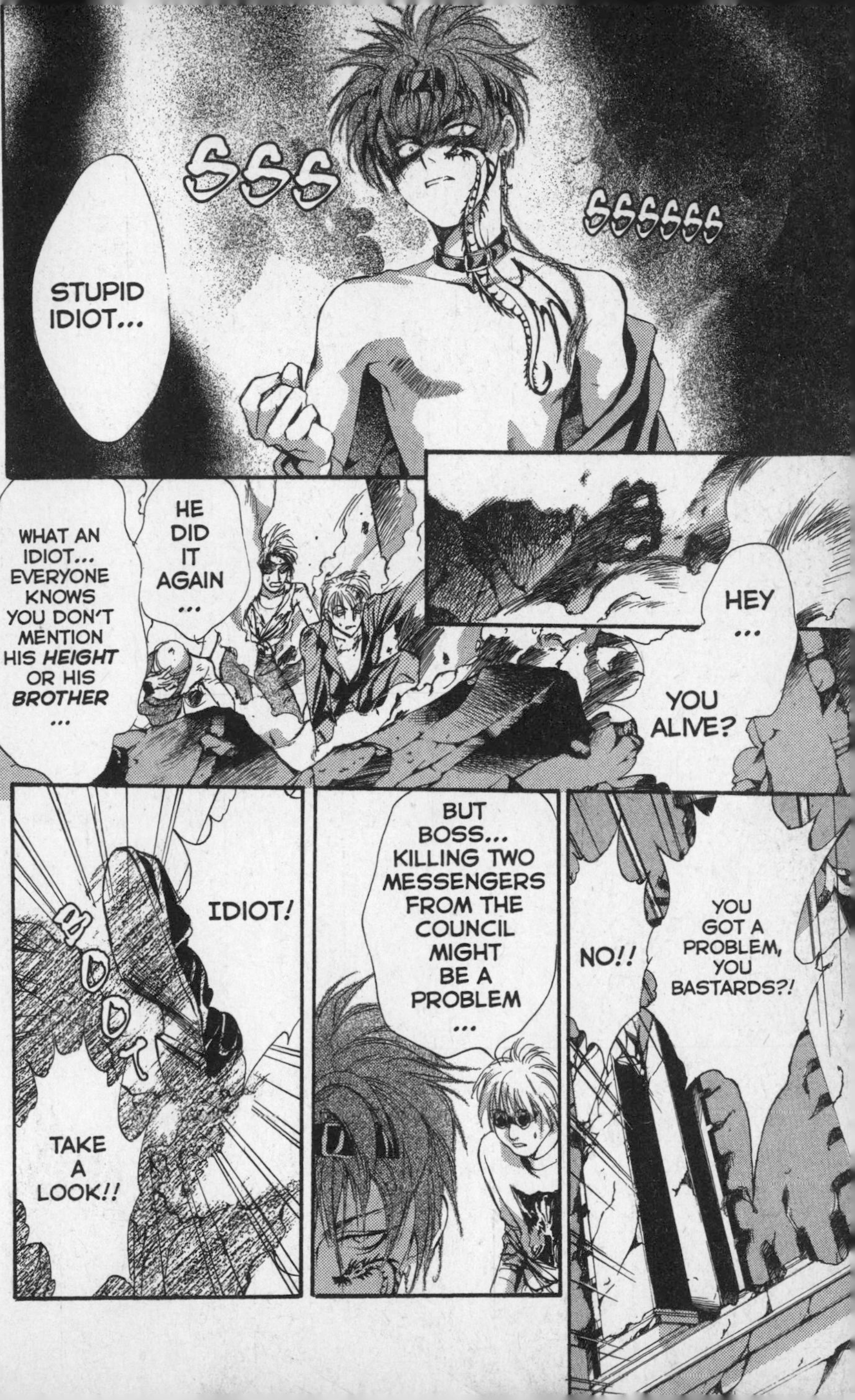
SSSSSS
SSS
STUPID IDIOT...
HEY ... YOU ALIVE?
HE DID IT AGAIN ...
WHAT AN IDIOT... EVERYONE KNOWS YOU DON'T MENTION HIS *HEIGHT* OR HIS *BROTHER* ...
YOU GOT A PROBLEM, YOU BASTARDS?!
NO!!
BUT BOSS... KILLING TWO MESSENGERS FROM THE COUNCIL MIGHT BE A PROBLEM ...
IDIOT!
TAKE A LOOK!!

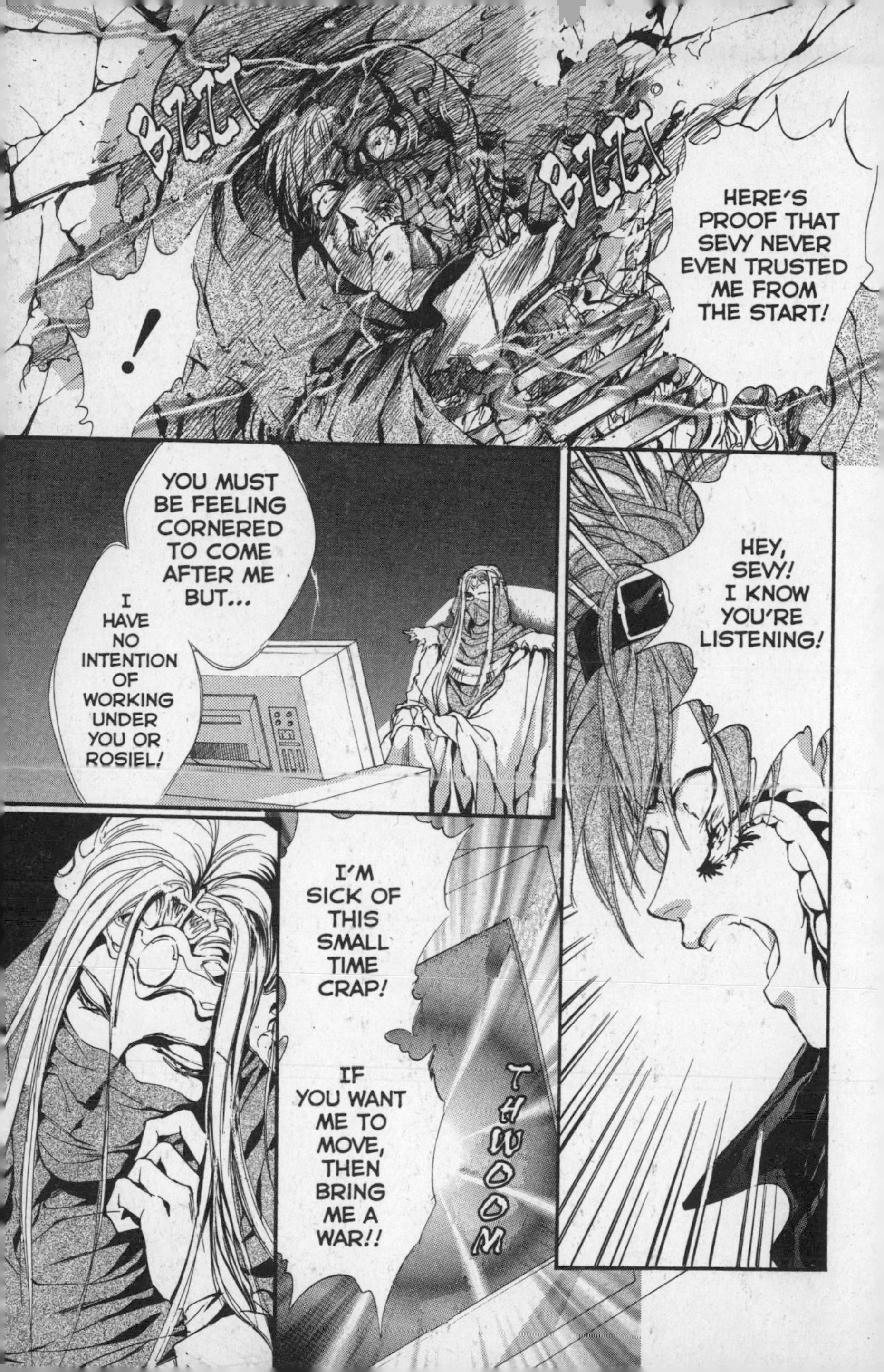
BZZT
BZZT
HERE'S PROOF THAT SEVY NEVER EVEN TRUSTED ME FROM THE START!
!
HEY, SEVY! I KNOW YOU'RE LISTENING!
YOU MUST BE FEELING CORNERED TO COME AFTER ME BUT...
I HAVE NO INTENTION OF WORKING UNDER YOU OR ROSIEL!
I'M SICK OF THIS SMALL TIME CRAP!
IF YOU WANT ME TO MOVE, THEN BRING ME A WAR!!
THWOOM

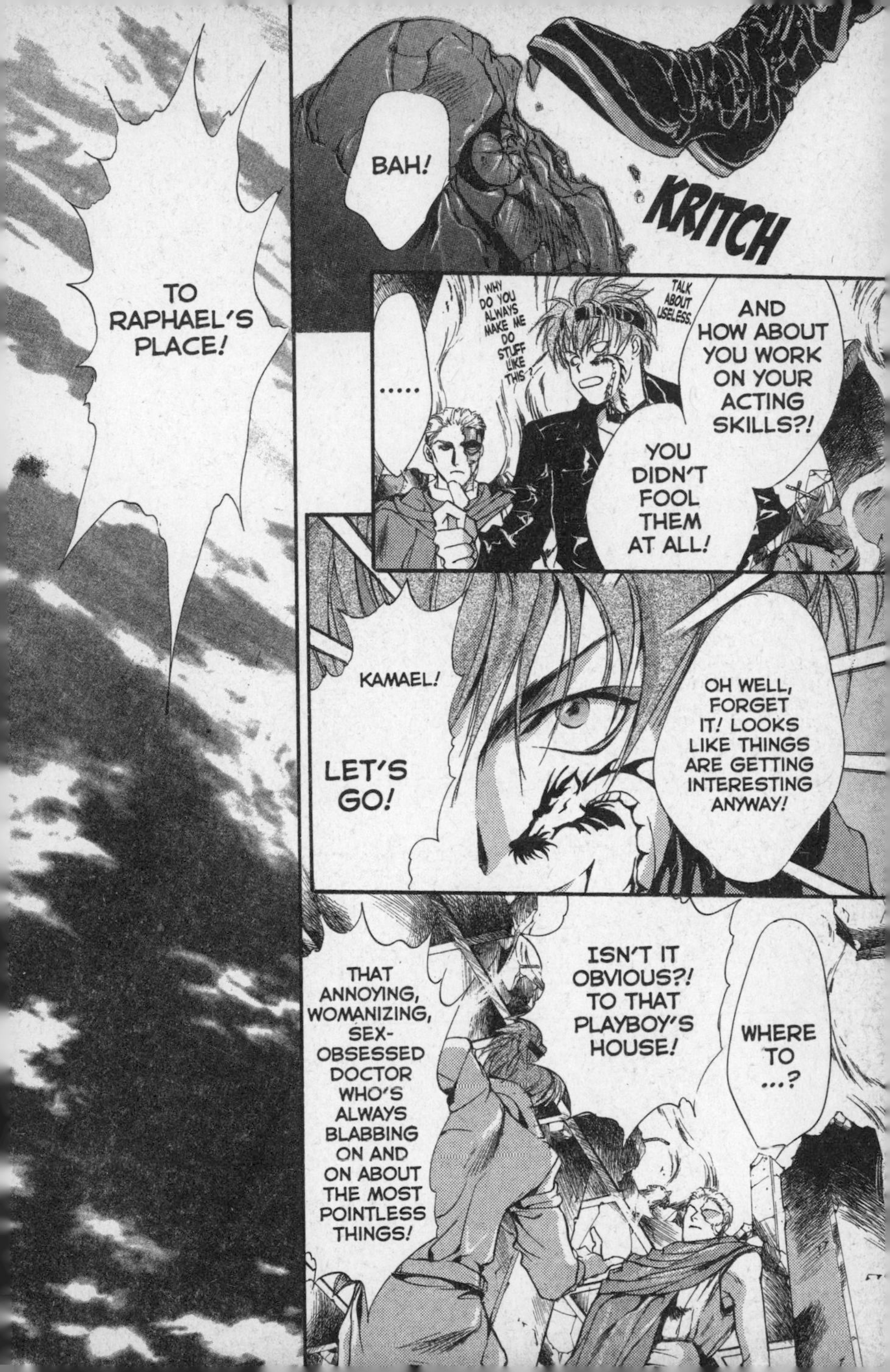
BAH!
KRITCH
AND HOW ABOUT YOU WORK ON YOUR ACTING SKILLS?!
YOU DIDN'T FOOL THEM AT ALL!
TALK ABOUT USELESS.
WHY DO YOU ALWAYS MAKE ME DO STUFF LIKE THIS?
.....
OH WELL, FORGET IT! LOOKS LIKE THINGS ARE GETTING INTERESTING ANYWAY!
KAMAEL!
LET'S GO!
WHERE TO ...?
ISN'T IT OBVIOUS?! TO THAT PLAYBOY'S HOUSE!
THAT ANNOYING, WOMANIZING, SEX-OBSESSED DOCTOR WHO'S ALWAYS BLABBING ON AND ON ABOUT THE MOST POINTLESS THINGS!
TO RAPHAEL'S PLACE!

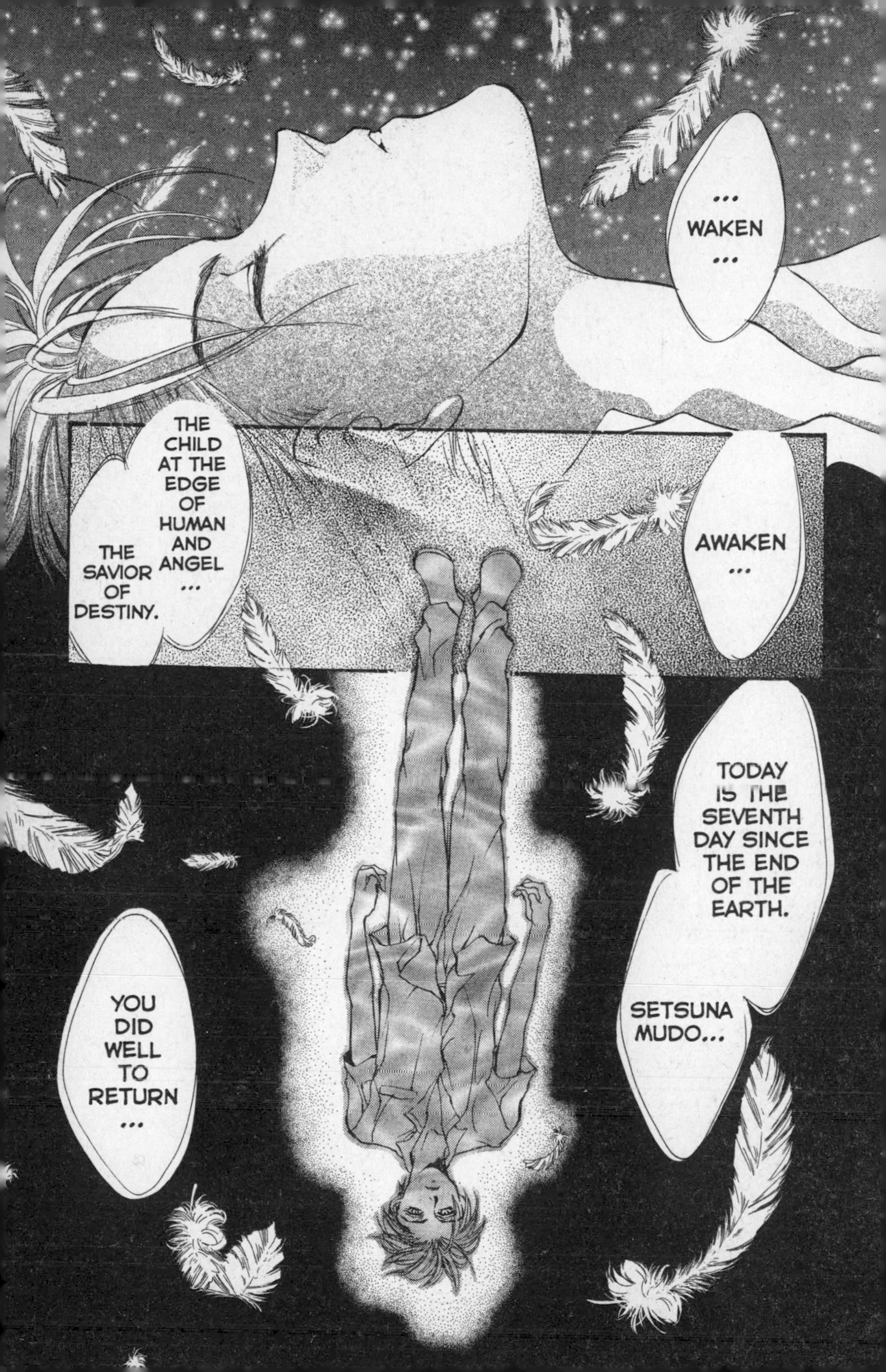
... WAKEN ...
AWAKEN ...
THE CHILD AT THE EDGE OF HUMAN AND ANGEL ...
THE SAVIOR OF DESTINY.
TODAY IS THE SEVENTH DAY SINCE THE END OF THE EARTH.
SETSUNA MUDO...
YOU DID WELL TO RETURN ...

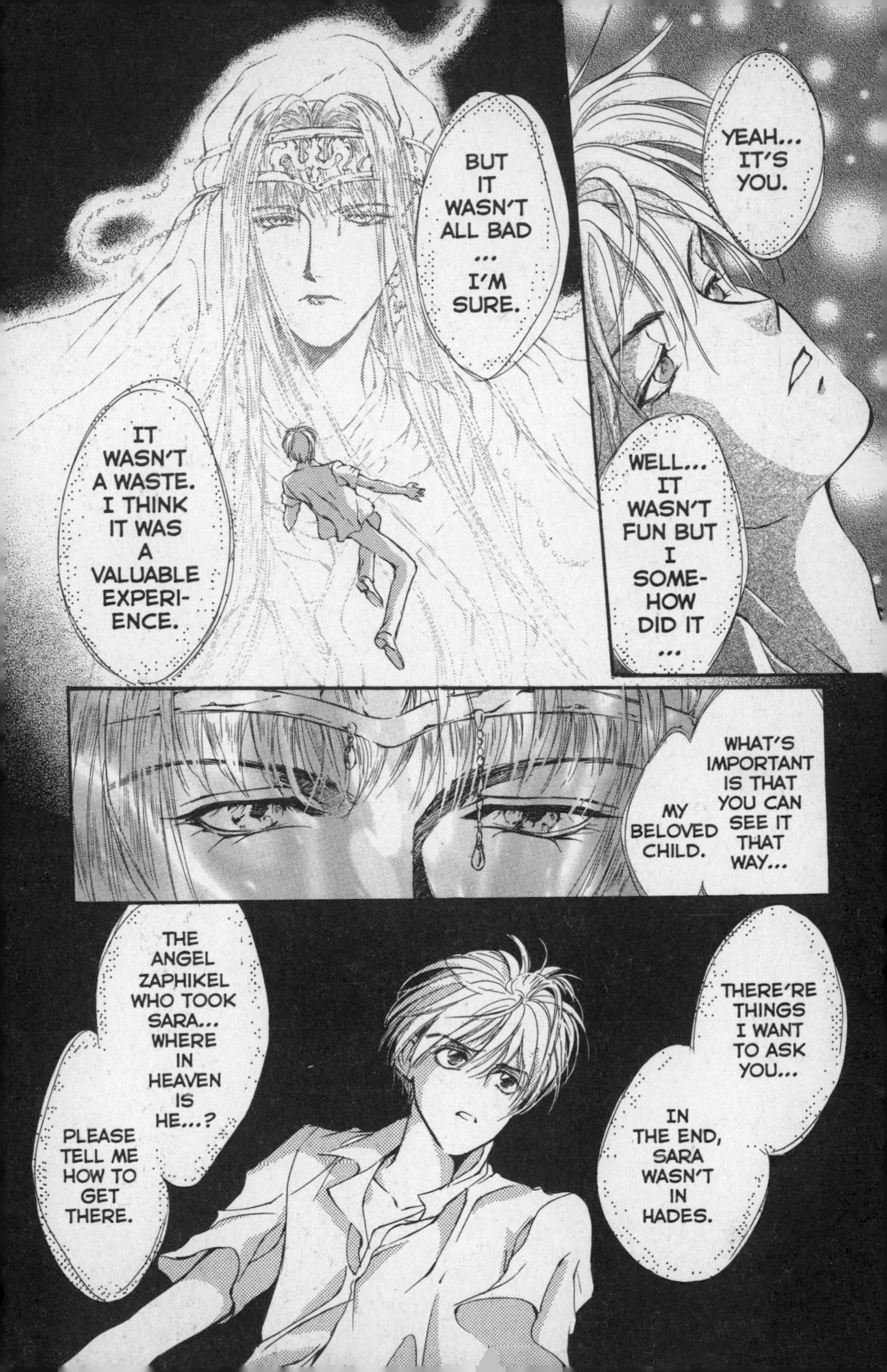
YEAH... IT'S YOU.
WELL... IT WASN'T FUN BUT I SOME-HOW DID IT ...
BUT IT WASN'T ALL BAD ... I'M SURE.
IT WASN'T A WASTE. I THINK IT WAS A VALUABLE EXPERI-ENCE.
WHAT'S IMPORTANT IS THAT YOU CAN SEE IT THAT WAY...
MY BELOVED CHILD.
THERE'RE THINGS I WANT TO ASK YOU...
IN THE END, SARA WASN'T IN HADES.
THE ANGEL ZAPHIKEL WHO TOOK SARA... WHERE IN HEAVEN IS HE...?
PLEASE TELL ME HOW TO GET THERE.

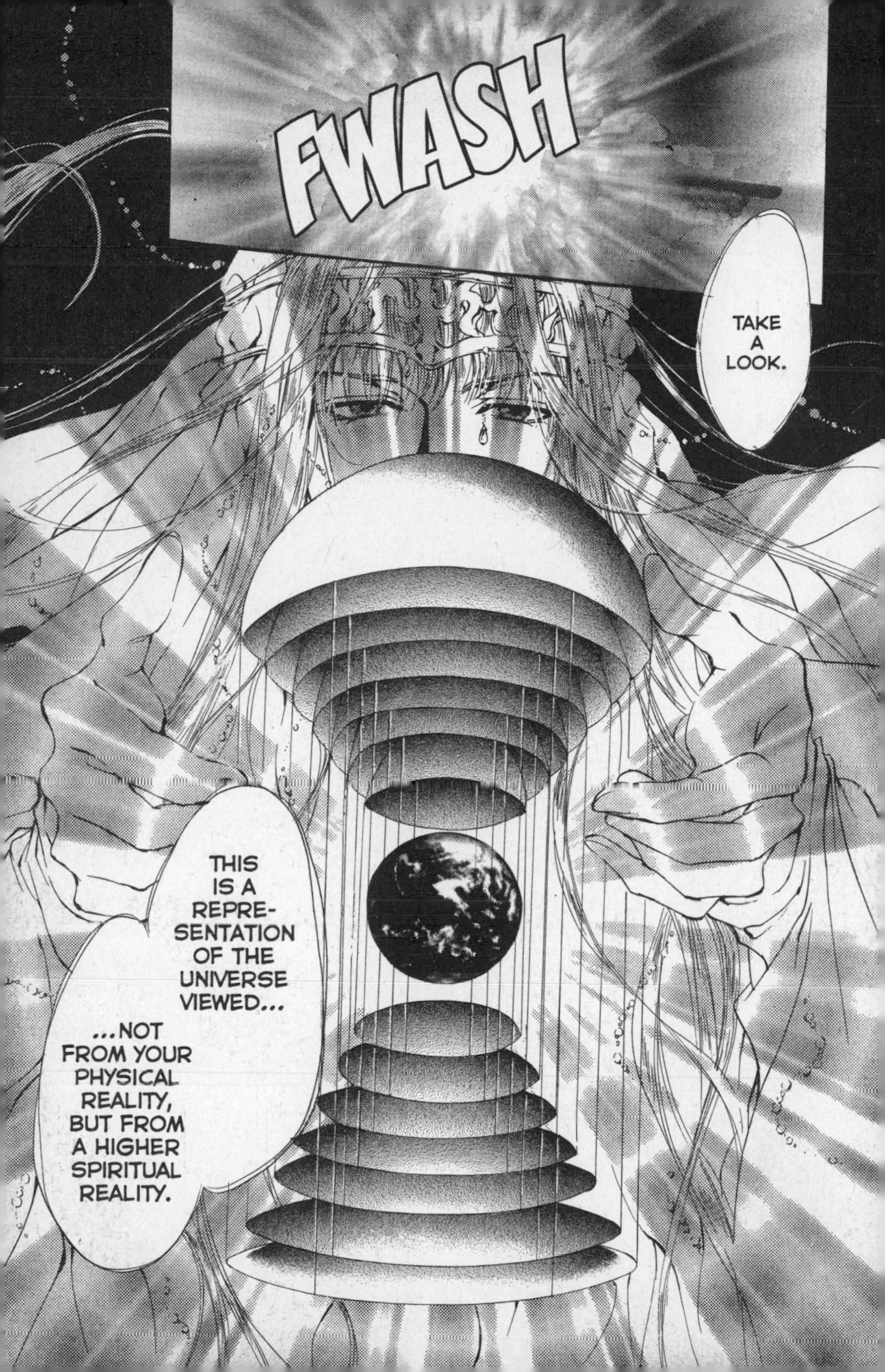
FWASH
TAKE A LOOK.
THIS IS A REPRESENTATION OF THE UNIVERSE VIEWED...
...NOT FROM YOUR PHYSICAL REALITY, BUT FROM A HIGHER SPIRITUAL REALITY.

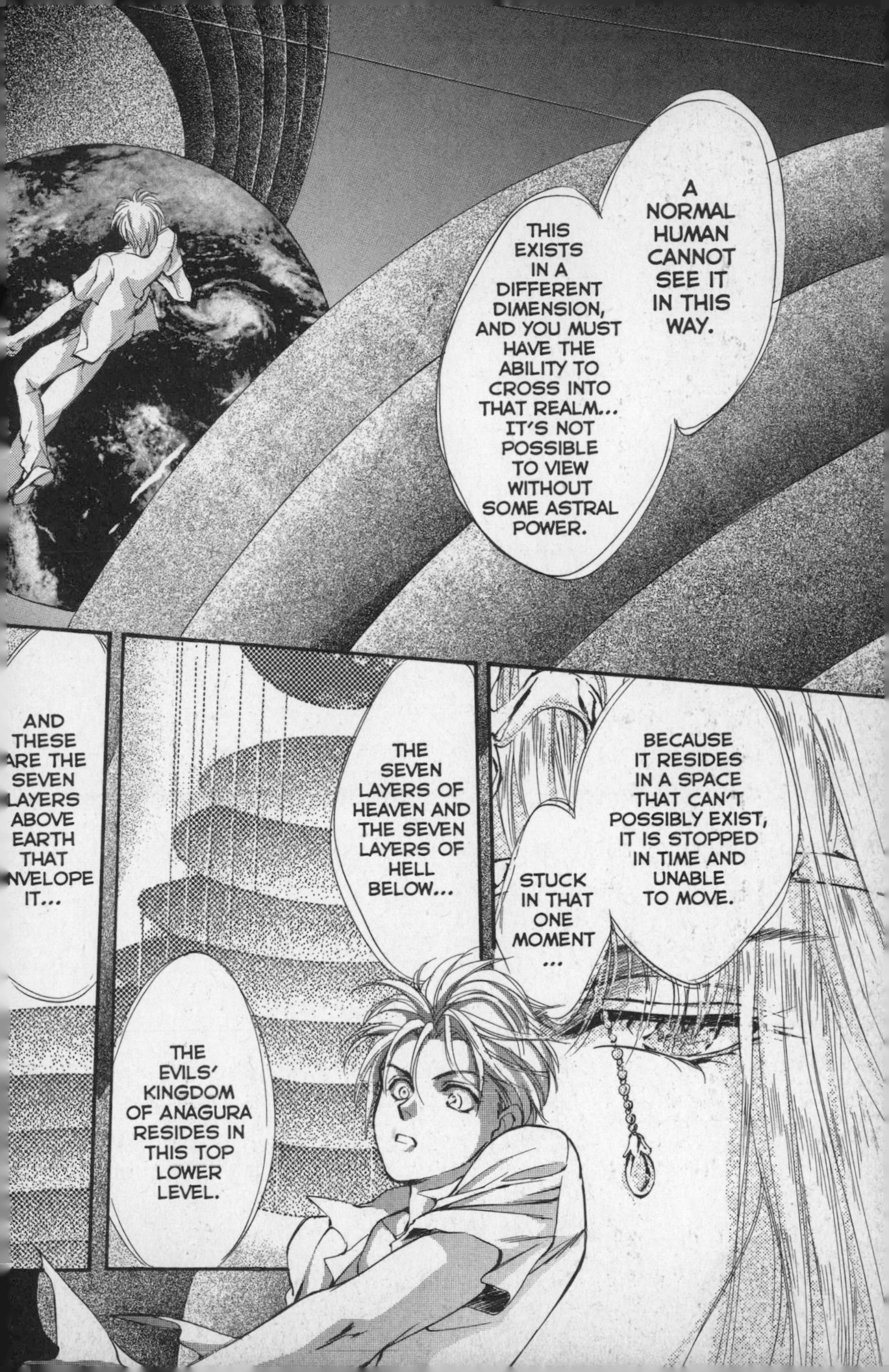
A NORMAL HUMAN CANNOT SEE IT IN THIS WAY.
THIS EXISTS IN A DIFFERENT DIMENSION, AND YOU MUST HAVE THE ABILITY TO CROSS INTO THAT REALM... IT'S NOT POSSIBLE TO VIEW WITHOUT SOME ASTRAL POWER.
BECAUSE IT RESIDES IN A SPACE THAT CAN'T POSSIBLY EXIST, IT IS STOPPED IN TIME AND UNABLE TO MOVE.
STUCK IN THAT ONE MOMENT...
THE SEVEN LAYERS OF HEAVEN AND THE SEVEN LAYERS OF HELL BELOW...
THE EVILS' KINGDOM OF ANAGURA RESIDES IN THIS TOP LOWER LEVEL.
AND THESE ARE THE SEVEN LAYERS ABOVE EARTH THAT NVELOPE IT...

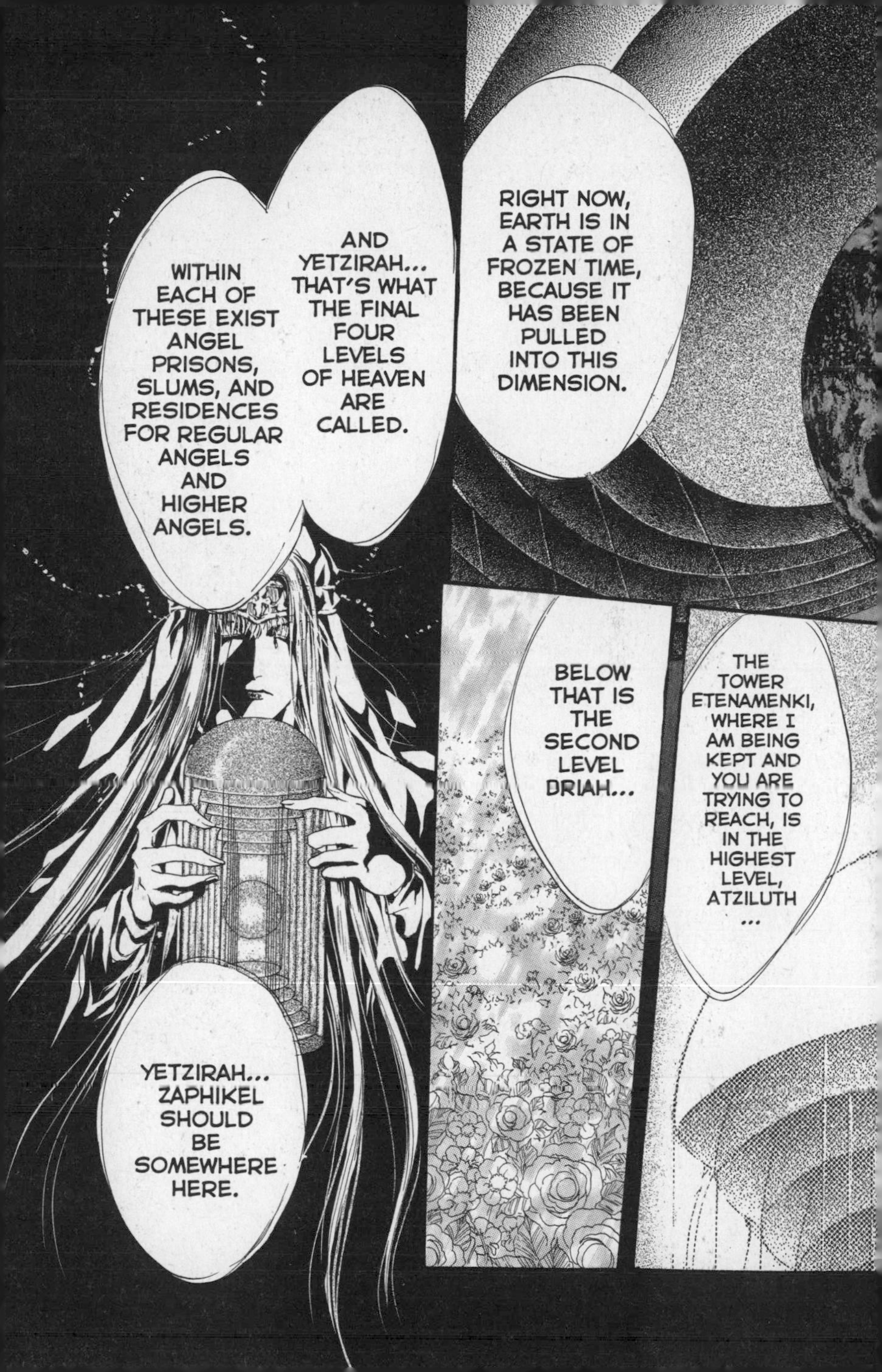
RIGHT NOW, EARTH IS IN A STATE OF FROZEN TIME, BECAUSE IT HAS BEEN PULLED INTO THIS DIMENSION.
THE TOWER ETENAMENKI, WHERE I AM BEING KEPT AND YOU ARE TRYING TO REACH, IS IN THE HIGHEST LEVEL, ATZILUTH ...
BELOW THAT IS THE SECOND LEVEL DRIAH...
AND YETZIRAH... THAT'S WHAT THE FINAL FOUR LEVELS OF HEAVEN ARE CALLED.
WITHIN EACH OF THESE EXIST ANGEL PRISONS, SLUMS, AND RESIDENCES FOR REGULAR ANGELS AND HIGHER ANGELS.
YETZIRAH... ZAPHIKEL SHOULD BE SOMEWHERE HERE.

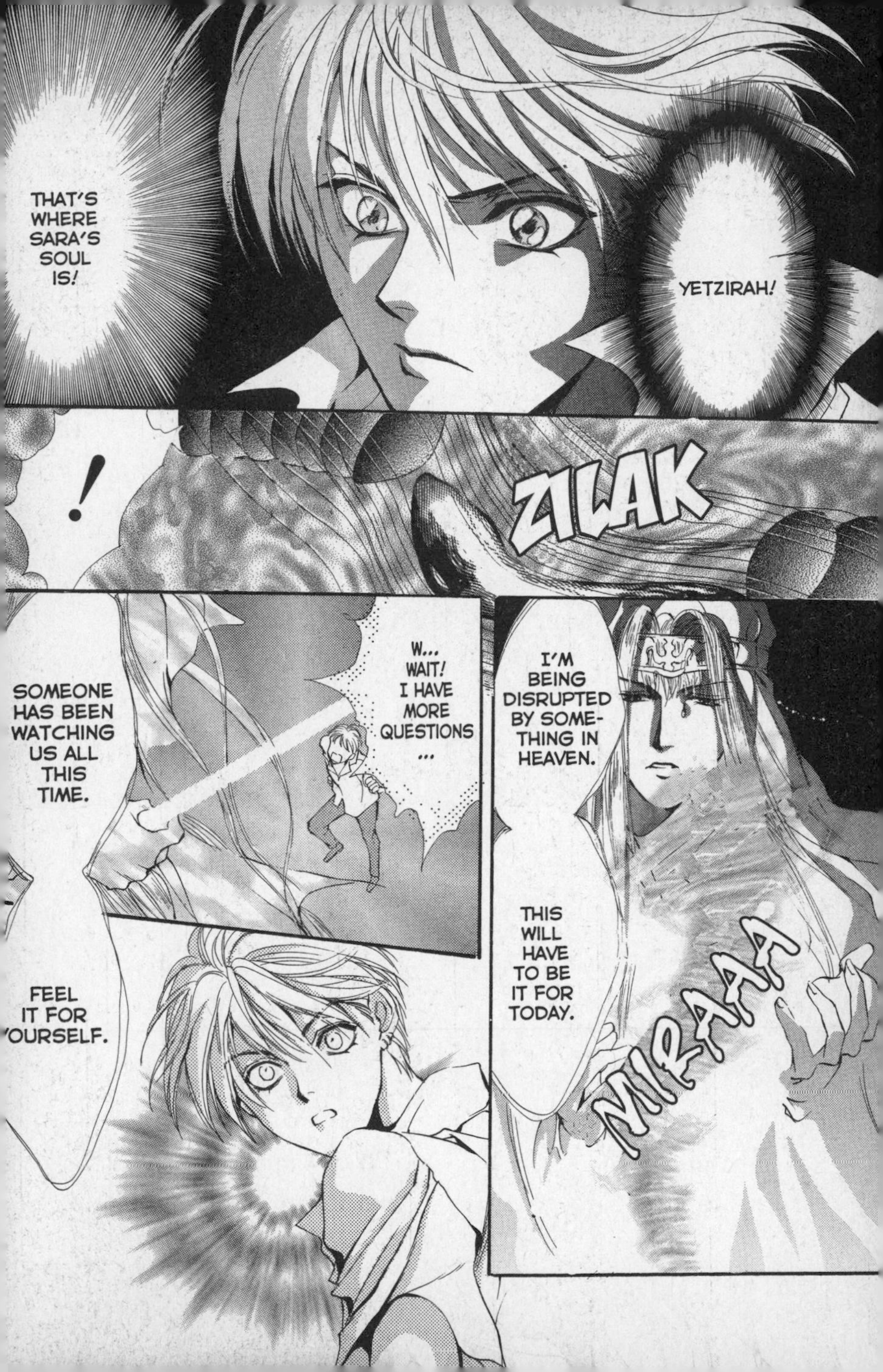
YETZIRAH!
THAT'S WHERE SARA'S SOUL IS!
ZILAK
!
I'M BEING DISRUPTED BY SOME-THING IN HEAVEN.
THIS WILL HAVE TO BE IT FOR TODAY.
MIRAAA
W... WAIT! I HAVE MORE QUESTIONS ...
SOMEONE HAS BEEN WATCHING US ALL THIS TIME.
FEEL IT FOR YOURSELF.

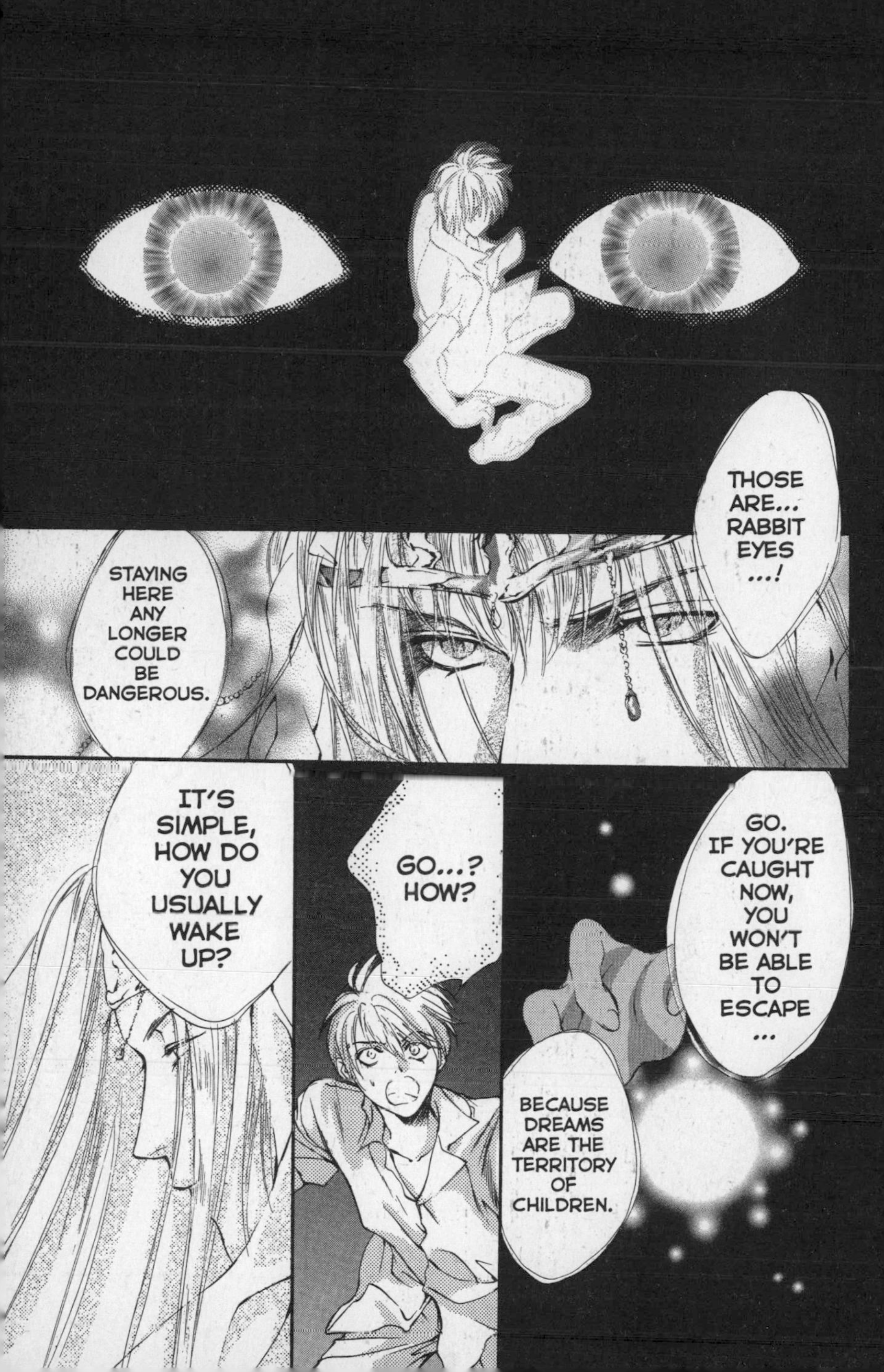
THOSE ARE... RABBIT EYES ...!
STAYING HERE ANY LONGER COULD BE DANGEROUS.
GO. IF YOU'RE CAUGHT NOW, YOU WON'T BE ABLE TO ESCAPE ...
BECAUSE DREAMS ARE THE TERRITORY OF CHILDREN.
GO...? HOW?
IT'S SIMPLE, HOW DO YOU USUALLY WAKE UP?

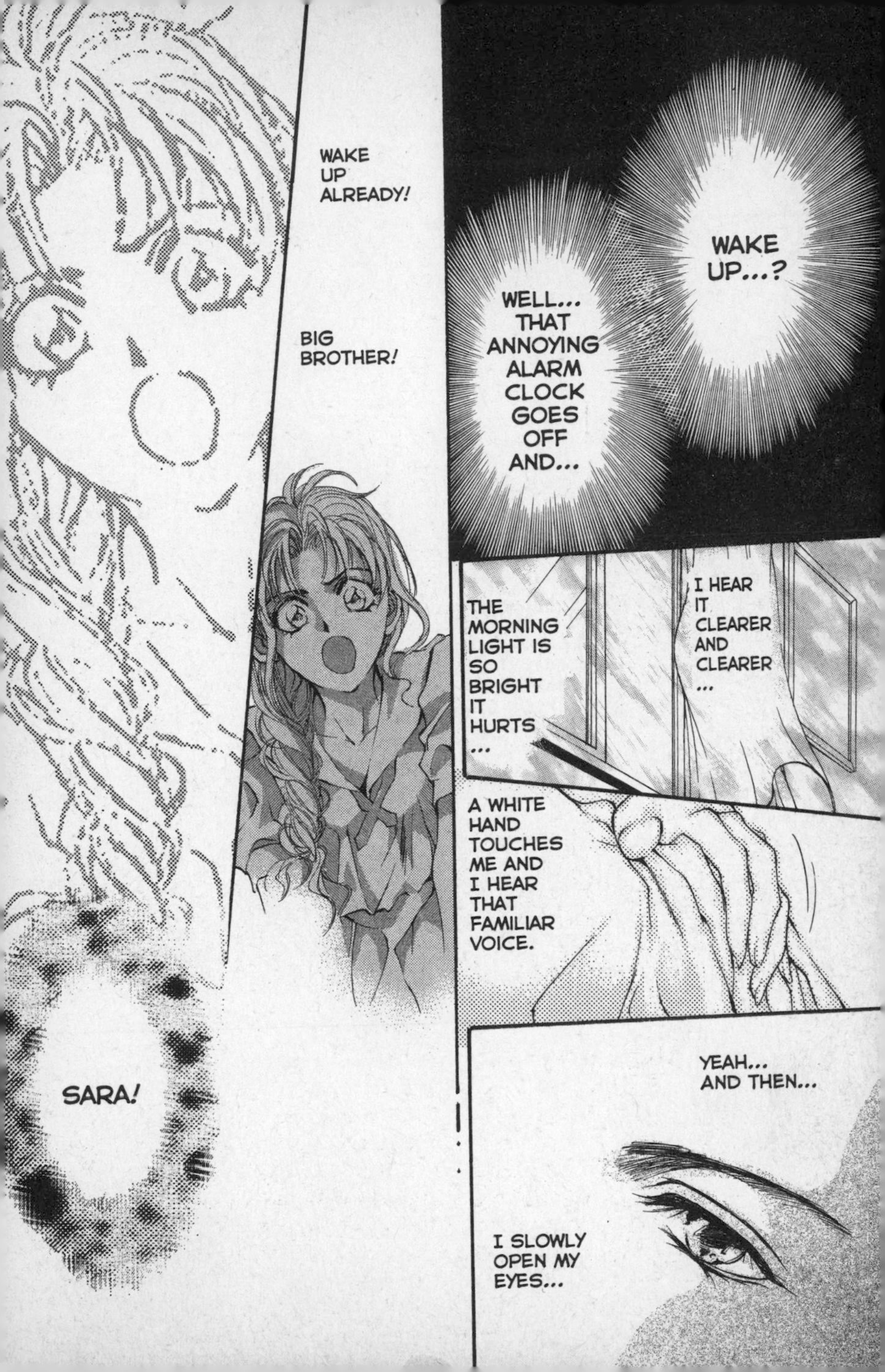
WAKE UP...?
WELL... THAT ANNOYING ALARM CLOCK GOES OFF AND...
I HEAR IT CLEARER AND CLEARER...
THE MORNING LIGHT IS SO BRIGHT IT HURTS...
A WHITE HAND TOUCHES ME AND I HEAR THAT FAMILIAR VOICE.
YEAH... AND THEN...
I SLOWLY OPEN MY EYES...
WAKE UP ALREADY!
BIG BROTHER!
SARA!

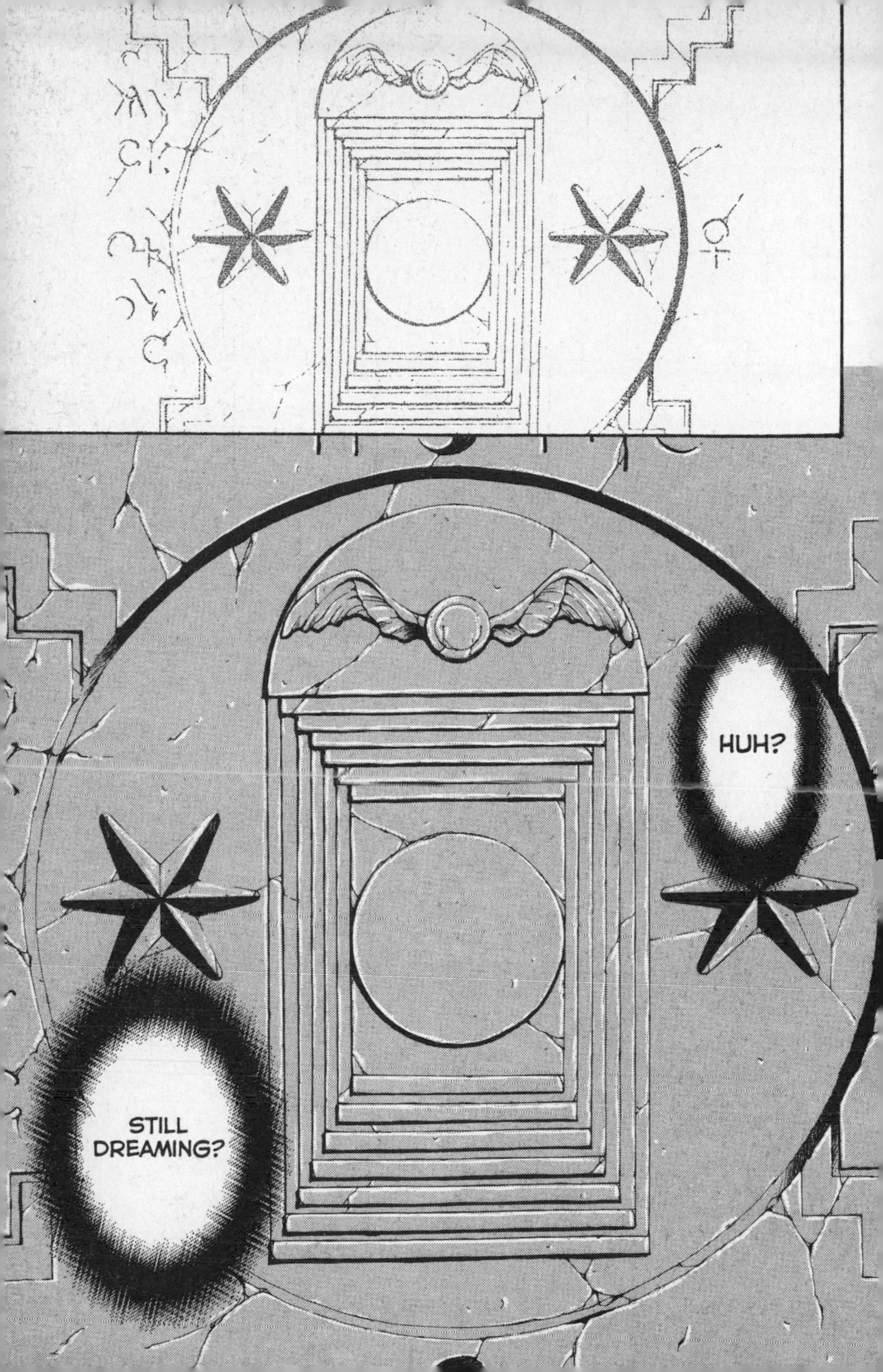
HUH?
STILL DREAMING?

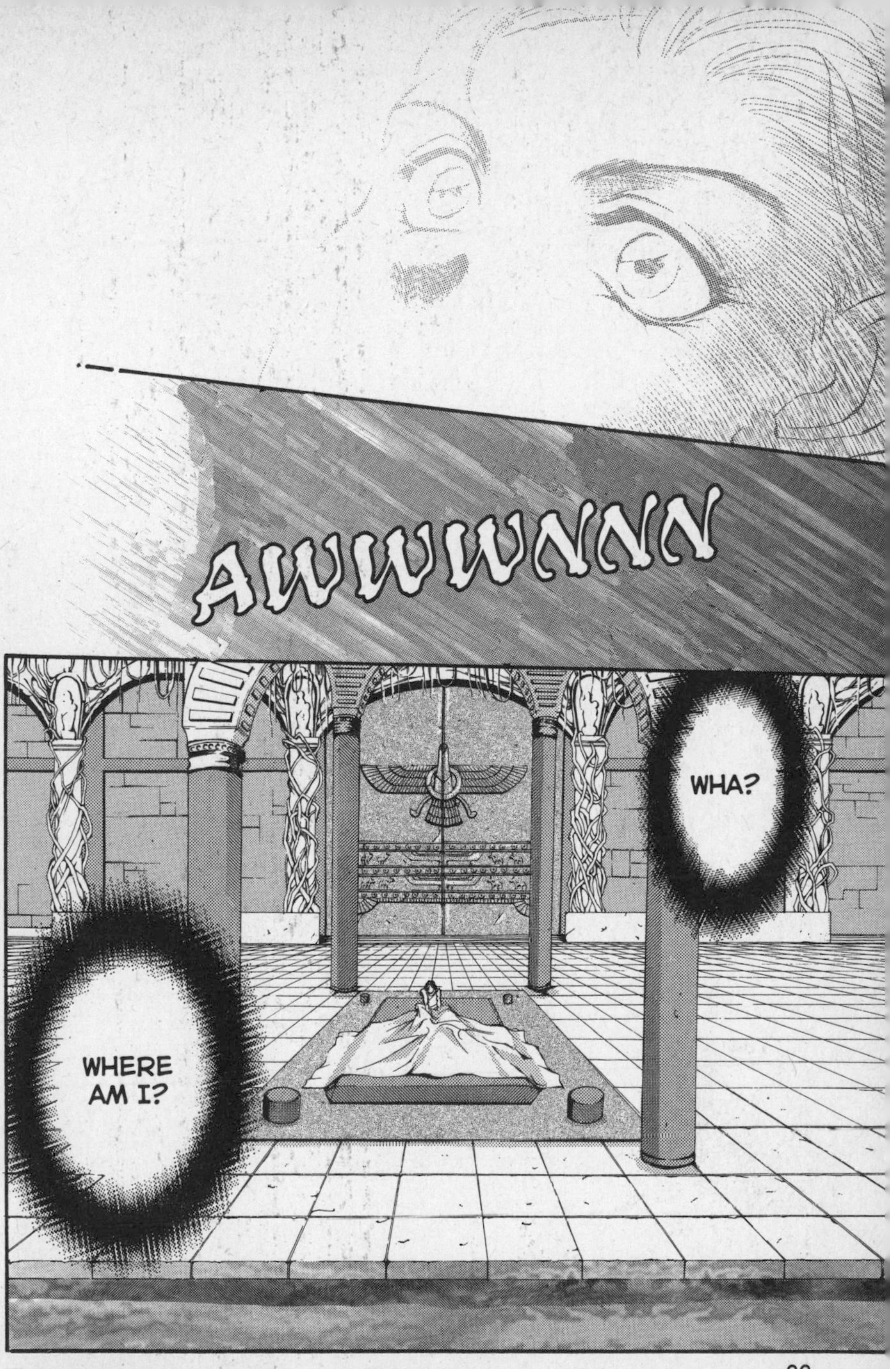
AWWWNNN
WHA?
WHERE AM I?

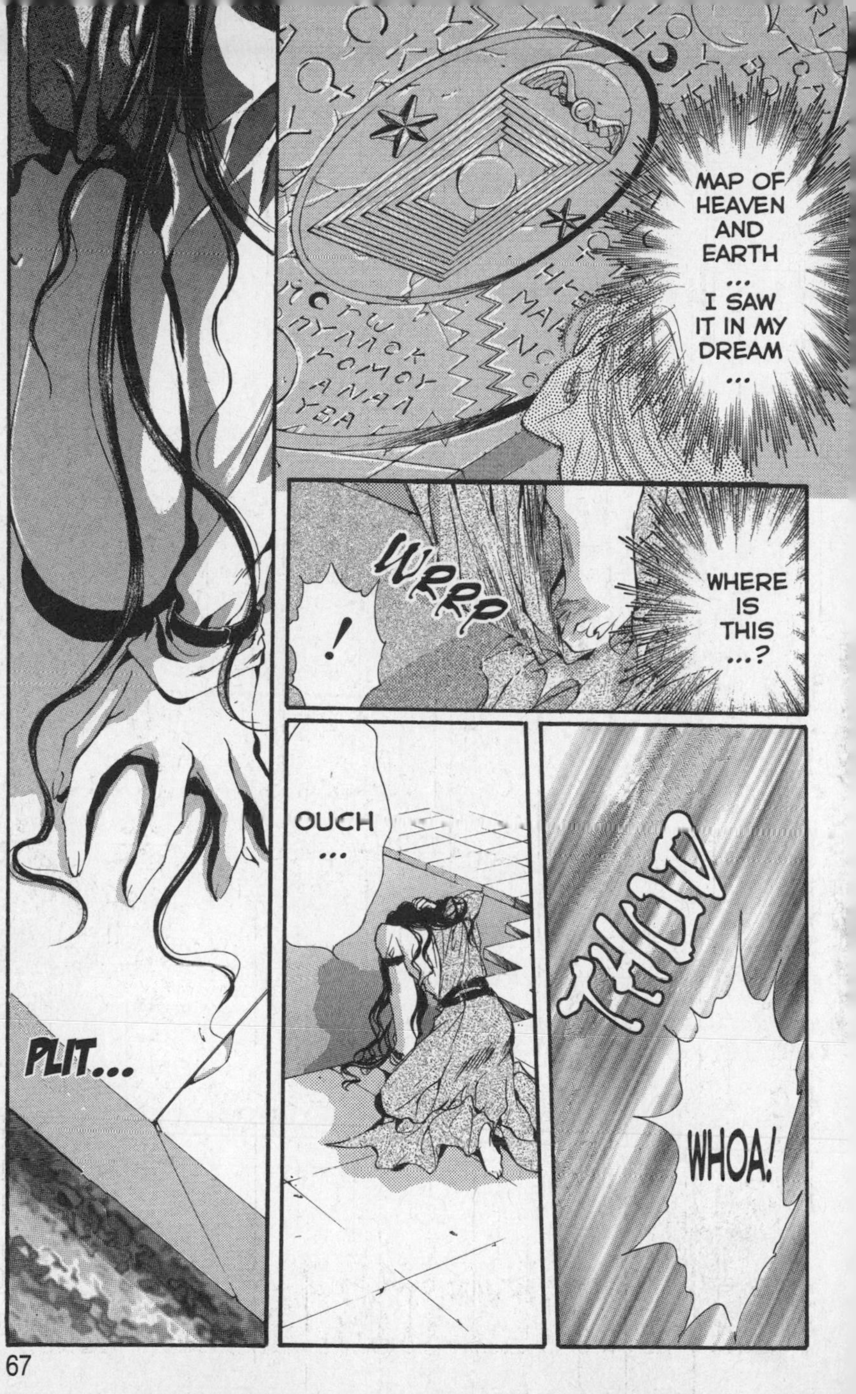
MAP OF HEAVEN AND EARTH ... I SAW IT IN MY DREAM ...
WHERE IS THIS ...?
WRRP
!
THUD
WHOA!
OUCH ...
PLIT...

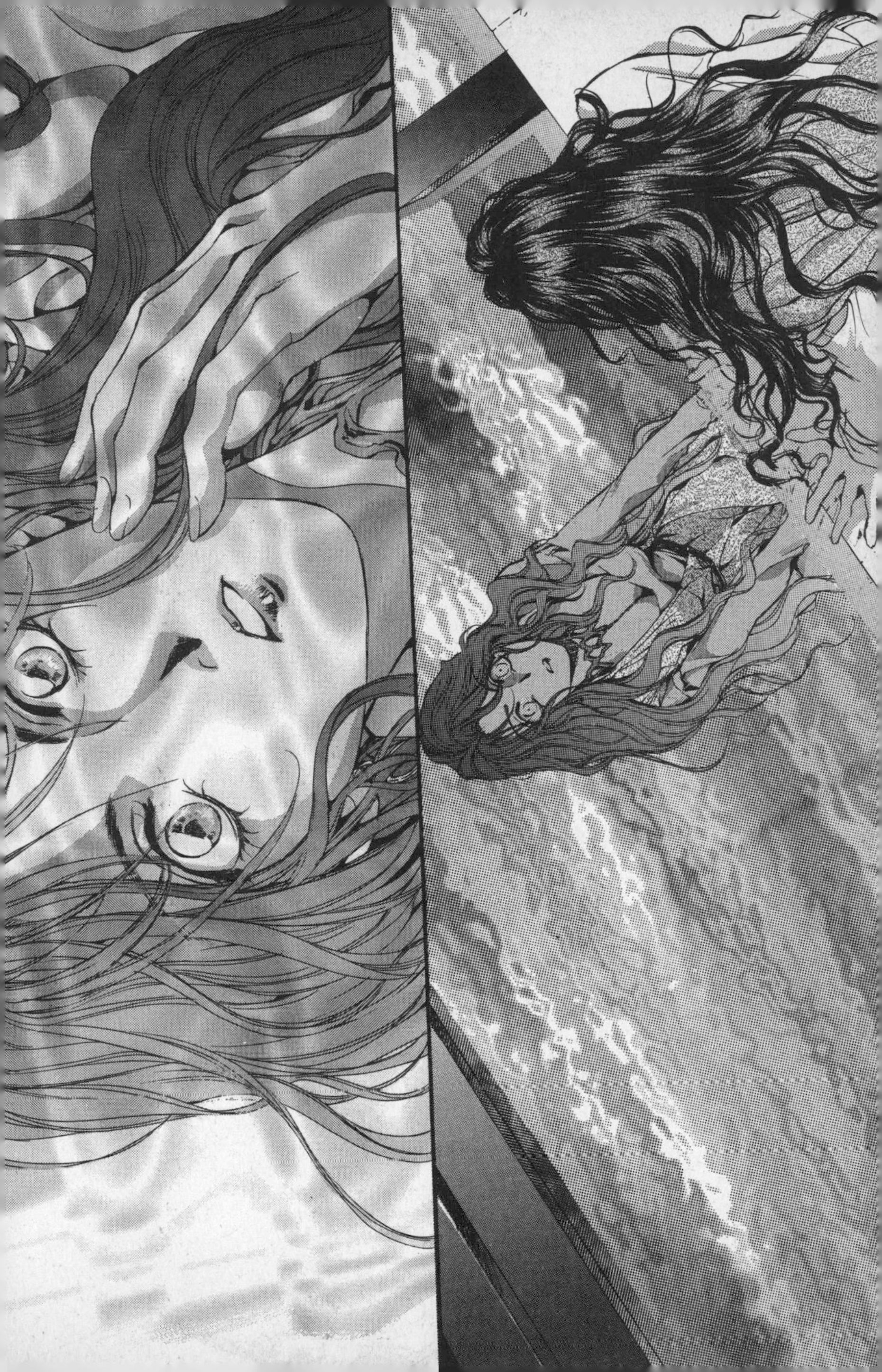

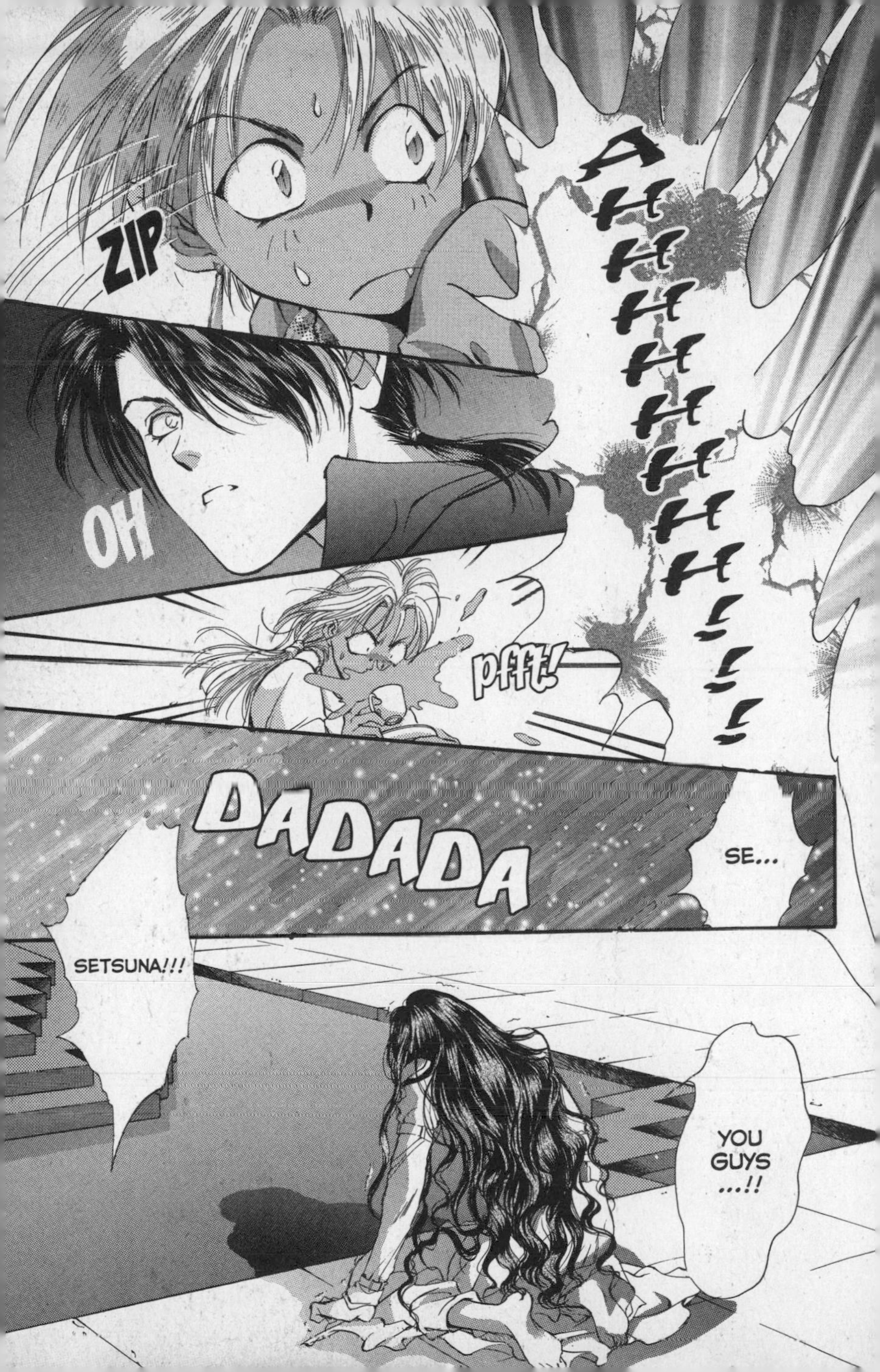
AHHHHHHHH!!!
ZIP
OH
pfft!
SE...
DADADA
SETSUNA!!!
YOU GUYS ...!!

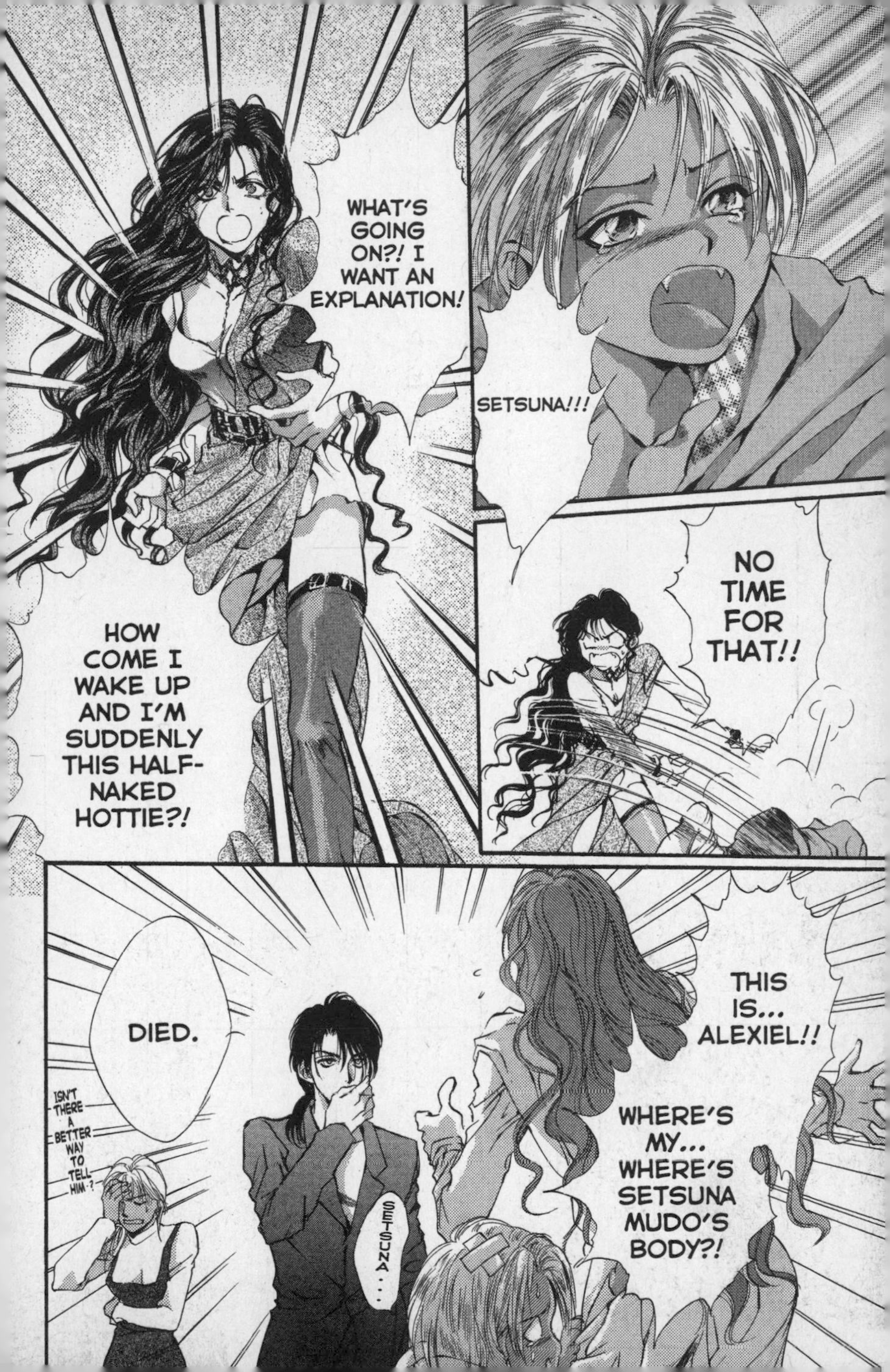
SETSUNA!!!
NO TIME FOR THAT!!
WHAT'S GOING ON?! I WANT AN EXPLANATION!
HOW COME I WAKE UP AND I'M SUDDENLY THIS HALF-NAKED HOTTIE?!
THIS IS... ALEXIEL!!
WHERE'S MY... WHERE'S SETSUNA MUDO'S BODY?!
DIED.
SETSUNA...
ISN'T THERE A BETTER WAY TO TELL HIM?

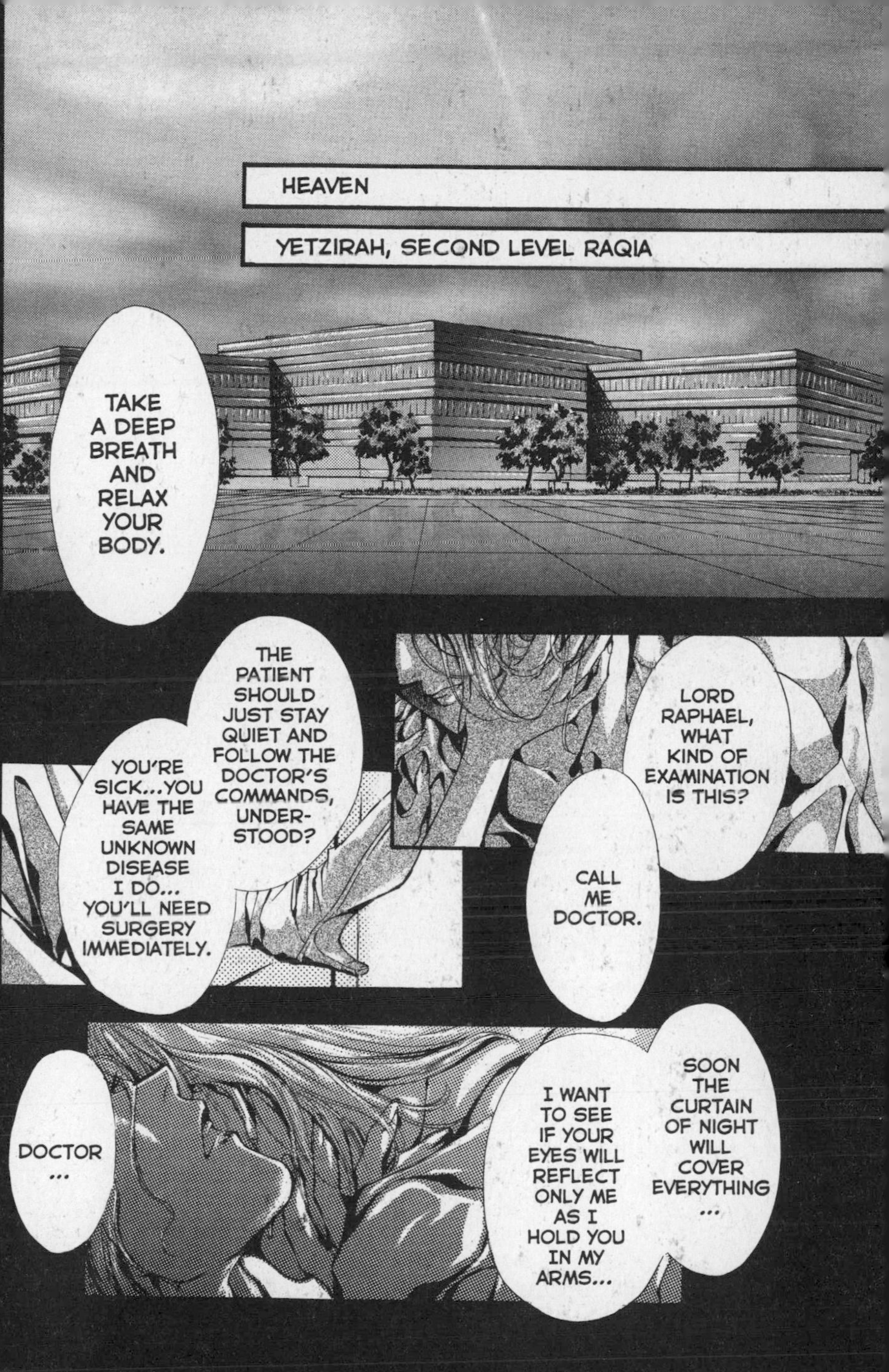
HEAVEN
YETZIRAH, SECOND LEVEL RAQIA
TAKE A DEEP BREATH AND RELAX YOUR BODY.
LORD RAPHAEL, WHAT KIND OF EXAMINATION IS THIS?
CALL ME DOCTOR.
THE PATIENT SHOULD JUST STAY QUIET AND FOLLOW THE DOCTOR'S COMMANDS, UNDER-STOOD?
YOU'RE SICK...YOU HAVE THE SAME UNKNOWN DISEASE I DO... YOU'LL NEED SURGERY IMMEDIATELY.
SOON THE CURTAIN OF NIGHT WILL COVER EVERYTHING...
I WANT TO SEE IF YOUR EYES WILL REFLECT ONLY ME AS I HOLD YOU IN MY ARMS...
DOCTOR...

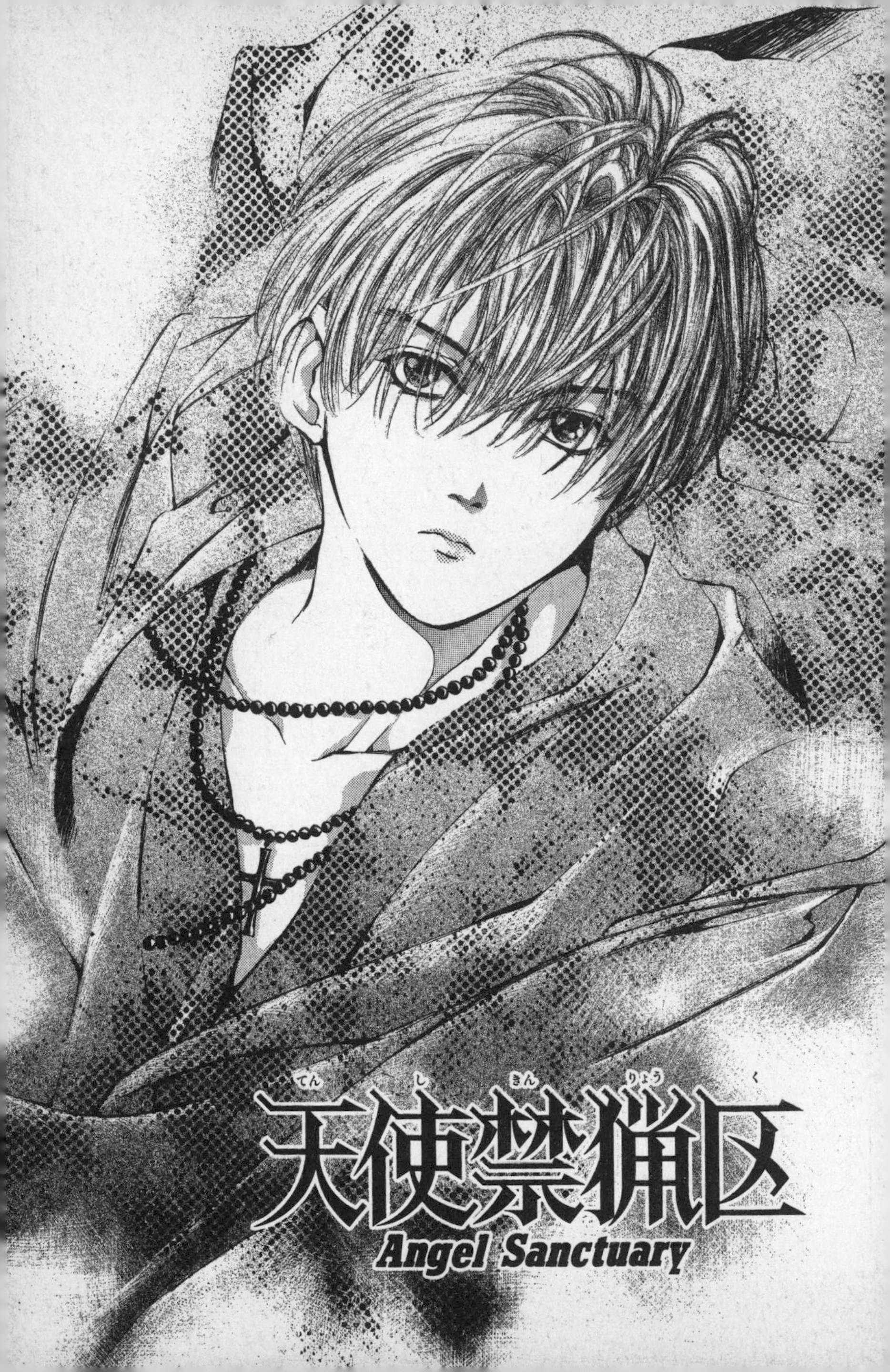
天使禁猟区
Angel Sanctuary

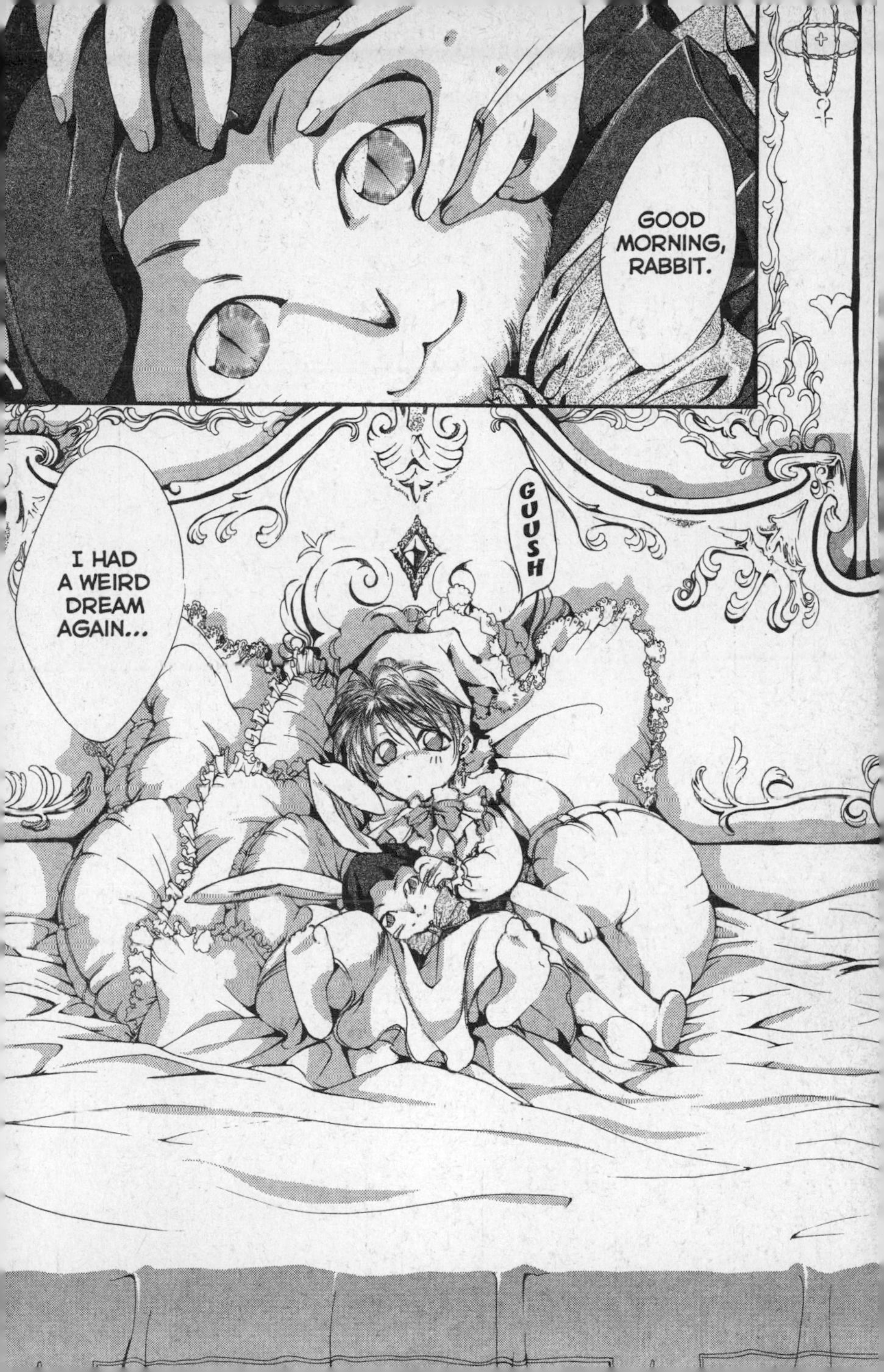
GOOD MORNING, RABBIT.
GUUSH
I HAD A WEIRD DREAM AGAIN...

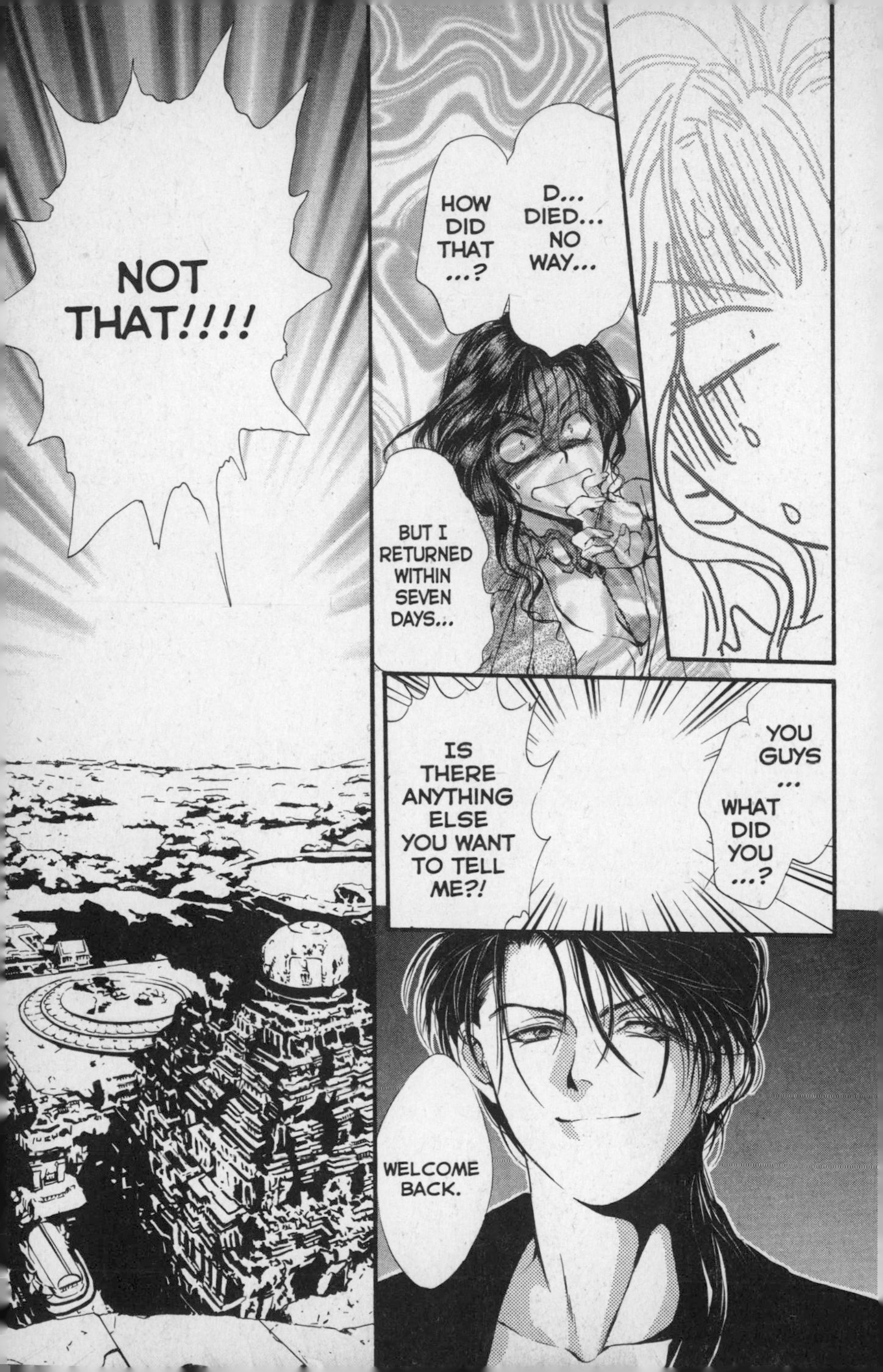
D... DIED... NO WAY...
HOW DID THAT ...?
BUT I RETURNED WITHIN SEVEN DAYS...
YOU GUYS ... WHAT DID YOU ...?
IS THERE ANYTHING ELSE YOU WANT TO TELL ME?!
WELCOME BACK.
NOT THAT!!!!

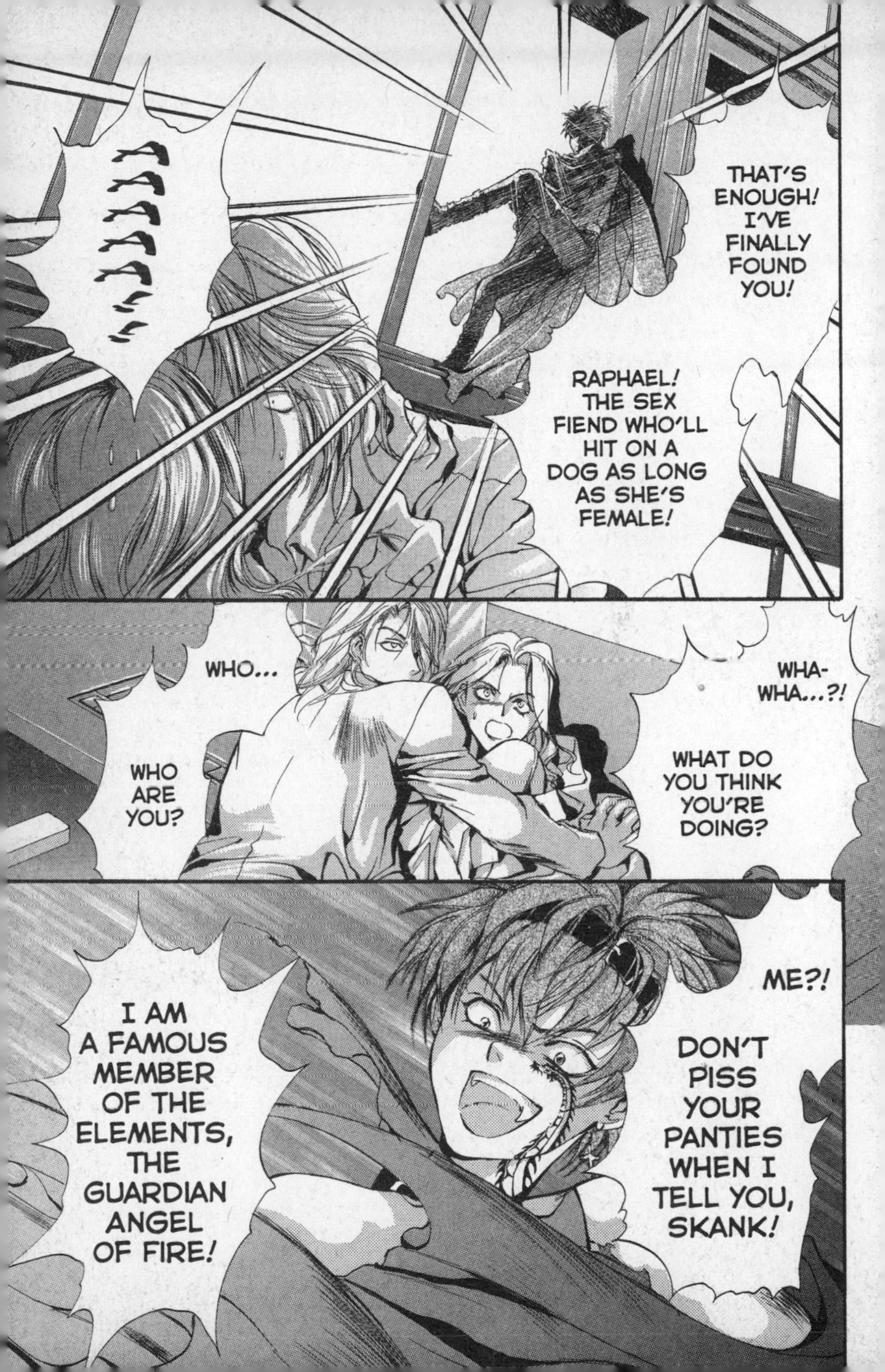
THAT'S ENOUGH! I'VE FINALLY FOUND YOU!
RAPHAEL! THE SEX FIEND WHO'LL HIT ON A DOG AS LONG AS SHE'S FEMALE!
AAAAA!!
WHA-WHA...?!
WHAT DO YOU THINK YOU'RE DOING?
WHO...
WHO ARE YOU?
ME?!
DON'T PISS YOUR PANTIES WHEN I TELL YOU, SKANK!
I AM A FAMOUS MEMBER OF THE ELEMENTS, THE GUARDIAN ANGEL OF FIRE!

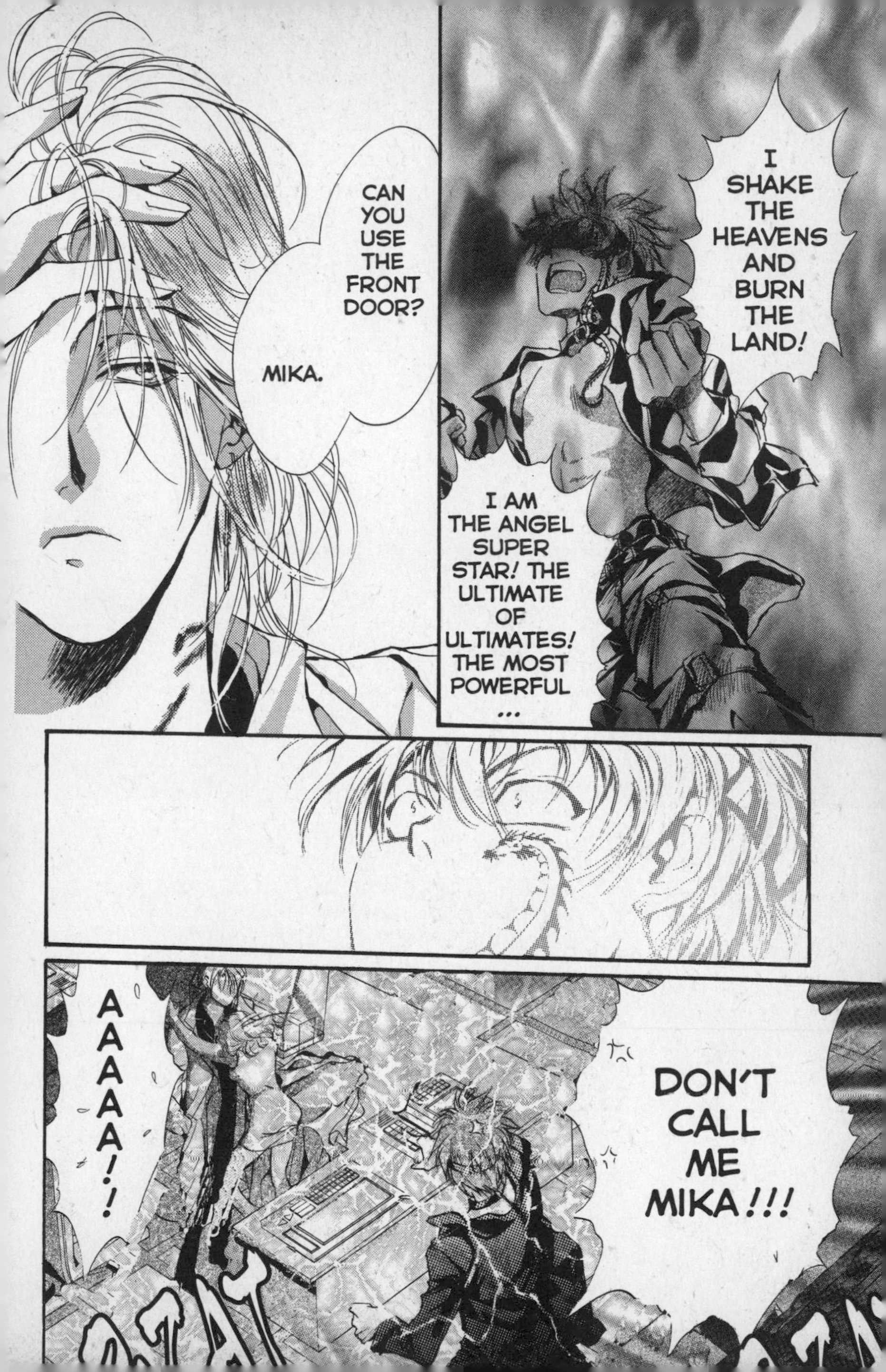
I SHAKE THE HEAVENS AND BURN THE LAND!
I AM THE ANGEL SUPER STAR! THE ULTIMATE OF ULTIMATES! THE MOST POWERFUL ...
CAN YOU USE THE FRONT DOOR?
MIKA.
DON'T CALL ME MIKA!!!
AAAAA!!!

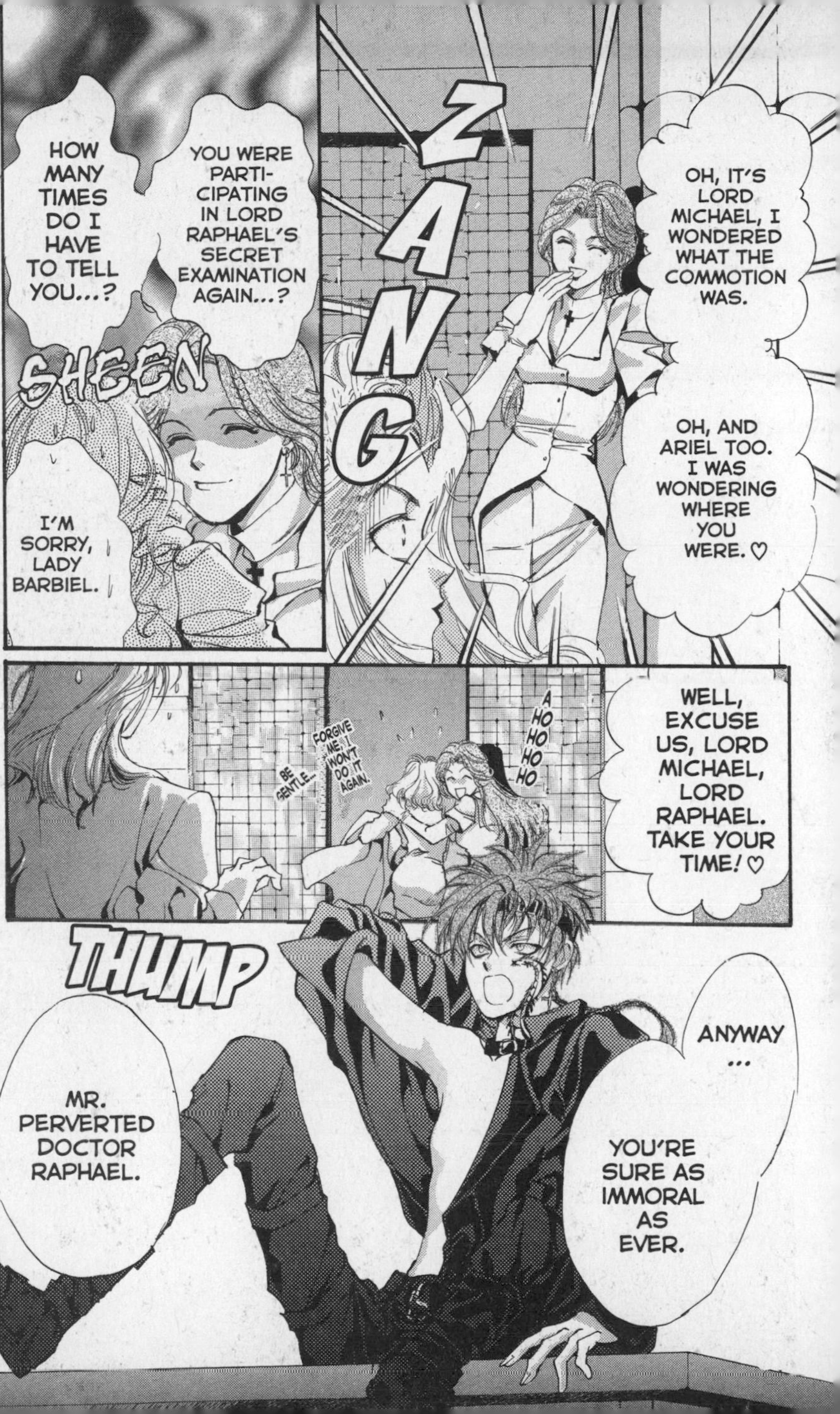
OH, IT'S LORD MICHAEL, I WONDERED WHAT THE COMMOTION WAS.
ZANG
OH, AND ARIEL TOO. I WAS WONDERING WHERE YOU WERE. ♡
YOU WERE PARTI-CIPATING IN LORD RAPHAEL'S SECRET EXAMINATION AGAIN...?
HOW MANY TIMES DO I HAVE TO TELL YOU...?
SHEEN
I'M SORRY, LADY BARBIEL.
WELL, EXCUSE US, LORD MICHAEL, LORD RAPHAEL. TAKE YOUR TIME! ♡
A HO HO HO HO
FORGIVE ME, I WON'T DO IT AGAIN.
BE GENTLE...
THUMP
ANYWAY ...
YOU'RE SURE AS IMMORAL AS EVER.
MR. PERVERTED DOCTOR RAPHAEL.

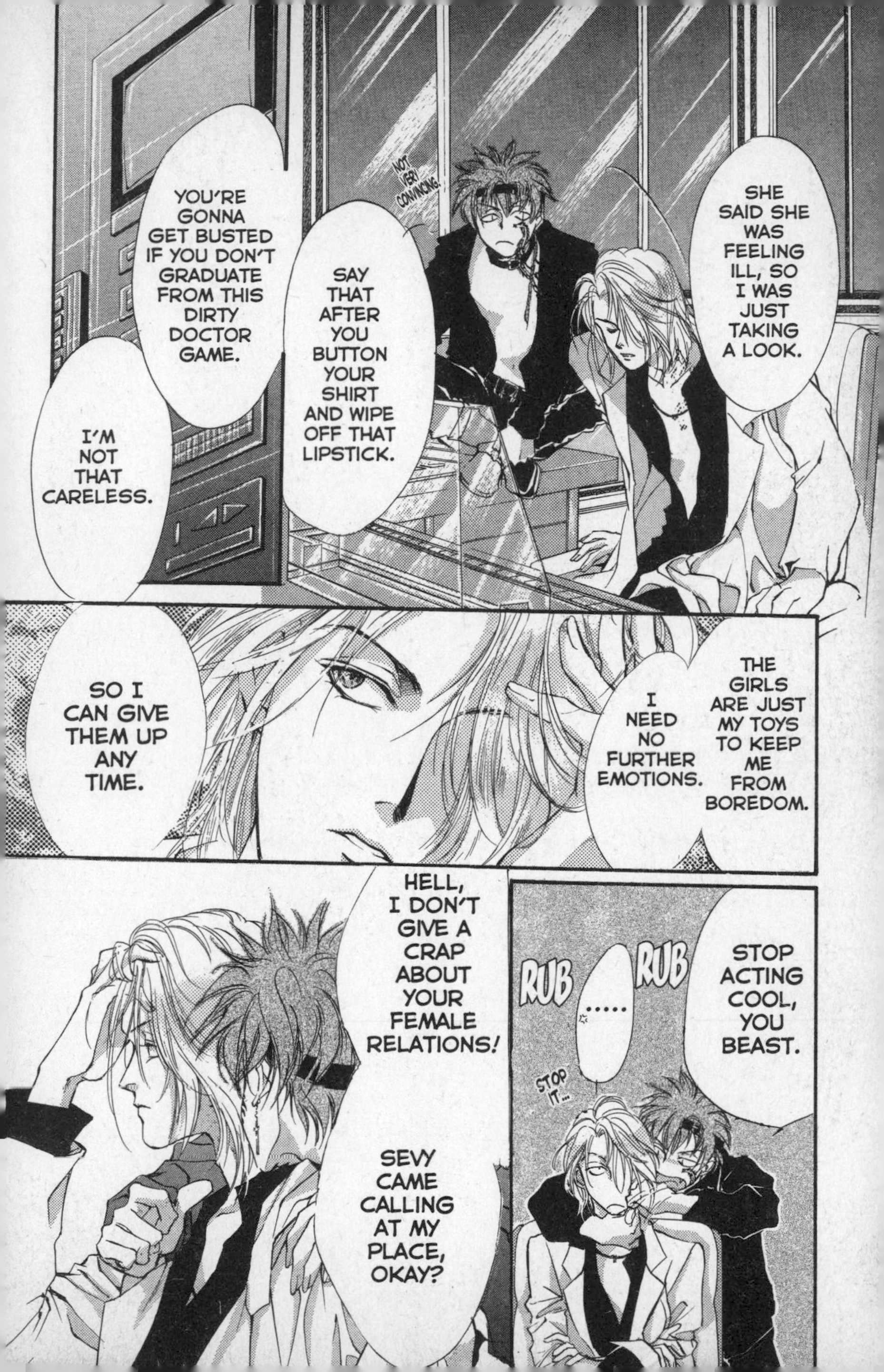
SHE SAID SHE WAS FEELING ILL, SO I WAS JUST TAKING A LOOK.
NOT VERY CONVINCING.
SAY THAT AFTER YOU BUTTON YOUR SHIRT AND WIPE OFF THAT LIPSTICK.
YOU'RE GONNA GET BUSTED IF YOU DON'T GRADUATE FROM THIS DIRTY DOCTOR GAME.
I'M NOT THAT CARELESS.
THE GIRLS ARE JUST MY TOYS TO KEEP ME FROM BOREDOM.
I NEED NO FURTHER EMOTIONS.
SO I CAN GIVE THEM UP ANY TIME.
STOP ACTING COOL, YOU BEAST.
RUB
RUB
.....
STOP IT...
HELL, I DON'T GIVE A CRAP ABOUT YOUR FEMALE RELATIONS!
SEVY CAME CALLING AT MY PLACE, OKAY?

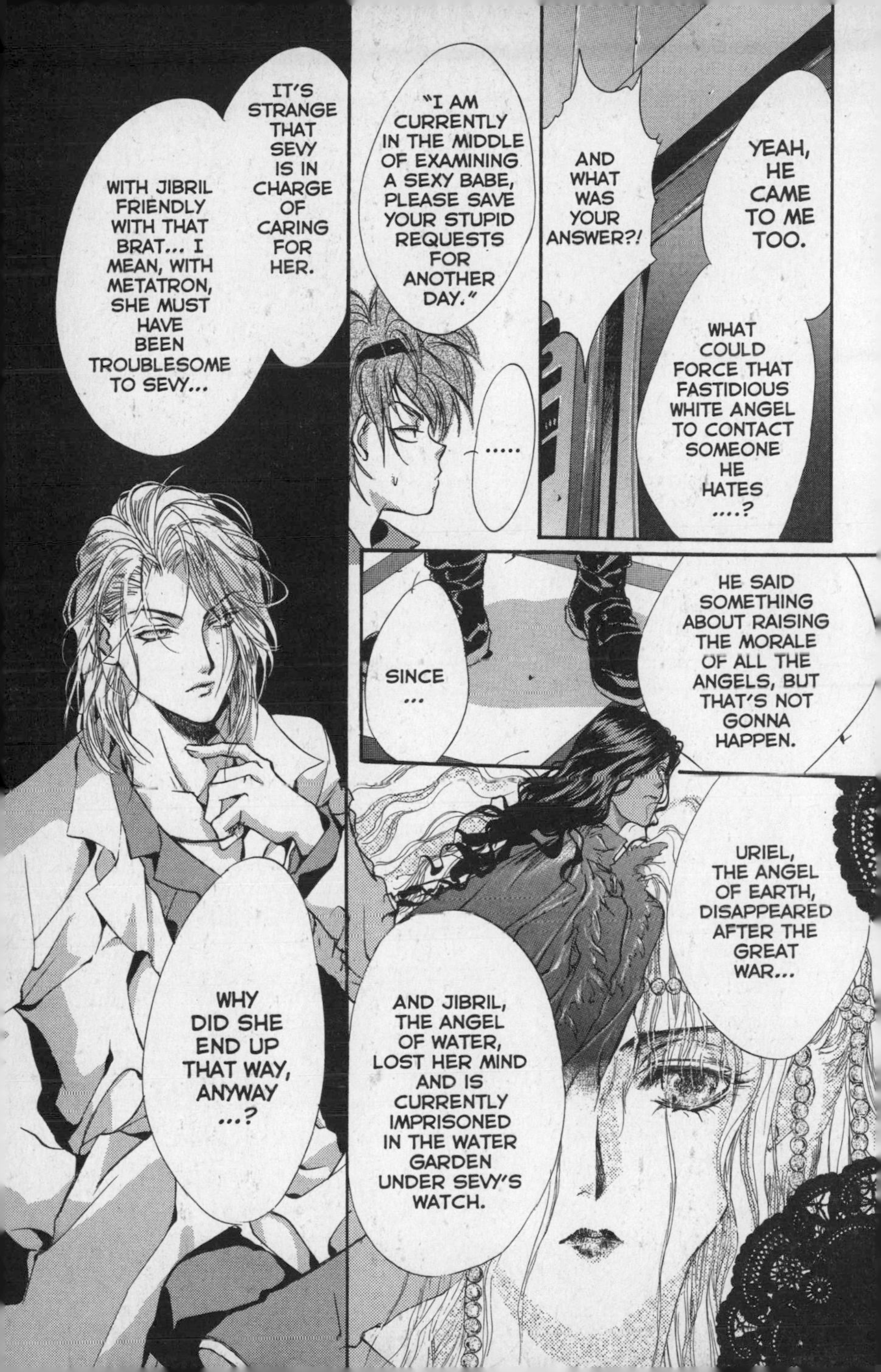
YEAH, HE CAME TO ME TOO.
AND WHAT WAS YOUR ANSWER?!
WHAT COULD FORCE THAT FASTIDIOUS WHITE ANGEL TO CONTACT SOMEONE HE HATES ....?
"I AM CURRENTLY IN THE MIDDLE OF EXAMINING A SEXY BABE, PLEASE SAVE YOUR STUPID REQUESTS FOR ANOTHER DAY."
.....
HE SAID SOMETHING ABOUT RAISING THE MORALE OF ALL THE ANGELS, BUT THAT'S NOT GONNA HAPPEN.
SINCE ...
URIEL, THE ANGEL OF EARTH, DISAPPEARED AFTER THE GREAT WAR...
AND JIBRIL, THE ANGEL OF WATER, LOST HER MIND AND IS CURRENTLY IMPRISONED IN THE WATER GARDEN UNDER SEVY'S WATCH.
IT'S STRANGE THAT SEVY IS IN CHARGE OF CARING FOR HER.
WITH JIBRIL FRIENDLY WITH THAT BRAT... I MEAN, WITH METATRON, SHE MUST HAVE BEEN TROUBLESOME TO SEVY...
WHY DID SHE END UP THAT WAY, ANYWAY ...?

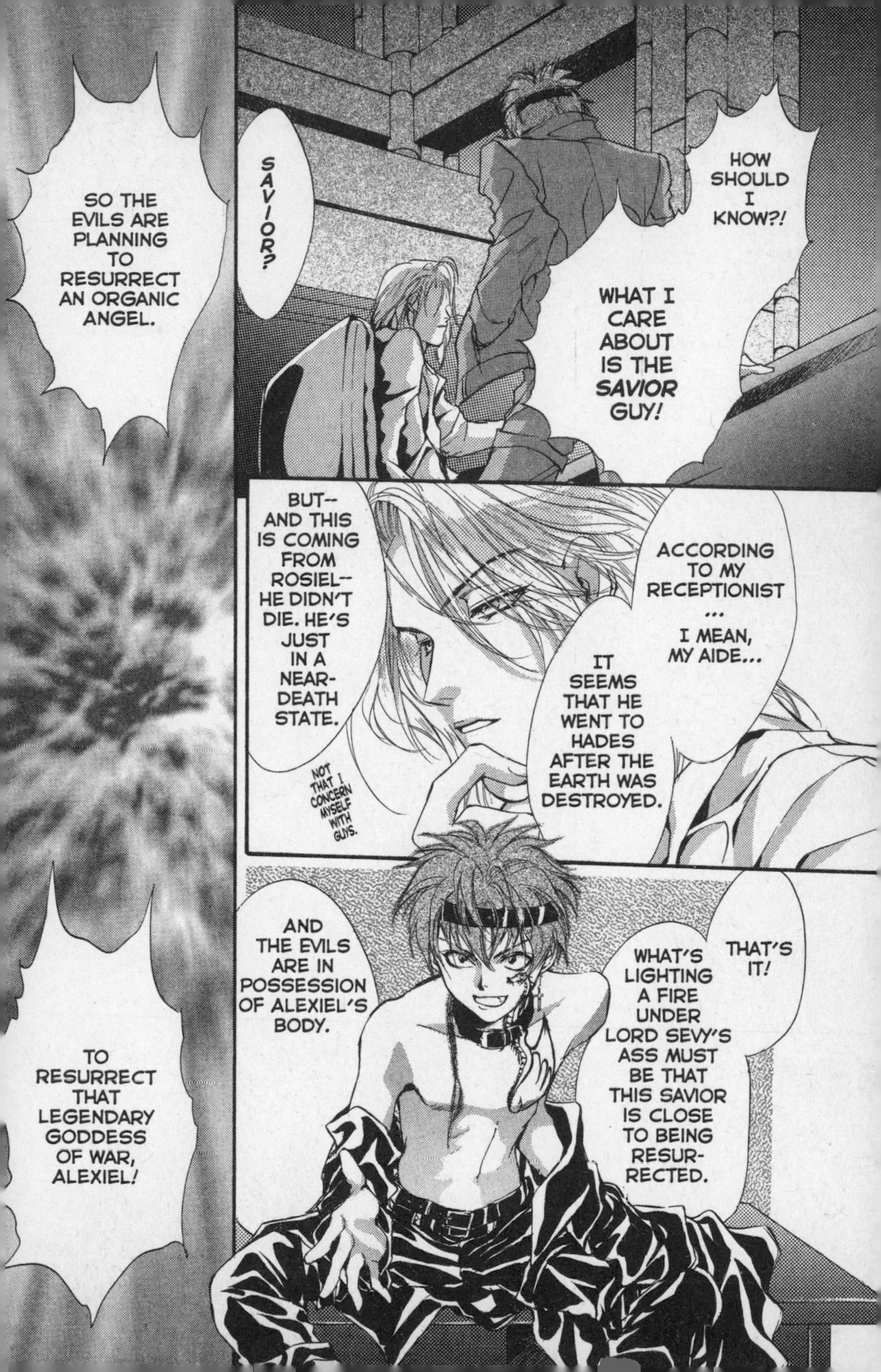
HOW SHOULD I KNOW?!
SAVIOR?
WHAT I CARE ABOUT IS THE SAVIOR GUY!
ACCORDING TO MY RECEPTIONIST... I MEAN, MY AIDE...
IT SEEMS THAT HE WENT TO HADES AFTER THE EARTH WAS DESTROYED.
BUT-- AND THIS IS COMING FROM ROSIEL-- HE DIDN'T DIE. HE'S JUST IN A NEAR-DEATH STATE.
NOT THAT I CONCERN MYSELF WITH GUYS.
THAT'S IT!
WHAT'S LIGHTING A FIRE UNDER LORD SEVY'S ASS MUST BE THAT THIS SAVIOR IS CLOSE TO BEING RESURRECTED.
AND THE EVILS ARE IN POSSESSION OF ALEXIEL'S BODY.
SO THE EVILS ARE PLANNING TO RESURRECT AN ORGANIC ANGEL.
TO RESURRECT THAT LEGENDARY GODDESS OF WAR, ALEXIEL!

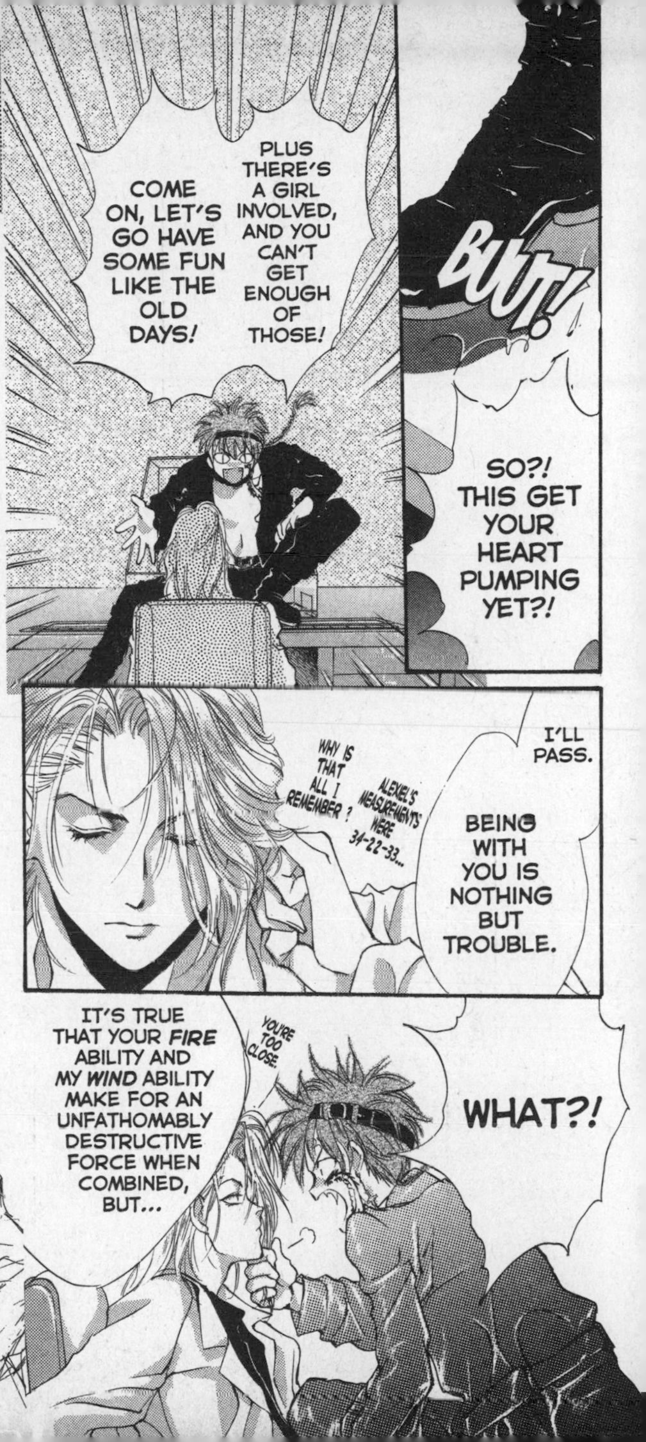
BUUT!
SO?! THIS GET YOUR HEART PUMPING YET?!
COME ON, LET'S GO HAVE SOME FUN LIKE THE OLD DAYS!
PLUS THERE'S A GIRL INVOLVED, AND YOU CAN'T GET ENOUGH OF THOSE!
I'LL PASS.
BEING WITH YOU IS NOTHING BUT TROUBLE.
ALEXIEL'S MEASUREMENTS WERE 34-22-33...
WHY IS THAT ALL I REMEMBER ?
WHAT?!
YOU'RE TOO CLOSE.
IT'S TRUE THAT YOUR *FIRE* ABILITY AND MY *WIND* ABILITY MAKE FOR AN UNFATHOMABLY DESTRUCTIVE FORCE WHEN COMBINED, BUT...

A S

And Lord Raphael makes his appearance too! He's a womanizing blabber-mouth doctor who calls the feared Michael "Mika." I had this set-up in mind for a long time. He's the angel of wind, so I wanted him to be whimsical... His main color is yellow. He has nice blond hair. He's always getting on Mika's case, but he's conniving and can't ignore his friend. Oh yeah! It took so long to draw Alexiel... It was tough! I couldn't draw her "beautiful" like I had planned. That hair is such a pain!

ARG!

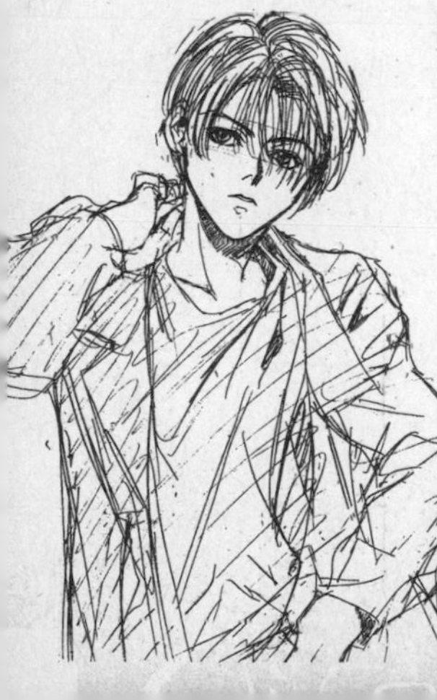

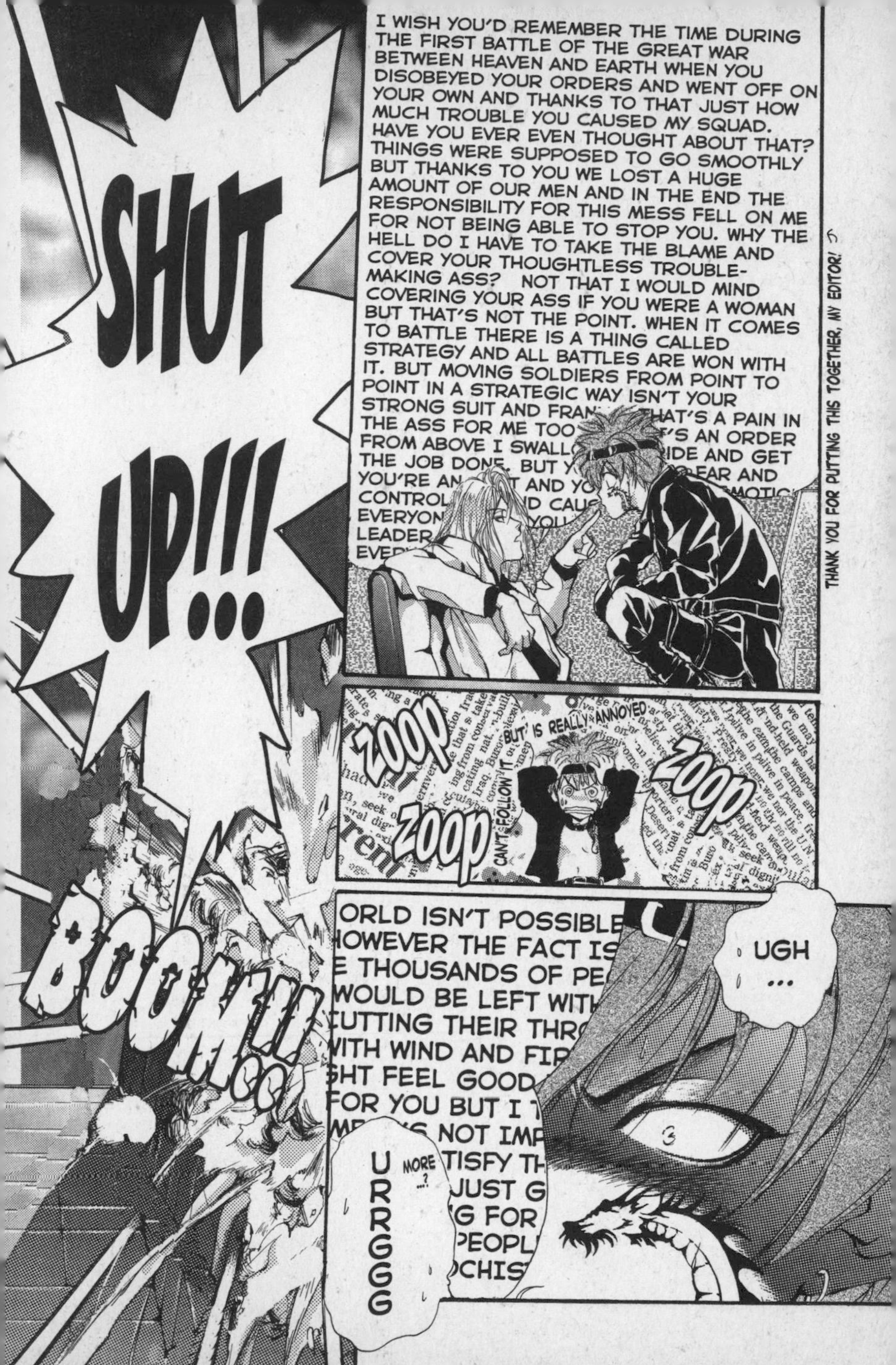
I WISH YOU'D REMEMBER THE TIME DURING THE FIRST BATTLE OF THE GREAT WAR BETWEEN HEAVEN AND EARTH WHEN YOU DISOBEYED YOUR ORDERS AND WENT OFF ON YOUR OWN AND THANKS TO THAT JUST HOW MUCH TROUBLE YOU CAUSED MY SQUAD. HAVE YOU EVER EVEN THOUGHT ABOUT THAT? THINGS WERE SUPPOSED TO GO SMOOTHLY BUT THANKS TO YOU WE LOST A HUGE AMOUNT OF OUR MEN AND IN THE END THE RESPONSIBILITY FOR THIS MESS FELL ON ME FOR NOT BEING ABLE TO STOP YOU. WHY THE HELL DO I HAVE TO TAKE THE BLAME AND COVER YOUR THOUGHTLESS TROUBLE-MAKING ASS? NOT THAT I WOULD MIND COVERING YOUR ASS IF YOU WERE A WOMAN BUT THAT'S NOT THE POINT. WHEN IT COMES TO BATTLE THERE IS A THING CALLED STRATEGY AND ALL BATTLES ARE WON WITH IT. BUT MOVING SOLDIERS FROM POINT TO POINT IN A STRATEGIC WAY ISN'T YOUR
STRONG SUIT AND FRAN
THAT'S A PAIN IN
THE ASS FOR ME TOO
'S AN ORDER
FROM ABOVE I SWALL
IDE AND GET
THE JOB DONE. BUT Y
FAR AND
YOU'RE AN
T AND YO
MOTIO
CONTROL
D CAUS
EVERYON
YOU
LEADER
EVER
ZOOP
BUT IS REALLY ANNOYED
CAN'T FOLLOW IT
ZOOP
ZOOP
ORLD ISN'T POSSIBLE
HOWEVER THE FACT IS
E THOUSANDS OF PE
WOULD BE LEFT WITH
CUTTING THEIR THRO
WITH WIND AND FIR
GHT FEEL GOOD
FOR YOU BUT I T
S NOT IMP
TISFY TH
JUST G
G FOR
PEOPL
OCHIS
UGH ...
URRGGG
MORE ...?
SHUT UP!!!...
BOOM!!...
THANK YOU FOR PUTTING THIS TOGETHER, MY EDITOR!

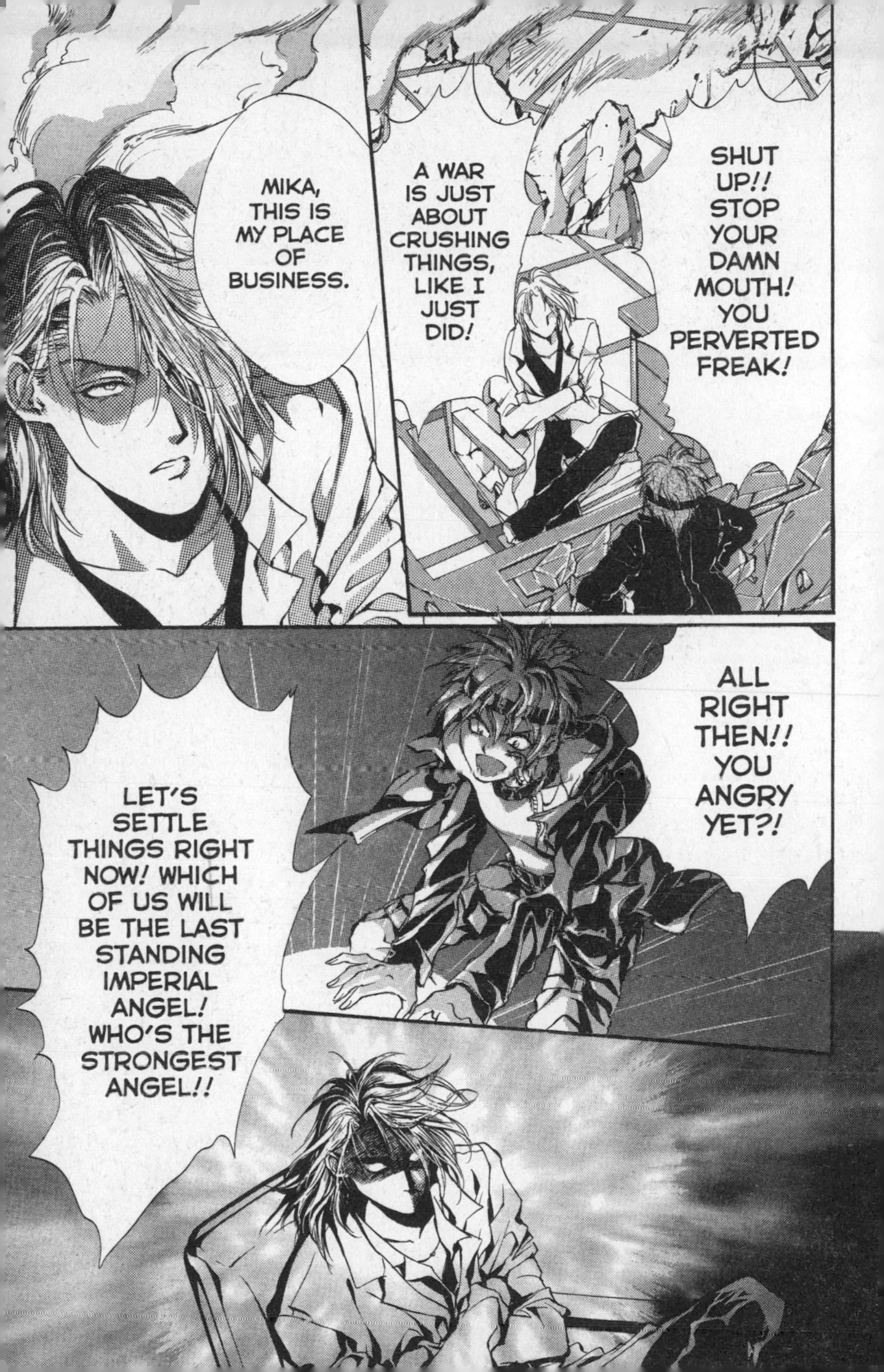
SHUT UP!! STOP YOUR DAMN MOUTH! YOU PERVERTED FREAK!
A WAR IS JUST ABOUT CRUSHING THINGS, LIKE I JUST DID!
MIKA, THIS IS MY PLACE OF BUSINESS.
ALL RIGHT THEN!! YOU ANGRY YET?!
LET'S SETTLE THINGS RIGHT NOW! WHICH OF US WILL BE THE LAST STANDING IMPERIAL ANGEL! WHO'S THE STRONGEST ANGEL!!

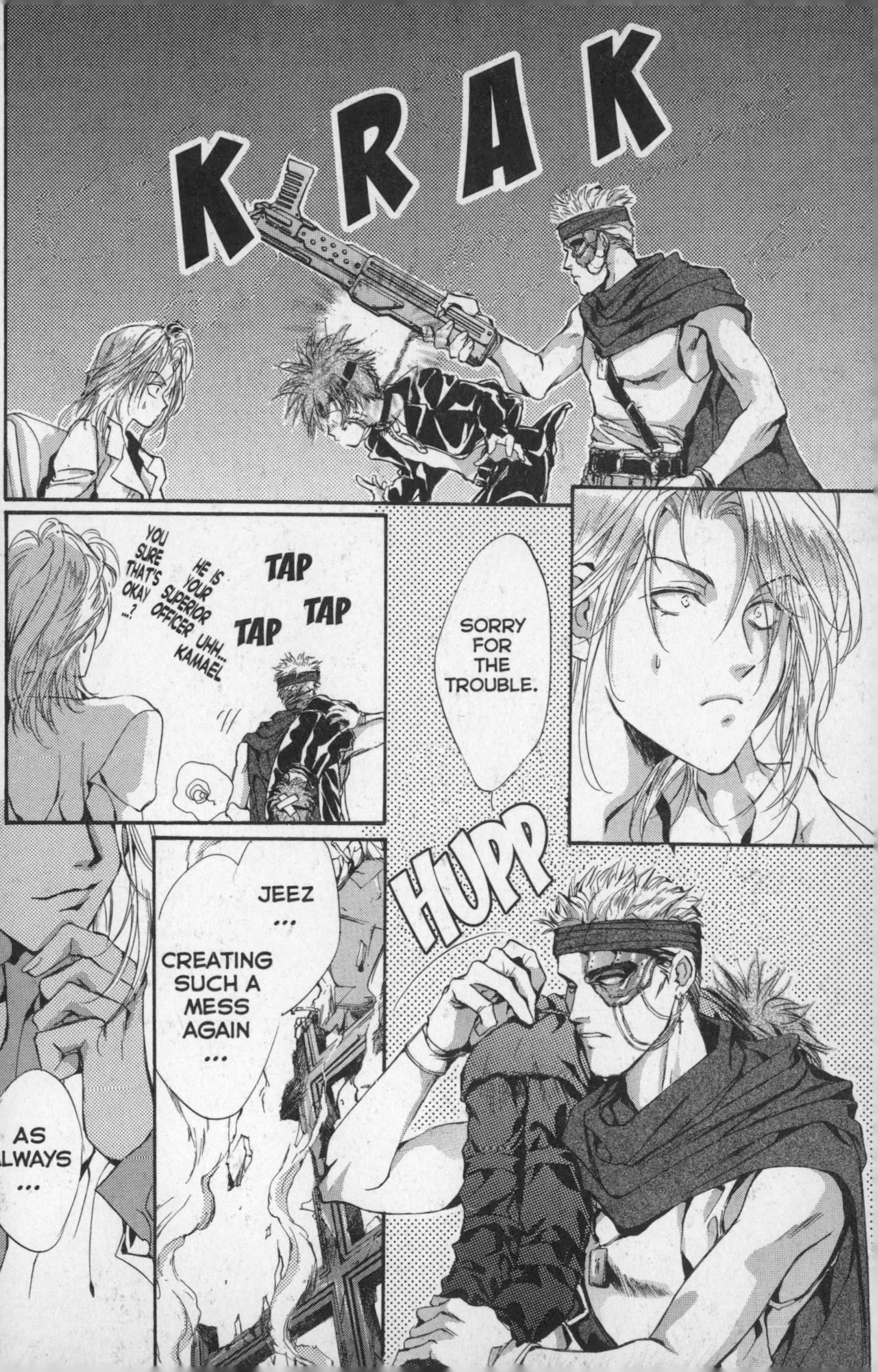
KRAK
SORRY FOR THE TROUBLE.
TAP TAP TAP
YOU SURE THAT'S OKAY ...? HE IS YOUR SUPERIOR OFFICER UHH... KAMAEL
HUPP
JEEZ ... CREATING SUCH A MESS AGAIN ...
AS ALWAYS ...

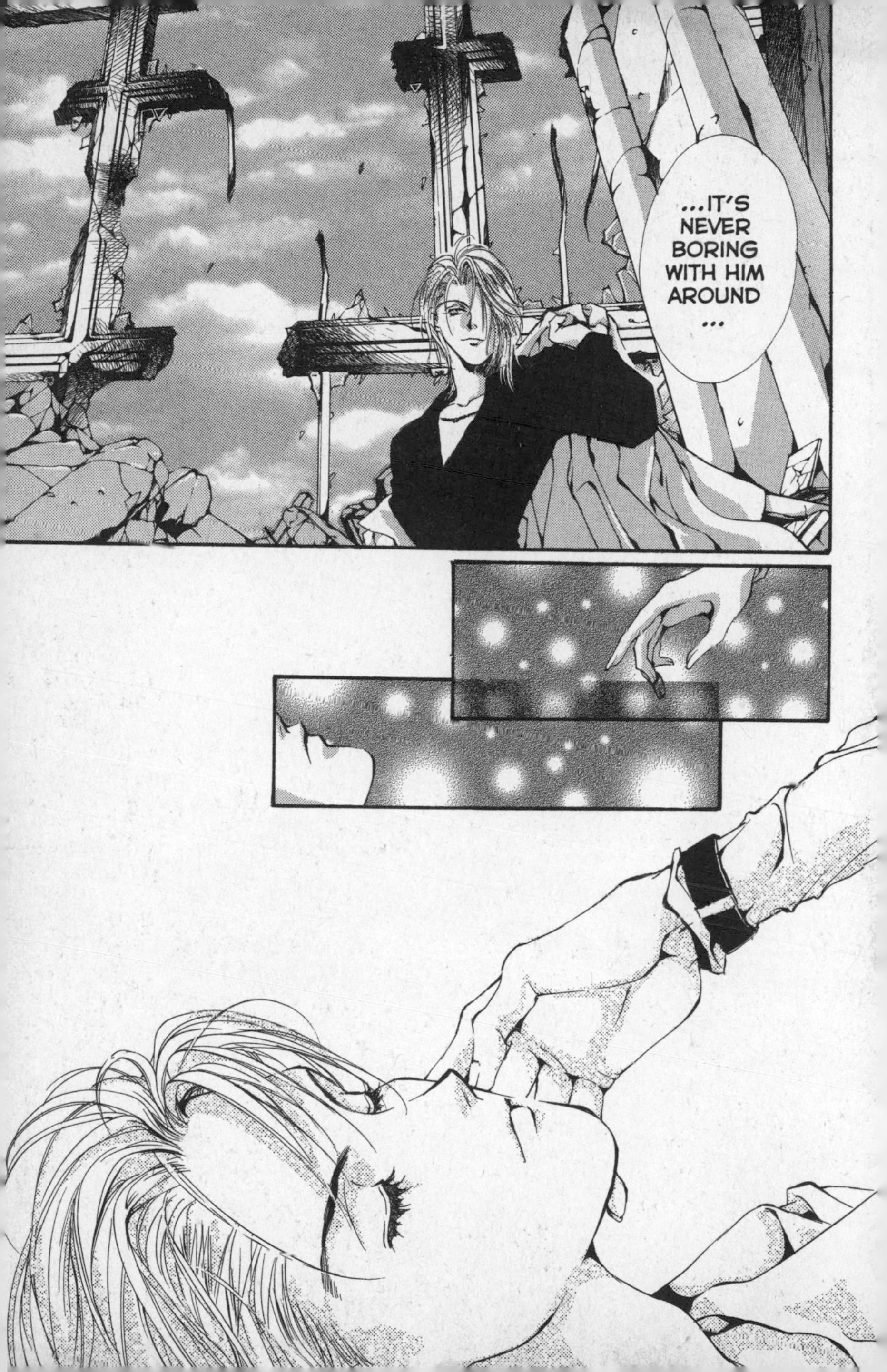
...IT'S NEVER BORING WITH HIM AROUND ...

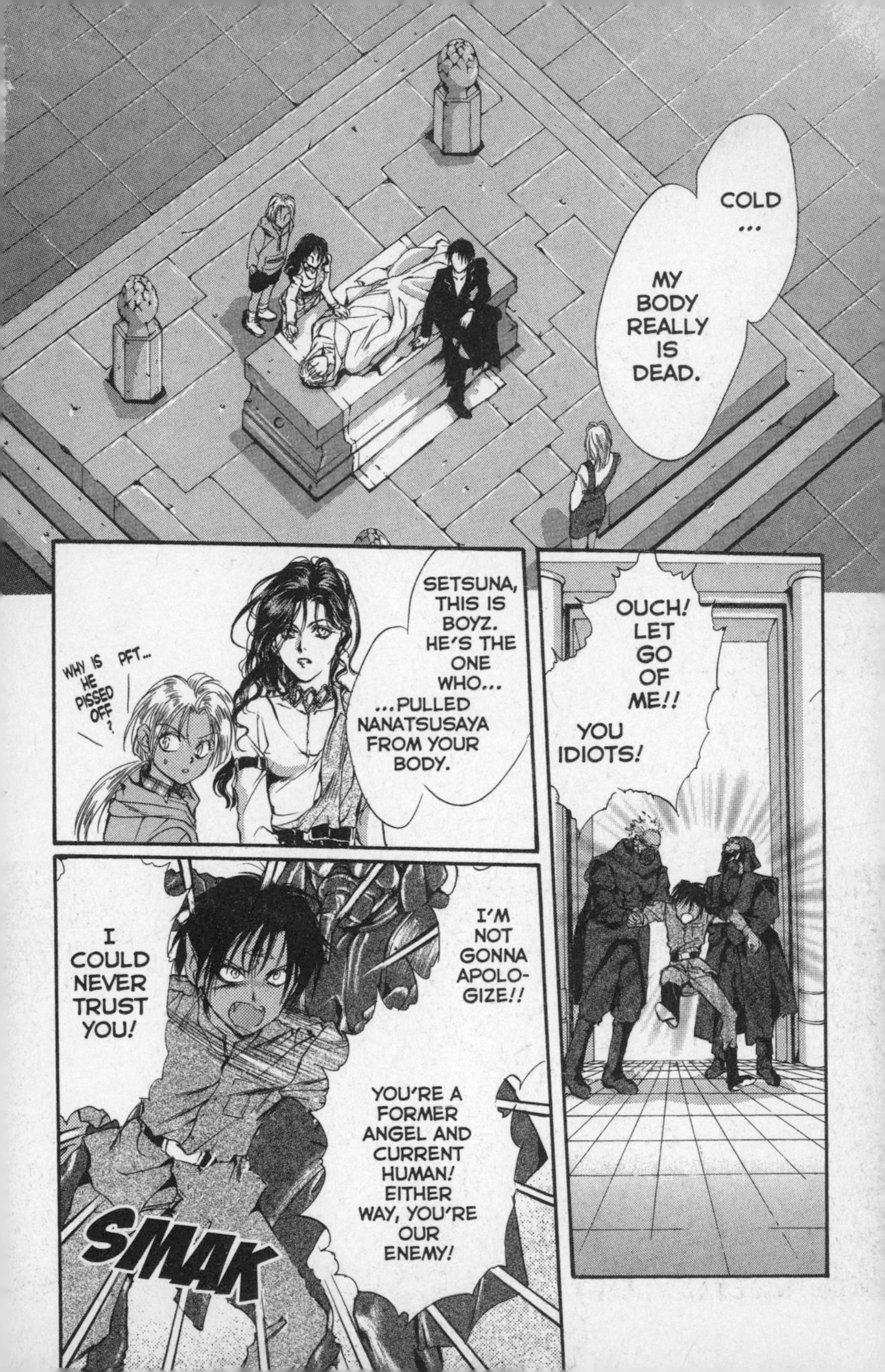
COLD ...
MY BODY REALLY IS DEAD.
OUCH! LET GO OF ME!!
YOU IDIOTS!
SETSUNA, THIS IS BOYZ. HE'S THE ONE WHO...
...PULLED NANATSUSAYA FROM YOUR BODY.
PFT...
WHY IS HE PISSED OFF?
I'M NOT GONNA APOLOGIZE!!
I COULD NEVER TRUST YOU!
YOU'RE A FORMER ANGEL AND CURRENT HUMAN! EITHER WAY, YOU'RE OUR ENEMY!
SMAK

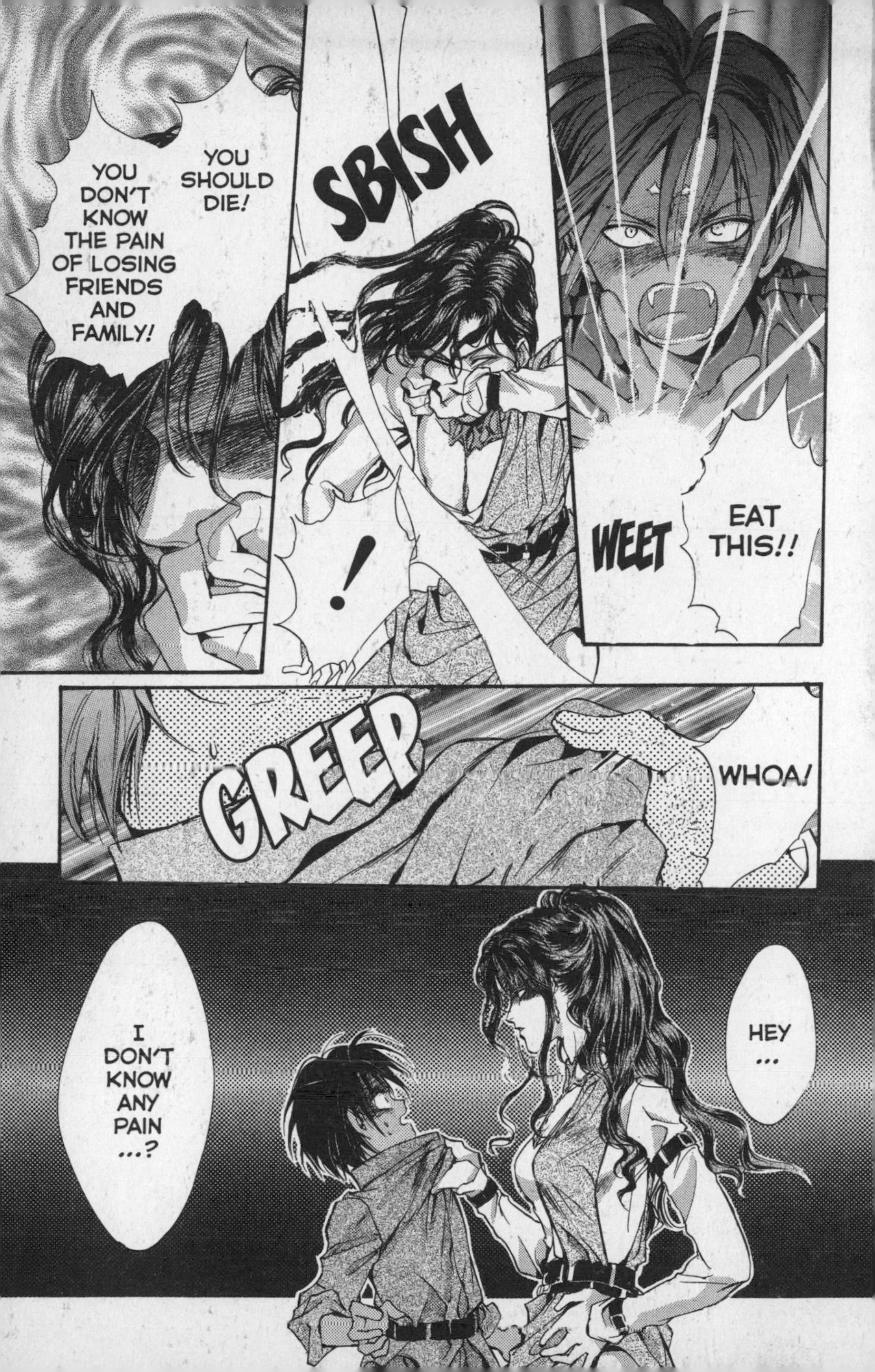
EAT THIS!!
WEET
SBISH
!
YOU SHOULD DIE!
YOU DON'T KNOW THE PAIN OF LOSING FRIENDS AND FAMILY!
WHOA!
GREEP
HEY ...
I DON'T KNOW ANY PAIN ...?

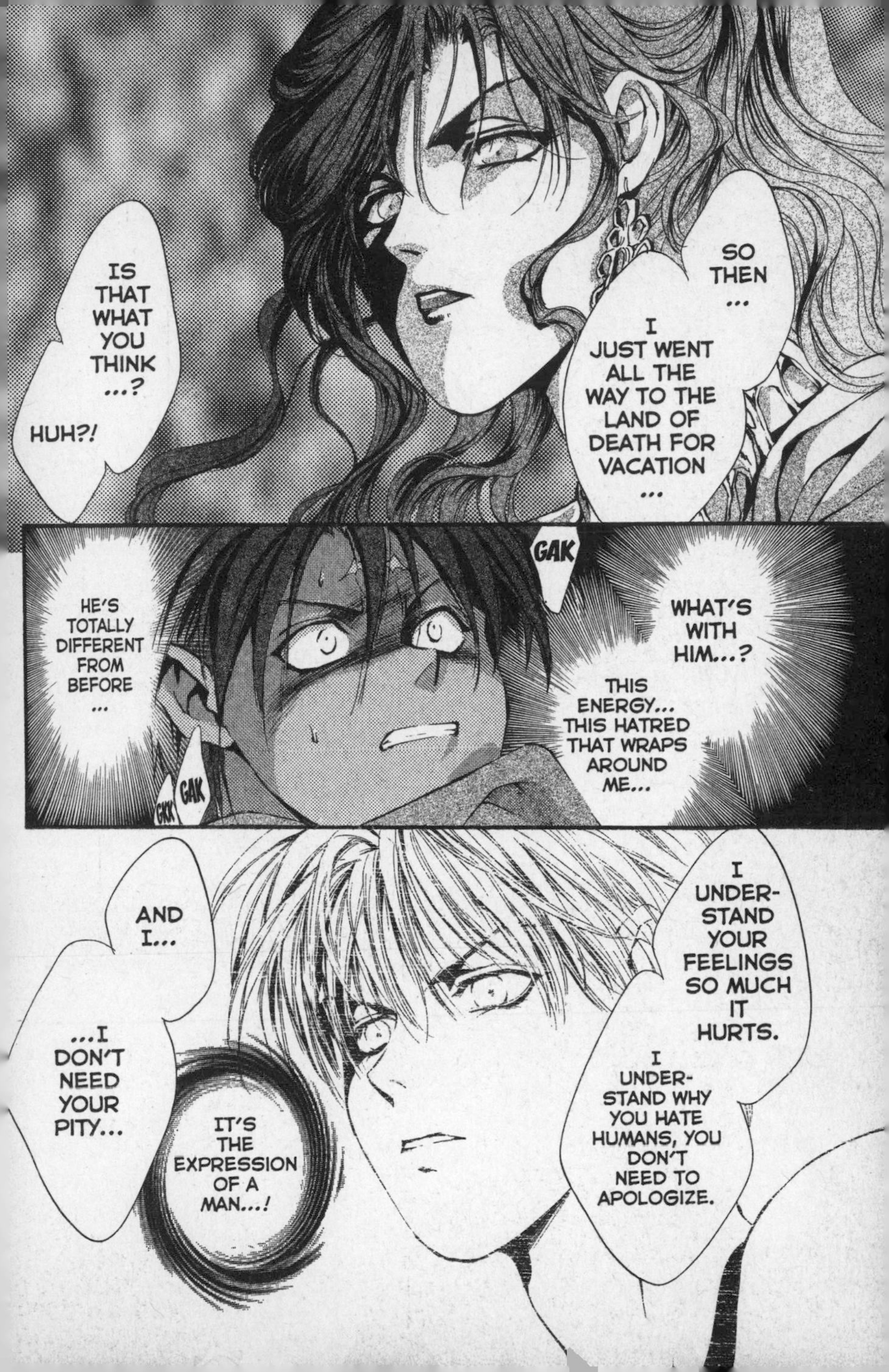
SO THEN...
I JUST WENT ALL THE WAY TO THE LAND OF DEATH FOR VACATION...
IS THAT WHAT YOU THINK...?
HUH?!
GAK
WHAT'S WITH HIM...?
THIS ENERGY... THIS HATRED THAT WRAPS AROUND ME...
HE'S TOTALLY DIFFERENT FROM BEFORE...
GAK
GKK
I UNDER-STAND YOUR FEELINGS SO MUCH IT HURTS.
I UNDER-STAND WHY YOU HATE HUMANS, YOU DON'T NEED TO APOLOGIZE.
IT'S THE EXPRESSION OF A MAN...!
AND I...
...I DON'T NEED YOUR PITY...

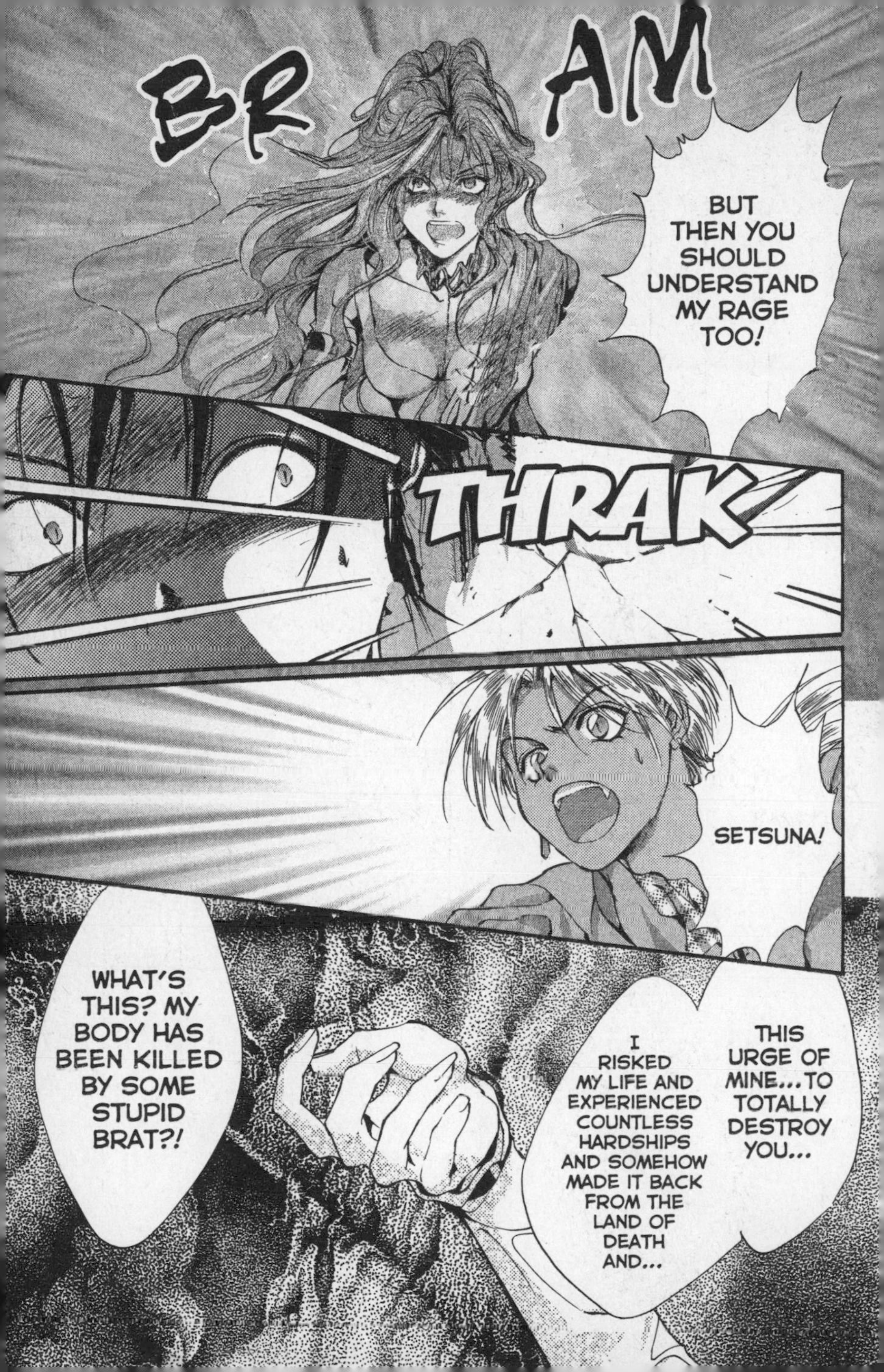
BR AM
BUT THEN YOU SHOULD UNDERSTAND MY RAGE TOO!
THRAK
SETSUNA!
THIS URGE OF MINE...TO TOTALLY DESTROY YOU...
I RISKED MY LIFE AND EXPERIENCED COUNTLESS HARDSHIPS AND SOMEHOW MADE IT BACK FROM THE LAND OF DEATH AND...
WHAT'S THIS? MY BODY HAS BEEN KILLED BY SOME STUPID BRAT?!

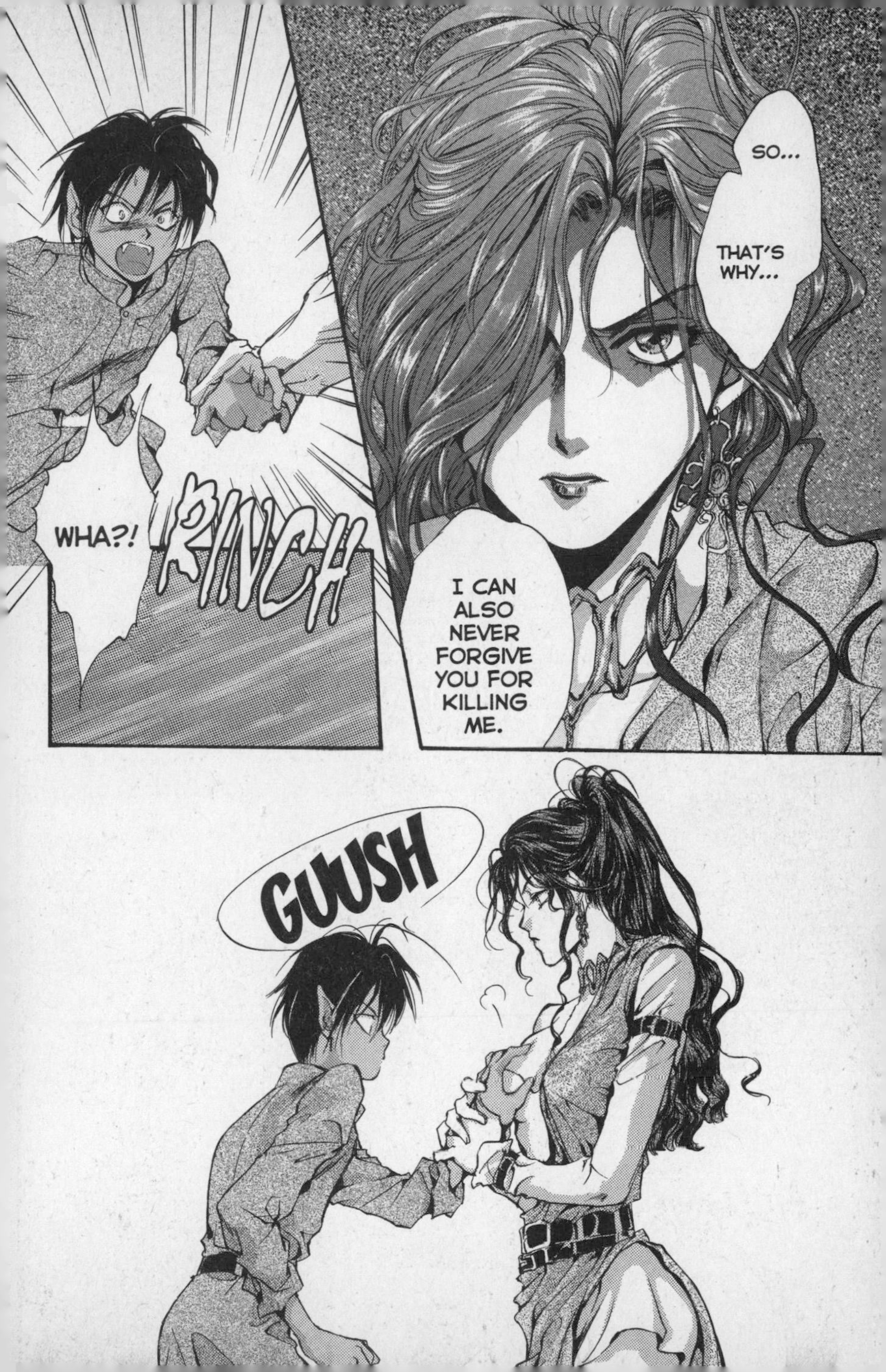
SO...
THAT'S WHY...
I CAN ALSO NEVER FORGIVE YOU FOR KILLING ME.
PINCH
WHA?!
GUUSH

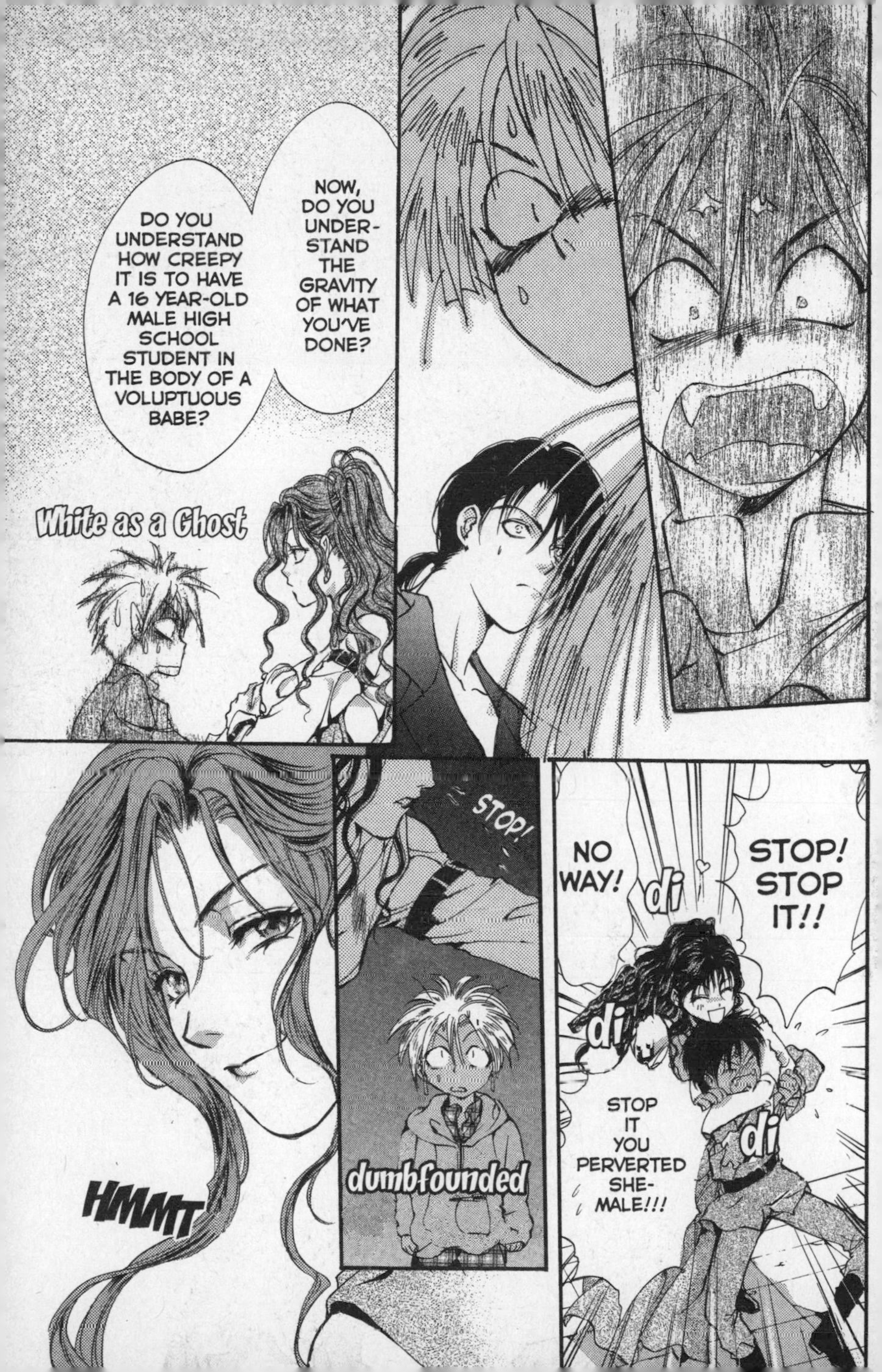
NOW, DO YOU UNDER-STAND THE GRAVITY OF WHAT YOU'VE DONE?
DO YOU UNDERSTAND HOW CREEPY IT IS TO HAVE A 16 YEAR-OLD MALE HIGH SCHOOL STUDENT IN THE BODY OF A VOLUPTUOUS BABE?
White as a Ghost
STOP! STOP IT!!
NO WAY!
di
di
di
STOP IT YOU PERVERTED SHE-MALE!!!
STOP!
dumbfounded
HMMT

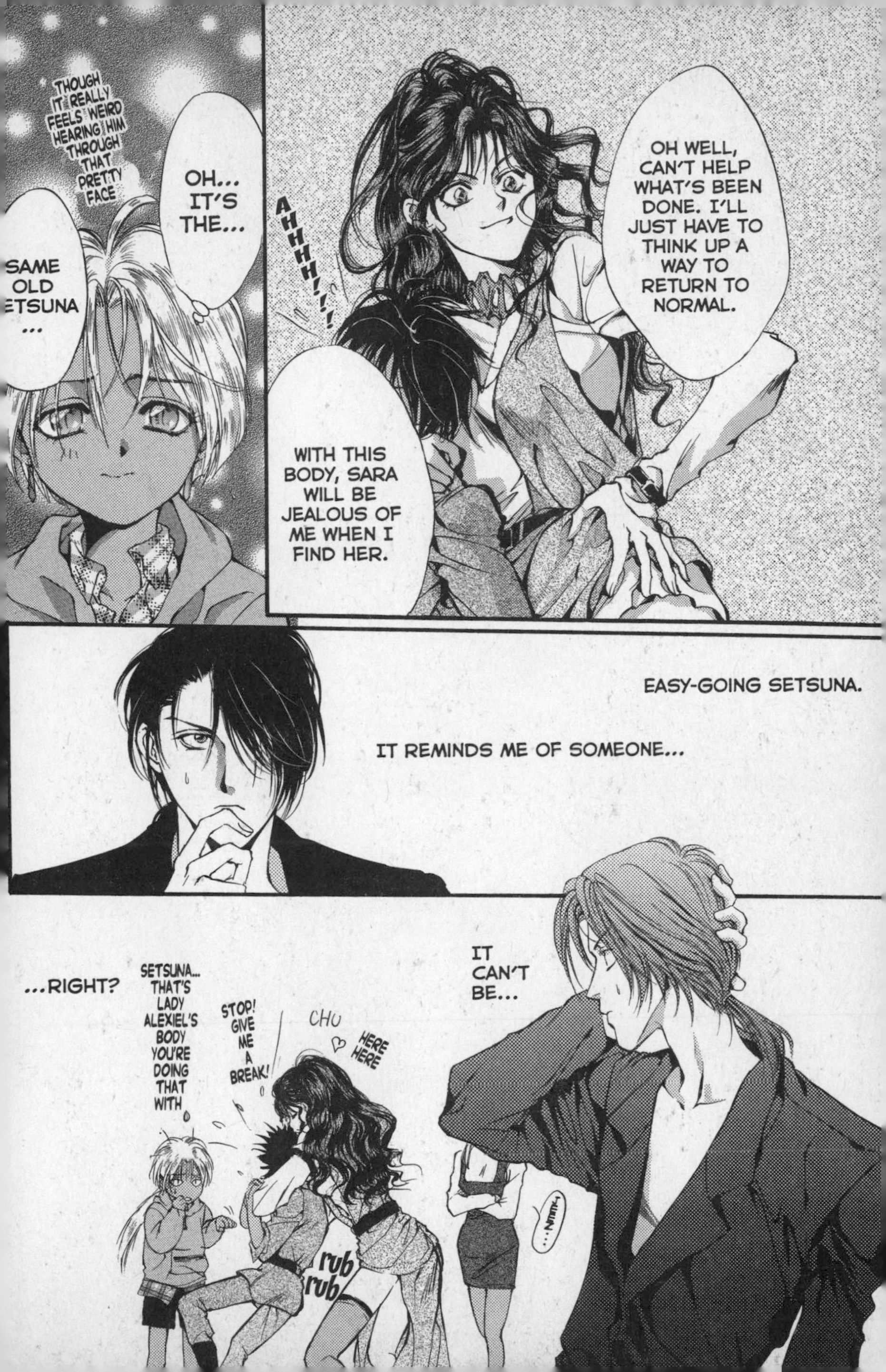
OH WELL, CAN'T HELP WHAT'S BEEN DONE. I'LL JUST HAVE TO THINK UP A WAY TO RETURN TO NORMAL.
AHHHH!!!
WITH THIS BODY, SARA WILL BE JEALOUS OF ME WHEN I FIND HER.
OH... IT'S THE...
SAME OLD SETSUNA...
THOUGH IT REALLY FEELS WEIRD HEARING HIM THROUGH THAT PRETTY FACE
EASY-GOING SETSUNA.
IT REMINDS ME OF SOMEONE...
IT CAN'T BE...
...RIGHT?
...NNNH!
HERE HERE
CHU
STOP! GIVE ME A BREAK!
SETSUNA... THAT'S LADY ALEXIEL'S BODY YOU'RE DOING THAT WITH
rub rub

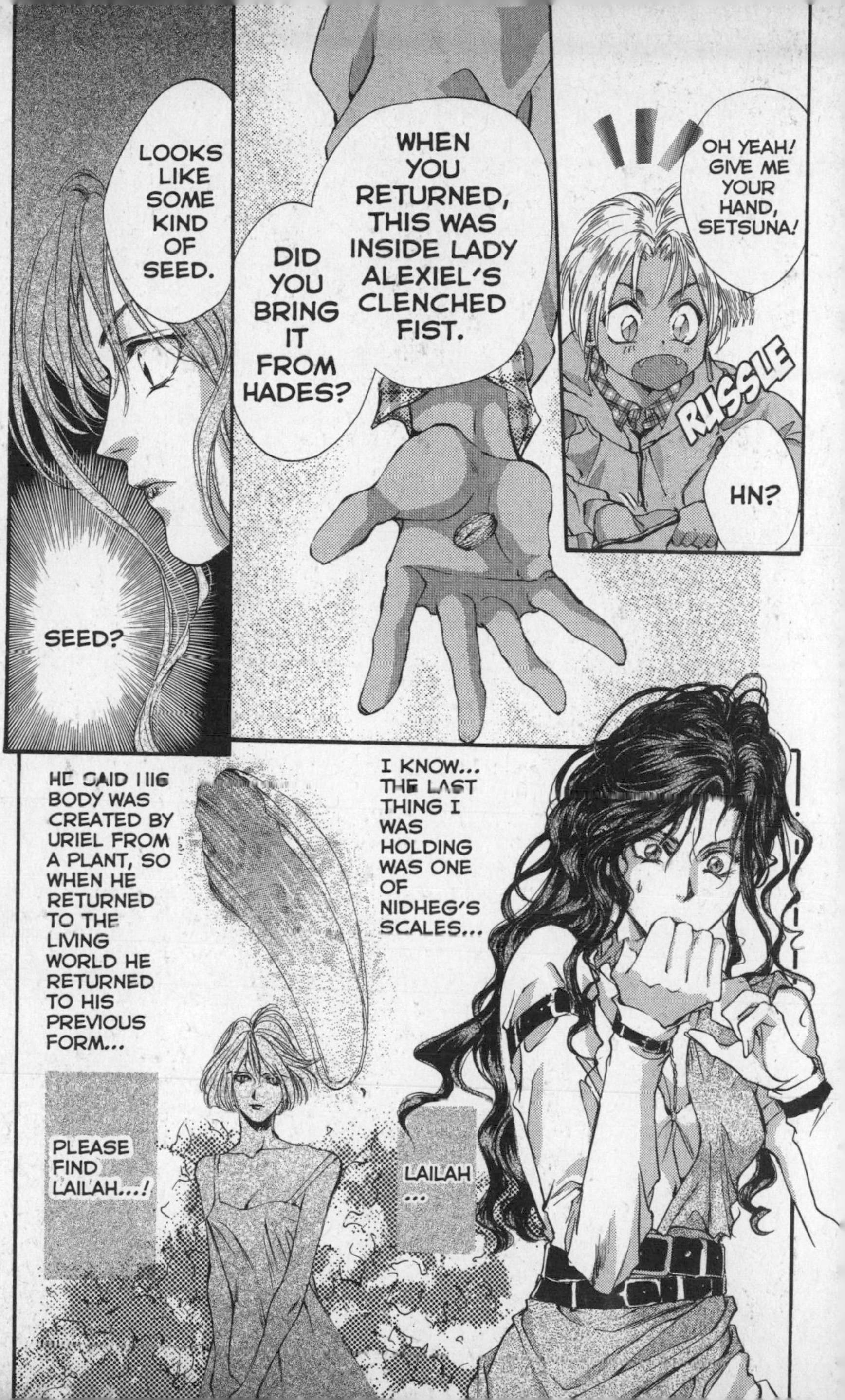
OH YEAH! GIVE ME YOUR HAND, SETSUNA!
RUSSLE
HN?
WHEN YOU RETURNED, THIS WAS INSIDE LADY ALEXIEL'S CLENCHED FIST.
DID YOU BRING IT FROM HADES?
LOOKS LIKE SOME KIND OF SEED.
SEED?
I KNOW... THE LAST THING I WAS HOLDING WAS ONE OF NIDHEG'S SCALES...
LAILAH ...
HE SAID HIS BODY WAS CREATED BY URIEL FROM A PLANT, SO WHEN HE RETURNED TO THE LIVING WORLD HE RETURNED TO HIS PREVIOUS FORM...
PLEASE FIND LAILAH...!

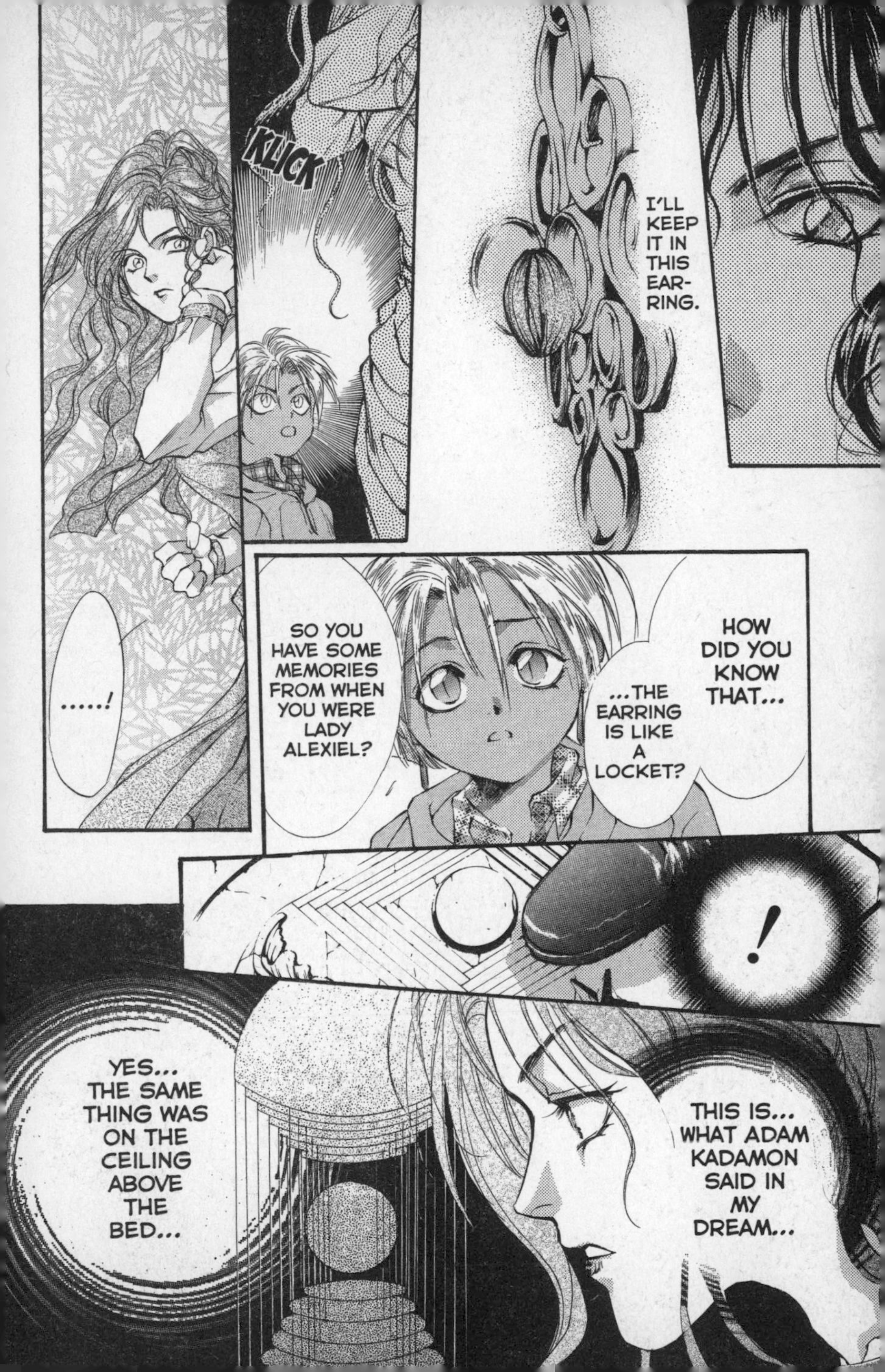
I'LL KEEP IT IN THIS EAR-RING.
KLICK
HOW DID YOU KNOW THAT...
...THE EARRING IS LIKE A LOCKET?
SO YOU HAVE SOME MEMORIES FROM WHEN YOU WERE LADY ALEXIEL?
......!
!
THIS IS... WHAT ADAM KADAMON SAID IN MY DREAM...
YES... THE SAME THING WAS ON THE CEILING ABOVE THE BED...

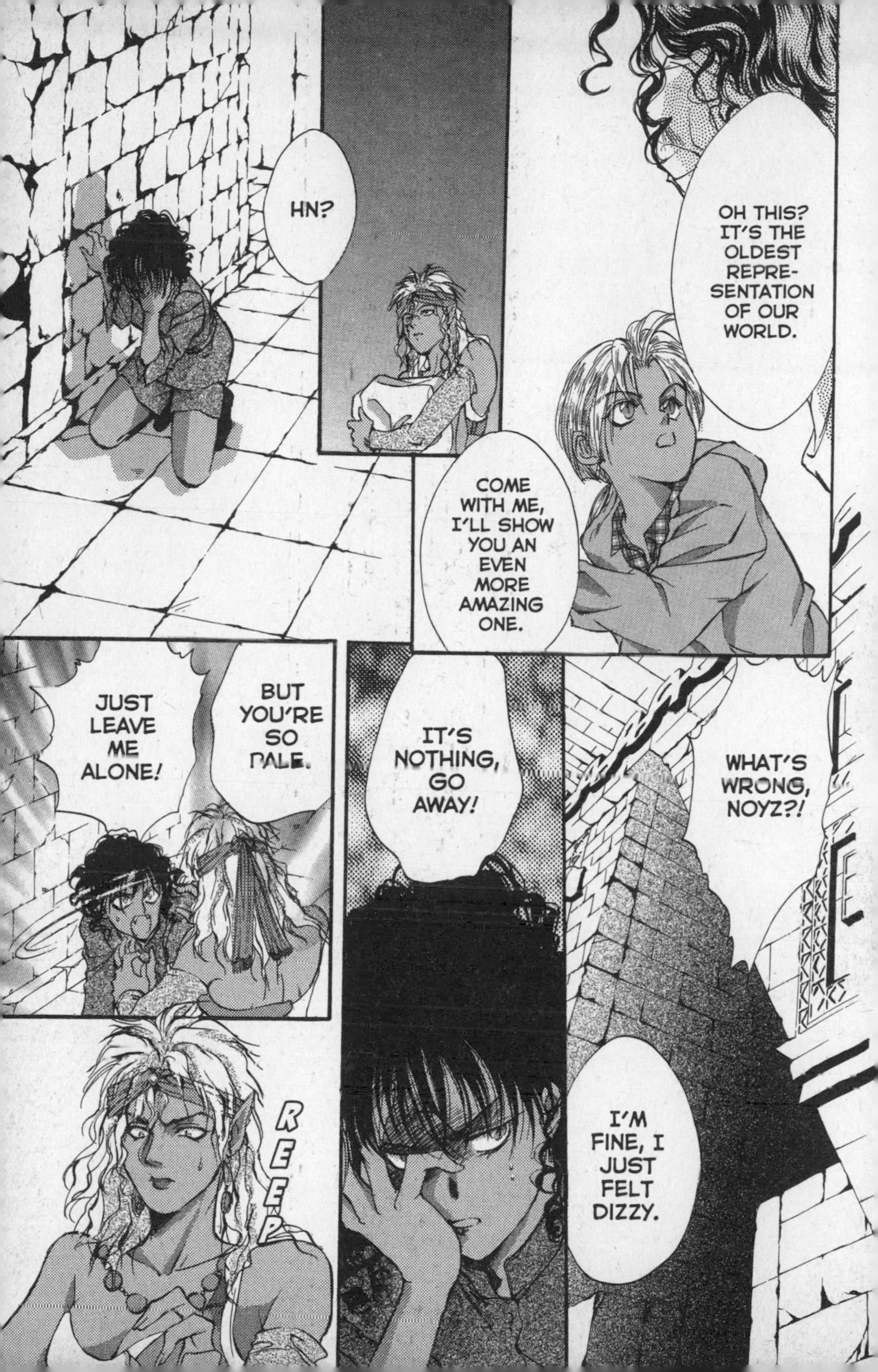
OH THIS? IT'S THE OLDEST REPRE-SENTATION OF OUR WORLD.
COME WITH ME, I'LL SHOW YOU AN EVEN MORE AMAZING ONE.
HN?
WHAT'S WRONG, NOYZ?!
I'M FINE, I JUST FELT DIZZY.
IT'S NOTHING, GO AWAY!
BUT YOU'RE SO PALE.
JUST LEAVE ME ALONE!
REEP

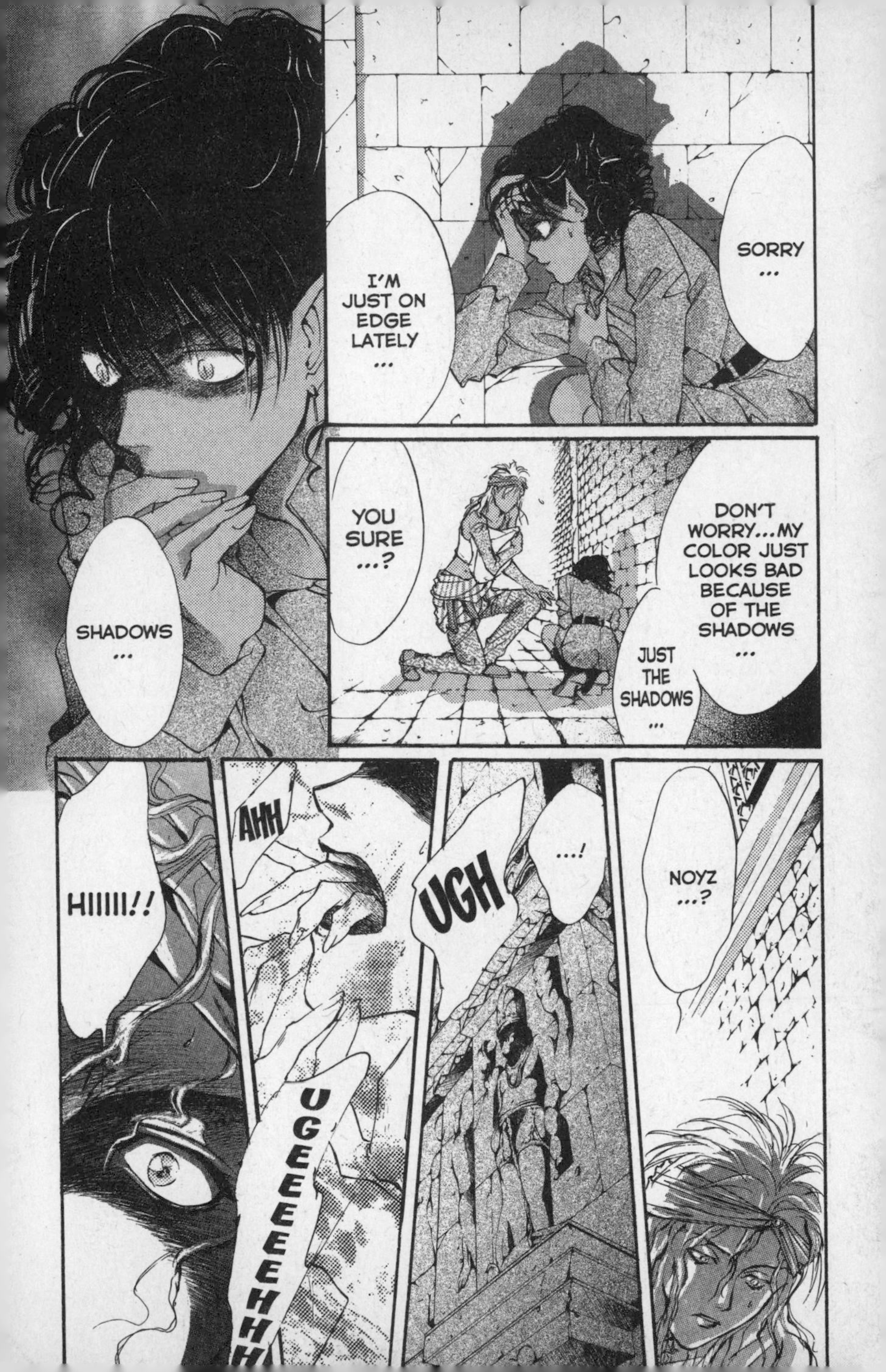
SORRY ...
I'M JUST ON EDGE LATELY ...
DON'T WORRY...MY COLOR JUST LOOKS BAD BECAUSE OF THE SHADOWS ...
JUST THE SHADOWS ...
YOU SURE ...?
SHADOWS ...
NOYZ ...?
...!
UGH
AHH
UGEEEEEEEHHH
HIIIIII!!

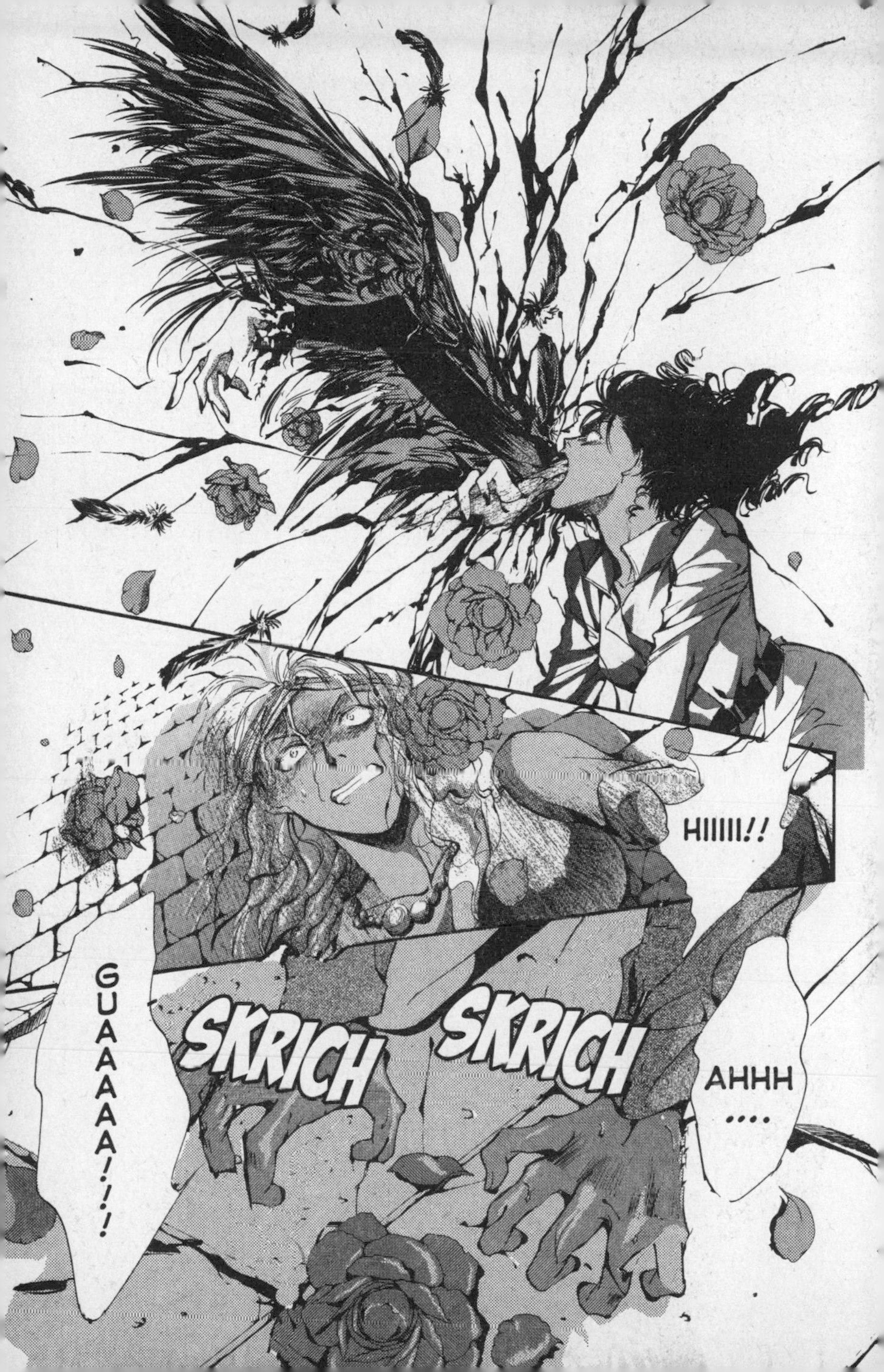
HIIIII!!
AHHH ....
SKRICH
SKRICH
GUAAAAAA!!!!

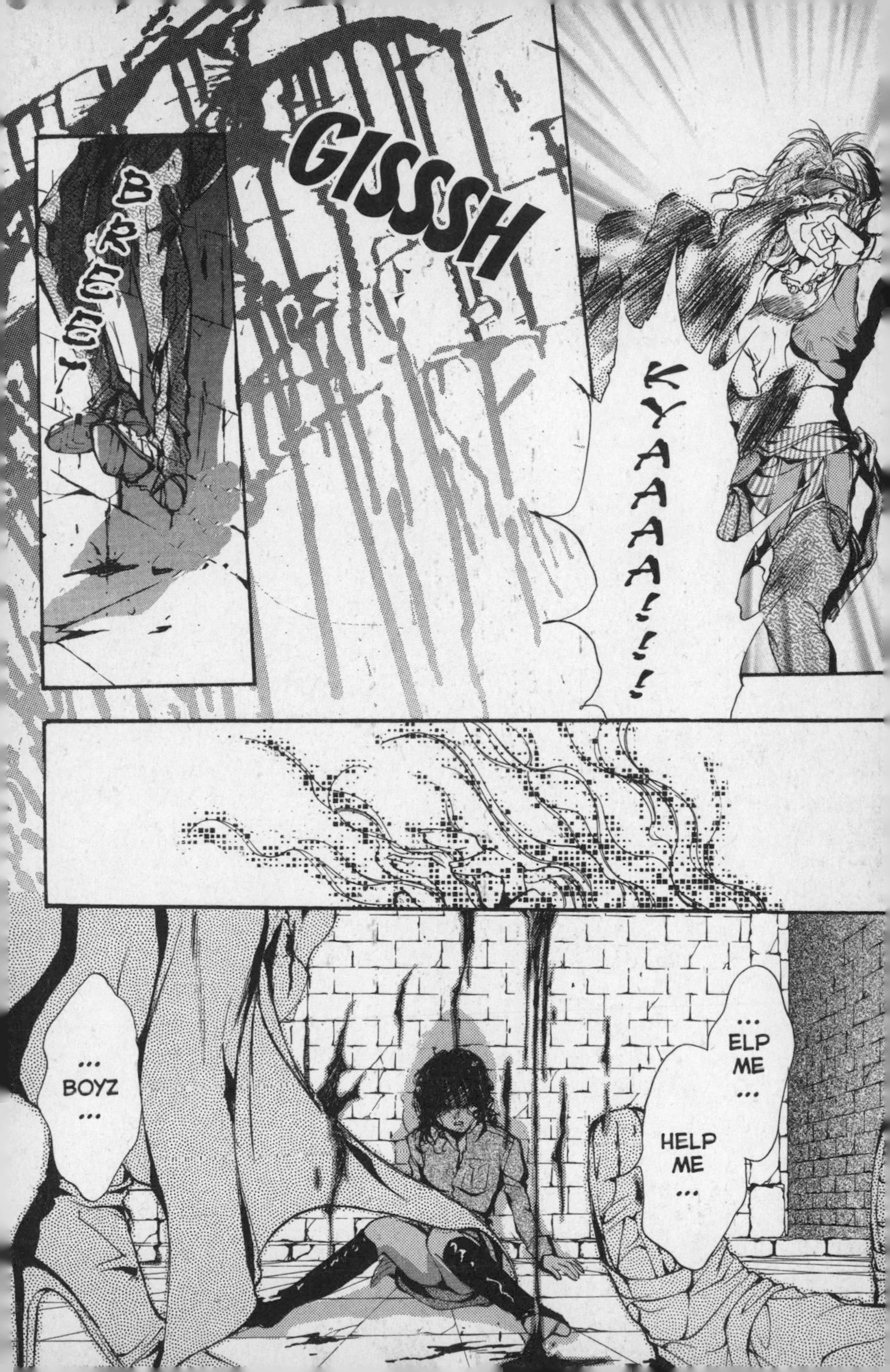
KYAAAAA!!!
GISSSH
BREEE!
... ELP ME ... HELP ME ...
... BOYZ ...

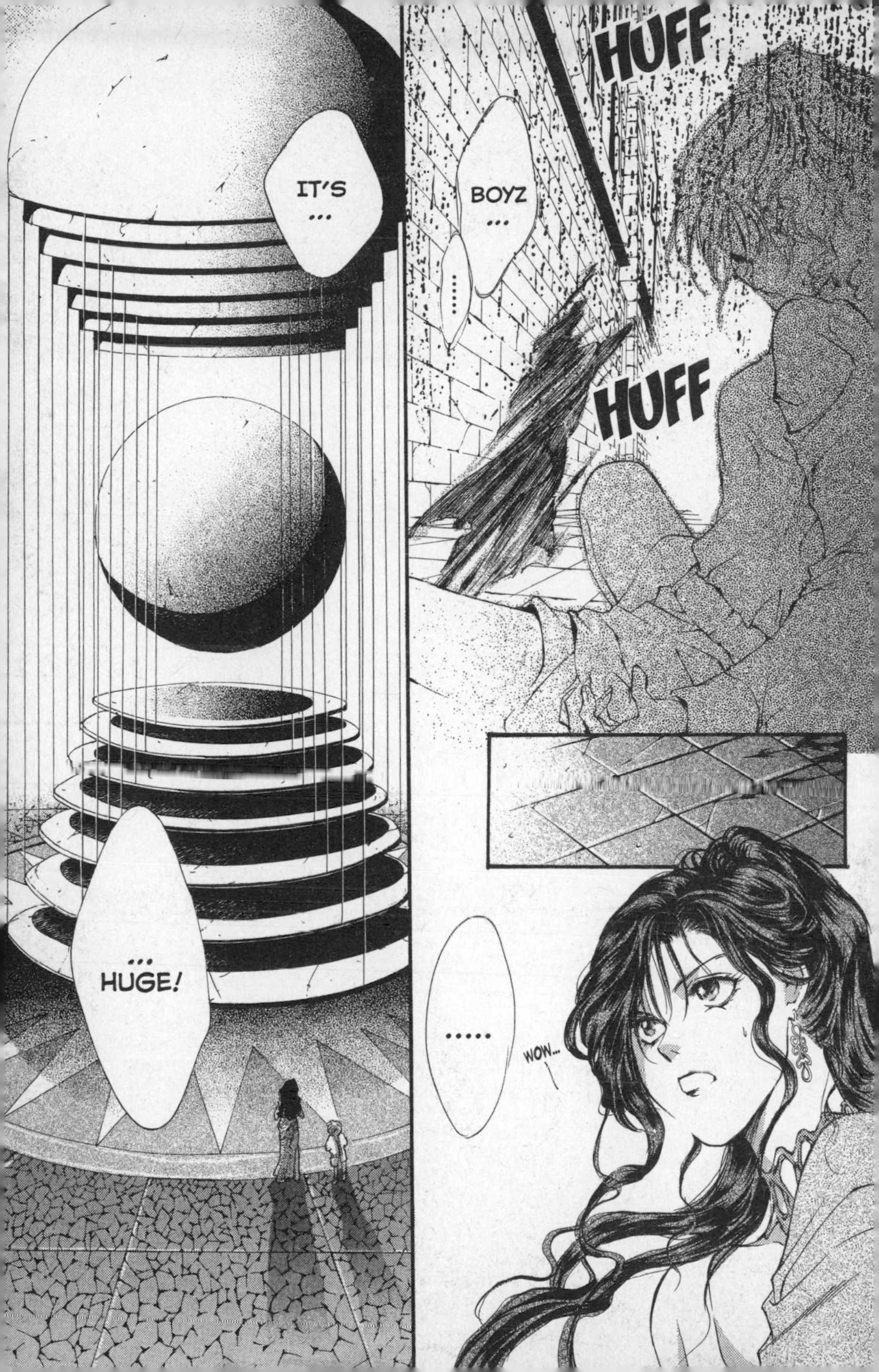
HUFF
BOYZ ...
......
HUFF
.....
WOW...
IT'S ...
... HUGE!

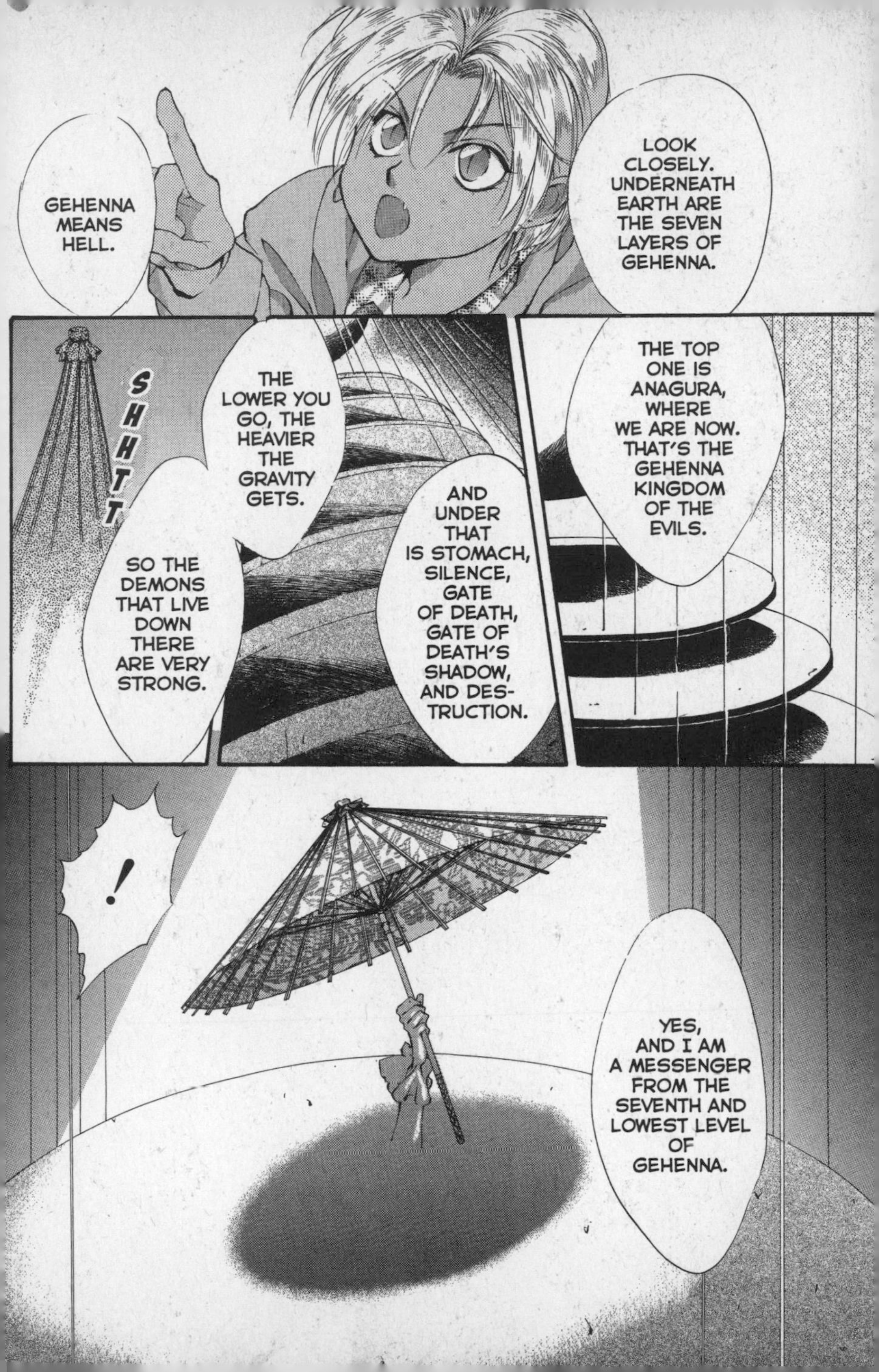
LOOK CLOSELY. UNDERNEATH EARTH ARE THE SEVEN LAYERS OF GEHENNA.
GEHENNA MEANS HELL.
THE TOP ONE IS ANAGURA, WHERE WE ARE NOW. THAT'S THE GEHENNA KINGDOM OF THE EVILS.
AND UNDER THAT IS STOMACH, SILENCE, GATE OF DEATH, GATE OF DEATH'S SHADOW, AND DES-TRUCTION.
THE LOWER YOU GO, THE HEAVIER THE GRAVITY GETS.
SHHTT
SO THE DEMONS THAT LIVE DOWN THERE ARE VERY STRONG.
YES, AND I AM A MESSENGER FROM THE SEVENTH AND LOWEST LEVEL OF GEHENNA.
!

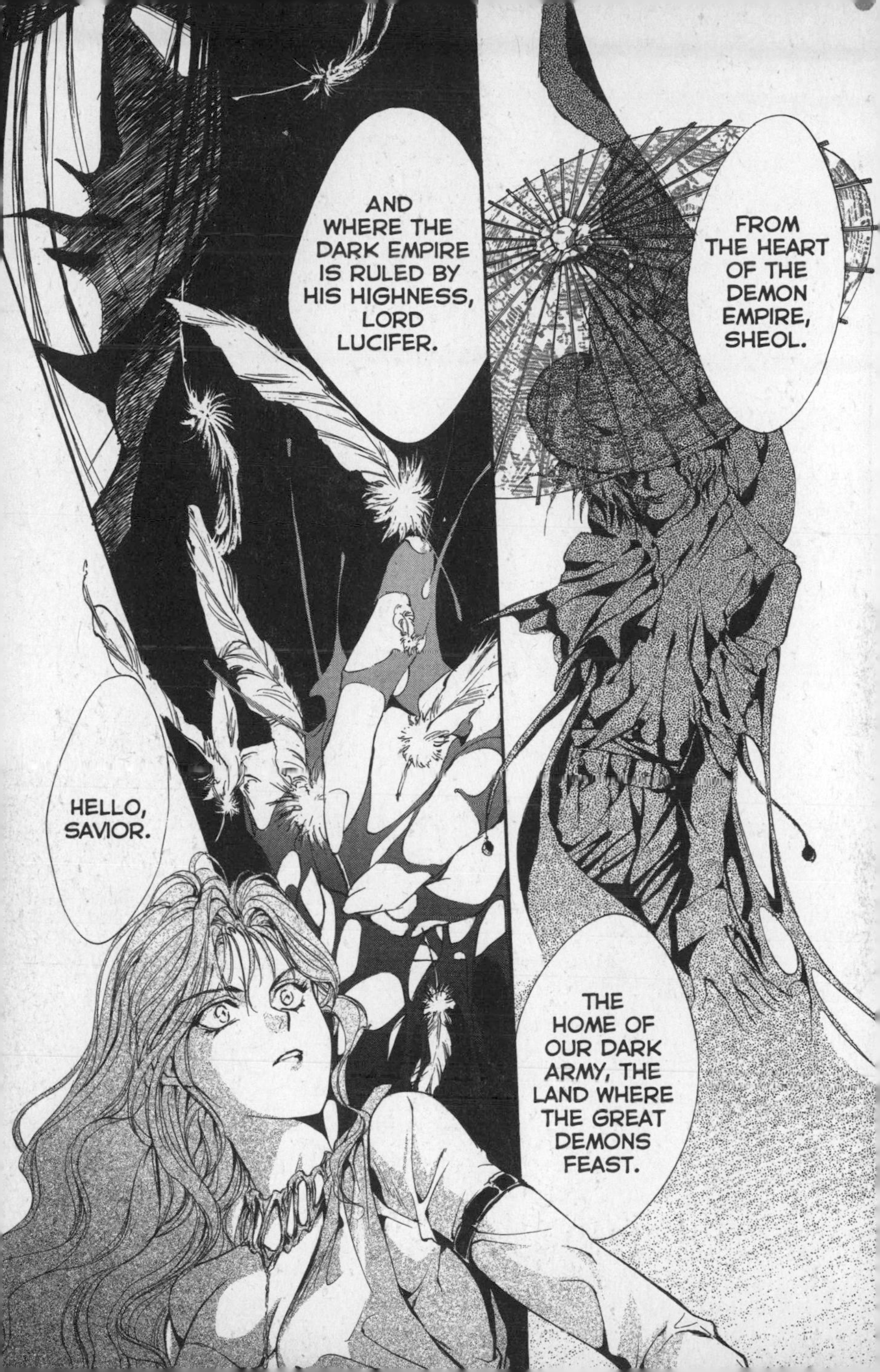
FROM THE HEART OF THE DEMON EMPIRE, SHEOL.
THE HOME OF OUR DARK ARMY, THE LAND WHERE THE GREAT DEMONS FEAST.
AND WHERE THE DARK EMPIRE IS RULED BY HIS HIGHNESS, LORD LUCIFER.
HELLO, SAVIOR.

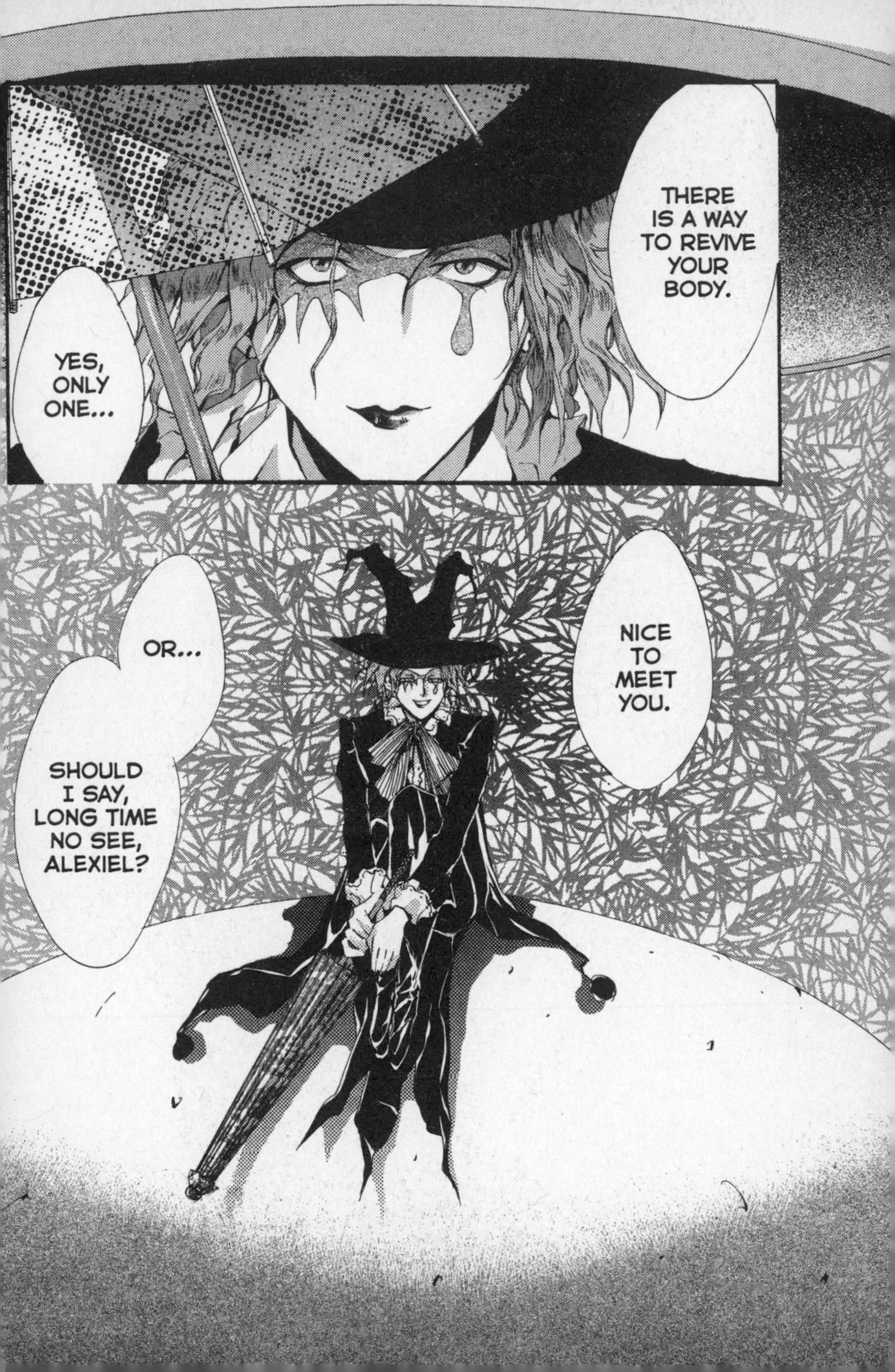
THERE IS A WAY TO REVIVE YOUR BODY.
YES, ONLY ONE...
NICE TO MEET YOU.
OR...
SHOULD I SAY, LONG TIME NO SEE, ALEXIEL?

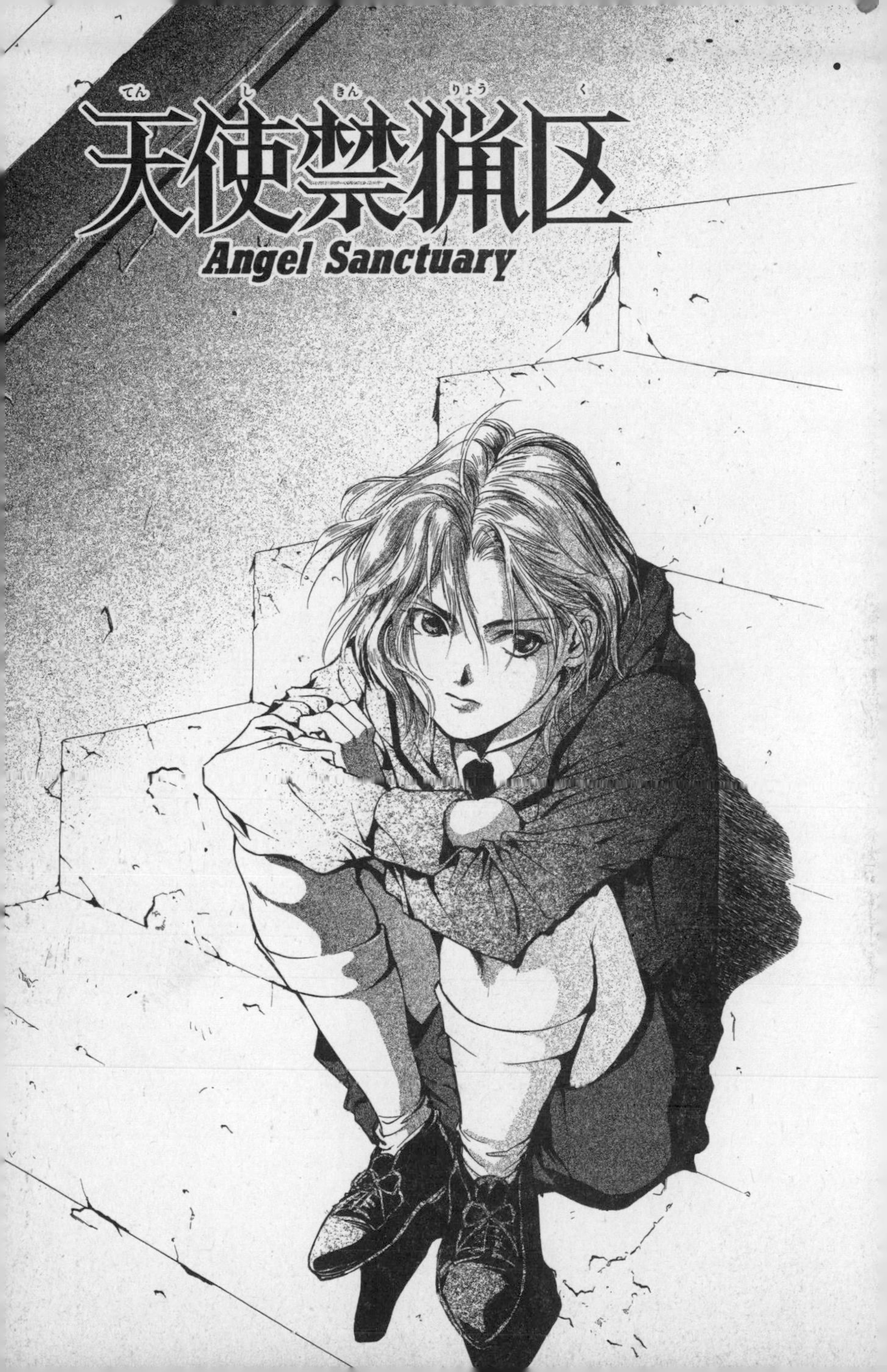
天使禁猟区
てんしきんりょうく
Angel Sanctuary

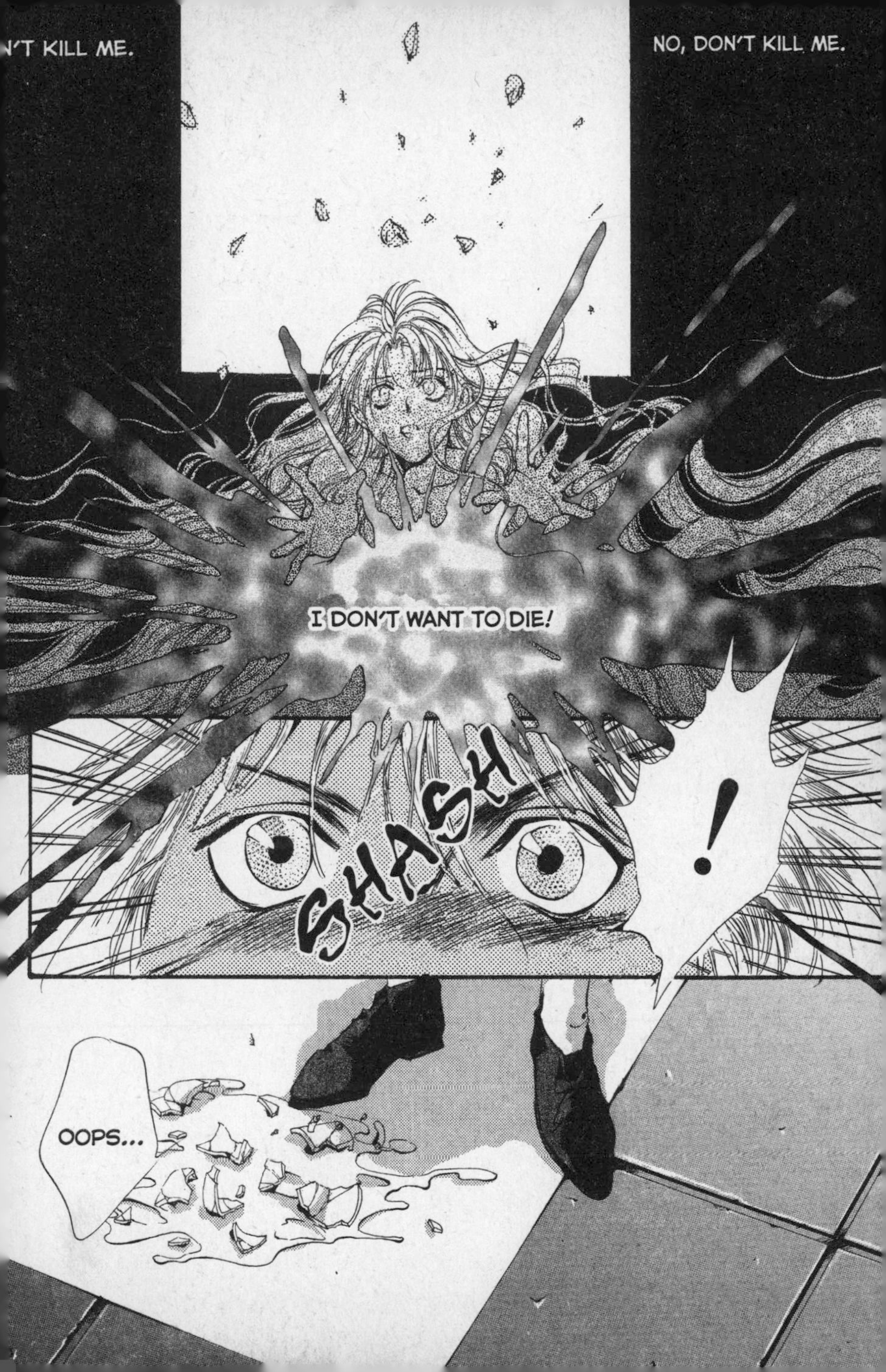
NO, DON'T KILL ME.
N'T KILL ME.
I DON'T WANT TO DIE!
SHASH
!
OOPS...

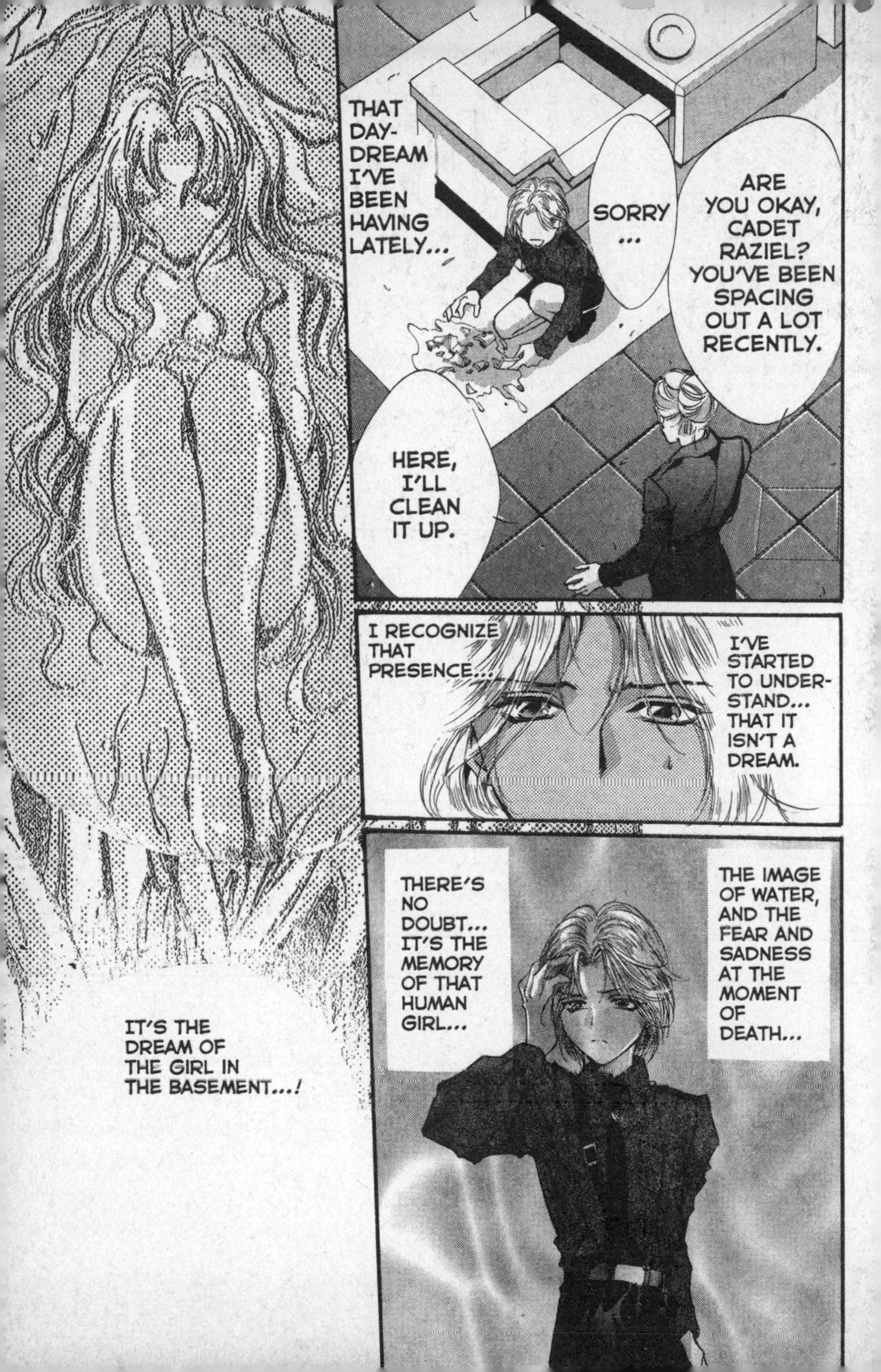
ARE YOU OKAY, CADET RAZIEL? YOU'VE BEEN SPACING OUT A LOT RECENTLY.
SORRY...
THAT DAY-DREAM I'VE BEEN HAVING LATELY...
HERE, I'LL CLEAN IT UP.
I'VE STARTED TO UNDER-STAND... THAT IT ISN'T A DREAM.
I RECOGNIZE THAT PRESENCE...
THE IMAGE OF WATER, AND THE FEAR AND SADNESS AT THE MOMENT OF DEATH...
THERE'S NO DOUBT... IT'S THE MEMORY OF THAT HUMAN GIRL...
IT'S THE DREAM OF THE GIRL IN THE BASEMENT...!

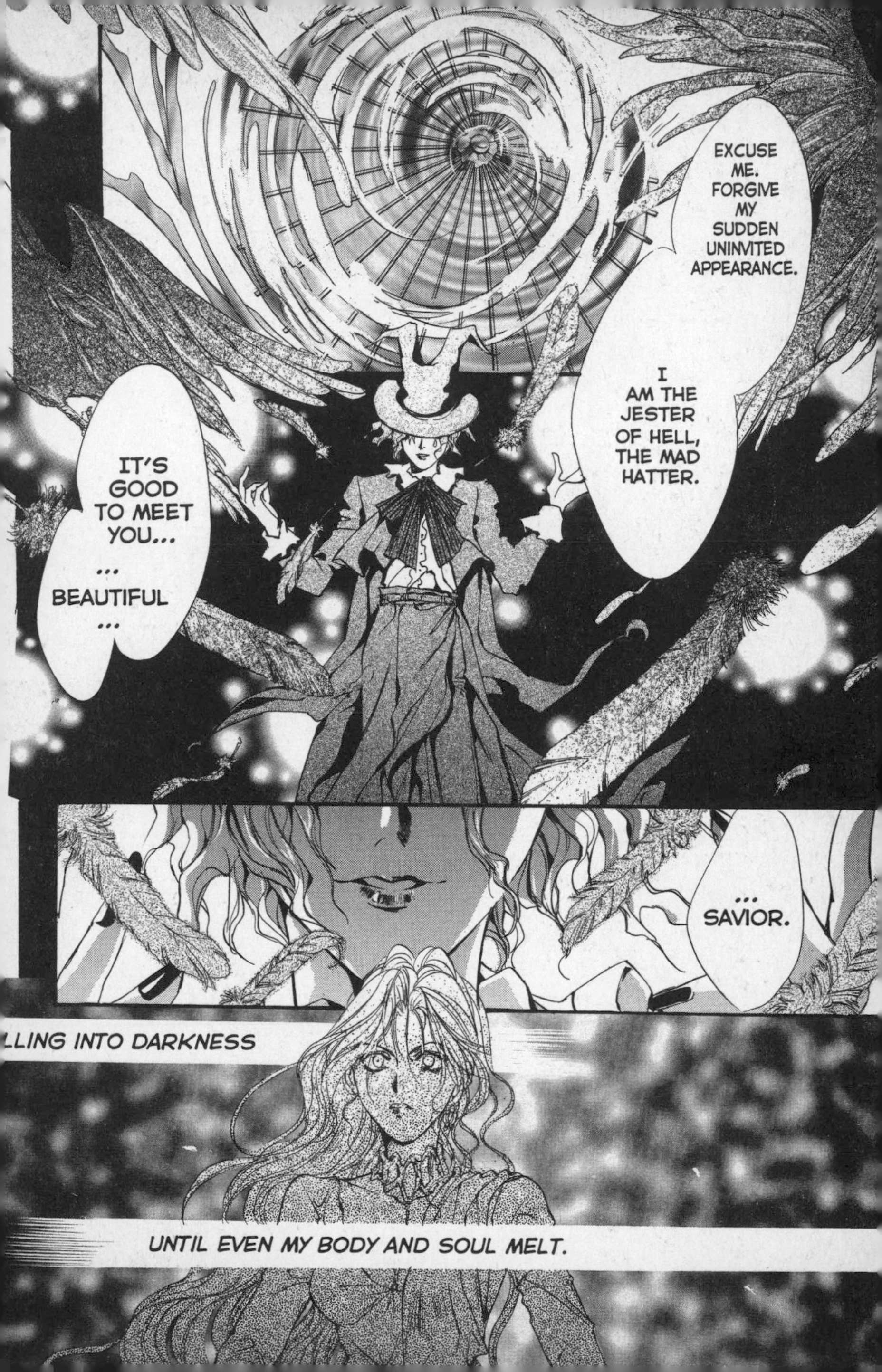
EXCUSE ME. FORGIVE MY SUDDEN UNINVITED APPEARANCE.
I AM THE JESTER OF HELL, THE MAD HATTER.
IT'S GOOD TO MEET YOU... ... BEAUTIFUL ...
... SAVIOR.
LLING INTO DARKNESS
UNTIL EVEN MY BODY AND SOUL MELT.

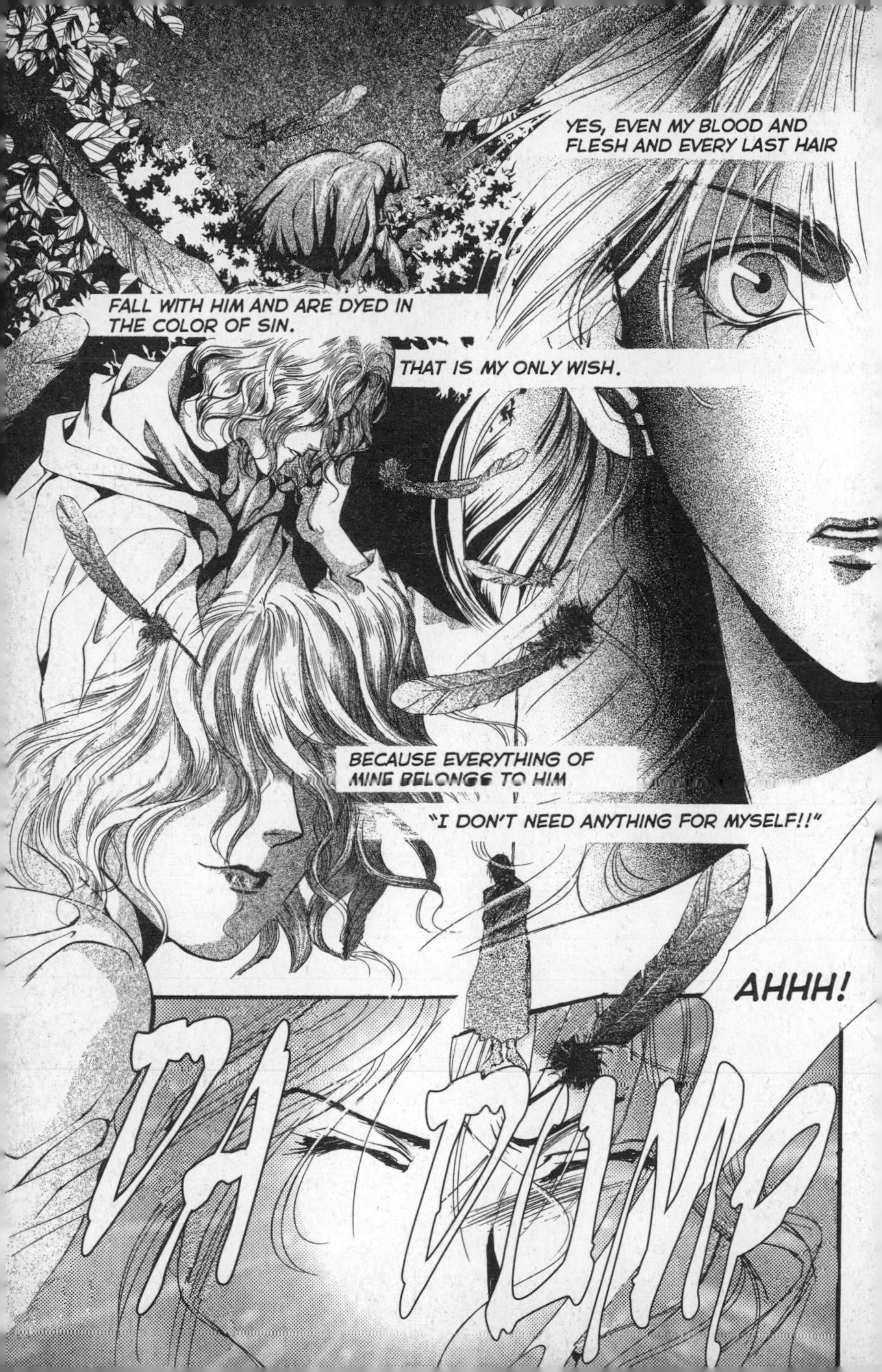
YES, EVEN MY BLOOD AND FLESH AND EVERY LAST HAIR
FALL WITH HIM AND ARE DYED IN THE COLOR OF SIN.
THAT IS MY ONLY WISH.
BECAUSE EVERYTHING OF MINE BELONGS TO HIM
"I DON'T NEED ANYTHING FOR MYSELF!!"
AHHH!
DA DUMP

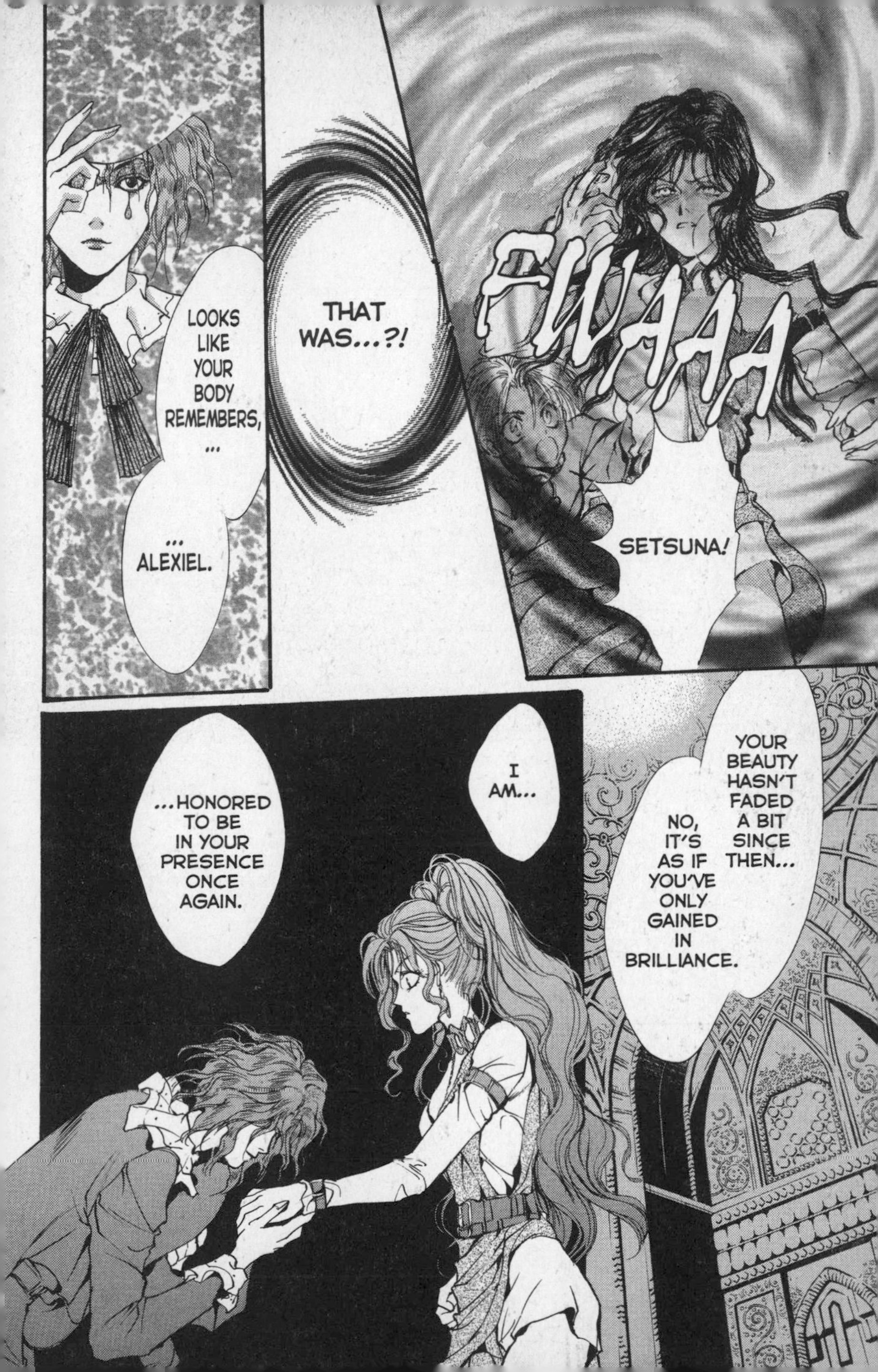
FWAAA
SETSUNA!
THAT WAS...?!
LOOKS LIKE YOUR BODY REMEMBERS, ...
... ALEXIEL.
YOUR BEAUTY HASN'T FADED A BIT SINCE THEN...
NO, IT'S AS IF YOU'VE ONLY GAINED IN BRILLIANCE.
I AM...
...HONORED TO BE IN YOUR PRESENCE ONCE AGAIN.

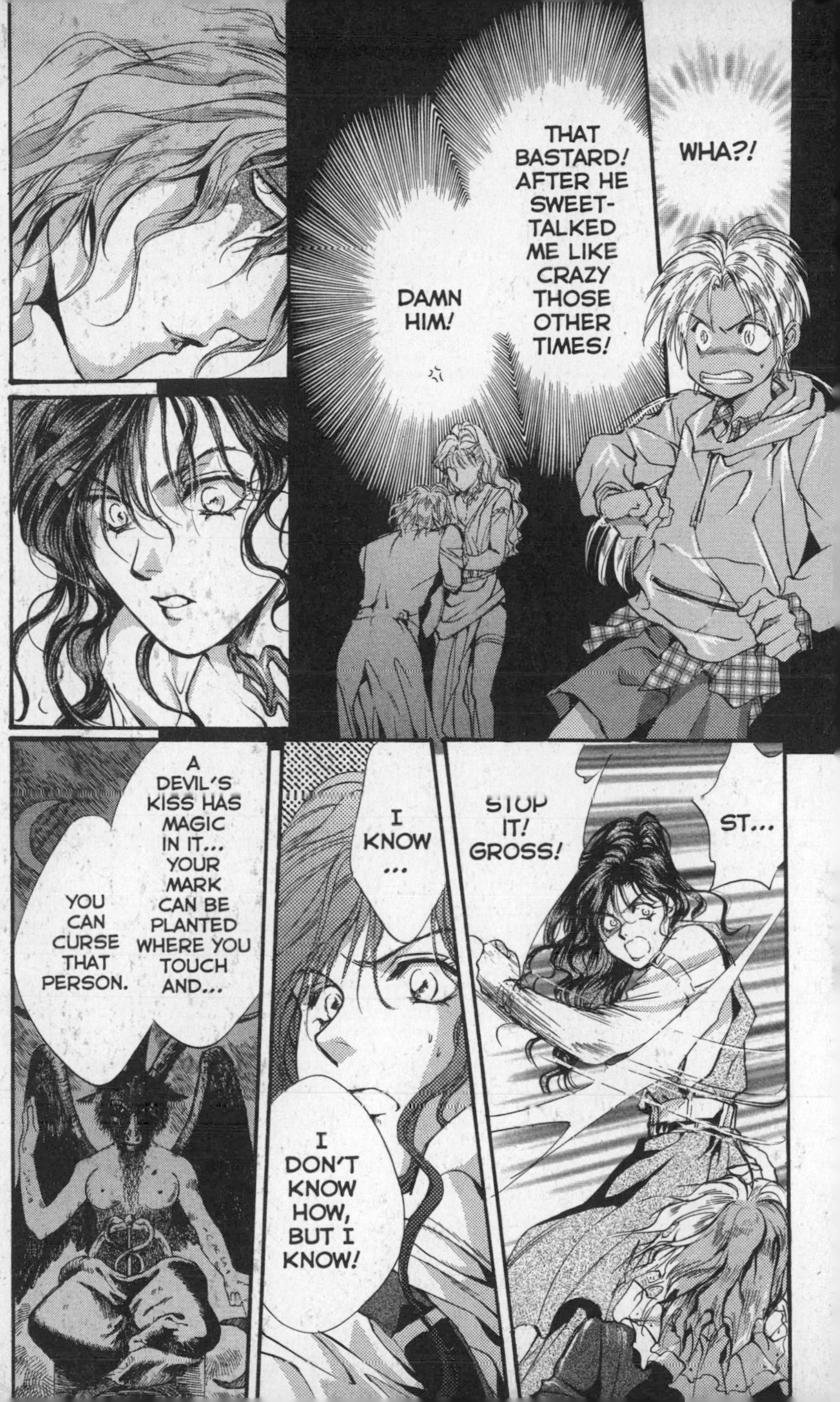
WHA?!
THAT BASTARD! AFTER HE SWEET-TALKED ME LIKE CRAZY THOSE OTHER TIMES!
DAMN HIM!
ST...
STOP IT! GROSS!
I KNOW...
I DON'T KNOW HOW, BUT I KNOW!
A DEVIL'S KISS HAS MAGIC IN IT... YOUR MARK CAN BE PLANTED WHERE YOU TOUCH AND...
YOU CAN CURSE THAT PERSON.

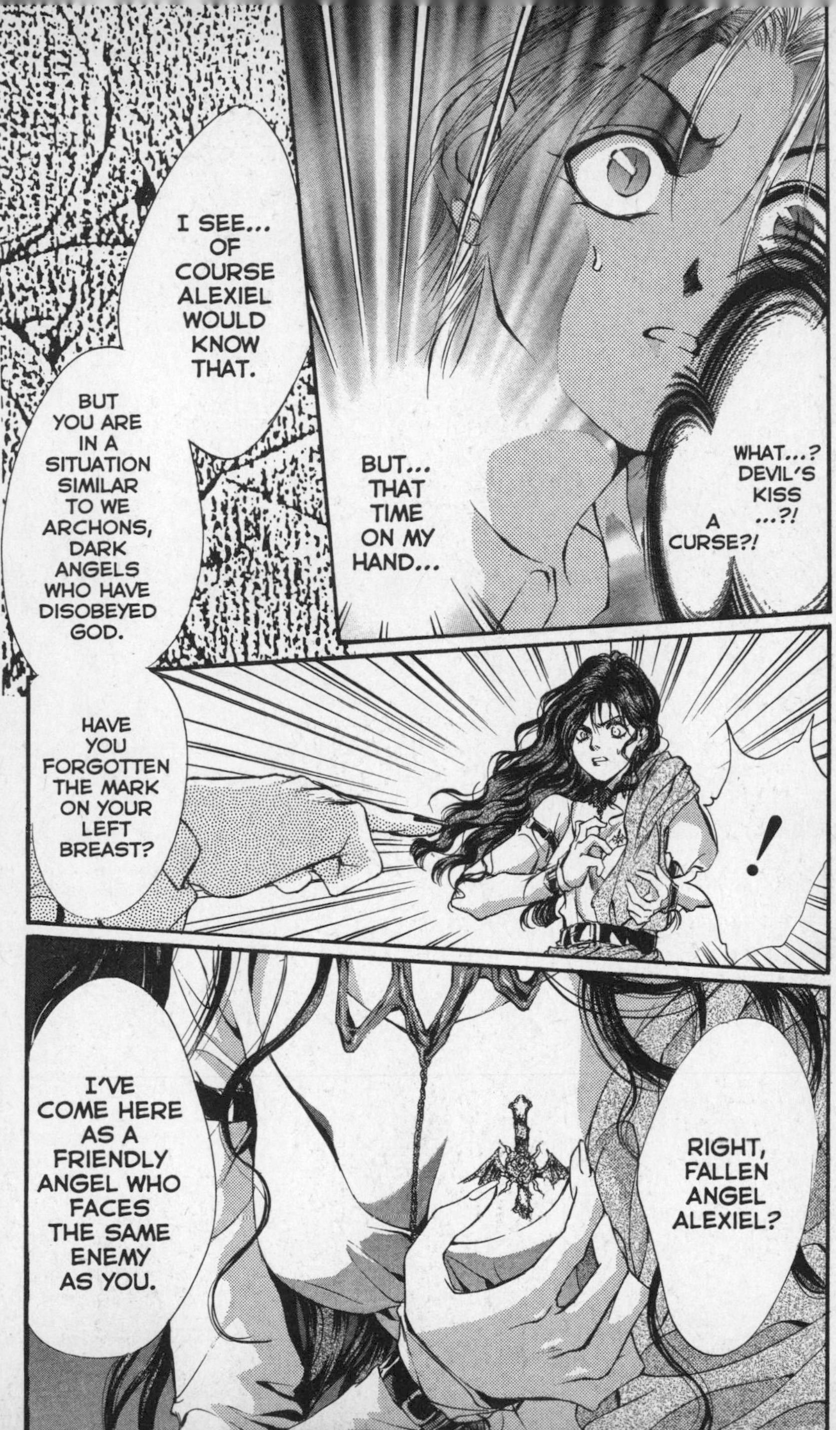
WHAT...? DEVIL'S KISS ...?!
A CURSE?!
BUT... THAT TIME ON MY HAND...
I SEE... OF COURSE ALEXIEL WOULD KNOW THAT.
BUT YOU ARE IN A SITUATION SIMILAR TO WE ARCHONS, DARK ANGELS WHO HAVE DISOBEYED GOD.
!
HAVE YOU FORGOTTEN THE MARK ON YOUR LEFT BREAST?
I'VE COME HERE AS A FRIENDLY ANGEL WHO FACES THE SAME ENEMY AS YOU.
RIGHT, FALLEN ANGEL ALEXIEL?

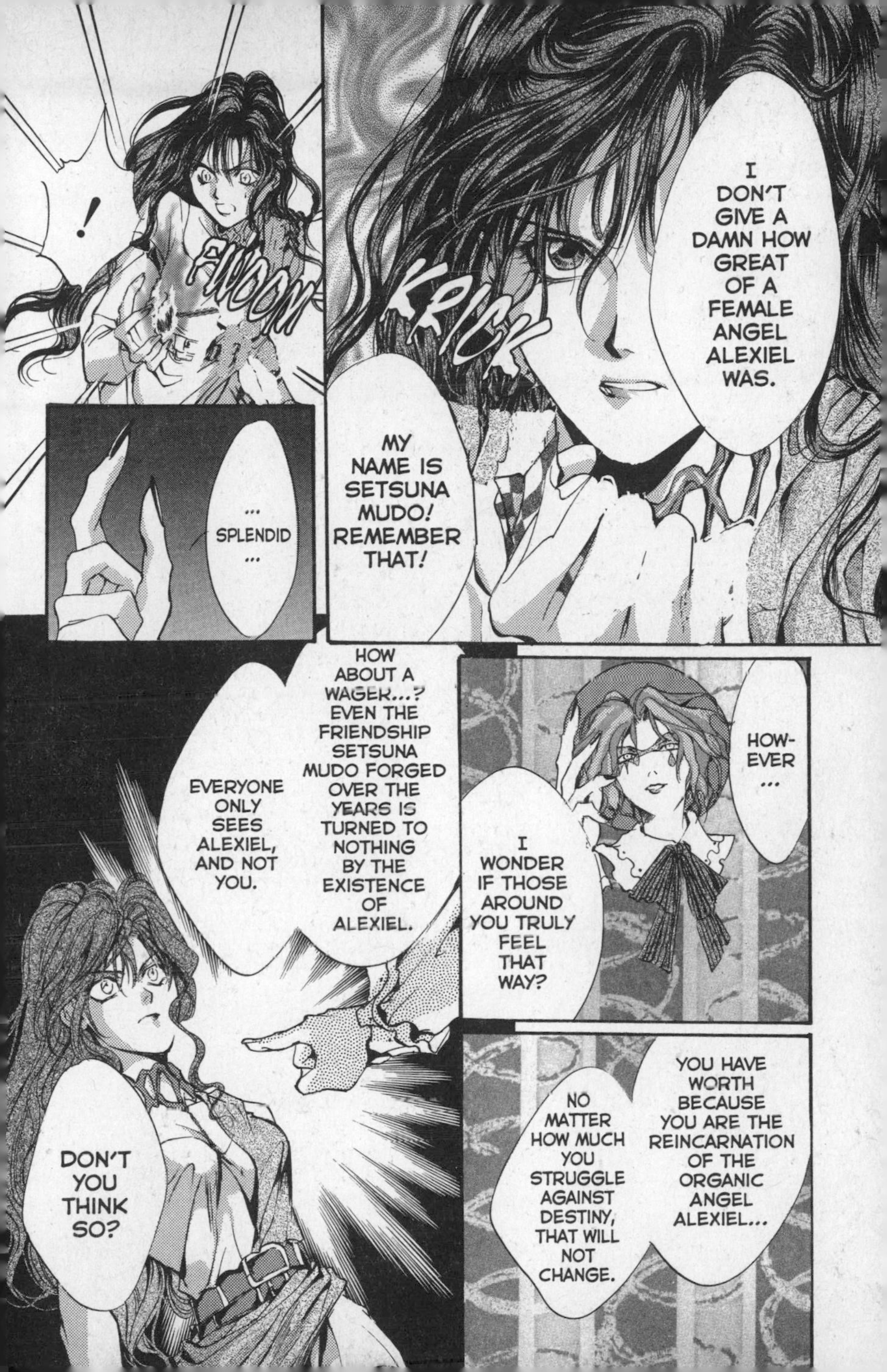
KRICK
I DON'T GIVE A DAMN HOW GREAT OF A FEMALE ANGEL ALEXIEL WAS.
MY NAME IS SETSUNA MUDO! REMEMBER THAT!
!
FWOOM
... SPLENDID ...
HOW-EVER ...
I WONDER IF THOSE AROUND YOU TRULY FEEL THAT WAY?
YOU HAVE WORTH BECAUSE YOU ARE THE REINCARNATION OF THE ORGANIC ANGEL ALEXIEL...
NO MATTER HOW MUCH YOU STRUGGLE AGAINST DESTINY, THAT WILL NOT CHANGE.
HOW ABOUT A WAGER...? EVEN THE FRIENDSHIP SETSUNA MUDO FORGED OVER THE YEARS IS TURNED TO NOTHING BY THE EXISTENCE OF ALEXIEL.
EVERYONE ONLY SEES ALEXIEL, AND NOT YOU.
DON'T YOU THINK SO?

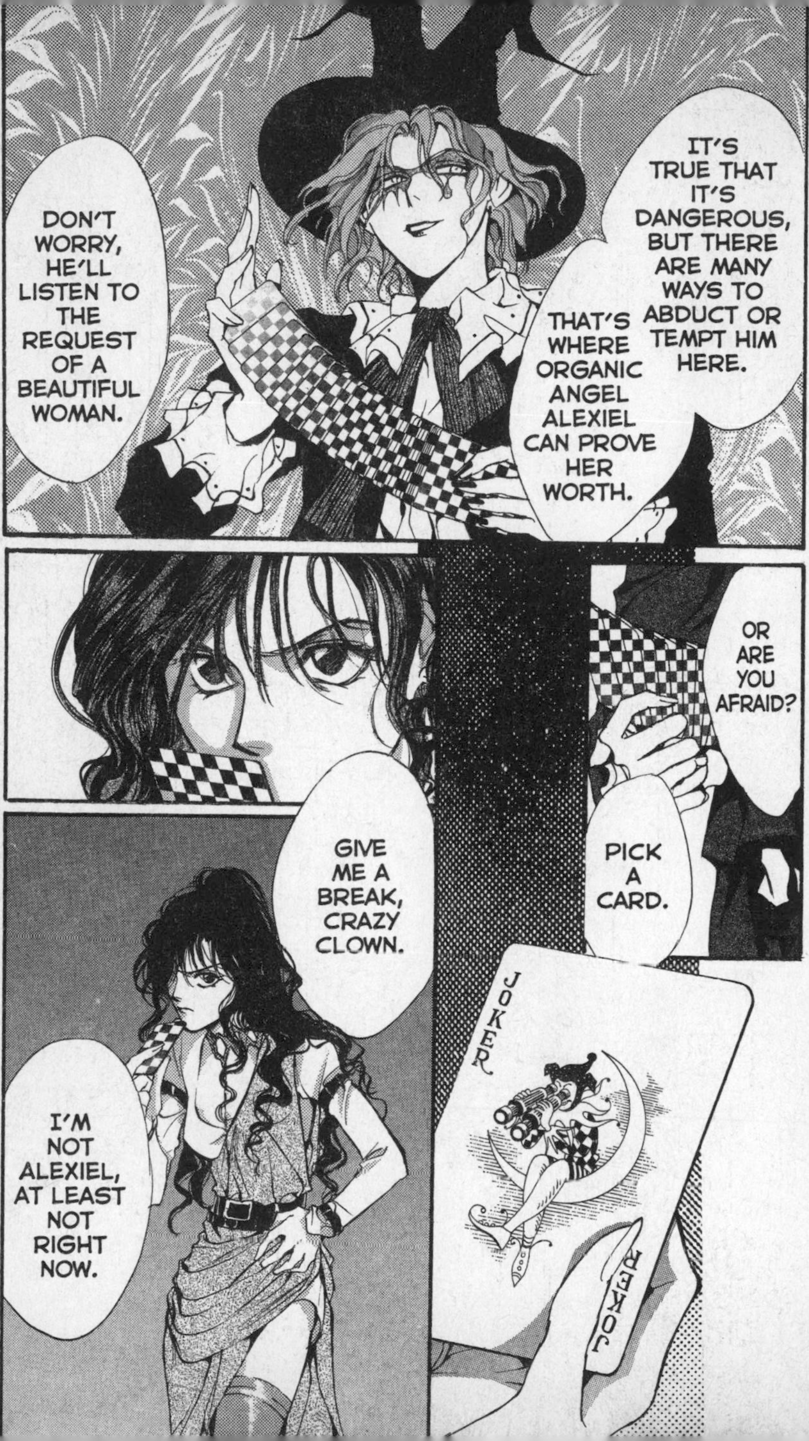
IT'S TRUE THAT IT'S DANGEROUS, BUT THERE ARE MANY WAYS TO ABDUCT OR TEMPT HIM HERE.
THAT'S WHERE ORGANIC ANGEL ALEXIEL CAN PROVE HER WORTH.
DON'T WORRY, HE'LL LISTEN TO THE REQUEST OF A BEAUTIFUL WOMAN.
OR ARE YOU AFRAID?
PICK A CARD.
JOKER
JOKER
GIVE ME A BREAK, CRAZY CLOWN.
I'M NOT ALEXIEL, AT LEAST NOT RIGHT NOW.

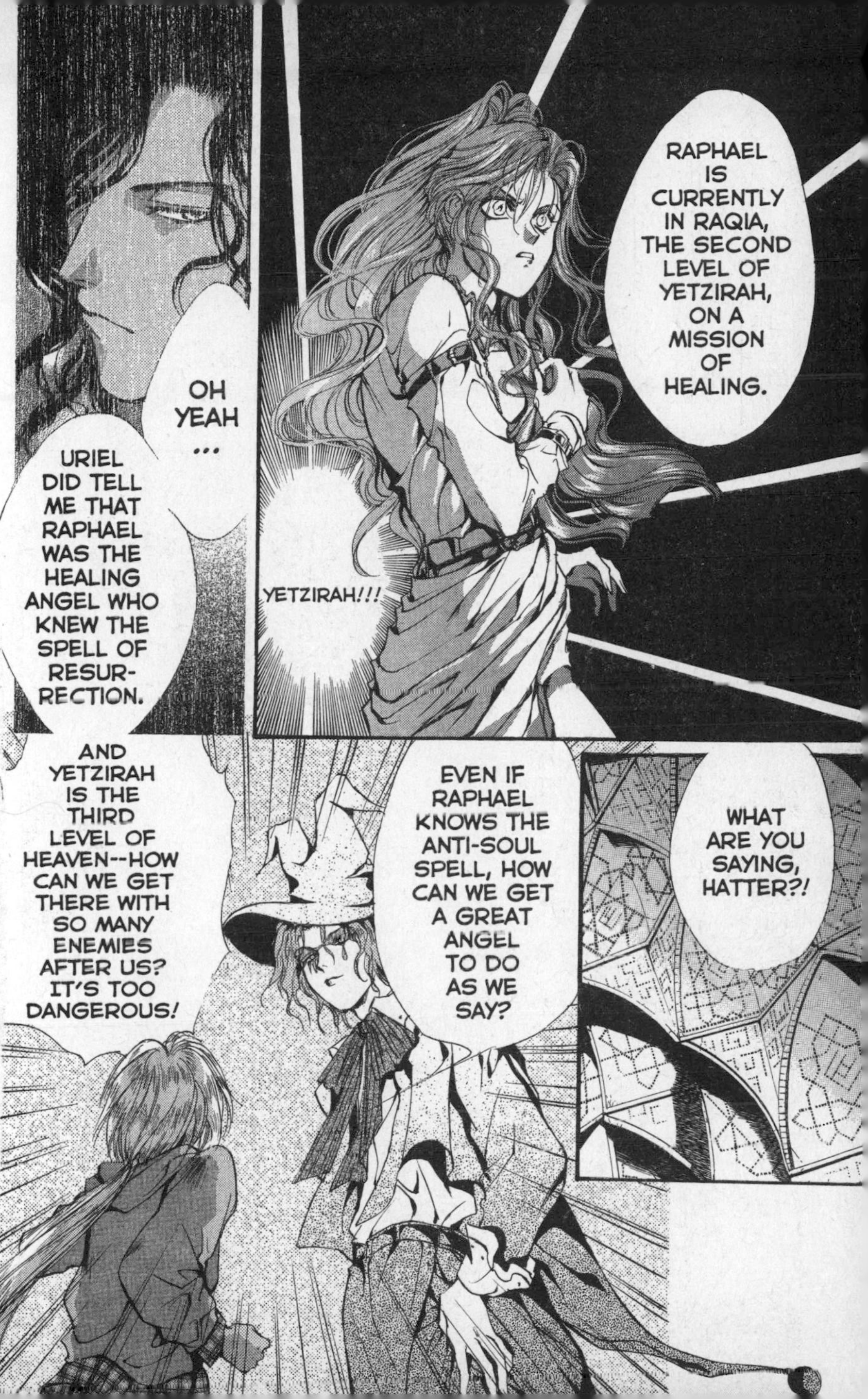
RAPHAEL IS CURRENTLY IN RAQIA, THE SECOND LEVEL OF YETZIRAH, ON A MISSION OF HEALING.
YETZIRAH!!!
OH YEAH ...
URIEL DID TELL ME THAT RAPHAEL WAS THE HEALING ANGEL WHO KNEW THE SPELL OF RESUR-RECTION.
WHAT ARE YOU SAYING, HATTER?!
EVEN IF RAPHAEL KNOWS THE ANTI-SOUL SPELL, HOW CAN WE GET A GREAT ANGEL TO DO AS WE SAY?
AND YETZIRAH IS THE THIRD LEVEL OF HEAVEN--HOW CAN WE GET THERE WITH SO MANY ENEMIES AFTER US? IT'S TOO DANGEROUS!

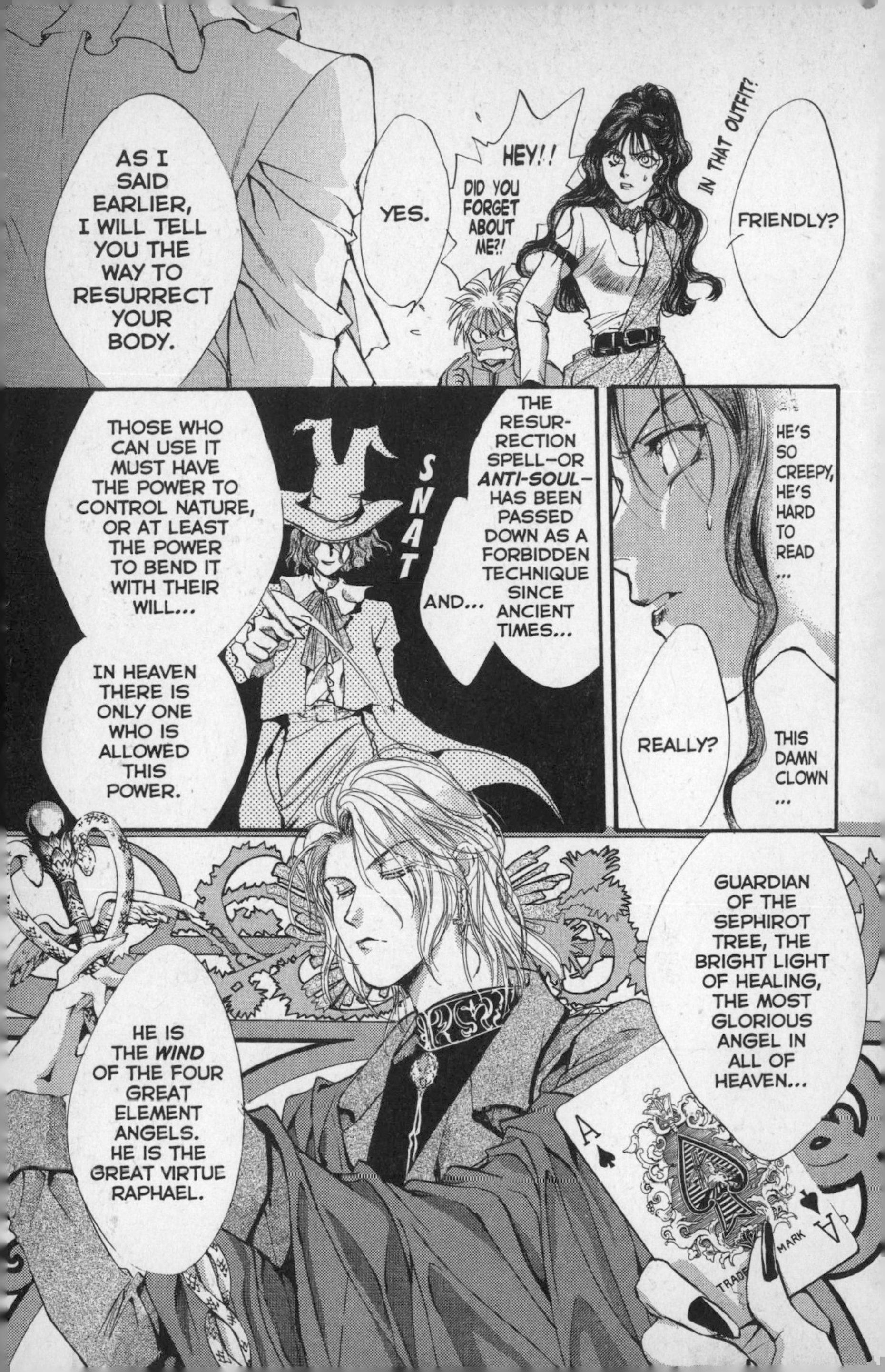
FRIENDLY?
IN THAT OUTFIT?
HEY!!
DID YOU FORGET ABOUT ME?!
YES.
AS I SAID EARLIER, I WILL TELL YOU THE WAY TO RESURRECT YOUR BODY.
HE'S SO CREEPY, HE'S HARD TO READ...
THIS DAMN CLOWN...
REALLY?
THE RESURRECTION SPELL—OR *ANTI-SOUL*—HAS BEEN PASSED DOWN AS A FORBIDDEN TECHNIQUE SINCE ANCIENT TIMES...
AND...
SNAT
THOSE WHO CAN USE IT MUST HAVE THE POWER TO CONTROL NATURE, OR AT LEAST THE POWER TO BEND IT WITH THEIR WILL...
IN HEAVEN THERE IS ONLY ONE WHO IS ALLOWED THIS POWER.
GUARDIAN OF THE SEPHIROT TREE, THE BRIGHT LIGHT OF HEALING, THE MOST GLORIOUS ANGEL IN ALL OF HEAVEN...
TRADE MARK
HE IS THE *WIND* OF THE FOUR GREAT ELEMENT ANGELS. HE IS THE GREAT VIRTUE RAPHAEL.

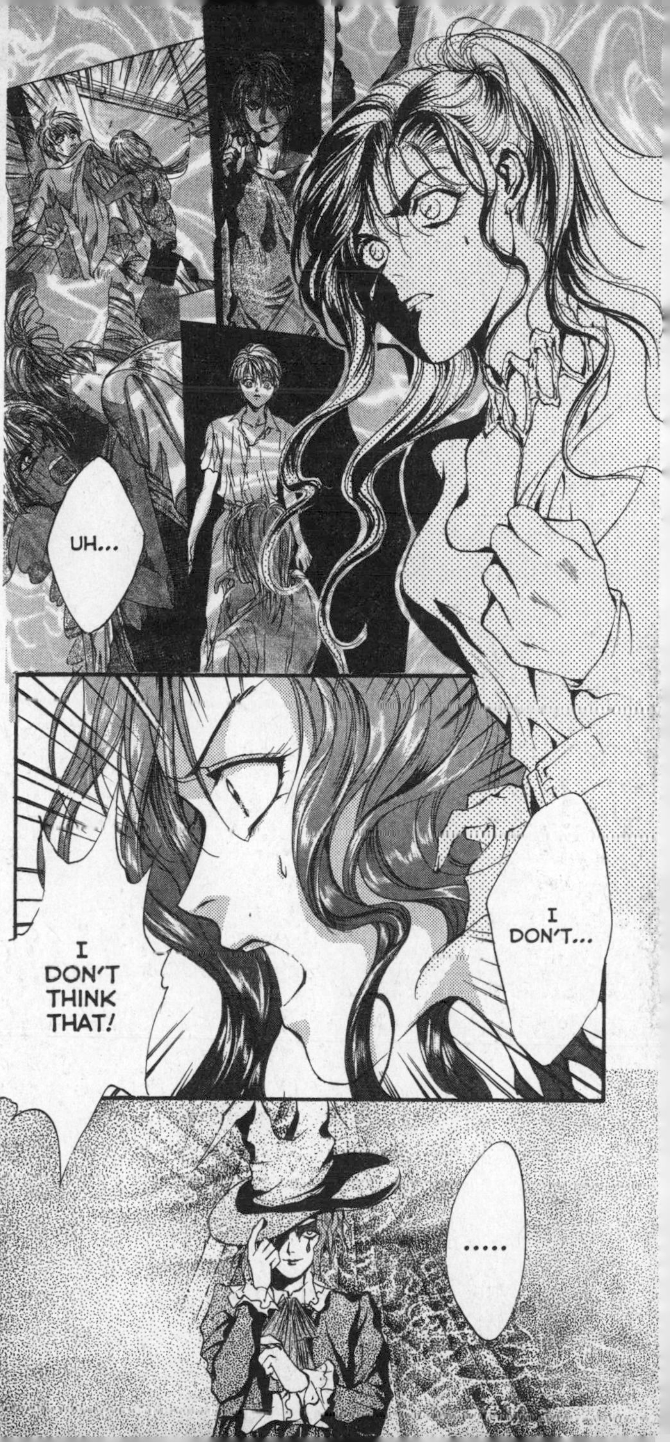
UH...
I DON'T...
I DON'T THINK THAT!
.....

Mr. Hatter, his hair, clothes, and hat are different every time, but it's the same person. When someone wrote "Who's that? He looks similar to that other guy but..." I freaked out. This person is actually popular. I had a model for him, but where did he go? He's totally different than how I first envisioned him being. But for how long do I have to keep drawing Alexiel (with Setsuna inside)? It's really a pain... It's kind of a problem if people forget what Setsuna looks like. That's why I try to draw Setsuna on the covers. But I get people saying "Hurry and change him back!" along with "Leave him like this forever"!! Forever...? I don't think so.

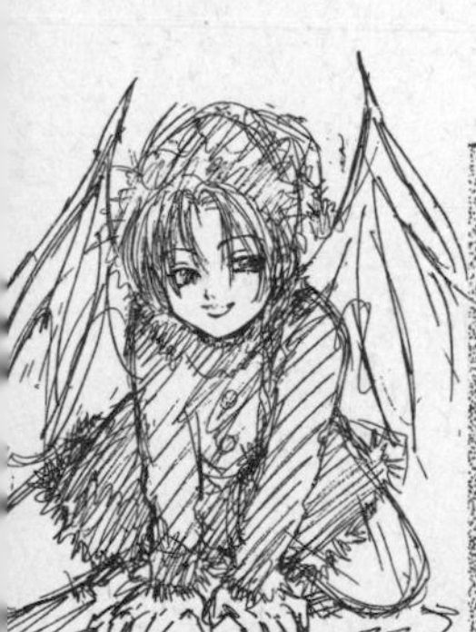

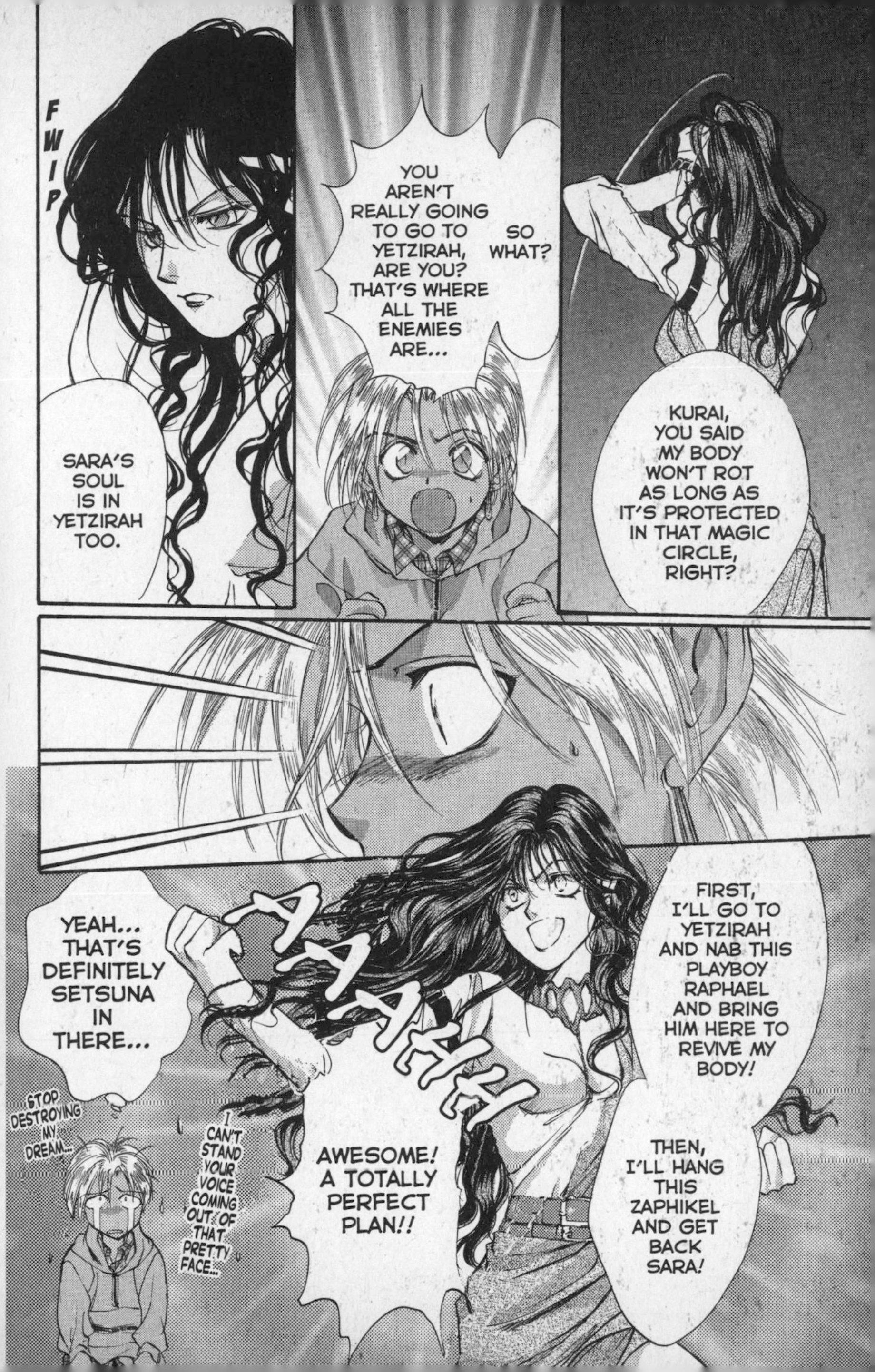
KURAI, YOU SAID MY BODY WON'T ROT AS LONG AS IT'S PROTECTED IN THAT MAGIC CIRCLE, RIGHT?
YOU AREN'T REALLY GOING TO GO TO YETZIRAH, ARE YOU? THAT'S WHERE ALL THE ENEMIES ARE...
SO WHAT?
FWIP
SARA'S SOUL IS IN YETZIRAH TOO.
FIRST, I'LL GO TO YETZIRAH AND NAB THIS PLAYBOY RAPHAEL AND BRING HIM HERE TO REVIVE MY BODY!
THEN, I'LL HANG THIS ZAPHIKEL AND GET BACK SARA!
AWESOME! A TOTALLY PERFECT PLAN!!
YEAH... THAT'S DEFINITELY SETSUNA IN THERE...
I CAN'T STAND YOUR VOICE COMING OUT OF THAT PRETTY FACE...
STOP DESTROYING MY DREAM...

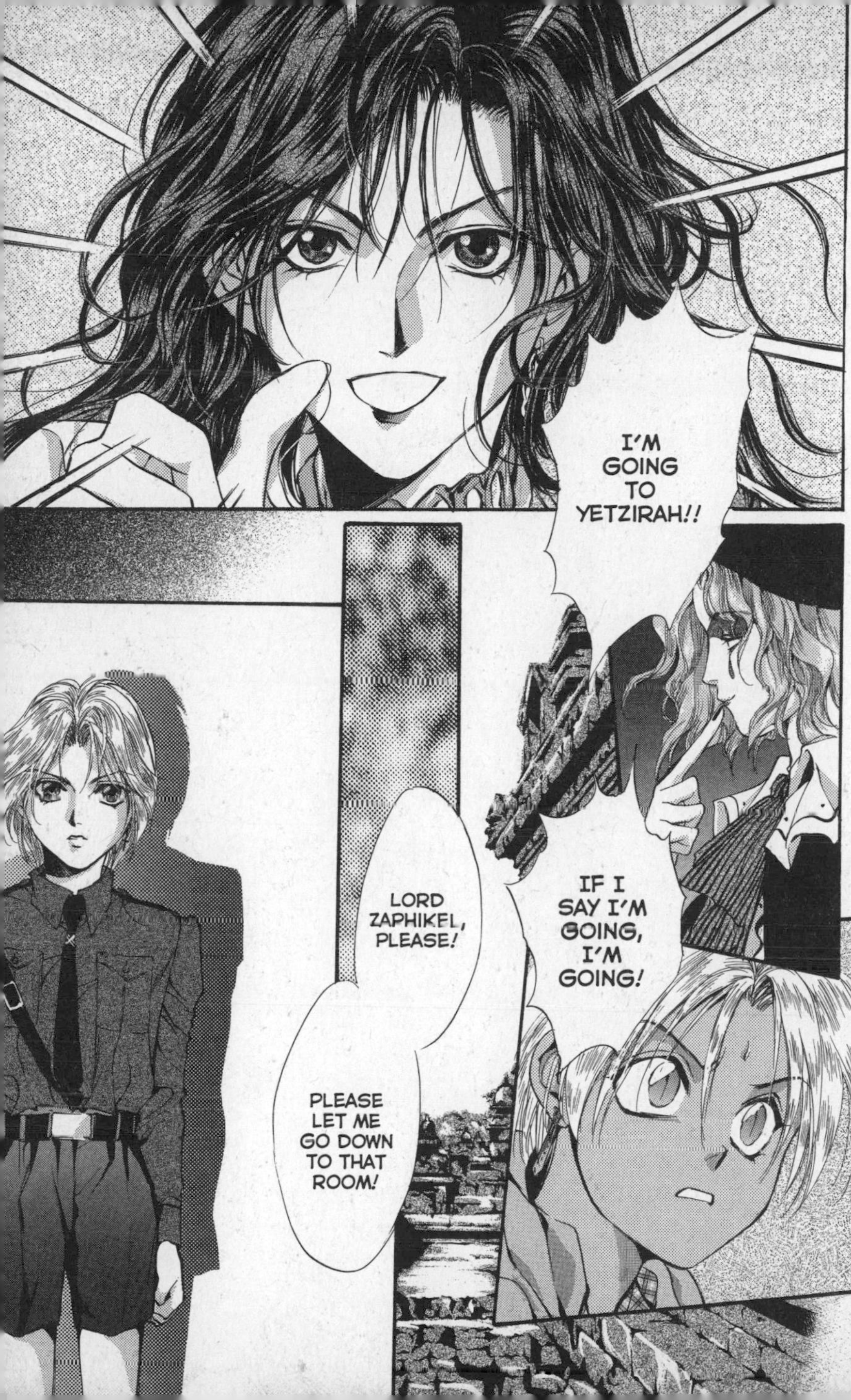
I'M GOING TO YETZIRAH!!
IF I SAY I'M GOING, I'M GOING!
LORD ZAPHIKEL, PLEASE!
PLEASE LET ME GO DOWN TO THAT ROOM!

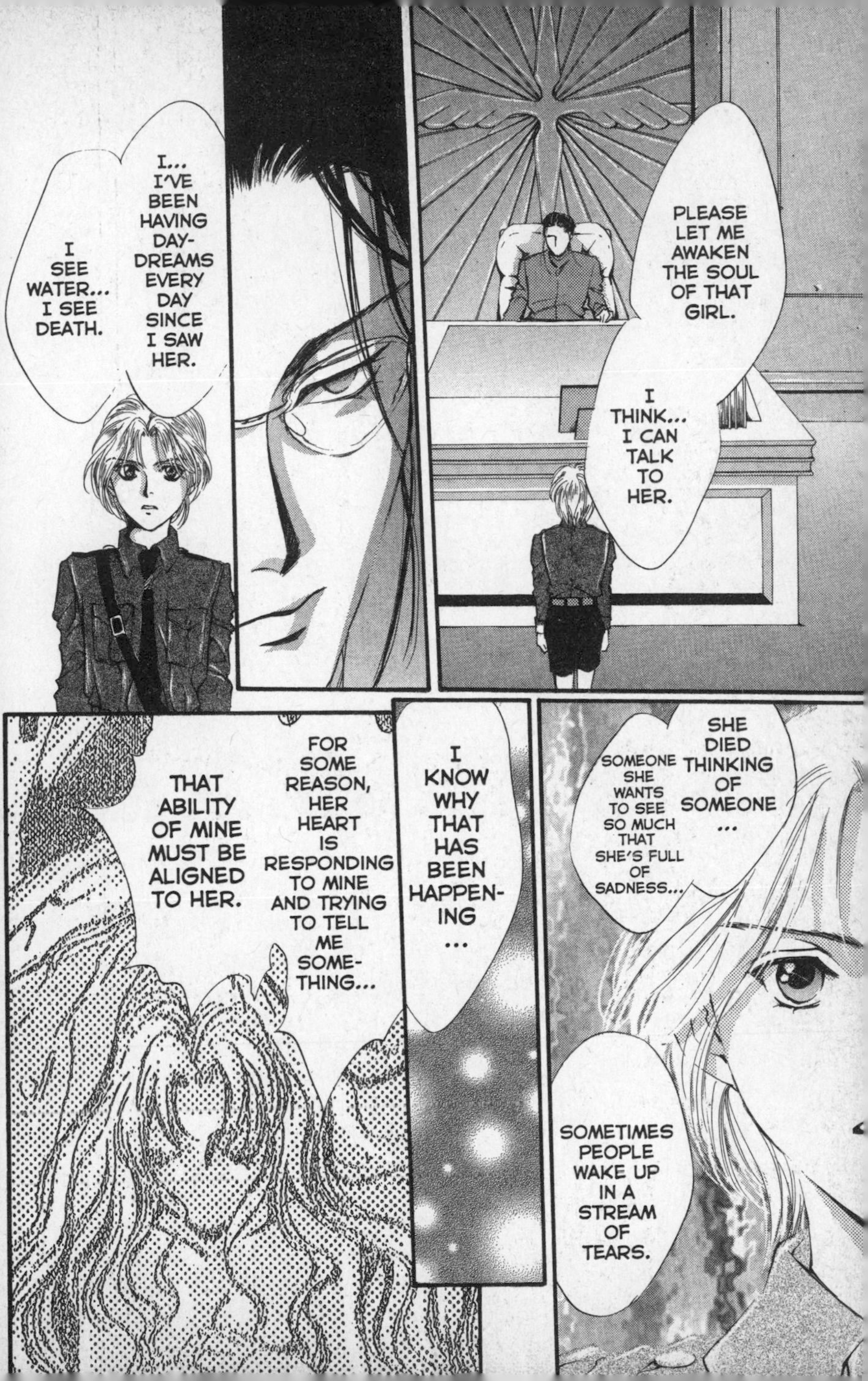
PLEASE LET ME AWAKEN THE SOUL OF THAT GIRL.
I THINK... I CAN TALK TO HER.
I... I'VE BEEN HAVING DAY-DREAMS EVERY DAY SINCE I SAW HER.
I SEE WATER... I SEE DEATH.
SHE DIED THINKING OF SOMEONE...
SOMEONE SHE WANTS TO SEE SO MUCH THAT SHE'S FULL OF SADNESS...
SOMETIMES PEOPLE WAKE UP IN A STREAM OF TEARS.
I KNOW WHY THAT HAS BEEN HAPPEN-ING...
FOR SOME REASON, HER HEART IS RESPONDING TO MINE AND TRYING TO TELL ME SOME-THING...
THAT ABILITY OF MINE MUST BE ALIGNED TO HER.

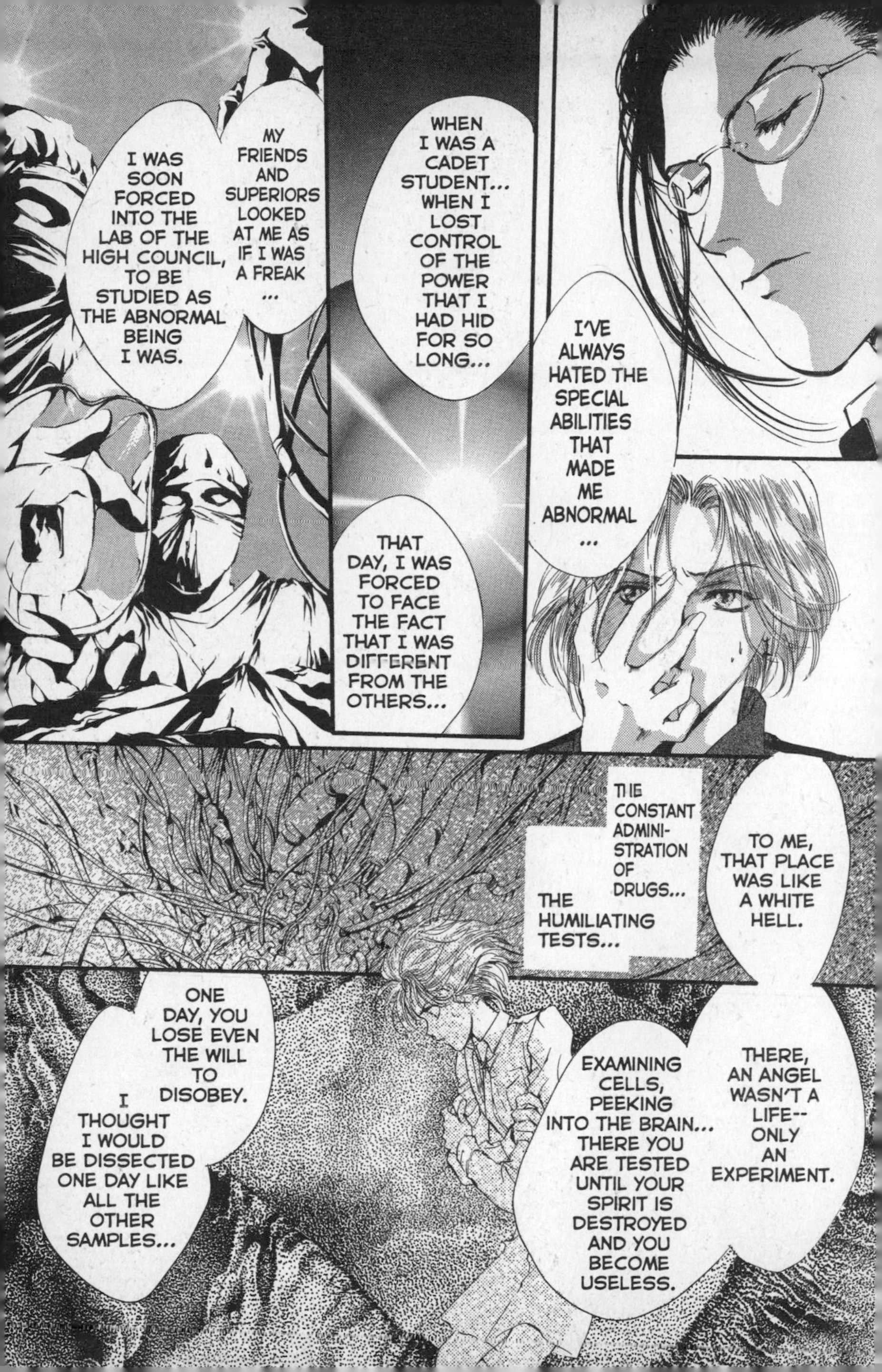
I'VE ALWAYS HATED THE SPECIAL ABILITIES THAT MADE ME ABNORMAL...
WHEN I WAS A CADET STUDENT... WHEN I LOST CONTROL OF THE POWER THAT I HAD HID FOR SO LONG...
THAT DAY, I WAS FORCED TO FACE THE FACT THAT I WAS DIFFERENT FROM THE OTHERS...
MY FRIENDS AND SUPERIORS LOOKED AT ME AS IF I WAS A FREAK...
I WAS SOON FORCED INTO THE LAB OF THE HIGH COUNCIL, TO BE STUDIED AS THE ABNORMAL BEING I WAS.
TO ME, THAT PLACE WAS LIKE A WHITE HELL.
THE CONSTANT ADMINISTRATION OF DRUGS... THE HUMILIATING TESTS...
THERE, AN ANGEL WASN'T A LIFE-- ONLY AN EXPERIMENT.
EXAMINING CELLS, PEEKING INTO THE BRAIN... THERE YOU ARE TESTED UNTIL YOUR SPIRIT IS DESTROYED AND YOU BECOME USELESS.
ONE DAY, YOU LOSE EVEN THE WILL TO DISOBEY.
I THOUGHT I WOULD BE DISSECTED ONE DAY LIKE ALL THE OTHER SAMPLES...

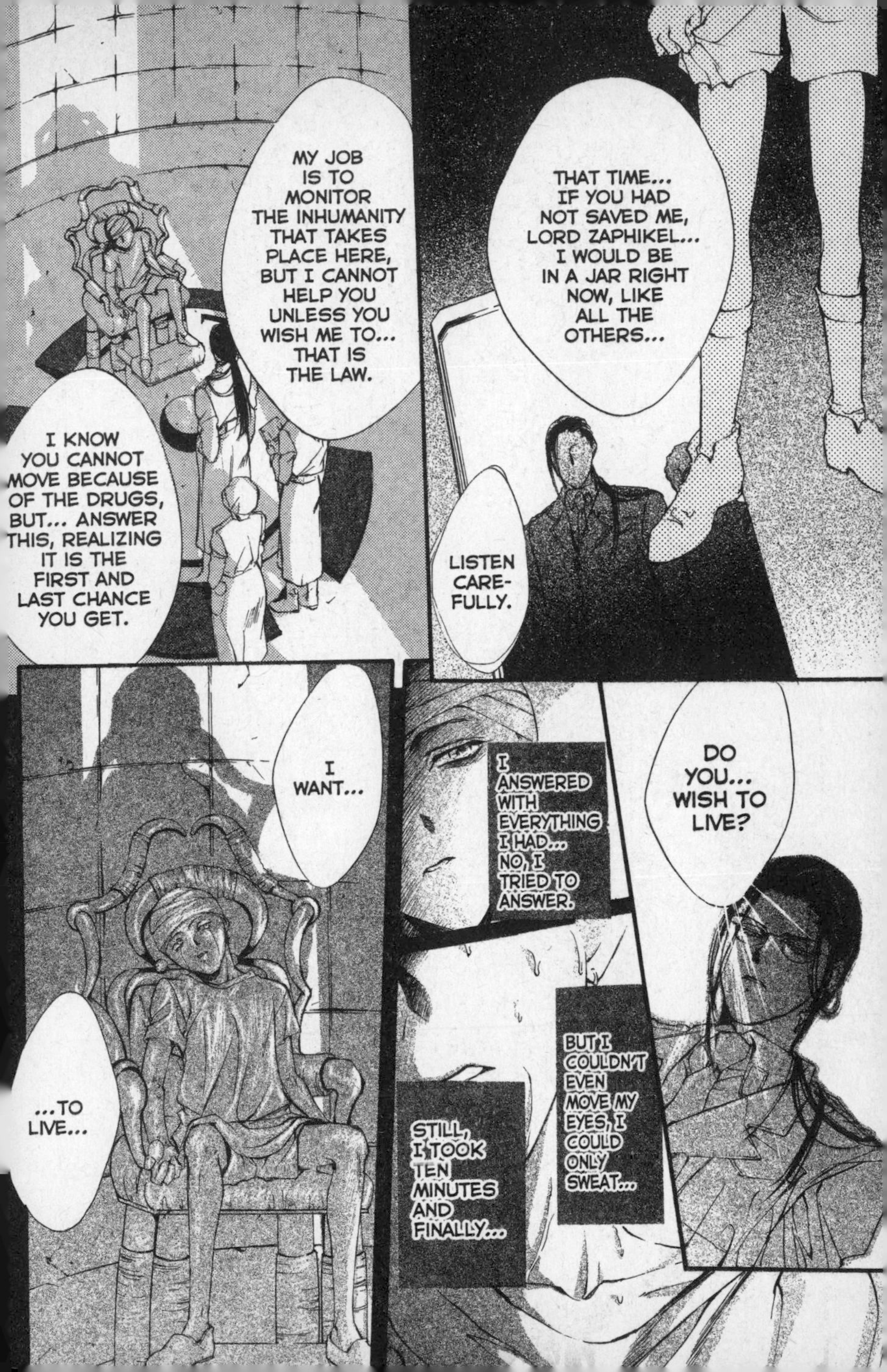
THAT TIME... IF YOU HAD NOT SAVED ME, LORD ZAPHIKEL... I WOULD BE IN A JAR RIGHT NOW, LIKE ALL THE OTHERS...
LISTEN CAREFULLY.
MY JOB IS TO MONITOR THE INHUMANITY THAT TAKES PLACE HERE, BUT I CANNOT HELP YOU UNLESS YOU WISH ME TO... THAT IS THE LAW.
I KNOW YOU CANNOT MOVE BECAUSE OF THE DRUGS, BUT... ANSWER THIS, REALIZING IT IS THE FIRST AND LAST CHANCE YOU GET.
DO YOU... WISH TO LIVE?
I ANSWERED WITH EVERYTHING I HAD... NO, I TRIED TO ANSWER.
BUT I COULDN'T EVEN MOVE MY EYES, I COULD ONLY SWEAT...
STILL, I TOOK TEN MINUTES AND FINALLY...
I WANT...
...TO LIVE...

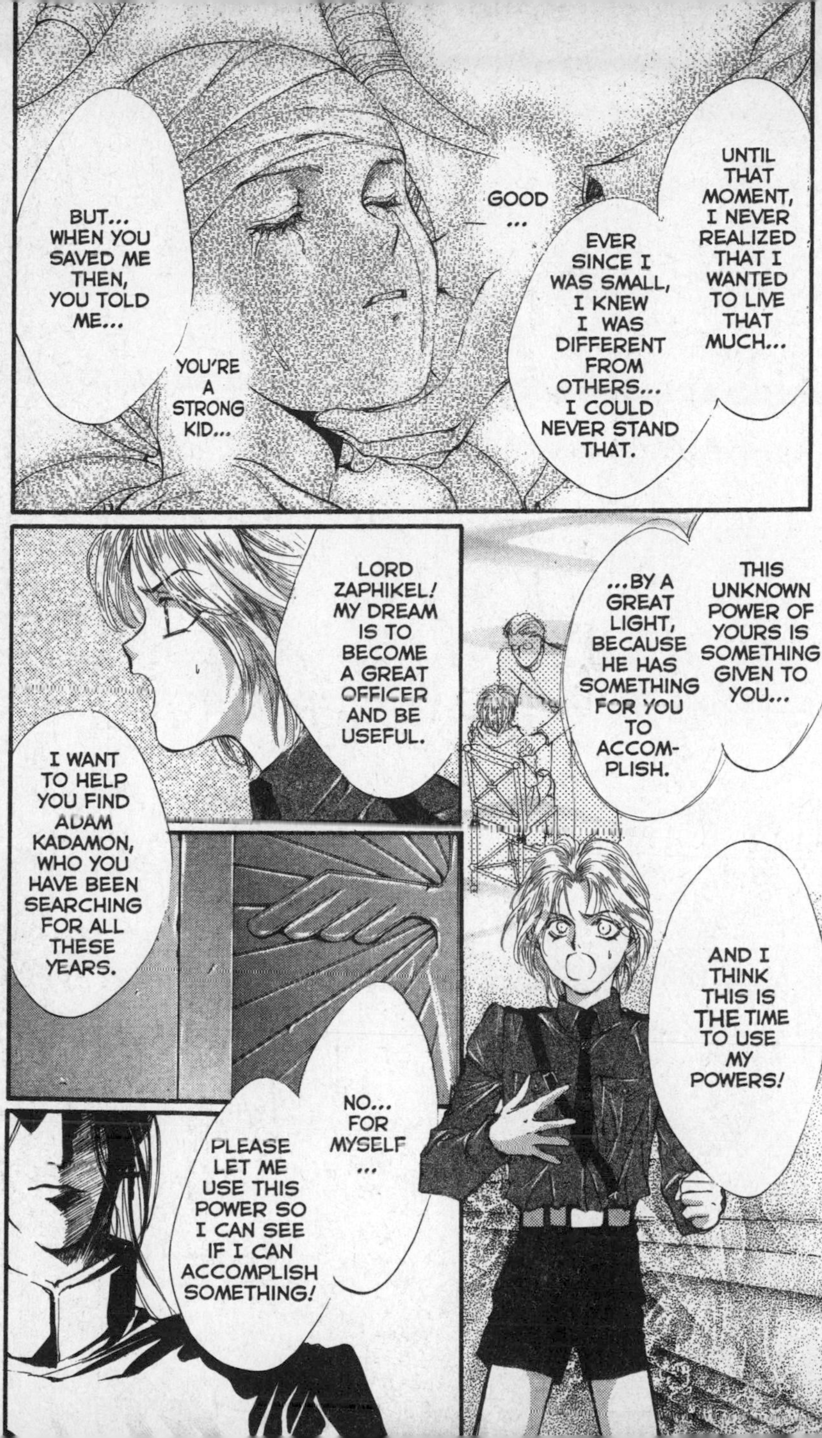
UNTIL THAT MOMENT, I NEVER REALIZED THAT I WANTED TO LIVE THAT MUCH...
EVER SINCE I WAS SMALL, I KNEW I WAS DIFFERENT FROM OTHERS... I COULD NEVER STAND THAT.
GOOD ...
BUT... WHEN YOU SAVED ME THEN, YOU TOLD ME...
YOU'RE A STRONG KID...
THIS UNKNOWN POWER OF YOURS IS SOMETHING GIVEN TO YOU...
...BY A GREAT LIGHT, BECAUSE HE HAS SOMETHING FOR YOU TO ACCOM-PLISH.
AND I THINK THIS IS THE TIME TO USE MY POWERS!
LORD ZAPHIKEL! MY DREAM IS TO BECOME A GREAT OFFICER AND BE USEFUL.
I WANT TO HELP YOU FIND ADAM KADAMON, WHO YOU HAVE BEEN SEARCHING FOR ALL THESE YEARS.
NO... FOR MYSELF ...
PLEASE LET ME USE THIS POWER SO I CAN SEE IF I CAN ACCOMPLISH SOMETHING!

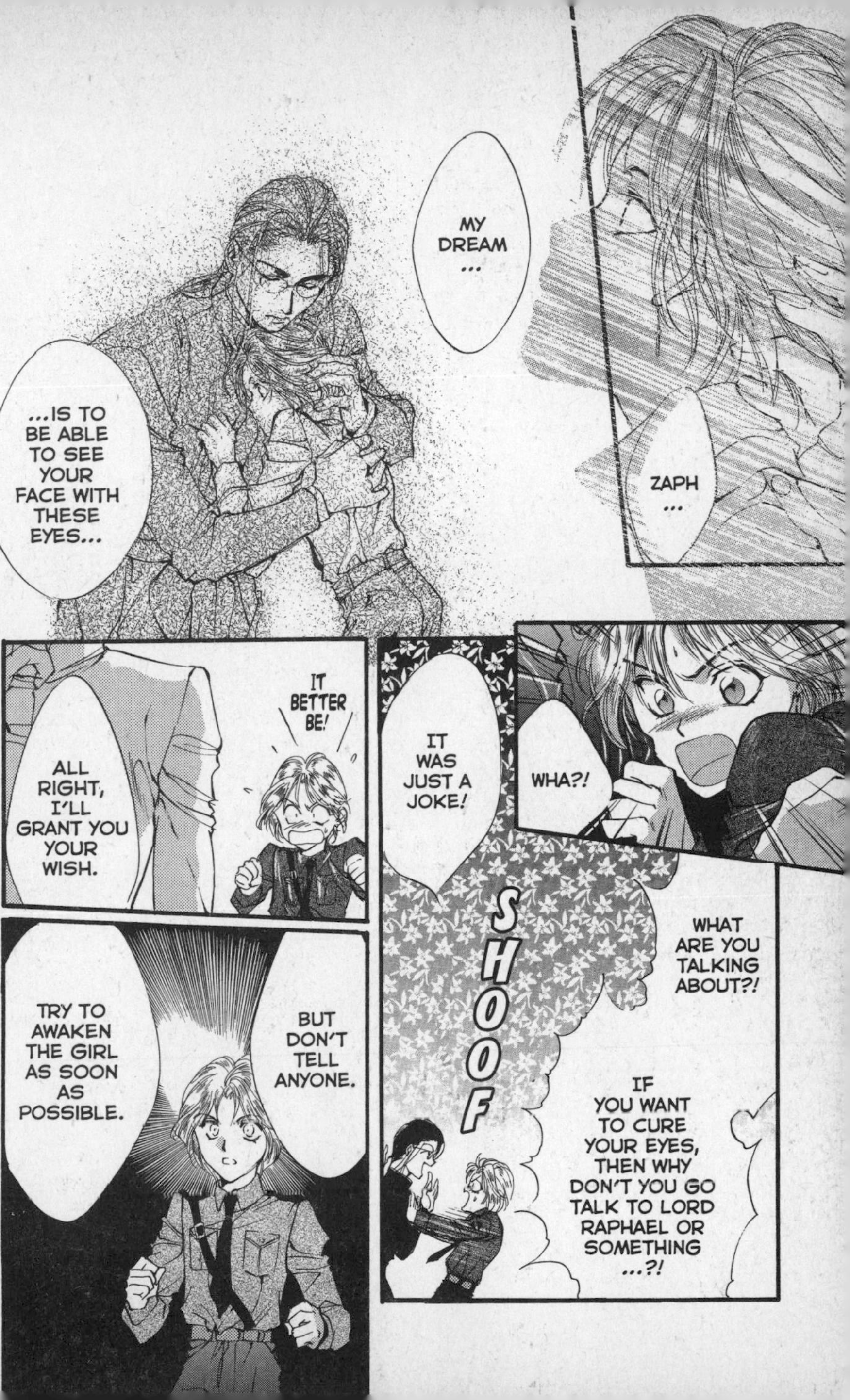
ZAPH ...
MY DREAM ...
...IS TO BE ABLE TO SEE YOUR FACE WITH THESE EYES...
WHA?!
WHAT ARE YOU TALKING ABOUT?!
IF YOU WANT TO CURE YOUR EYES, THEN WHY DON'T YOU GO TALK TO LORD RAPHAEL OR SOMETHING ...?!
SHOOF
IT WAS JUST A JOKE!
ALL RIGHT, I'LL GRANT YOU YOUR WISH.
IT BETTER BE!
TRY TO AWAKEN THE GIRL AS SOON AS POSSIBLE.
BUT DON'T TELL ANYONE.

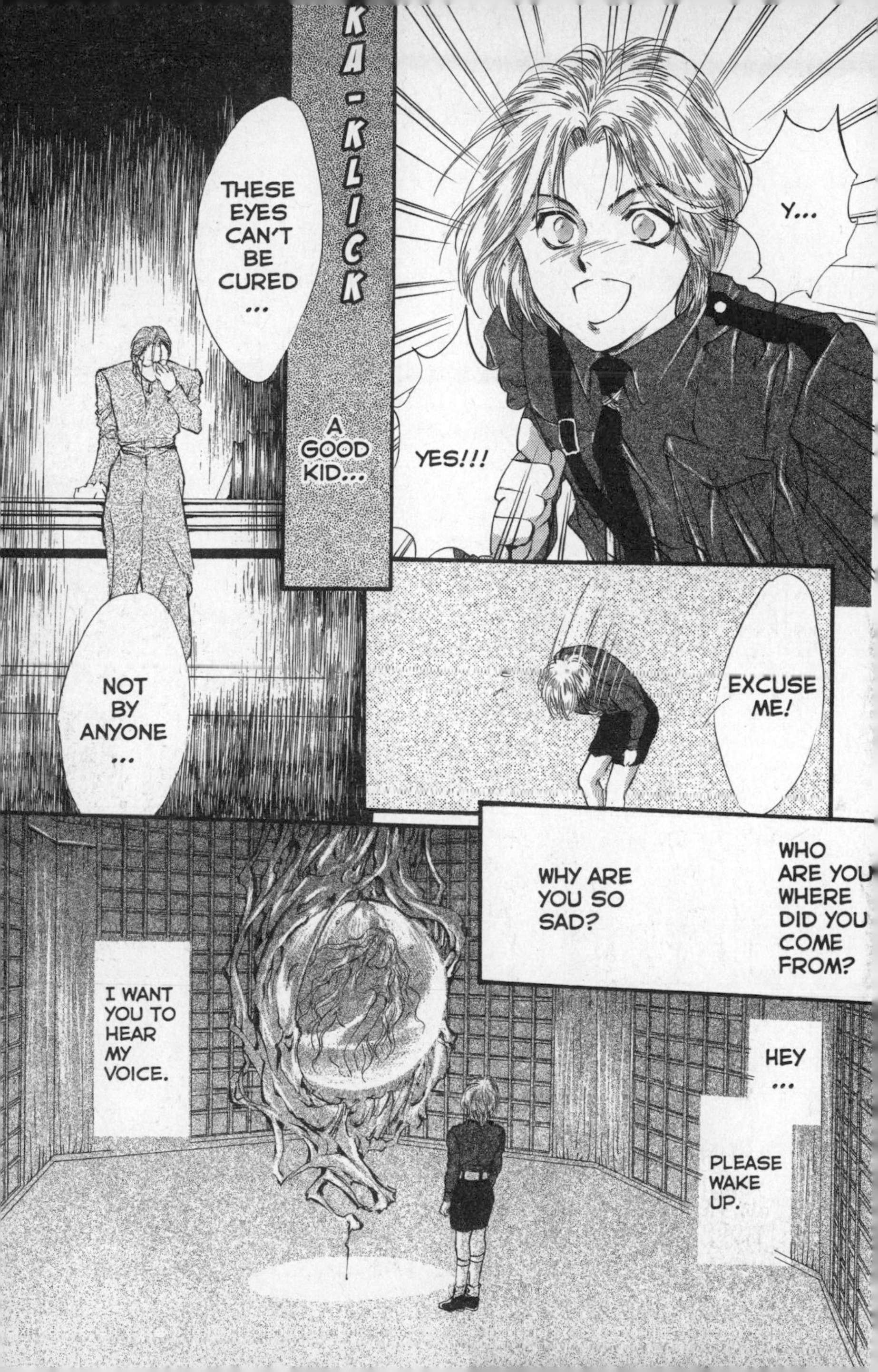
Y...
YES!!!
KA-KLICK
A GOOD KID...
EXCUSE ME!
THESE EYES CAN'T BE CURED...
NOT BY ANYONE...
WHO ARE YOU WHERE DID YOU COME FROM?
WHY ARE YOU SO SAD?
HEY...
PLEASE WAKE UP.
I WANT YOU TO HEAR MY VOICE.

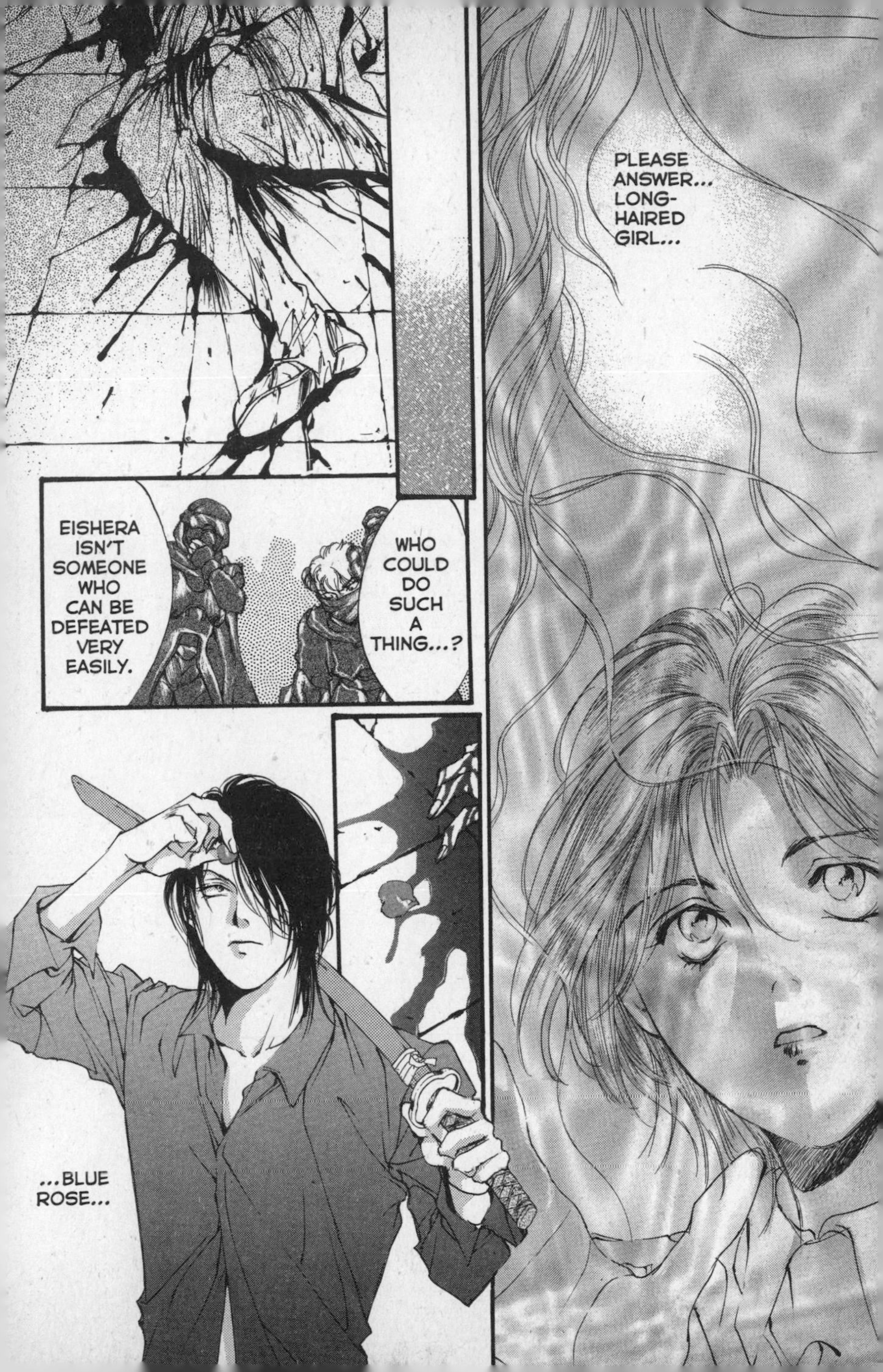
PLEASE ANSWER... LONG-HAIRED GIRL...
WHO COULD DO SUCH A THING...?
EISHERA ISN'T SOMEONE WHO CAN BE DEFEATED VERY EASILY.
...BLUE ROSE...

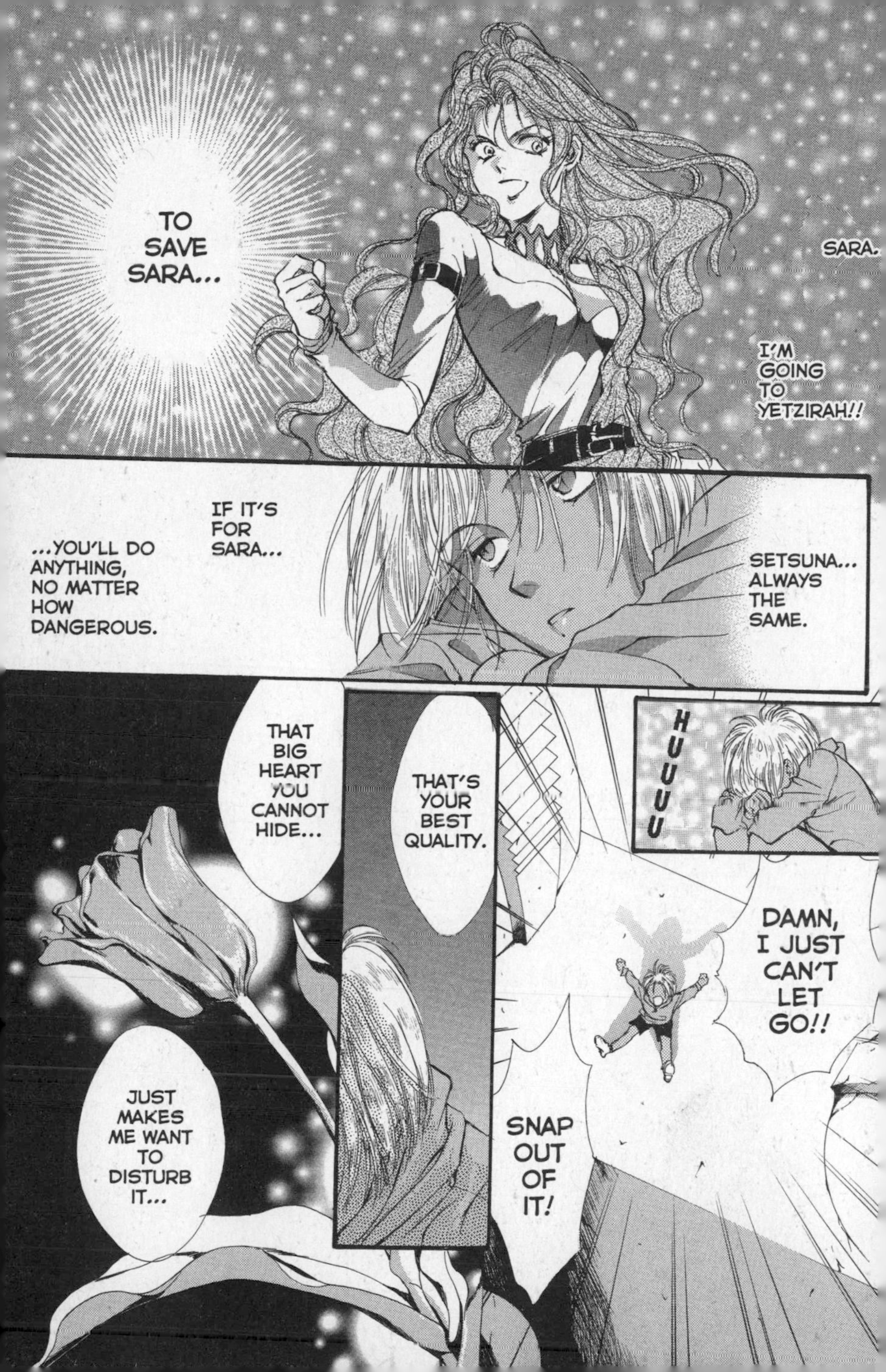
SARA.
I'M GOING TO YETZIRAH!!
TO SAVE SARA...
SETSUNA... ALWAYS THE SAME.
IF IT'S FOR SARA...
...YOU'LL DO ANYTHING, NO MATTER HOW DANGEROUS.
HUUUU
DAMN, I JUST CAN'T LET GO!!
SNAP OUT OF IT!
THAT'S YOUR BEST QUALITY.
THAT BIG HEART YOU CANNOT HIDE...
JUST MAKES ME WANT TO DISTURB IT...

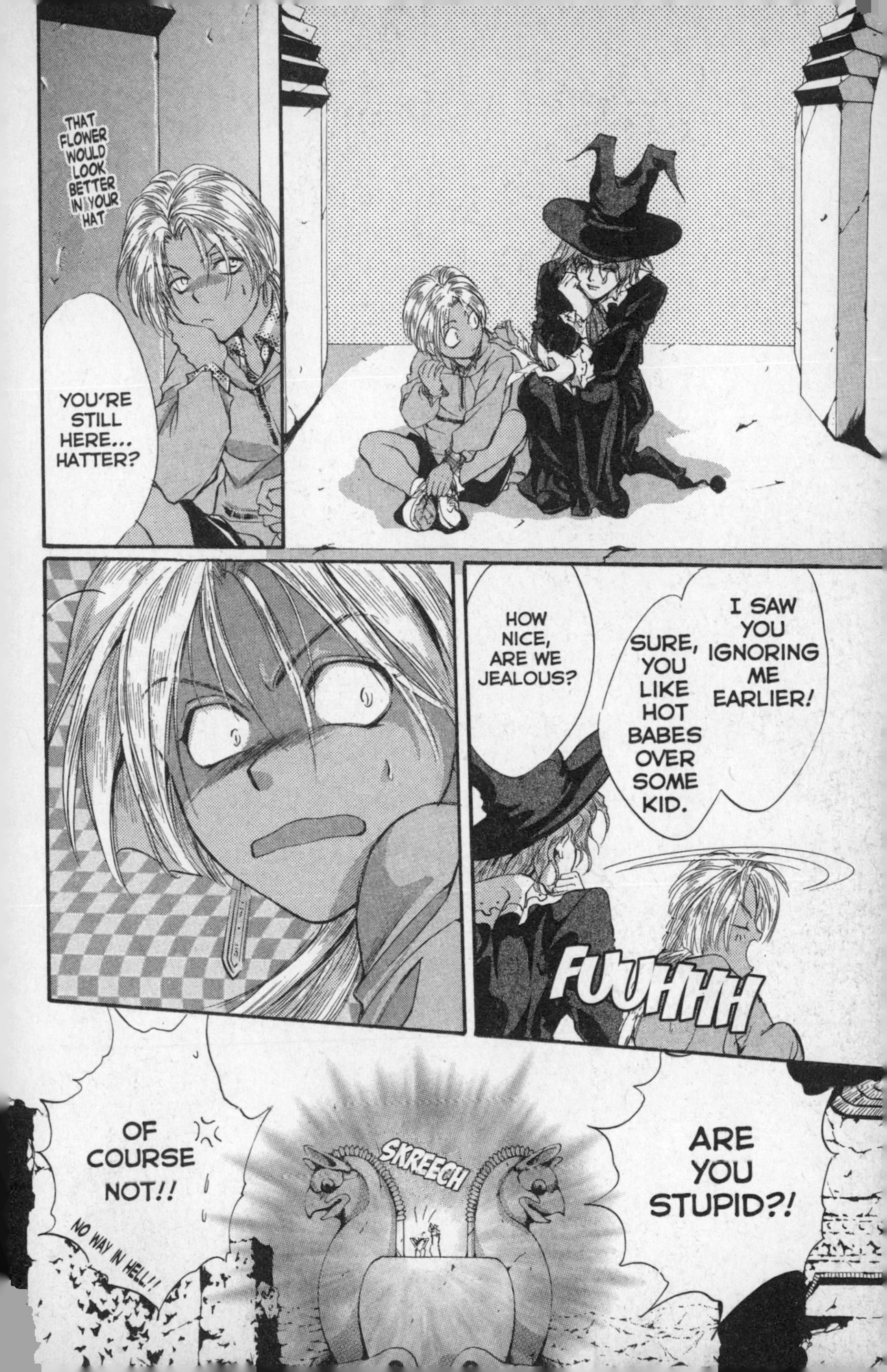
THAT FLOWER WOULD LOOK BETTER IN YOUR HAT
YOU'RE STILL HERE... HATTER?
I SAW YOU IGNORING ME EARLIER!
SURE, YOU LIKE HOT BABES OVER SOME KID.
HOW NICE, ARE WE JEALOUS?
FUUHHHH
ARE YOU STUPID?!
SKREECH
OF COURSE NOT!!
NO WAY IN HELL!!

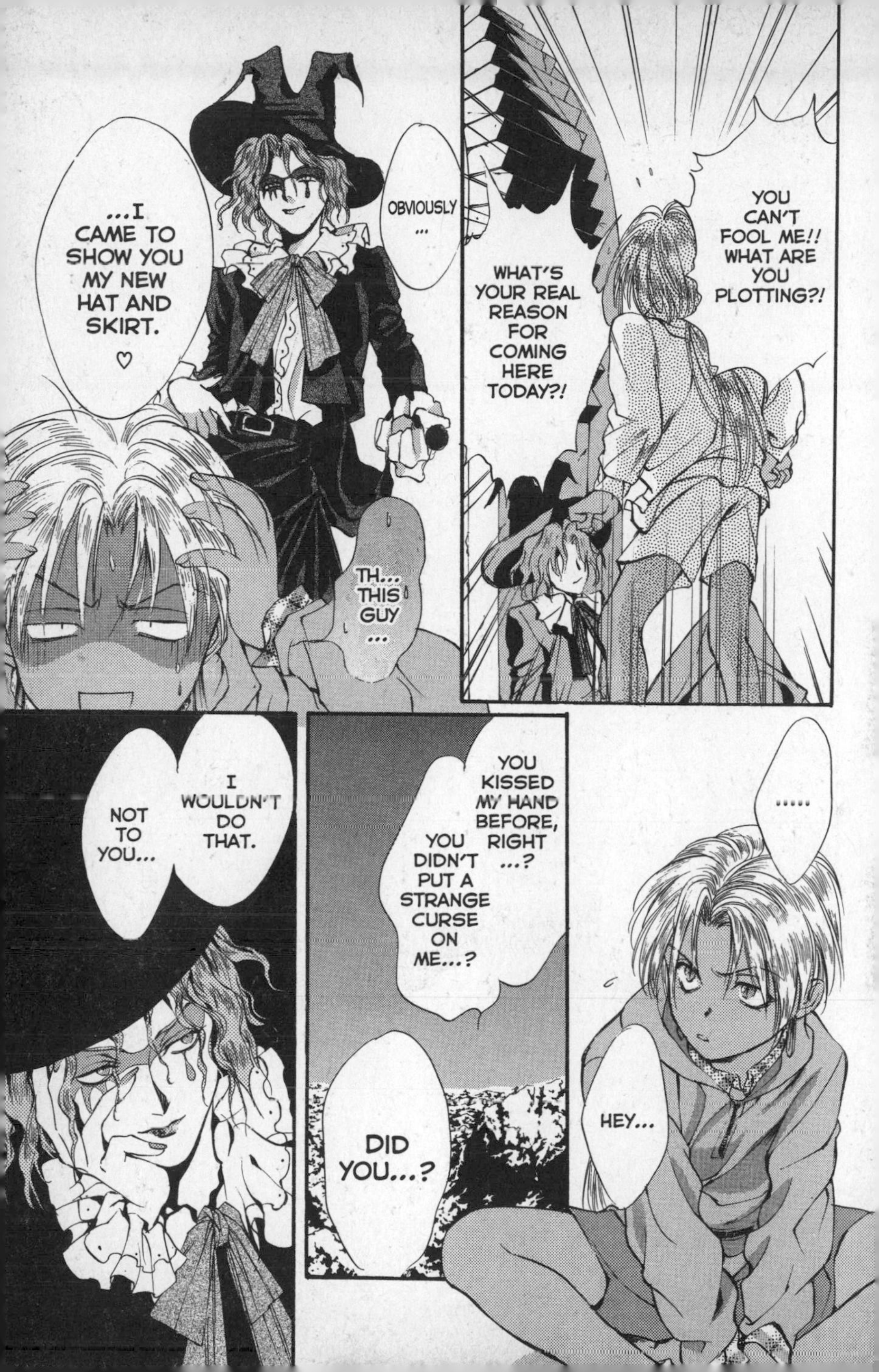
YOU CAN'T FOOL ME!! WHAT ARE YOU PLOTTING?!
WHAT'S YOUR REAL REASON FOR COMING HERE TODAY?!
OBVIOUSLY ...
...I CAME TO SHOW YOU MY NEW HAT AND SKIRT. ♡
TH... THIS GUY ...
.....
HEY...
YOU KISSED MY HAND BEFORE, RIGHT ...?
YOU DIDN'T PUT A STRANGE CURSE ON ME...?
DID YOU...?
I WOULDN'T DO THAT.
NOT TO YOU...

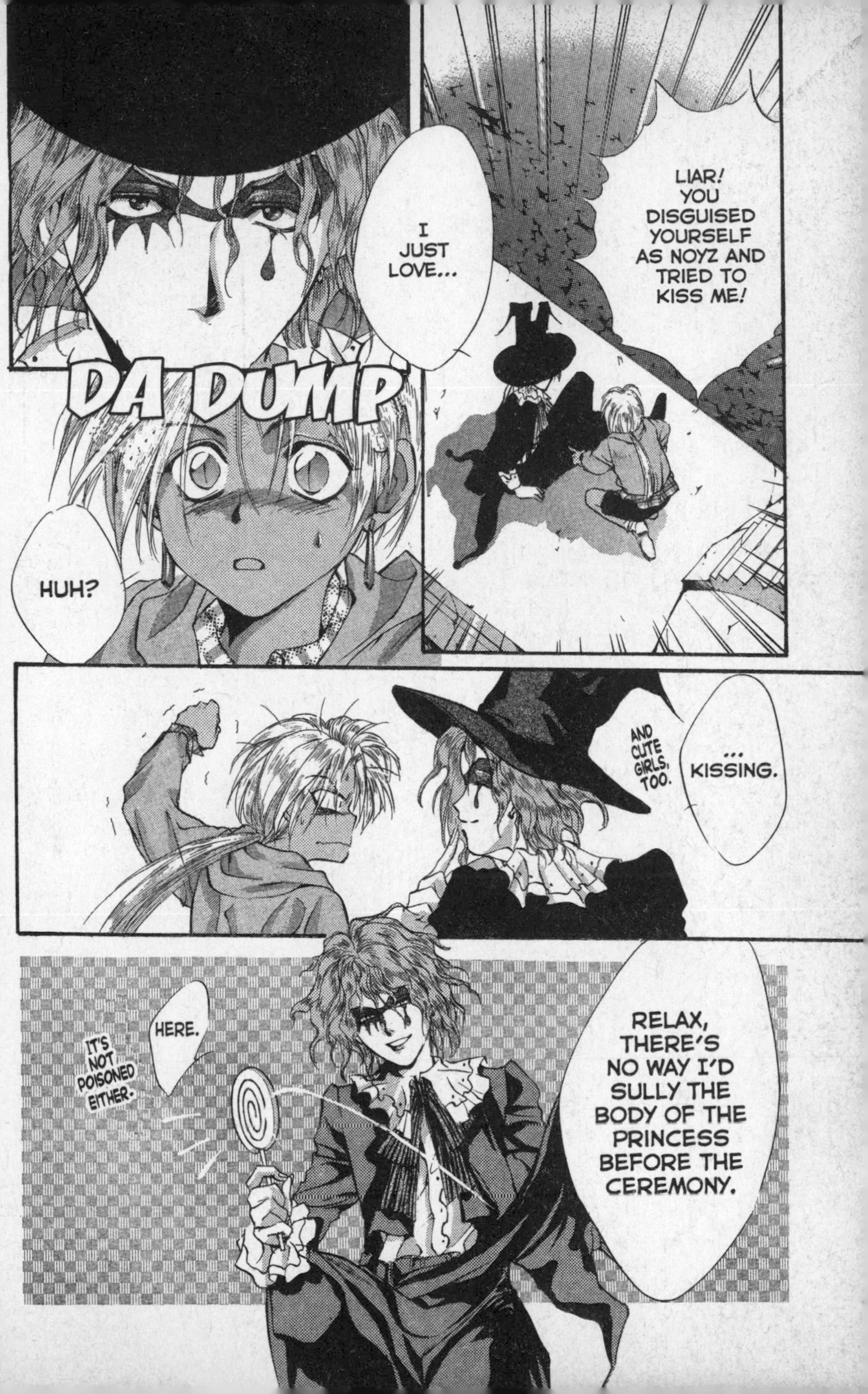
LIAR! YOU DISGUISED YOURSELF AS NOYZ AND TRIED TO KISS ME!
I JUST LOVE...
DA DUMP
HUH?
...KISSING.
AND CUTE GIRLS, TOO.
RELAX, THERE'S NO WAY I'D SULLY THE BODY OF THE PRINCESS BEFORE THE CEREMONY.
HERE.
IT'S NOT POISONED EITHER.

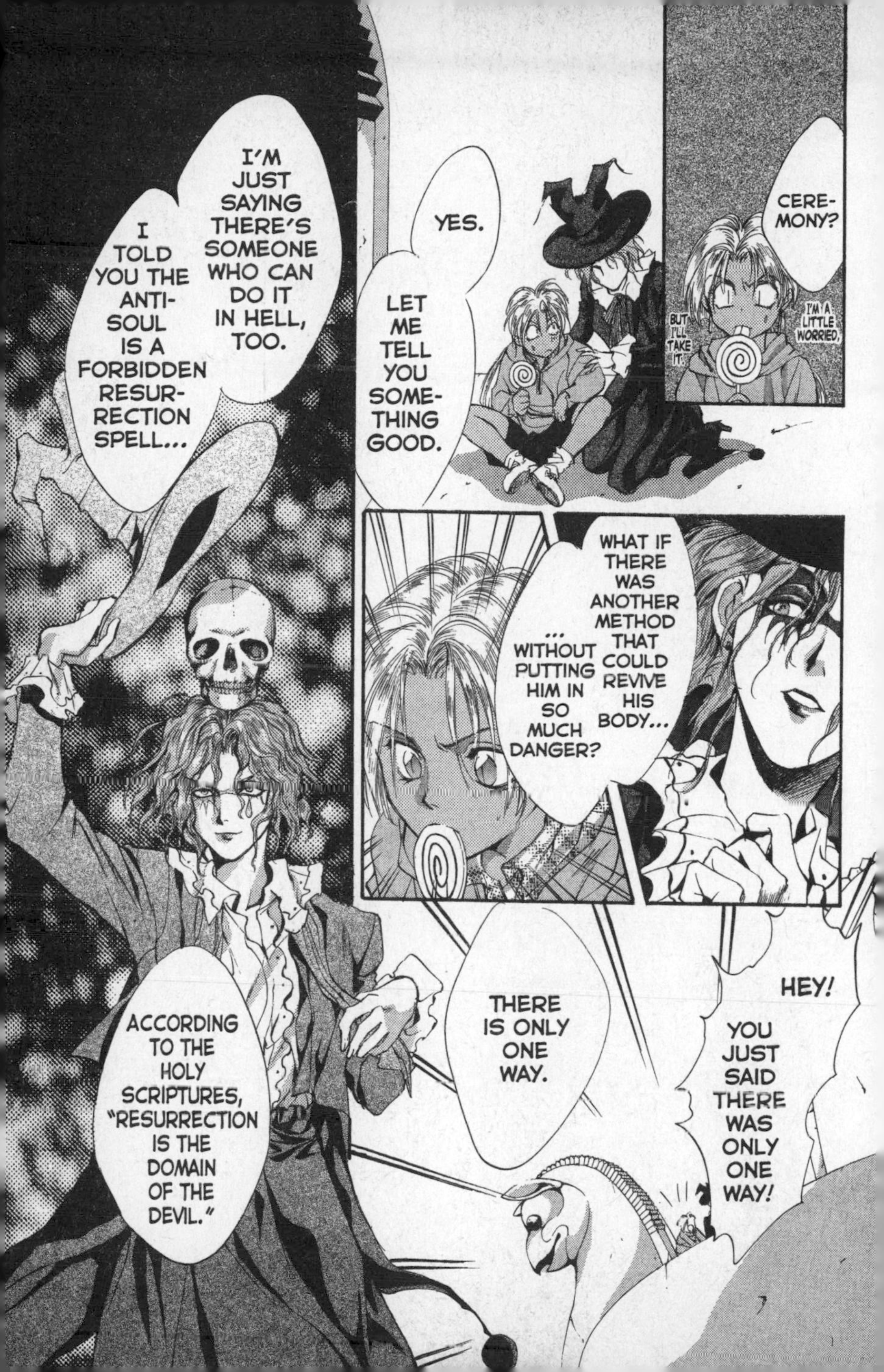
CERE-MONY?
I'M A LITTLE WORRIED,
BUT I'LL TAKE IT.
YES.
LET ME TELL YOU SOME-THING GOOD.
WHAT IF THERE WAS ANOTHER METHOD THAT COULD REVIVE HIS BODY...
...WITHOUT PUTTING HIM IN SO MUCH DANGER?
HEY!
YOU JUST SAID THERE WAS ONLY ONE WAY!
THERE IS ONLY ONE WAY.
I'M JUST SAYING THERE'S SOMEONE WHO CAN DO IT IN HELL, TOO.
I TOLD YOU THE ANTI-SOUL IS A FORBIDDEN RESUR-RECTION SPELL...
ACCORDING TO THE HOLY SCRIPTURES, "RESURRECTION IS THE DOMAIN OF THE DEVIL."

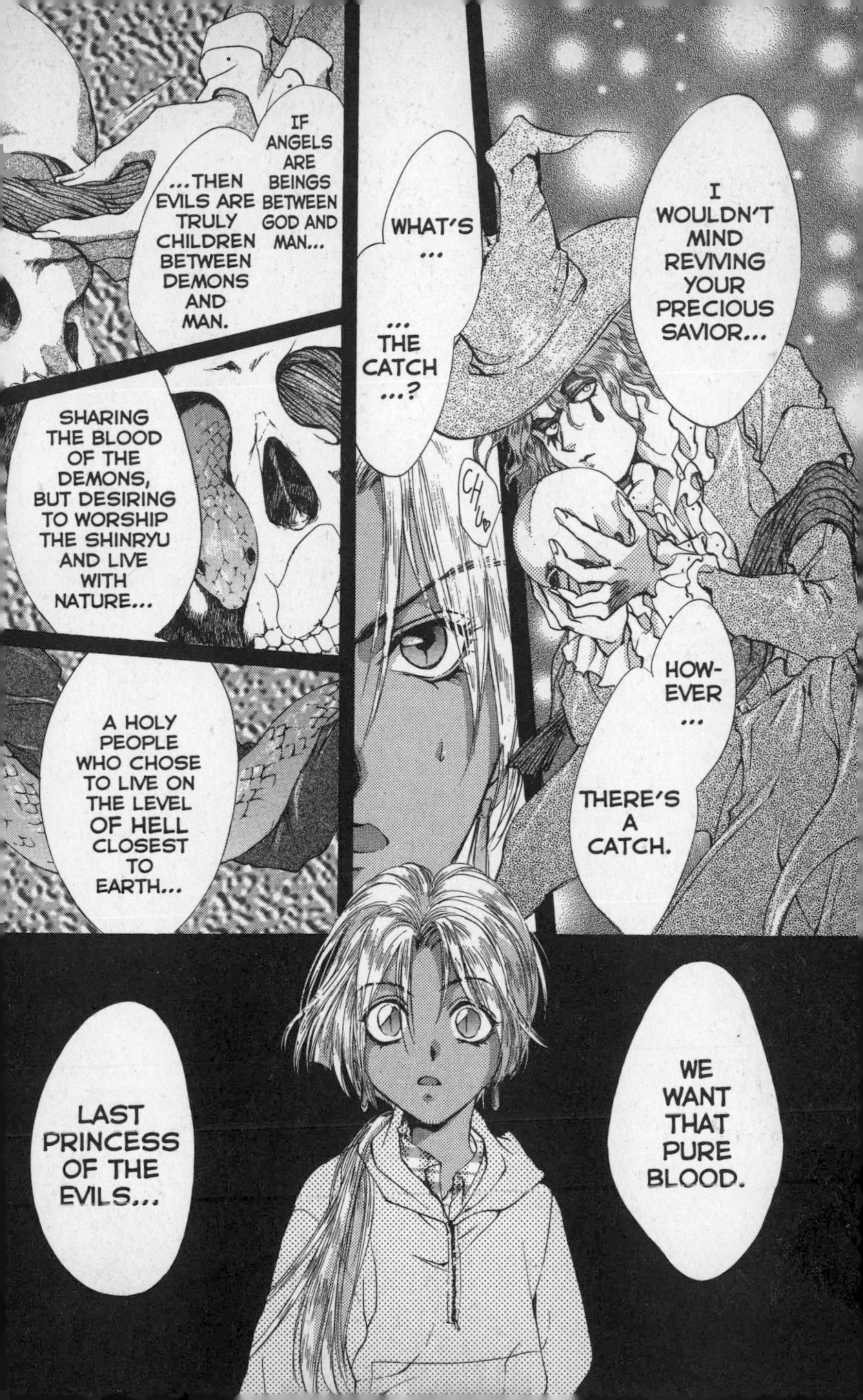
I WOULDN'T MIND REVIVING YOUR PRECIOUS SAVIOR...
CHU
HOW-EVER...
THERE'S A CATCH.
WHAT'S...
...THE CATCH...?
IF ANGELS ARE BEINGS BETWEEN GOD AND MAN...
...THEN EVILS ARE TRULY CHILDREN BETWEEN DEMONS AND MAN.
SHARING THE BLOOD OF THE DEMONS, BUT DESIRING TO WORSHIP THE SHINRYU AND LIVE WITH NATURE...
A HOLY PEOPLE WHO CHOSE TO LIVE ON THE LEVEL OF HELL CLOSEST TO EARTH...
WE WANT THAT PURE BLOOD.
LAST PRINCESS OF THE EVILS...

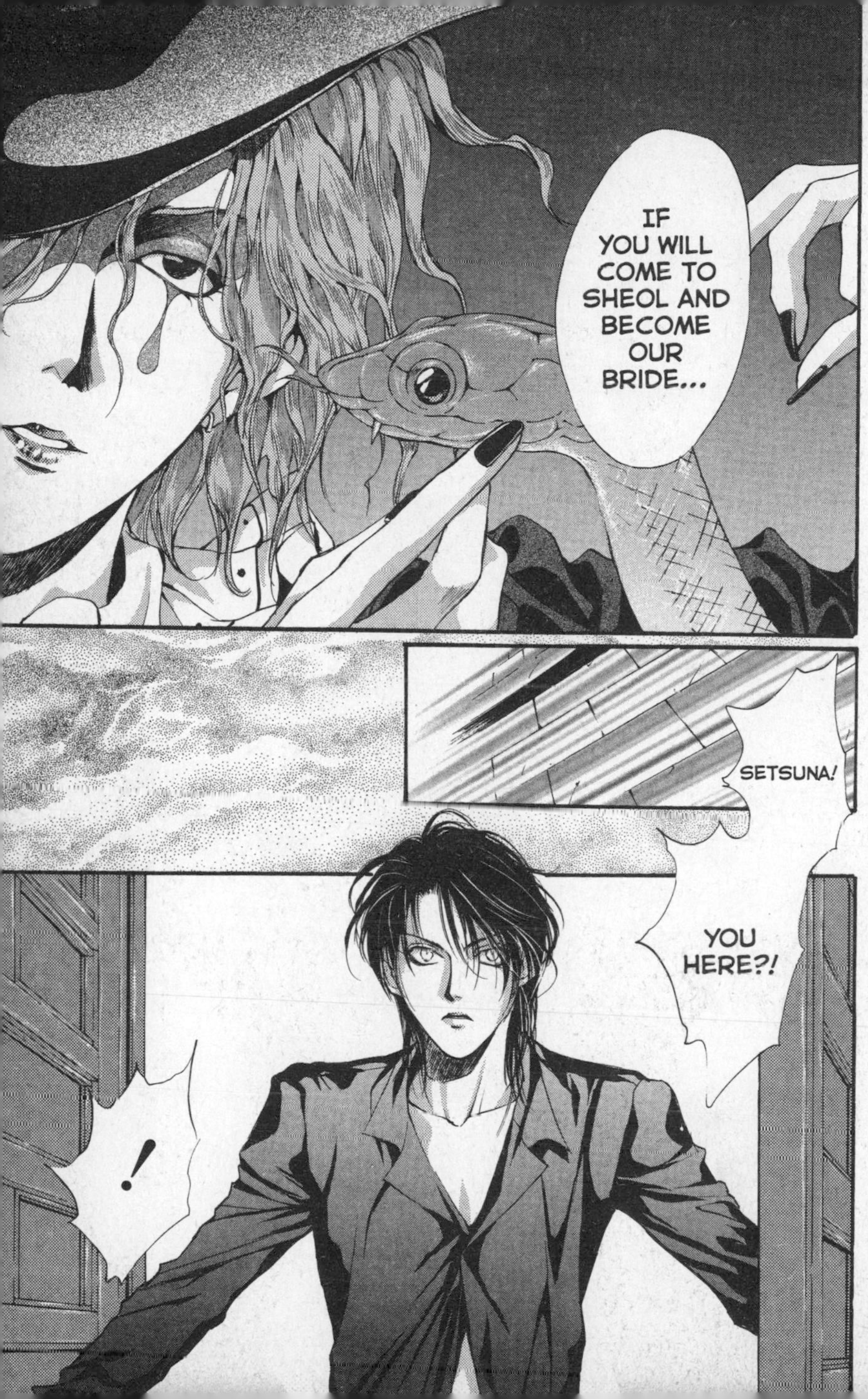
IF YOU WILL COME TO SHEOL AND BECOME OUR BRIDE...
SETSUNA!
YOU HERE?!
!

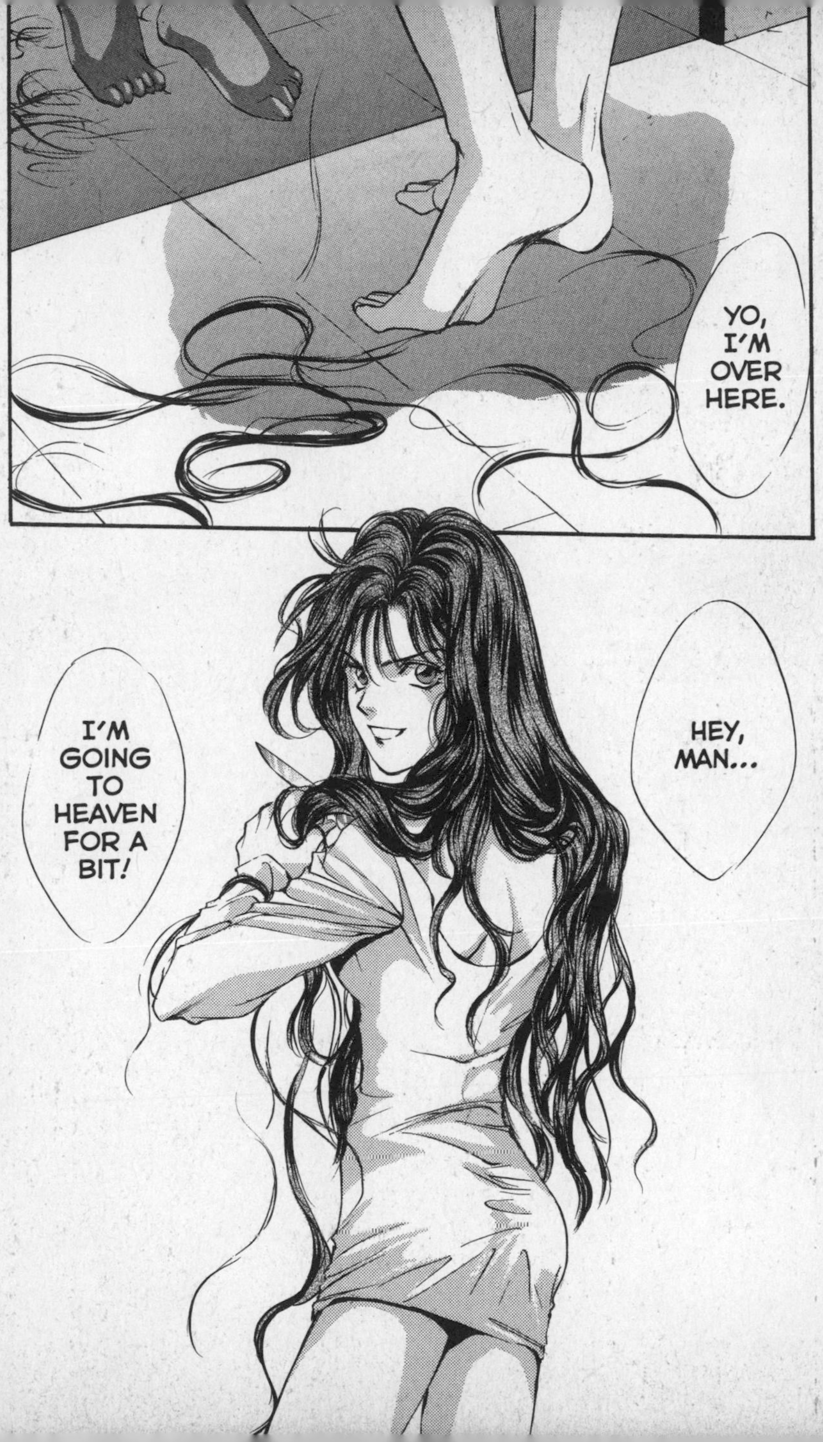
YO, I'M OVER HERE.
HEY, MAN...
I'M GOING TO HEAVEN FOR A BIT!

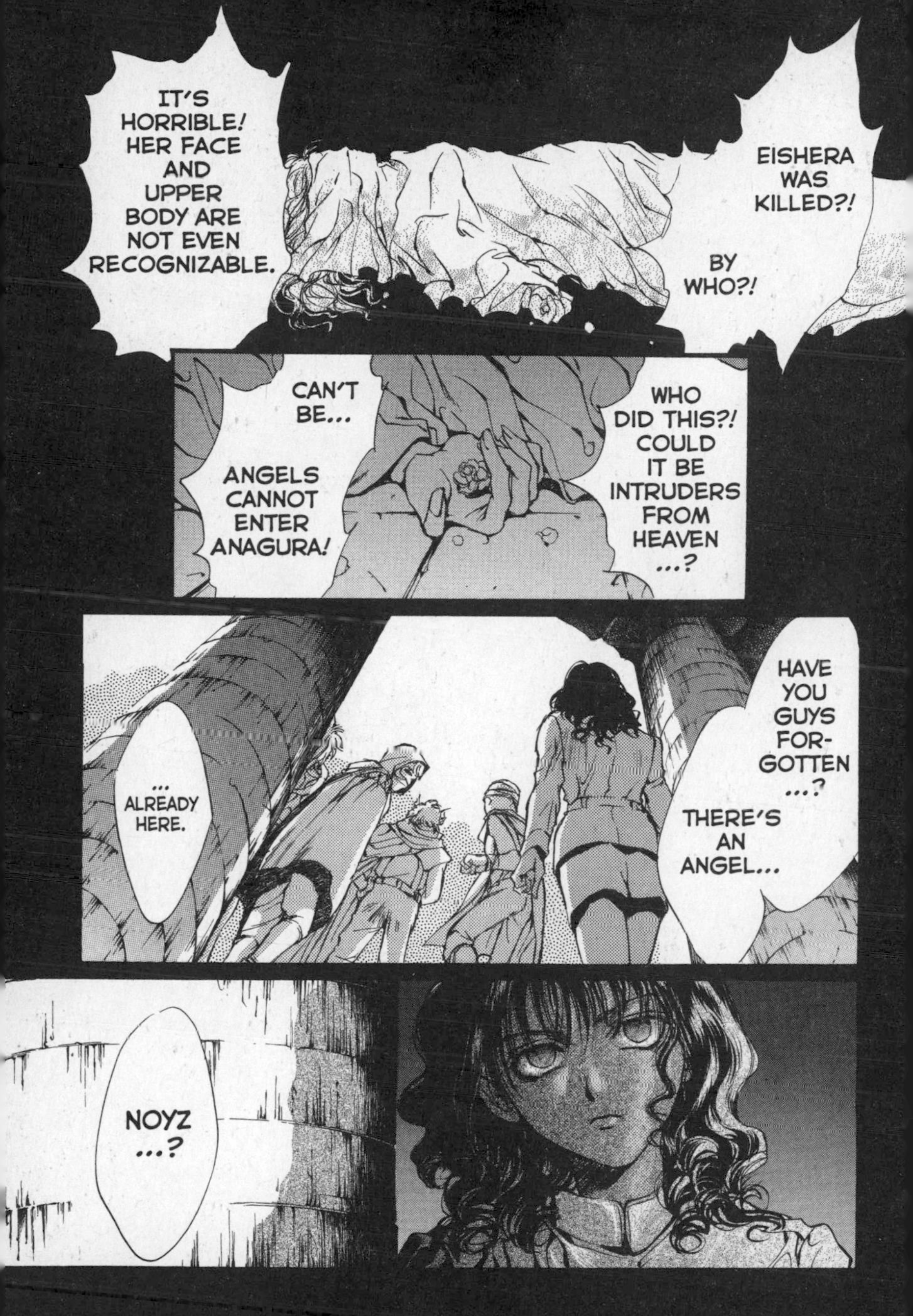
EISHERA WAS KILLED?!
BY WHO?!
IT'S HORRIBLE! HER FACE AND UPPER BODY ARE NOT EVEN RECOGNIZABLE.
WHO DID THIS?! COULD IT BE INTRUDERS FROM HEAVEN ...?
CAN'T BE...
ANGELS CANNOT ENTER ANAGURA!
HAVE YOU GUYS FOR-GOTTEN ...?
THERE'S AN ANGEL...
... ALREADY HERE.
NOYZ ...?

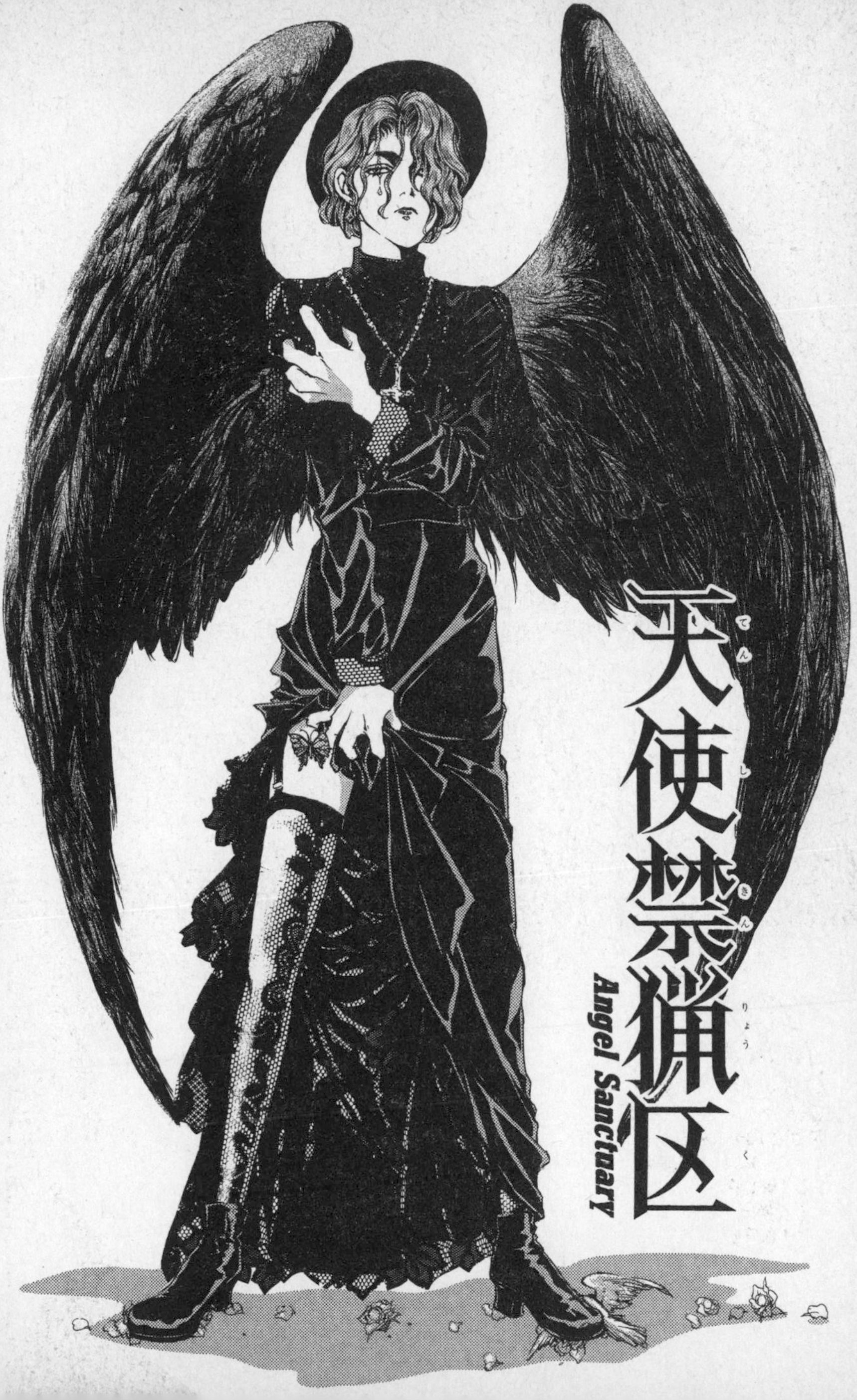
天使禁猟区
Angel Sanctuary

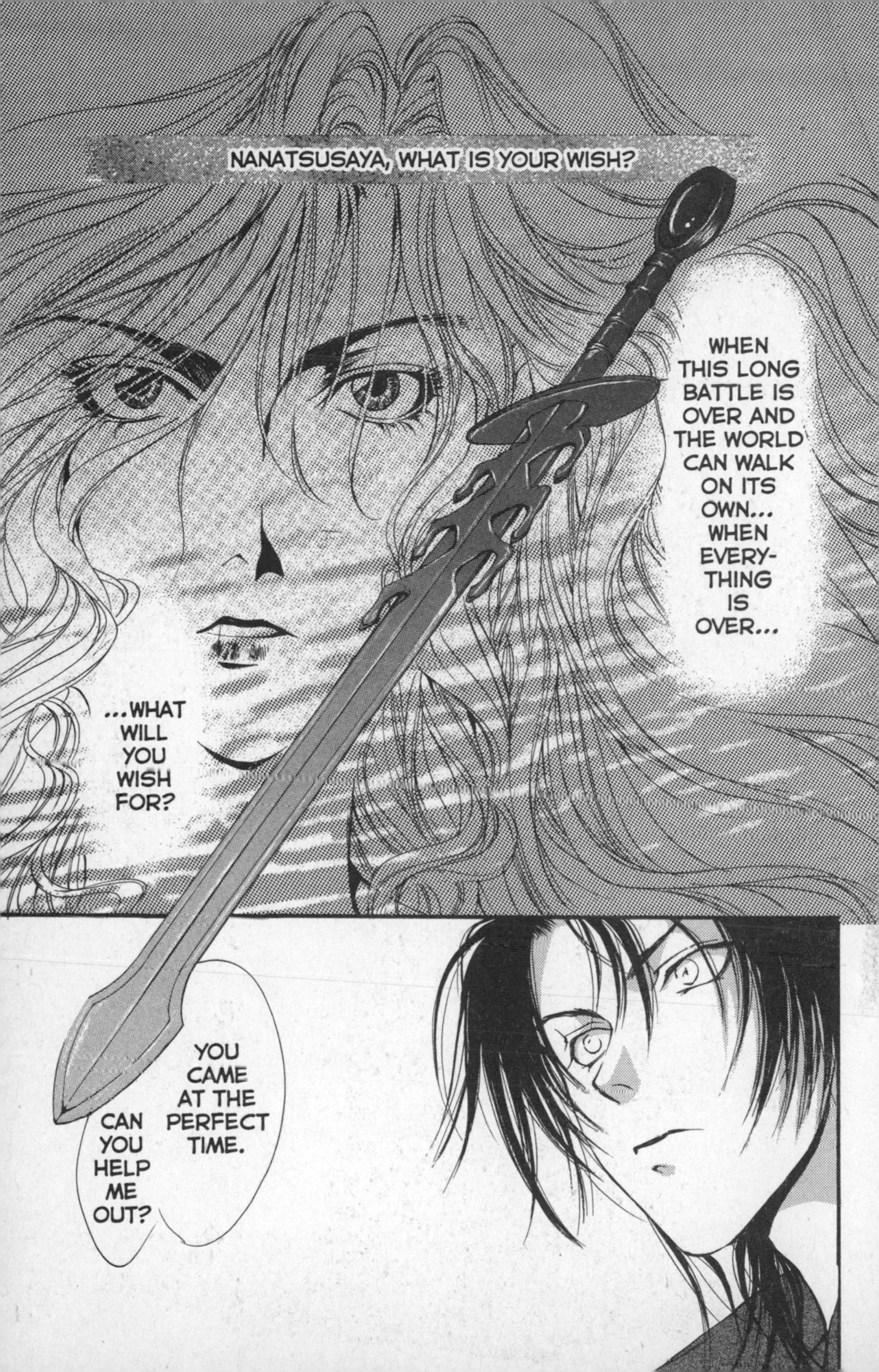
NANATSUSAYA, WHAT IS YOUR WISH?
WHEN THIS LONG BATTLE IS OVER AND THE WORLD CAN WALK ON ITS OWN... WHEN EVERY-THING IS OVER...
...WHAT WILL YOU WISH FOR?
YOU CAME AT THE PERFECT TIME.
CAN YOU HELP ME OUT?

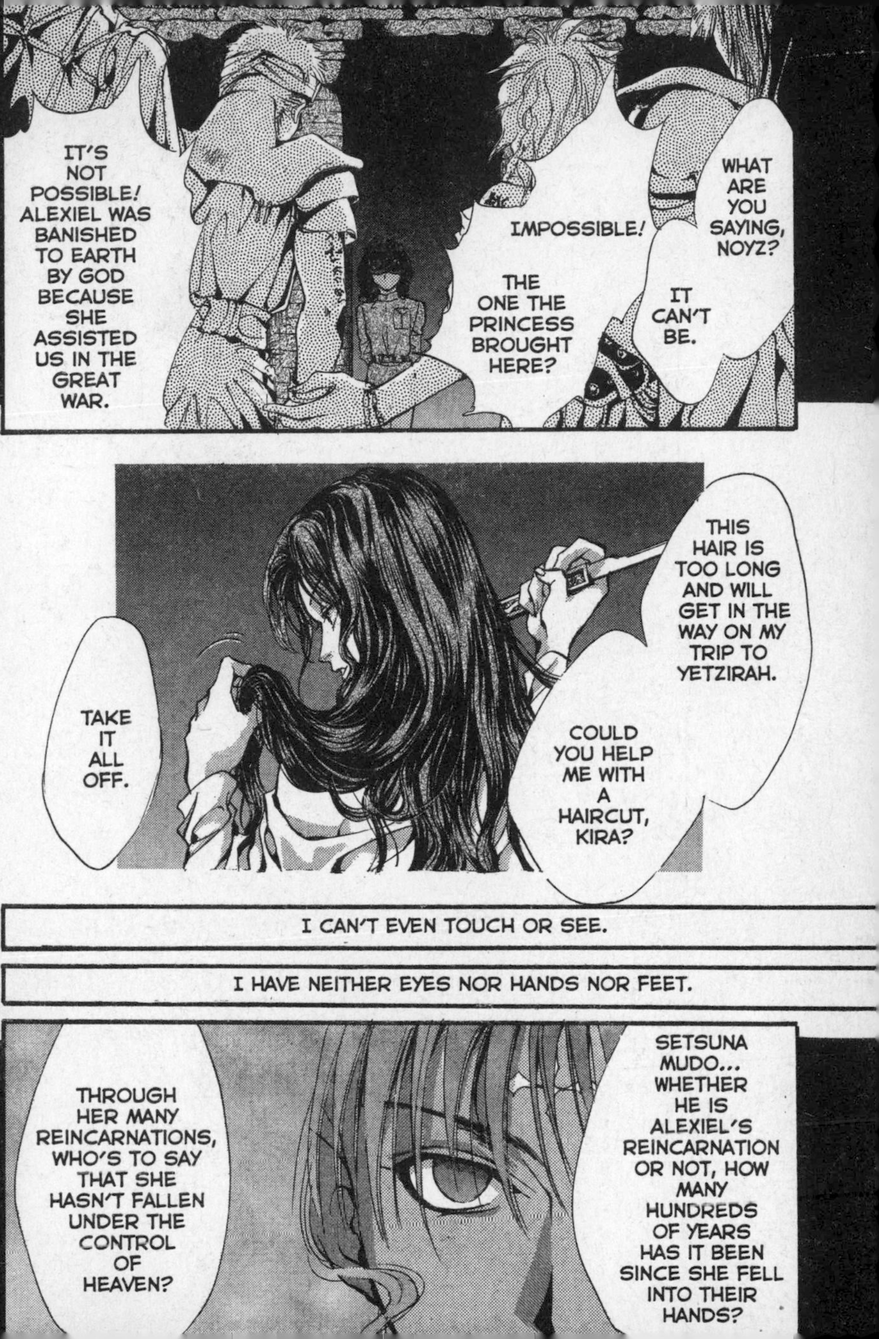
WHAT ARE YOU SAYING, NOYZ?
IT CAN'T BE.
IMPOSSIBLE!
THE ONE THE PRINCESS BROUGHT HERE?
IT'S NOT POSSIBLE! ALEXIEL WAS BANISHED TO EARTH BY GOD BECAUSE SHE ASSISTED US IN THE GREAT WAR.
THIS HAIR IS TOO LONG AND WILL GET IN THE WAY ON MY TRIP TO YETZIRAH.
COULD YOU HELP ME WITH A HAIRCUT, KIRA?
TAKE IT ALL OFF.
I CAN'T EVEN TOUCH OR SEE.
I HAVE NEITHER EYES NOR HANDS NOR FEET.
SETSUNA MUDO... WHETHER HE IS ALEXIEL'S REINCARNATION OR NOT, HOW MANY HUNDREDS OF YEARS HAS IT BEEN SINCE SHE FELL INTO THEIR HANDS?
THROUGH HER MANY REINCARNATIONS, WHO'S TO SAY THAT SHE HASN'T FALLEN UNDER THE CONTROL OF HEAVEN?

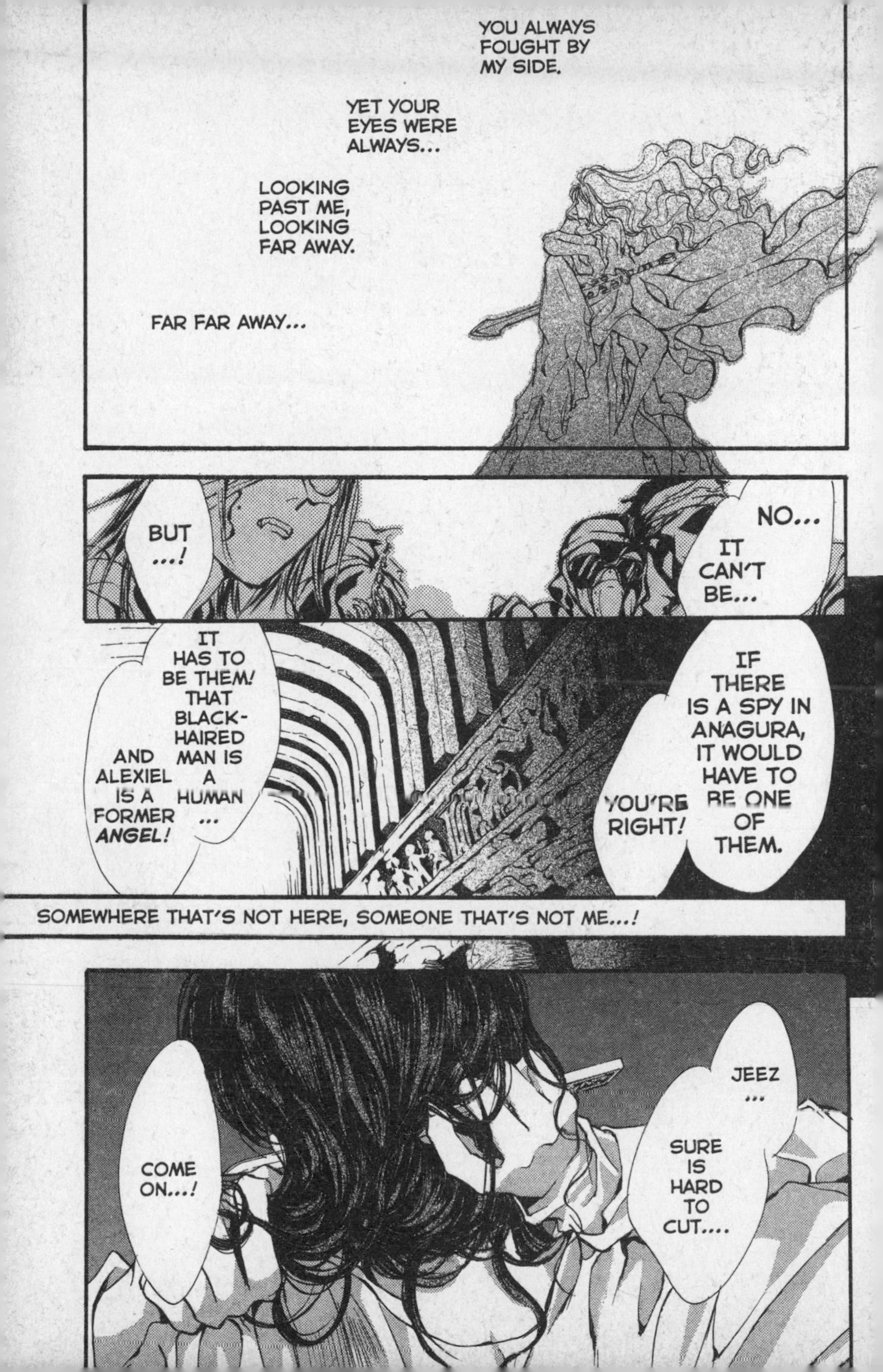
YOU ALWAYS FOUGHT BY MY SIDE.
YET YOUR EYES WERE ALWAYS...
LOOKING PAST ME, LOOKING FAR AWAY.
FAR FAR AWAY...
NO...
IT CAN'T BE...
BUT ...!
IF THERE IS A SPY IN ANAGURA, IT WOULD HAVE TO BE ONE OF THEM.
YOU'RE RIGHT!
IT HAS TO BE THEM! THAT BLACK-HAIRED MAN IS A HUMAN ...
AND ALEXIEL IS A FORMER *ANGEL*!
SOMEWHERE THAT'S NOT HERE, SOMEONE THAT'S NOT ME...!
JEEZ ...
SURE IS HARD TO CUT....
COME ON...!

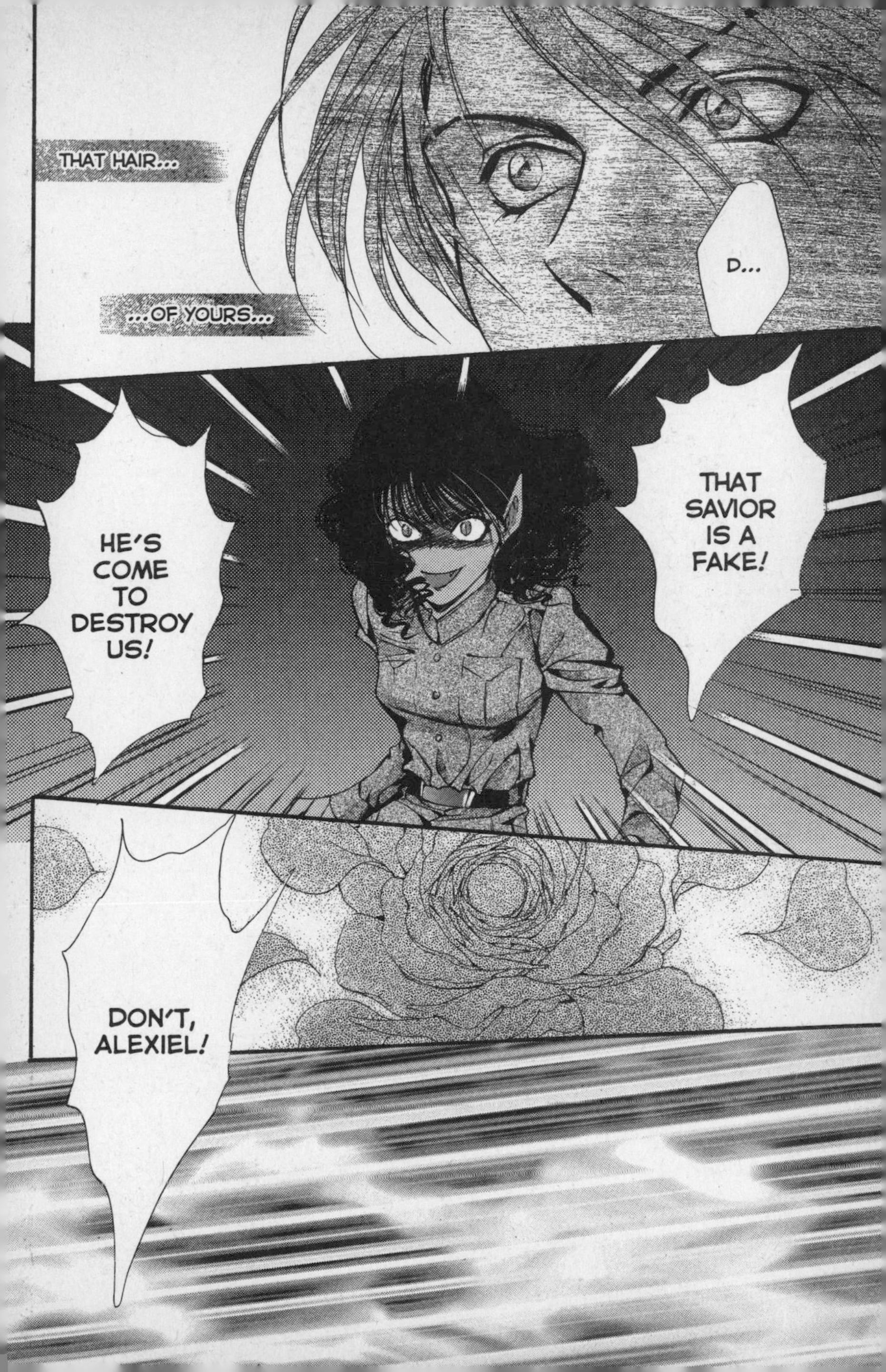
D...
THAT HAIR...
...OF YOURS...
THAT SAVIOR IS A FAKE!
HE'S COME TO DESTROY US!
DON'T, ALEXIEL!

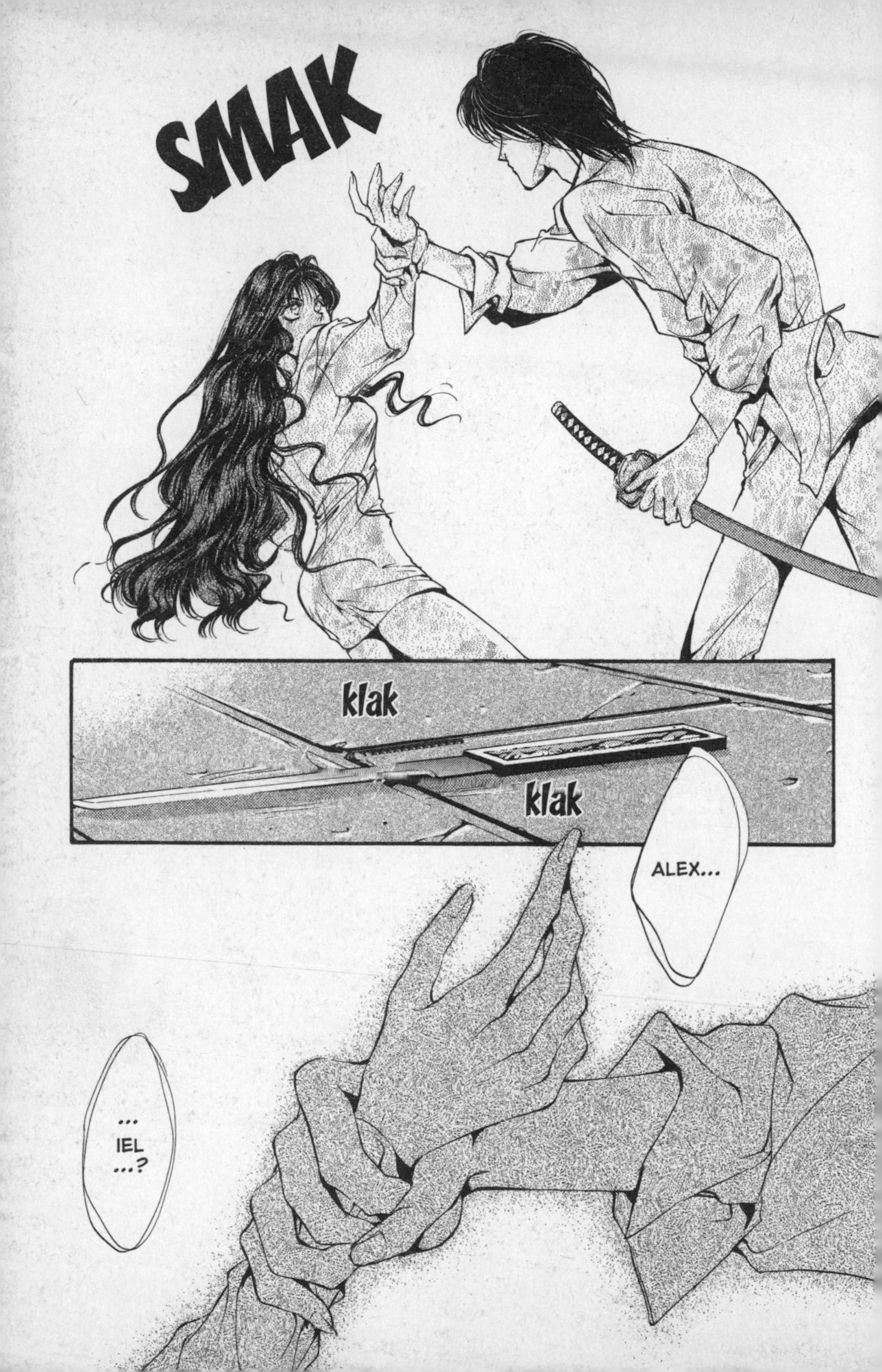
SMAK
klak
klak
ALEX...
... IEL ...?

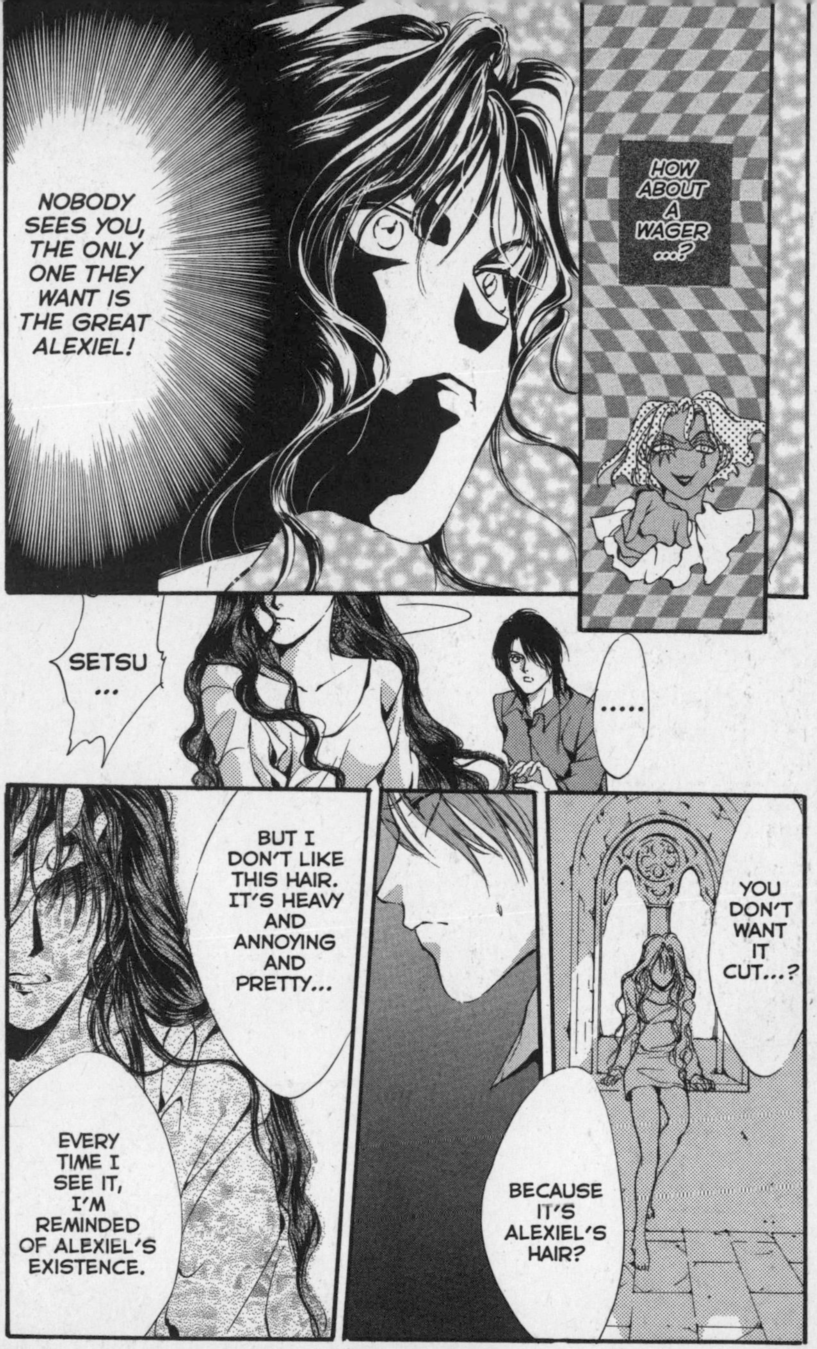
HOW ABOUT A WAGER ...?
NOBODY SEES YOU, THE ONLY ONE THEY WANT IS THE GREAT ALEXIEL!
.....
SETSU ...
YOU DON'T WANT IT CUT...?
BECAUSE IT'S ALEXIEL'S HAIR?
BUT I DON'T LIKE THIS HAIR. IT'S HEAVY AND ANNOYING AND PRETTY...
EVERY TIME I SEE IT, I'M REMINDED OF ALEXIEL'S EXISTENCE.

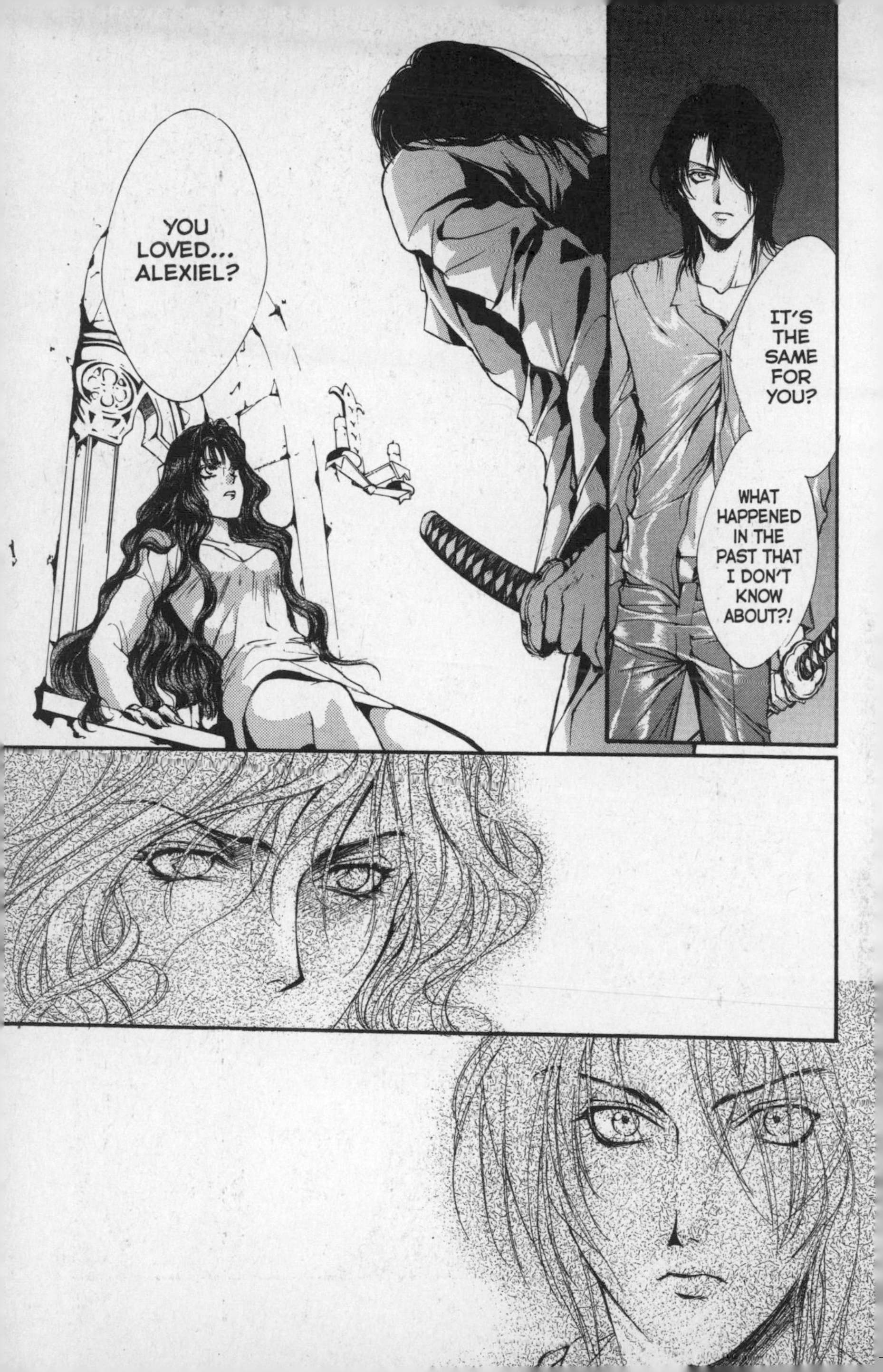
IT'S THE SAME FOR YOU?
WHAT HAPPENED IN THE PAST THAT I DON'T KNOW ABOUT?!
YOU LOVED... ALEXIEL?

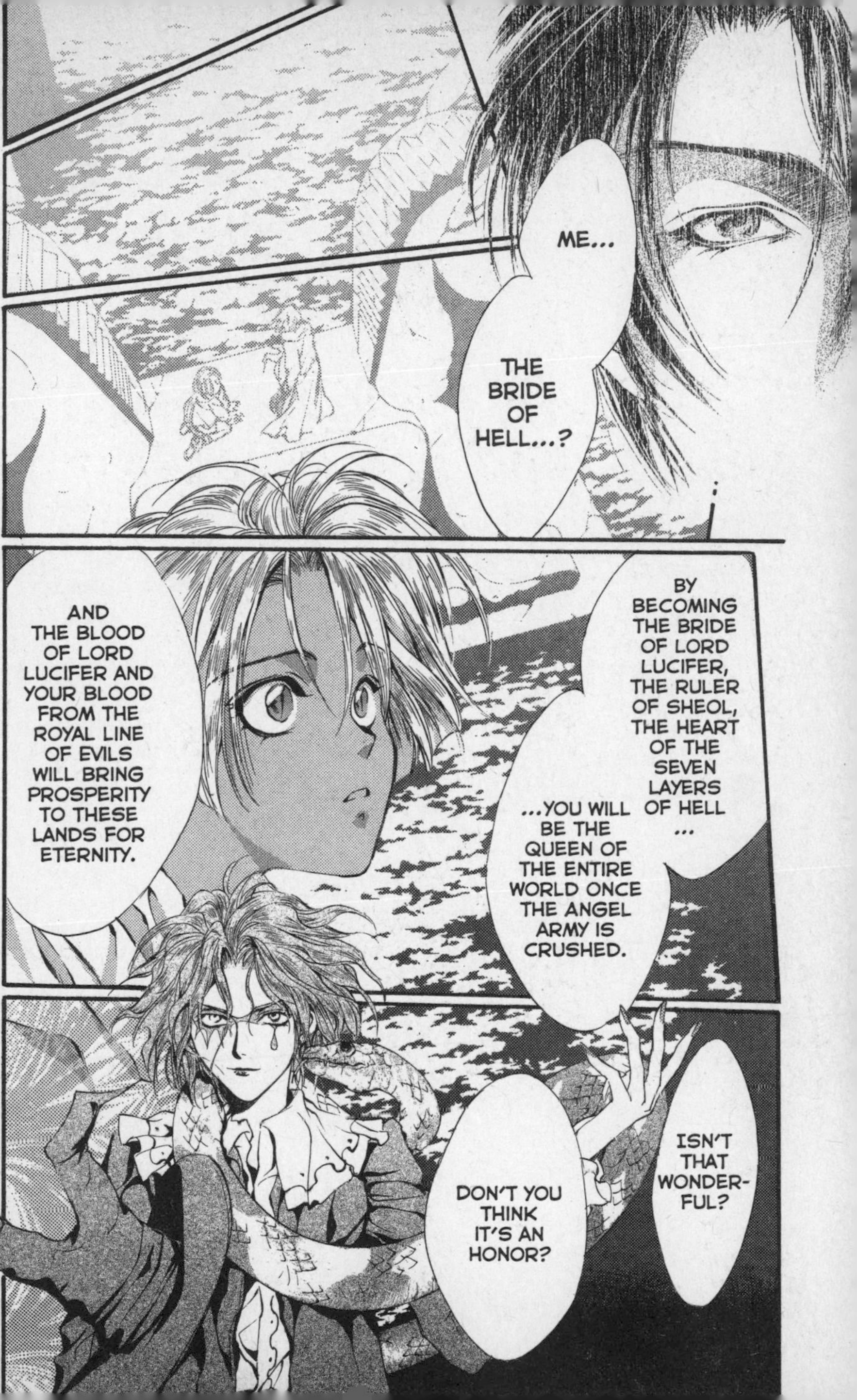
ME...
THE BRIDE OF HELL...?
BY BECOMING THE BRIDE OF LORD LUCIFER, THE RULER OF SHEOL, THE HEART OF THE SEVEN LAYERS OF HELL ...
...YOU WILL BE THE QUEEN OF THE ENTIRE WORLD ONCE THE ANGEL ARMY IS CRUSHED.
AND THE BLOOD OF LORD LUCIFER AND YOUR BLOOD FROM THE ROYAL LINE OF EVILS WILL BRING PROSPERITY TO THESE LANDS FOR ETERNITY.
ISN'T THAT WONDER-FUL?
DON'T YOU THINK IT'S AN HONOR?

Snakes... Making my assistants draw snakes and that tattoo on Michael... I'm not torturing them or anything. But it is hard to draw things you're not used to. Like the face of a smiling snake! It looks so cute with the smiley face, so I left it as is. And yes, I'm really bad at drawing snakes. Oh yeah, for this book I was really busy (well, I always am...). I only had a few days, so I can't include as many extras. There's not even a postscript... Sorry, please forgive me!

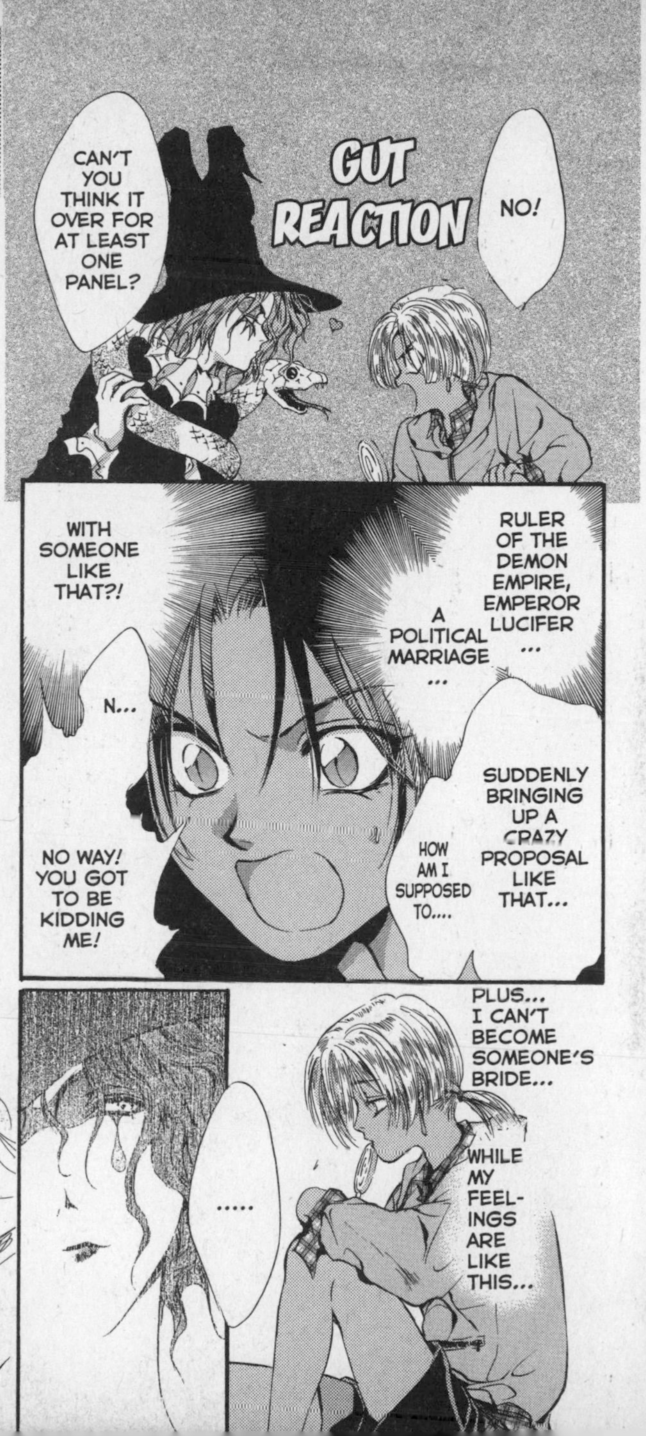
NO!
GUT REACTION
CAN'T YOU THINK IT OVER FOR AT LEAST ONE PANEL?
RULER OF THE DEMON EMPIRE, EMPEROR LUCIFER ...
A POLITICAL MARRIAGE ...
WITH SOMEONE LIKE THAT?!
N...
SUDDENLY BRINGING UP A CRAZY PROPOSAL LIKE THAT...
HOW AM I SUPPOSED TO....
NO WAY! YOU GOT TO BE KIDDING ME!
PLUS... I CAN'T BECOME SOMEONE'S BRIDE...
WHILE MY FEEL-INGS ARE LIKE THIS...
.....

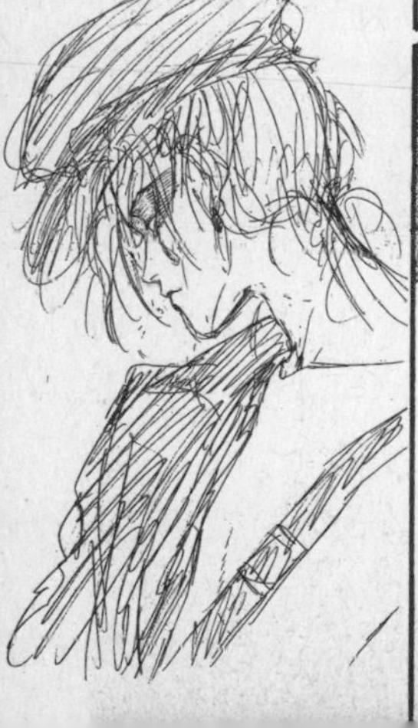

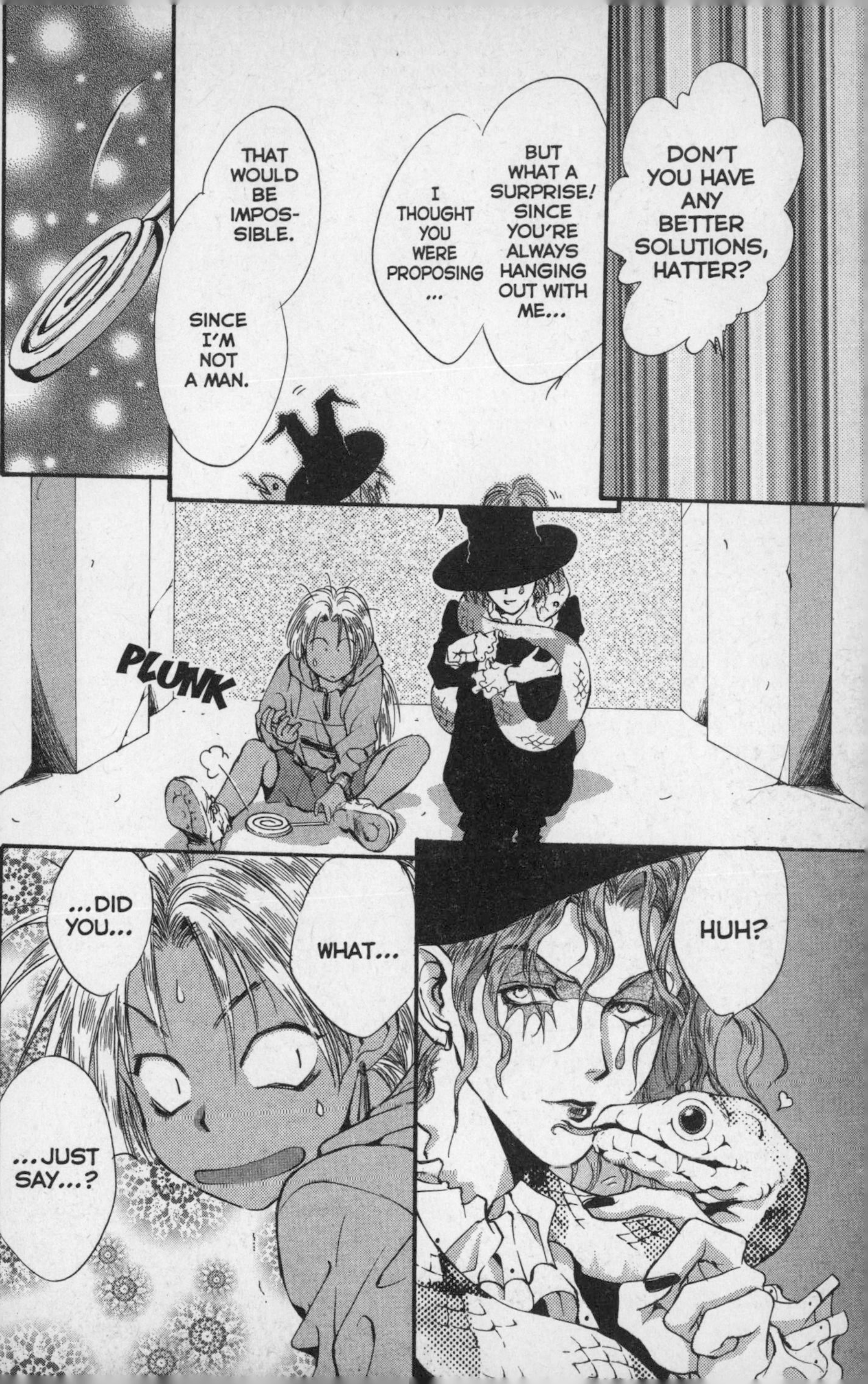
DON'T YOU HAVE ANY BETTER SOLUTIONS, HATTER?
BUT WHAT A SURPRISE! SINCE YOU'RE ALWAYS HANGING OUT WITH ME...
I THOUGHT YOU WERE PROPOSING...
THAT WOULD BE IMPOSSIBLE.
SINCE I'M NOT A MAN.
PLUNK
HUH?
WHAT...
...DID YOU...
...JUST SAY...?

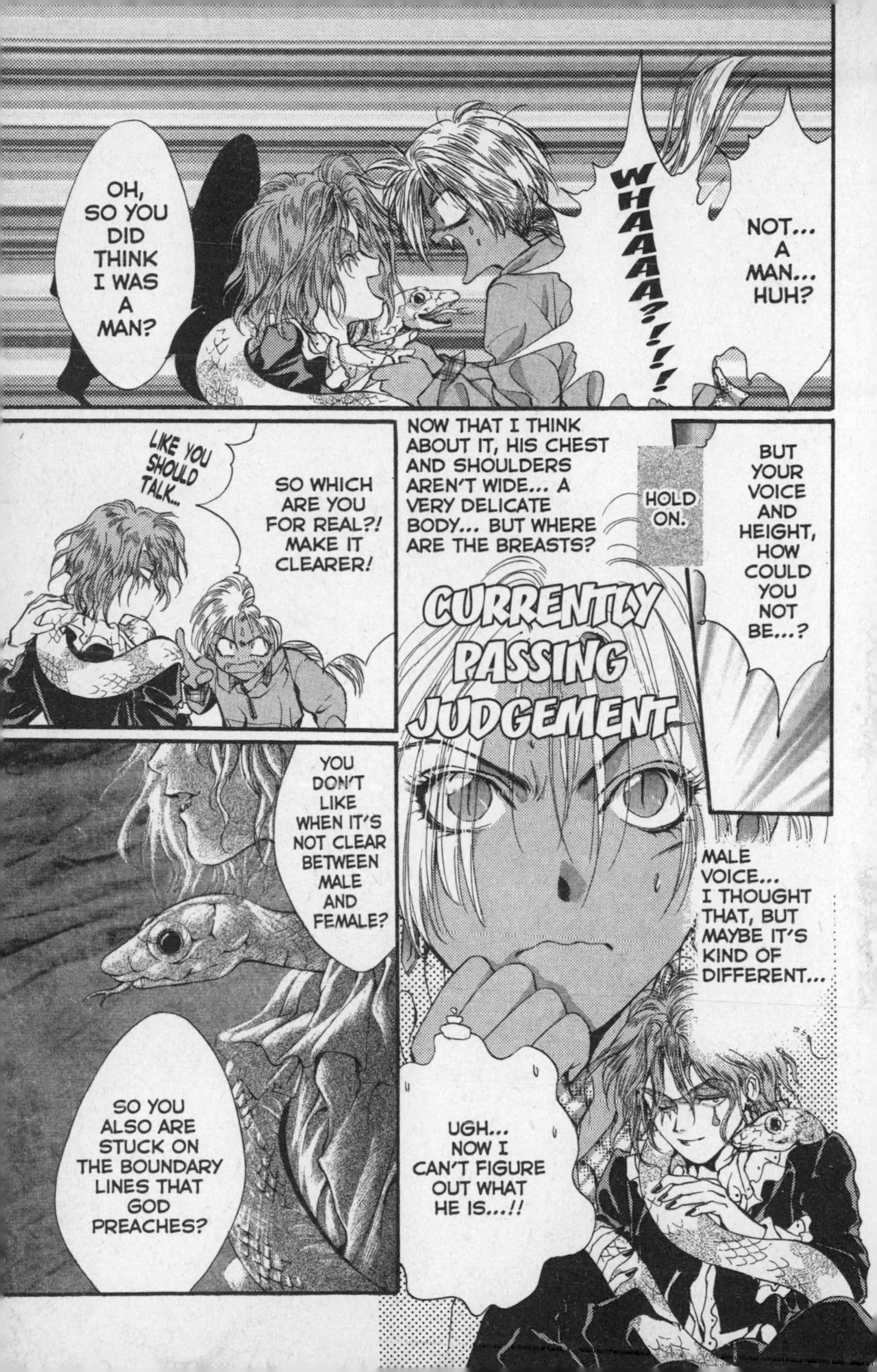
NOT... A MAN... HUH?
WHAAAA?!!!
OH, SO YOU DID THINK I WAS A MAN?
BUT YOUR VOICE AND HEIGHT, HOW COULD YOU NOT BE...?
HOLD ON.
NOW THAT I THINK ABOUT IT, HIS CHEST AND SHOULDERS AREN'T WIDE... A VERY DELICATE BODY... BUT WHERE ARE THE BREASTS?
CURRENTLY PASSING JUDGEMENT
MALE VOICE... I THOUGHT THAT, BUT MAYBE IT'S KIND OF DIFFERENT...
UGH... NOW I CAN'T FIGURE OUT WHAT HE IS...!!
SO WHICH ARE YOU FOR REAL?! MAKE IT CLEARER!
LIKE YOU SHOULD TALK...
YOU DON'T LIKE WHEN IT'S NOT CLEAR BETWEEN MALE AND FEMALE?
SO YOU ALSO ARE STUCK ON THE BOUNDARY LINES THAT GOD PREACHES?

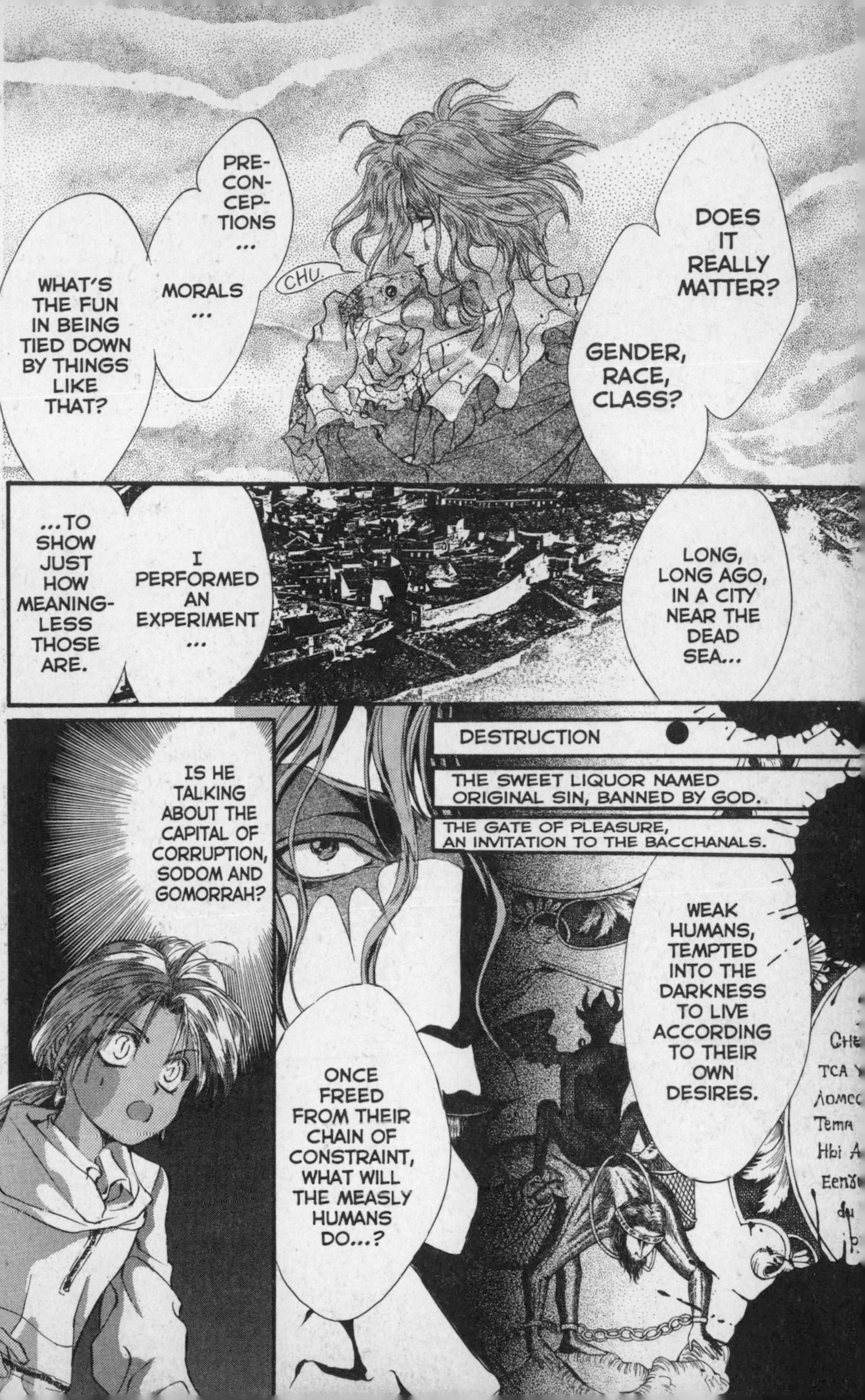
DOES IT REALLY MATTER?
GENDER, RACE, CLASS?
CHU.
PRE-CONCEPTIONS...
MORALS...
WHAT'S THE FUN IN BEING TIED DOWN BY THINGS LIKE THAT?
LONG, LONG AGO, IN A CITY NEAR THE DEAD SEA...
I PERFORMED AN EXPERIMENT...
...TO SHOW JUST HOW MEANINGLESS THOSE ARE.
DESTRUCTION
THE SWEET LIQUOR NAMED ORIGINAL SIN, BANNED BY GOD.
THE GATE OF PLEASURE, AN INVITATION TO THE BACCHANALS.
WEAK HUMANS, TEMPTED INTO THE DARKNESS TO LIVE ACCORDING TO THEIR OWN DESIRES.
ONCE FREED FROM THEIR CHAIN OF CONSTRAINT, WHAT WILL THE MEASLY HUMANS DO...?
IS HE TALKING ABOUT THE CAPITAL OF CORRUPTION, SODOM AND GOMORRAH?

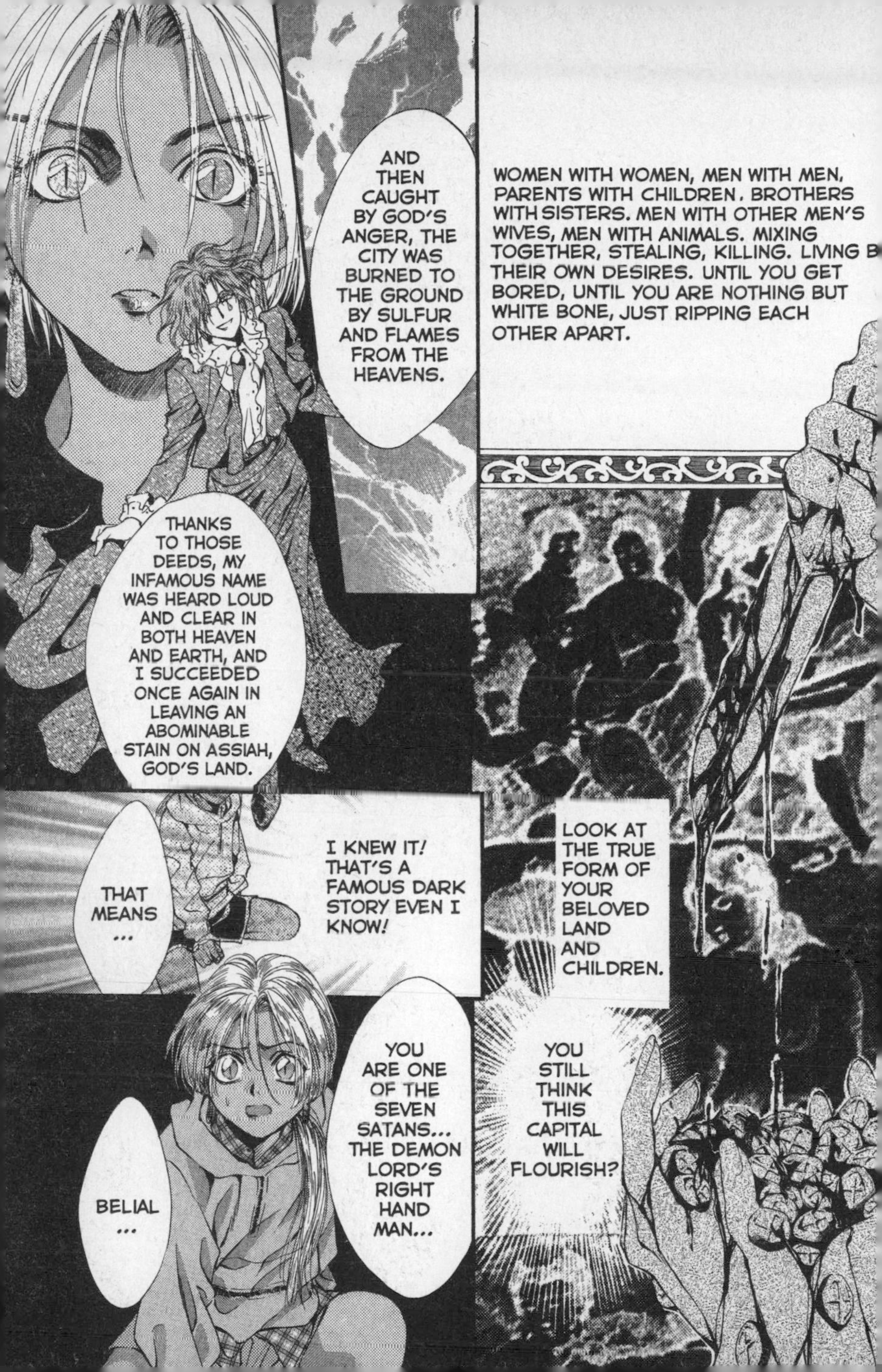
WOMEN WITH WOMEN, MEN WITH MEN, PARENTS WITH CHILDREN. BROTHERS WITH SISTERS. MEN WITH OTHER MEN'S WIVES, MEN WITH ANIMALS. MIXING TOGETHER, STEALING, KILLING. LIVING B THEIR OWN DESIRES. UNTIL YOU GET BORED, UNTIL YOU ARE NOTHING BUT WHITE BONE, JUST RIPPING EACH OTHER APART.
AND THEN CAUGHT BY GOD'S ANGER, THE CITY WAS BURNED TO THE GROUND BY SULFUR AND FLAMES FROM THE HEAVENS.
THANKS TO THOSE DEEDS, MY INFAMOUS NAME WAS HEARD LOUD AND CLEAR IN BOTH HEAVEN AND EARTH, AND I SUCCEEDED ONCE AGAIN IN LEAVING AN ABOMINABLE STAIN ON ASSIAH, GOD'S LAND.
LOOK AT THE TRUE FORM OF YOUR BELOVED LAND AND CHILDREN.
I KNEW IT! THAT'S A FAMOUS DARK STORY EVEN I KNOW!
THAT MEANS ...
YOU STILL THINK THIS CAPITAL WILL FLOURISH?
YOU ARE ONE OF THE SEVEN SATANS... THE DEMON LORD'S RIGHT HAND MAN...
BELIAL ...

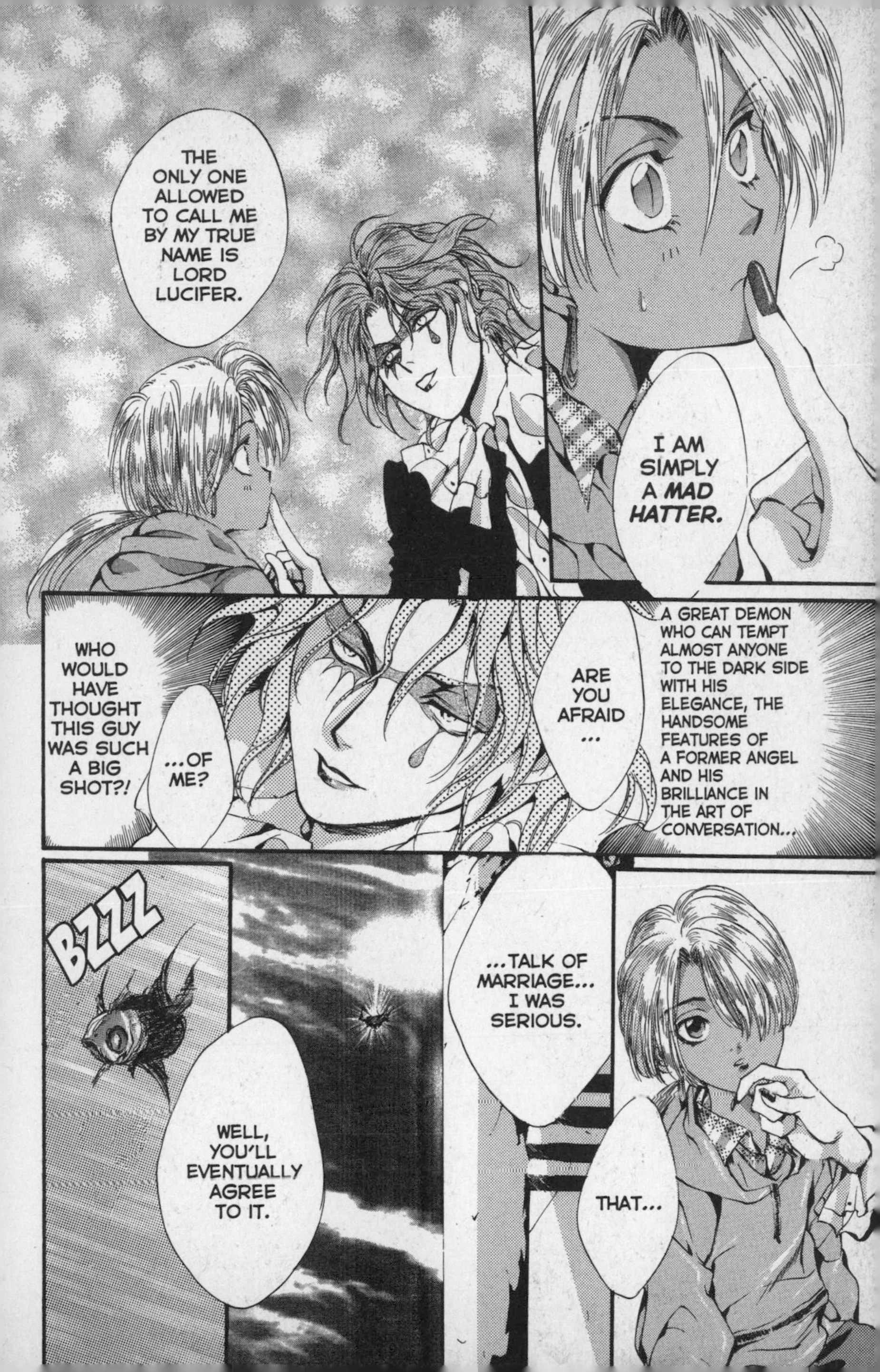
I AM SIMPLY A *MAD HATTER.*
THE ONLY ONE ALLOWED TO CALL ME BY MY TRUE NAME IS LORD LUCIFER.
A GREAT DEMON WHO CAN TEMPT ALMOST ANYONE TO THE DARK SIDE WITH HIS ELEGANCE, THE HANDSOME FEATURES OF A FORMER ANGEL AND HIS BRILLIANCE IN THE ART OF CONVERSATION...
ARE YOU AFRAID ...
...OF ME?
WHO WOULD HAVE THOUGHT THIS GUY WAS SUCH A BIG SHOT?!
THAT...
...TALK OF MARRIAGE... I WAS SERIOUS.
BZZZ
WELL, YOU'LL EVENTUALLY AGREE TO IT.

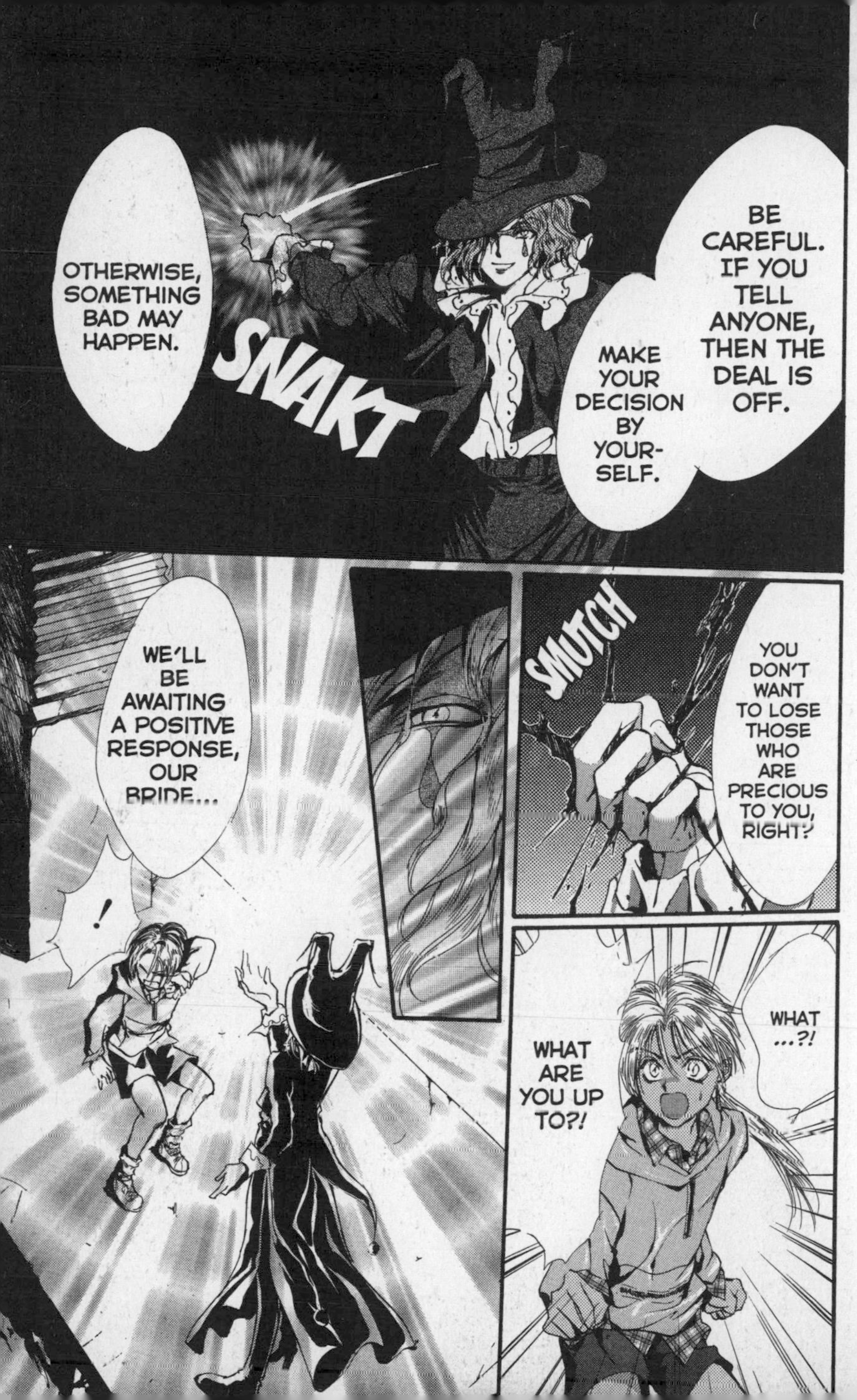
BE CAREFUL. IF YOU TELL ANYONE, THEN THE DEAL IS OFF.
MAKE YOUR DECISION BY YOURSELF.
SNAKT
OTHERWISE, SOMETHING BAD MAY HAPPEN.
SMUTCH
YOU DON'T WANT TO LOSE THOSE WHO ARE PRECIOUS TO YOU, RIGHT?
WHAT ...?!
WHAT ARE YOU UP TO?!
WE'LL BE AWAITING A POSITIVE RESPONSE, OUR BRIDE...
!

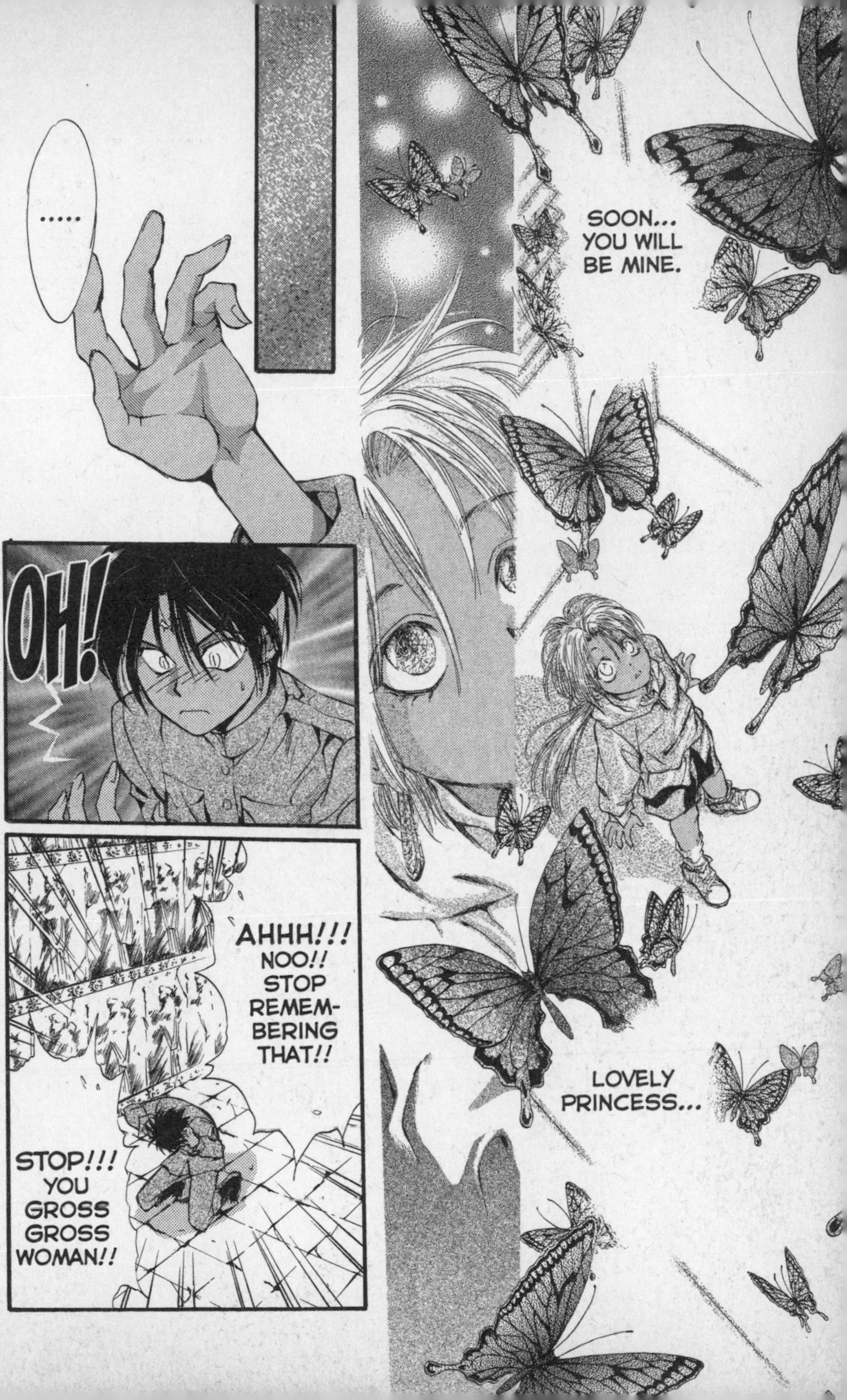
SOON... YOU WILL BE MINE.
LOVELY PRINCESS...
......
OH!
AHHH!!! NOO!! STOP REMEM-BERING THAT!!
STOP!!! YOU GROSS GROSS WOMAN!!

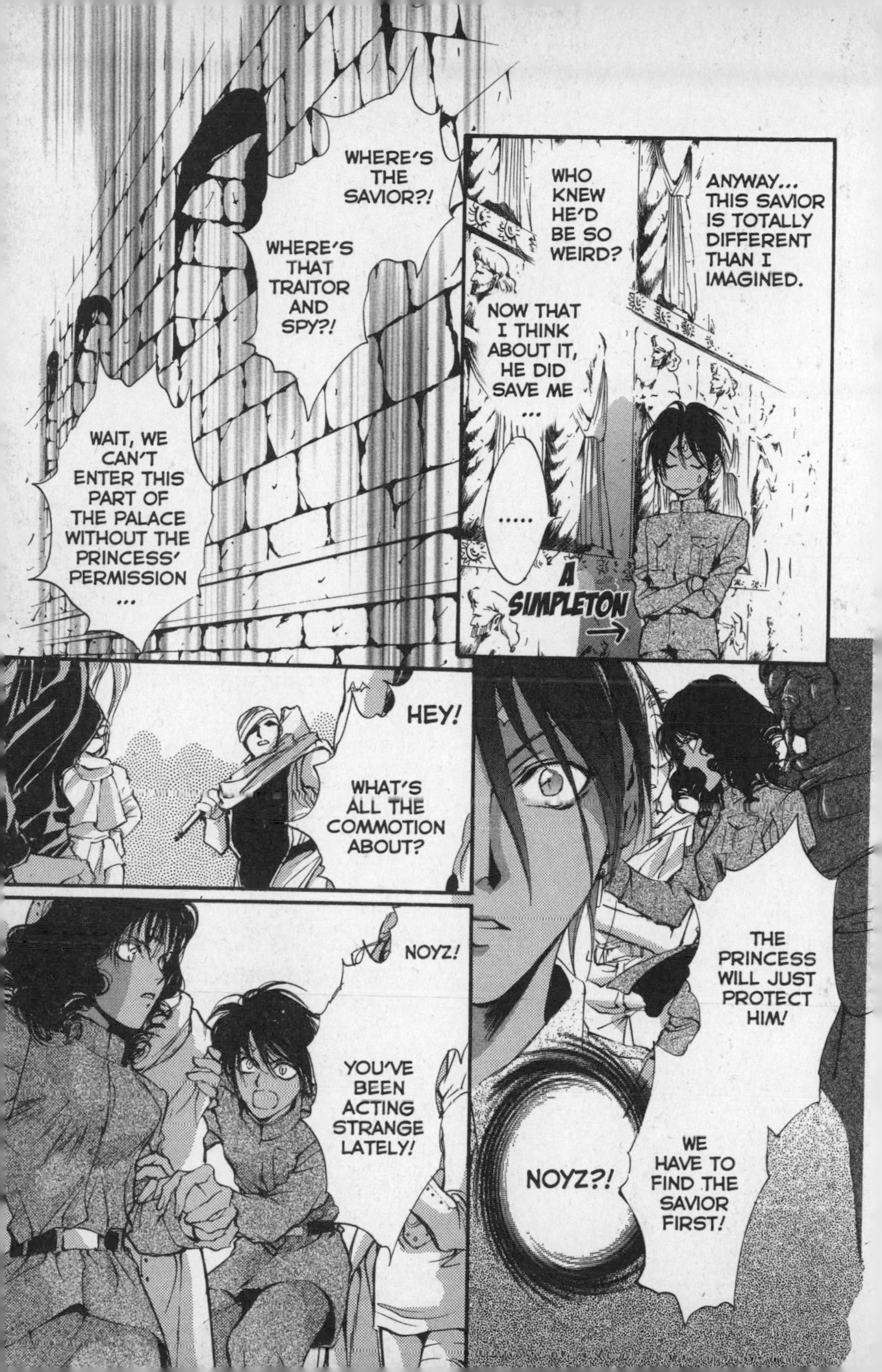
ANYWAY... THIS SAVIOR IS TOTALLY DIFFERENT THAN I IMAGINED.
WHO KNEW HE'D BE SO WEIRD?
NOW THAT I THINK ABOUT IT, HE DID SAVE ME ...
.....
A SIMPLETON →
WHERE'S THE SAVIOR?!
WHERE'S THAT TRAITOR AND SPY?!
WAIT, WE CAN'T ENTER THIS PART OF THE PALACE WITHOUT THE PRINCESS' PERMISSION ...
THE PRINCESS WILL JUST PROTECT HIM!
WE HAVE TO FIND THE SAVIOR FIRST!
NOYZ?!
HEY!
WHAT'S ALL THE COMMOTION ABOUT?
NOYZ!
YOU'VE BEEN ACTING STRANGE LATELY!

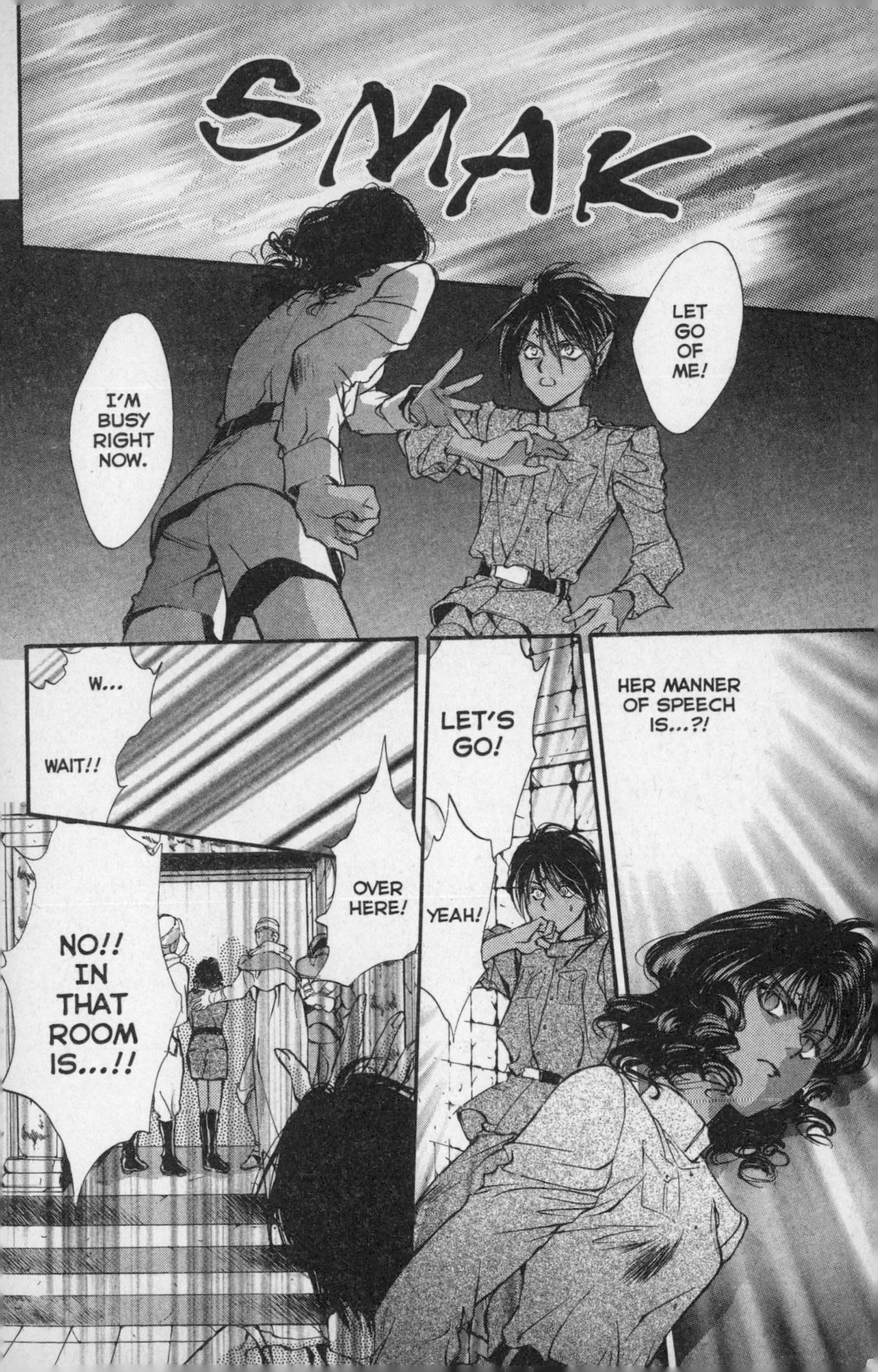
SMAK
LET GO OF ME!
I'M BUSY RIGHT NOW.
HER MANNER OF SPEECH IS...?!
LET'S GO!
YEAH!
W...
WAIT!!
OVER HERE!
NO!! IN THAT ROOM IS...!!

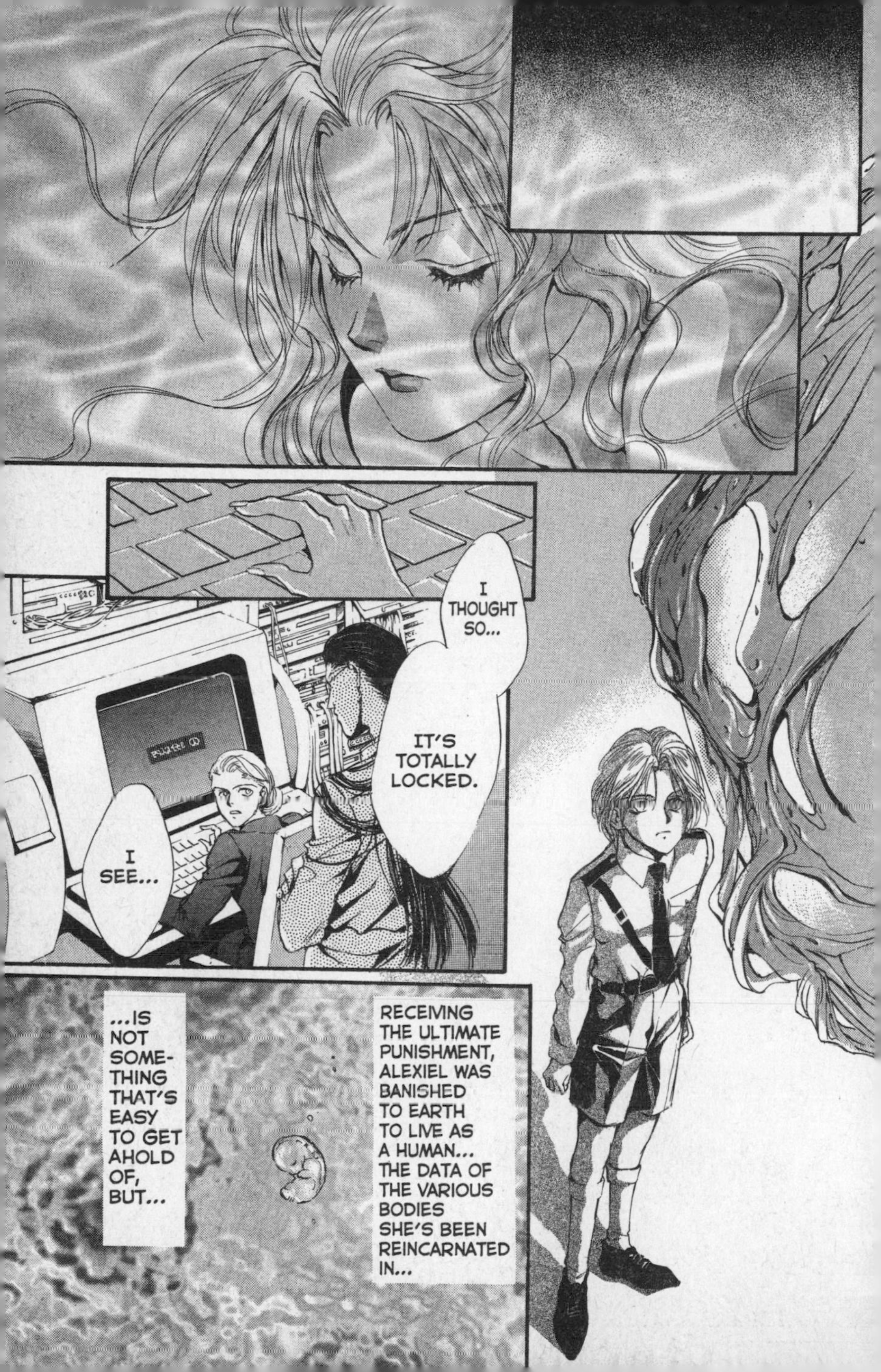
I THOUGHT SO...
IT'S TOTALLY LOCKED.
I SEE...
RECEIVING THE ULTIMATE PUNISHMENT, ALEXIEL WAS BANISHED TO EARTH TO LIVE AS A HUMAN... THE DATA OF THE VARIOUS BODIES SHE'S BEEN REINCARNATED IN...
...IS NOT SOMETHING THAT'S EASY TO GET AHOLD OF, BUT...

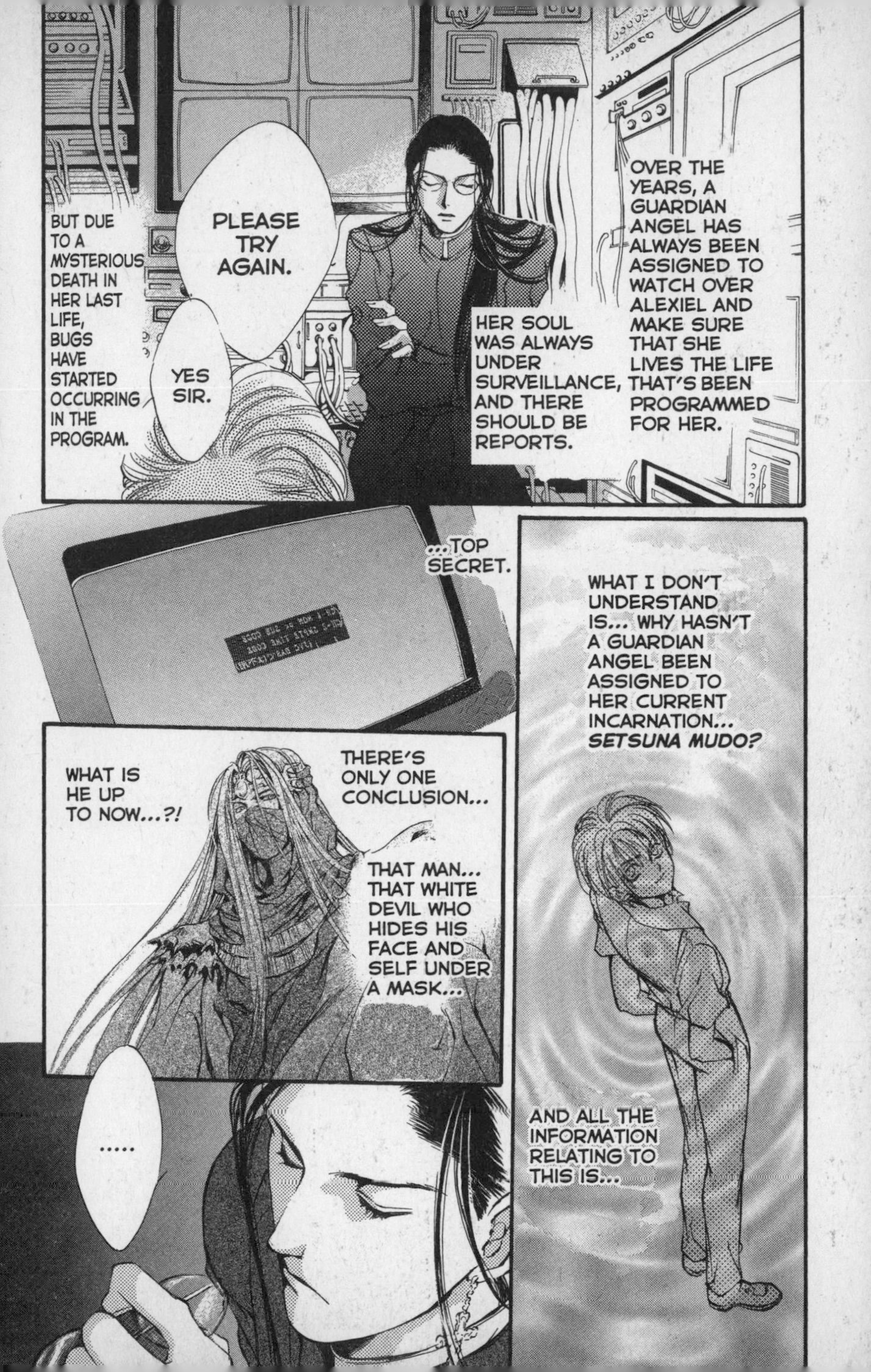
OVER THE YEARS, A GUARDIAN ANGEL HAS ALWAYS BEEN ASSIGNED TO WATCH OVER ALEXIEL AND MAKE SURE THAT SHE LIVES THE LIFE THAT'S BEEN PROGRAMMED FOR HER.
HER SOUL WAS ALWAYS UNDER SURVEILLANCE, AND THERE SHOULD BE REPORTS.
BUT DUE TO A MYSTERIOUS DEATH IN HER LAST LIFE, BUGS HAVE STARTED OCCURRING IN THE PROGRAM.
PLEASE TRY AGAIN.
YES SIR.
WHAT I DON'T UNDERSTAND IS... WHY HASN'T A GUARDIAN ANGEL BEEN ASSIGNED TO HER CURRENT INCARNATION... *SETSUNA MUDO?*
AND ALL THE INFORMATION RELATING TO THIS IS...
...TOP SECRET.
THERE'S ONLY ONE CONCLUSION...
THAT MAN... THAT WHITE DEVIL WHO HIDES HIS FACE AND SELF UNDER A MASK...
WHAT IS HE UP TO NOW...?!
.....

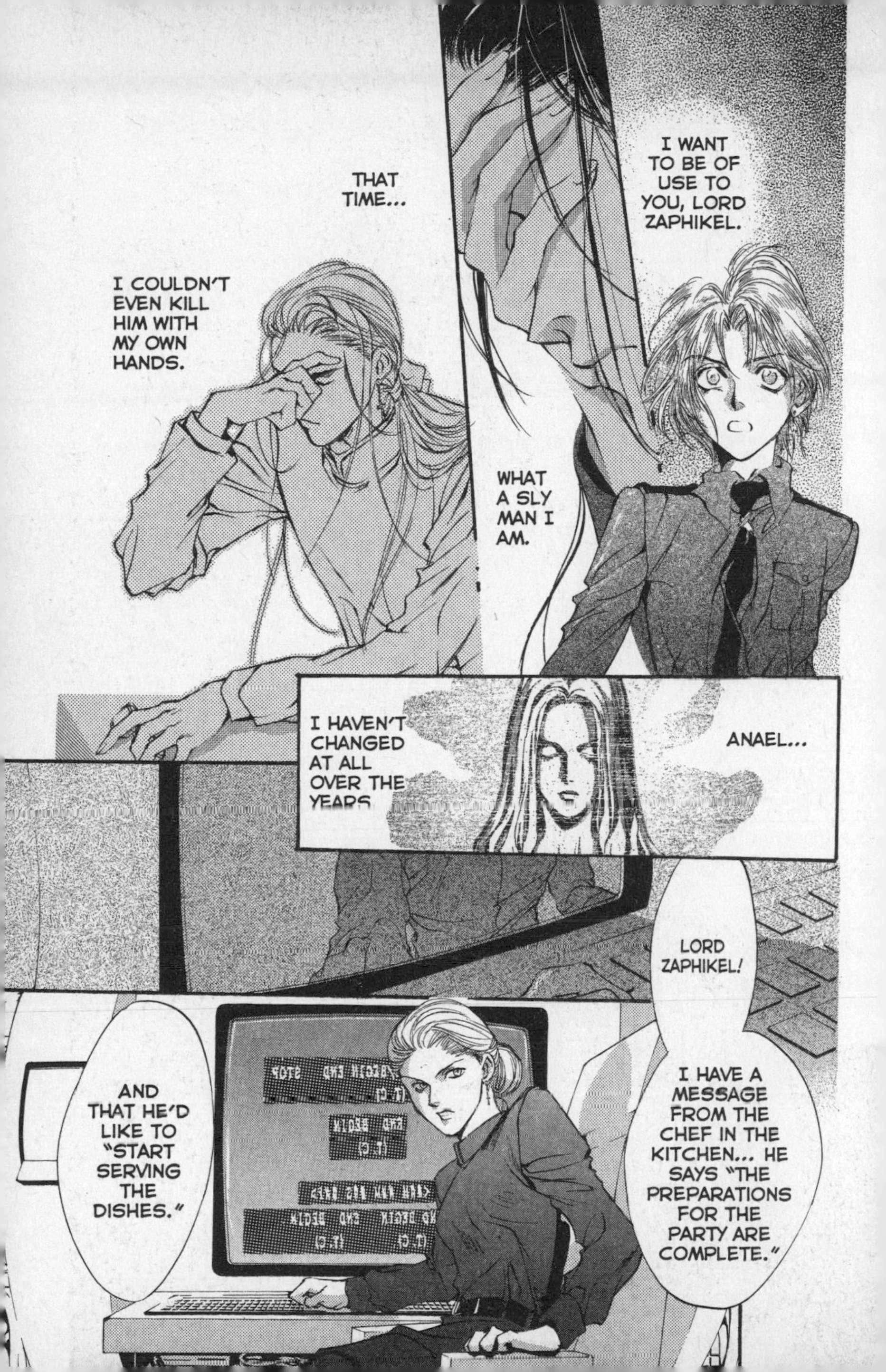
I WANT TO BE OF USE TO YOU, LORD ZAPHIKEL.
WHAT A SLY MAN I AM.
THAT TIME...
I COULDN'T EVEN KILL HIM WITH MY OWN HANDS.
ANAEL...
I HAVEN'T CHANGED AT ALL OVER THE YEARS.
LORD ZAPHIKEL!
I HAVE A MESSAGE FROM THE CHEF IN THE KITCHEN... HE SAYS "THE PREPARATIONS FOR THE PARTY ARE COMPLETE."
AND THAT HE'D LIKE TO "START SERVING THE DISHES."

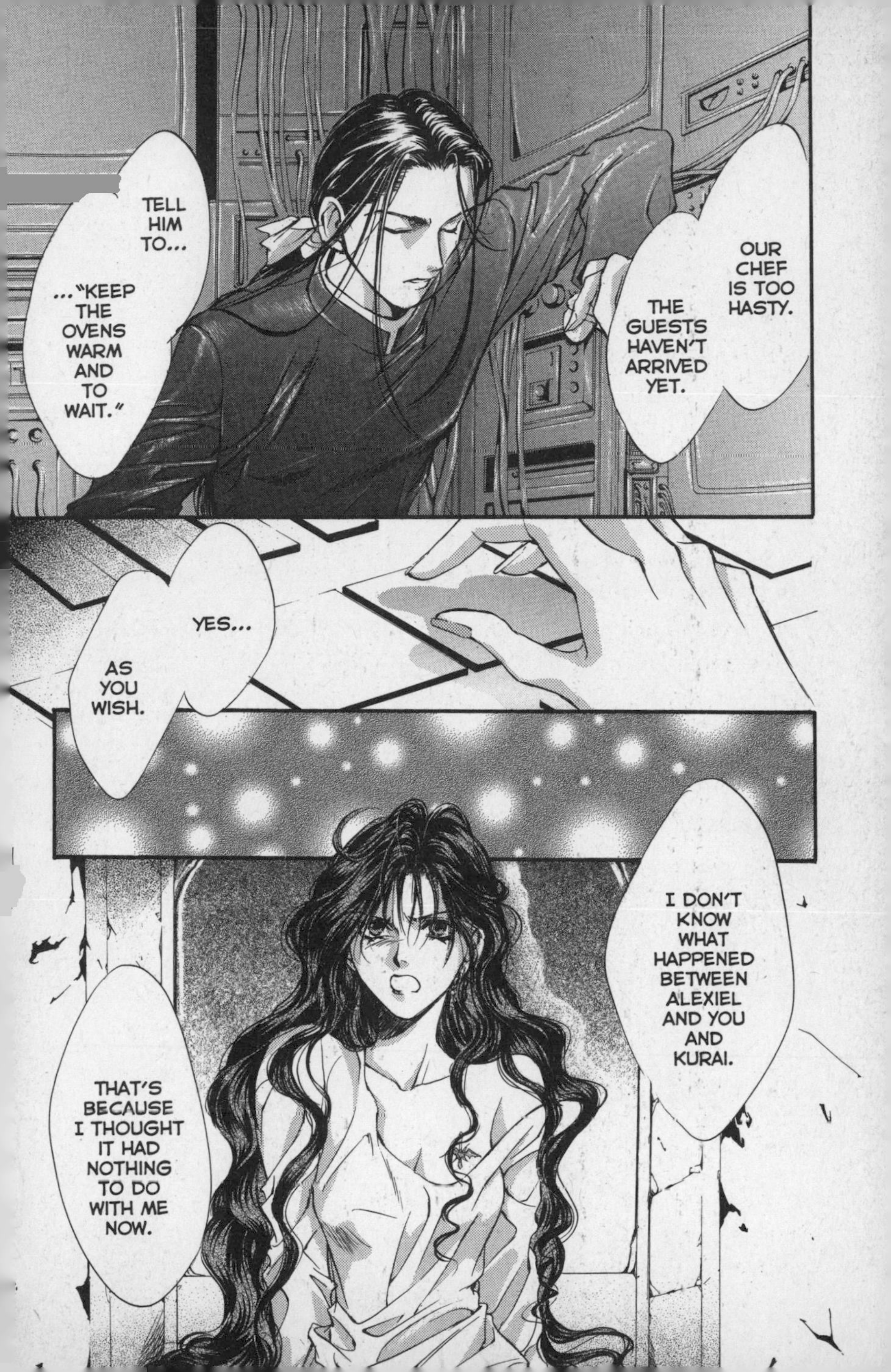
OUR CHEF IS TOO HASTY.
THE GUESTS HAVEN'T ARRIVED YET.
TELL HIM TO...
..."KEEP THE OVENS WARM AND TO WAIT."
YES...
AS YOU WISH.
I DON'T KNOW WHAT HAPPENED BETWEEN ALEXIEL AND YOU AND KURAI.
THAT'S BECAUSE I THOUGHT IT HAD NOTHING TO DO WITH ME NOW.

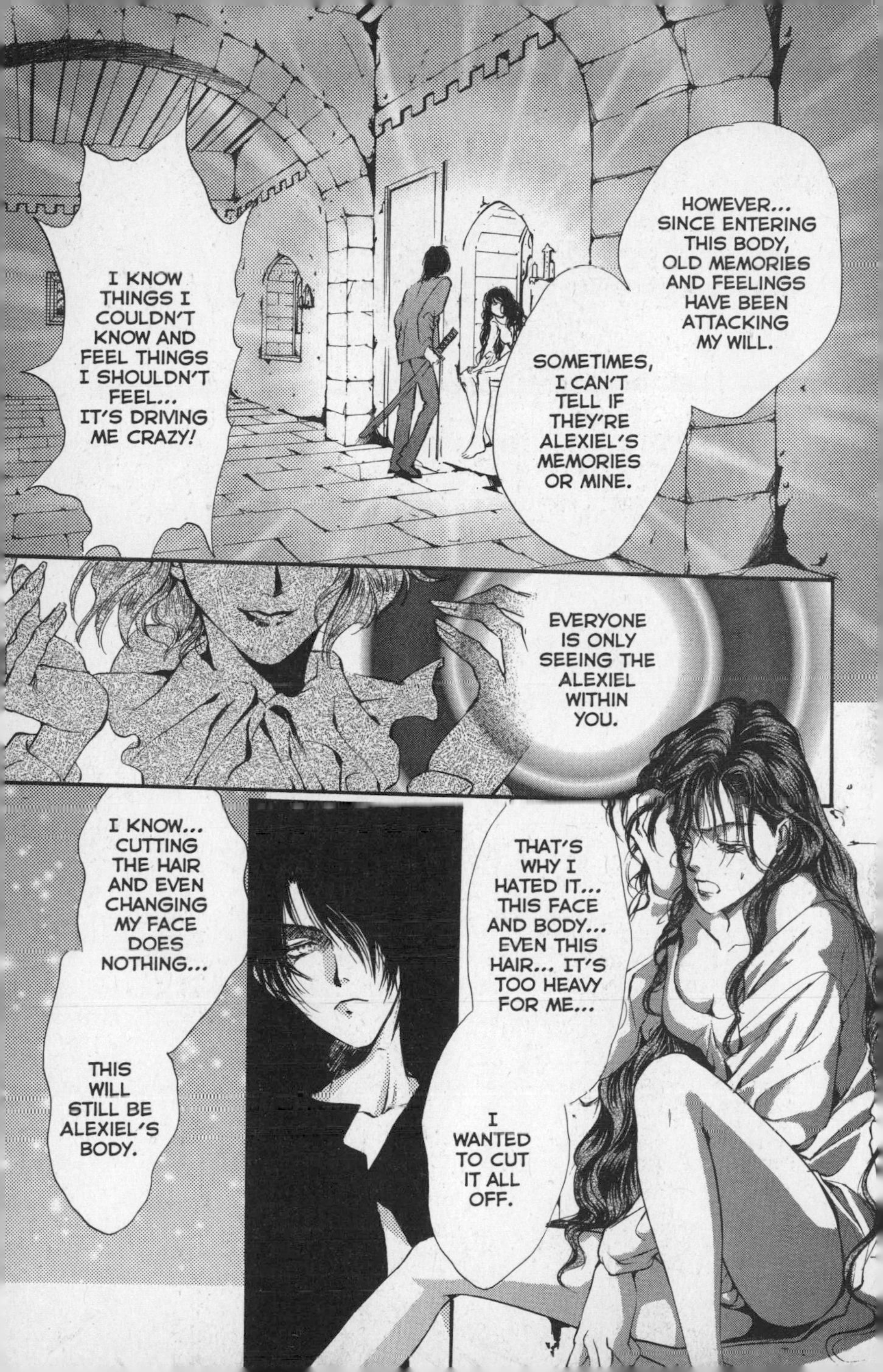
HOWEVER... SINCE ENTERING THIS BODY, OLD MEMORIES AND FEELINGS HAVE BEEN ATTACKING MY WILL.
SOMETIMES, I CAN'T TELL IF THEY'RE ALEXIEL'S MEMORIES OR MINE.
I KNOW THINGS I COULDN'T KNOW AND FEEL THINGS I SHOULDN'T FEEL... IT'S DRIVING ME CRAZY!
EVERYONE IS ONLY SEEING THE ALEXIEL WITHIN YOU.
THAT'S WHY I HATED IT... THIS FACE AND BODY... EVEN THIS HAIR... IT'S TOO HEAVY FOR ME...
I WANTED TO CUT IT ALL OFF.
I KNOW... CUTTING THE HAIR AND EVEN CHANGING MY FACE DOES NOTHING...
THIS WILL STILL BE ALEXIEL'S BODY.

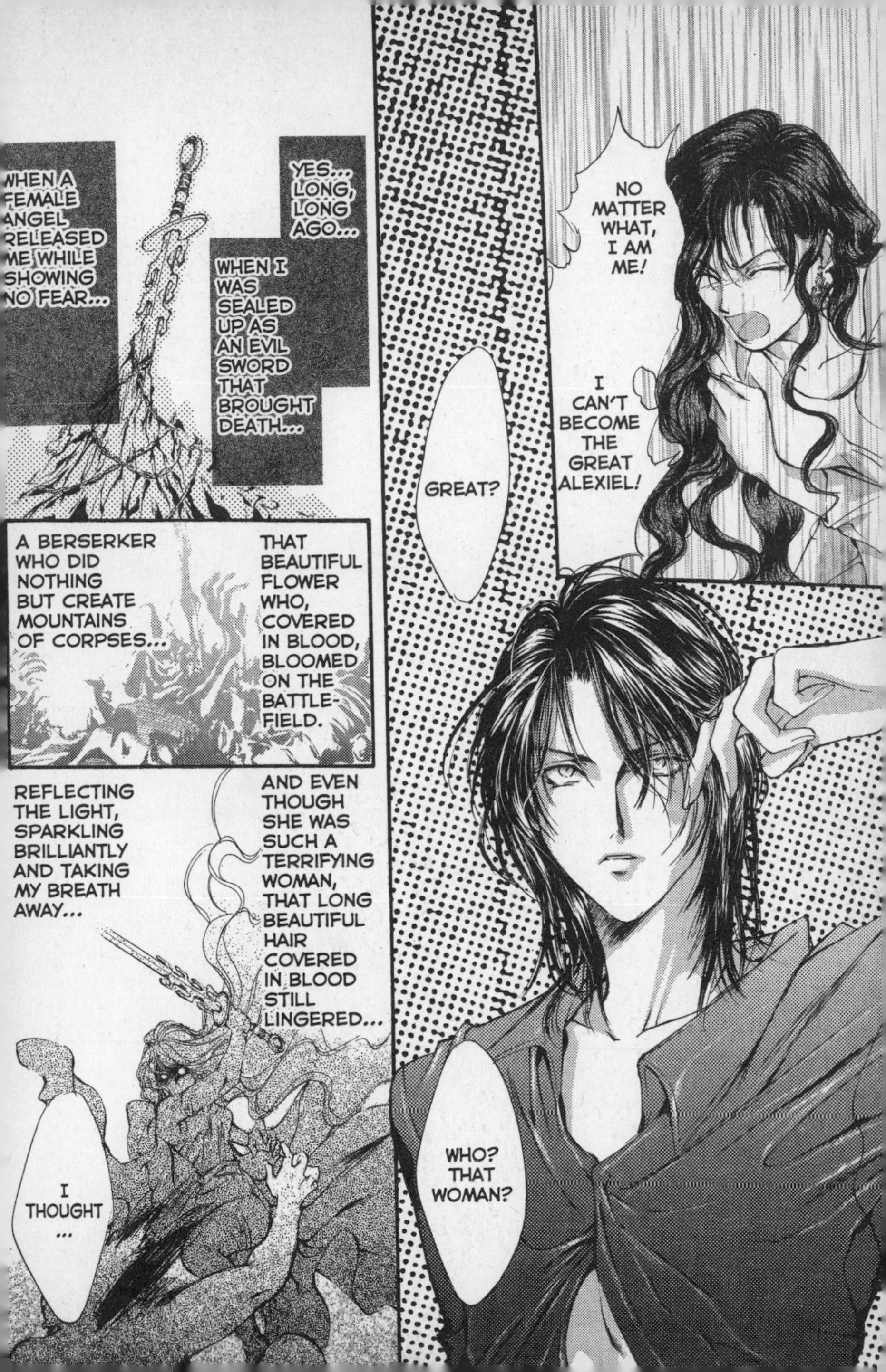
NO MATTER WHAT, I AM ME!
I CAN'T BECOME THE GREAT ALEXIEL!
GREAT?
WHO? THAT WOMAN?
YES... LONG, LONG AGO...
WHEN I WAS SEALED UP AS AN EVIL SWORD THAT BROUGHT DEATH...
WHEN A FEMALE ANGEL RELEASED ME WHILE SHOWING NO FEAR...
THAT BEAUTIFUL FLOWER WHO, COVERED IN BLOOD, BLOOMED ON THE BATTLE-FIELD.
A BERSERKER WHO DID NOTHING BUT CREATE MOUNTAINS OF CORPSES...
AND EVEN THOUGH SHE WAS SUCH A TERRIFYING WOMAN, THAT LONG BEAUTIFUL HAIR COVERED IN BLOOD STILL LINGERED...
REFLECTING THE LIGHT, SPARKLING BRILLIANTLY AND TAKING MY BREATH AWAY...
I THOUGHT ...

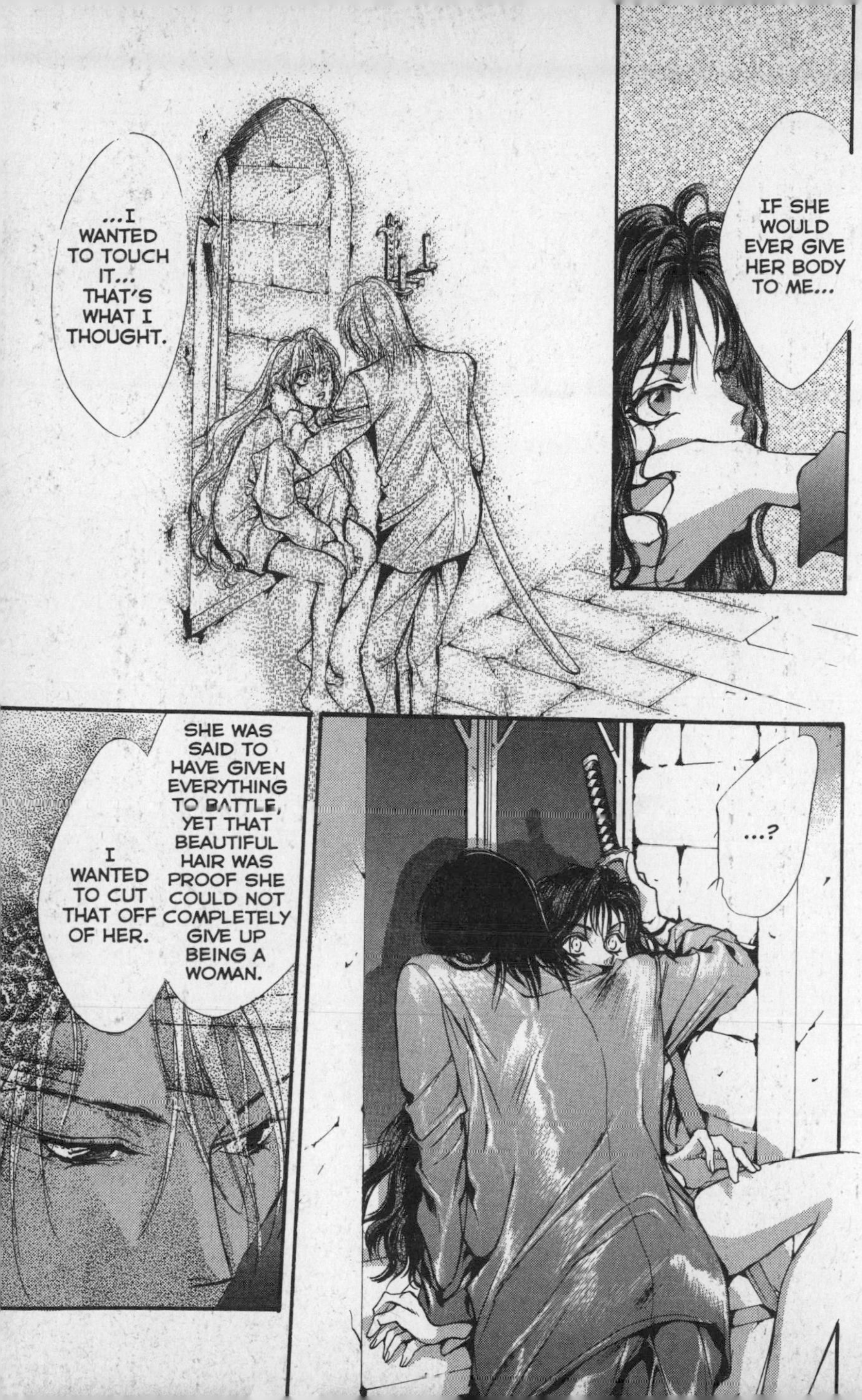
IF SHE WOULD EVER GIVE HER BODY TO ME...
...I WANTED TO TOUCH IT... THAT'S WHAT I THOUGHT.
...?
SHE WAS SAID TO HAVE GIVEN EVERYTHING TO BATTLE, YET THAT BEAUTIFUL HAIR WAS PROOF SHE COULD NOT COMPLETELY GIVE UP BEING A WOMAN.
I WANTED TO CUT THAT OFF OF HER.

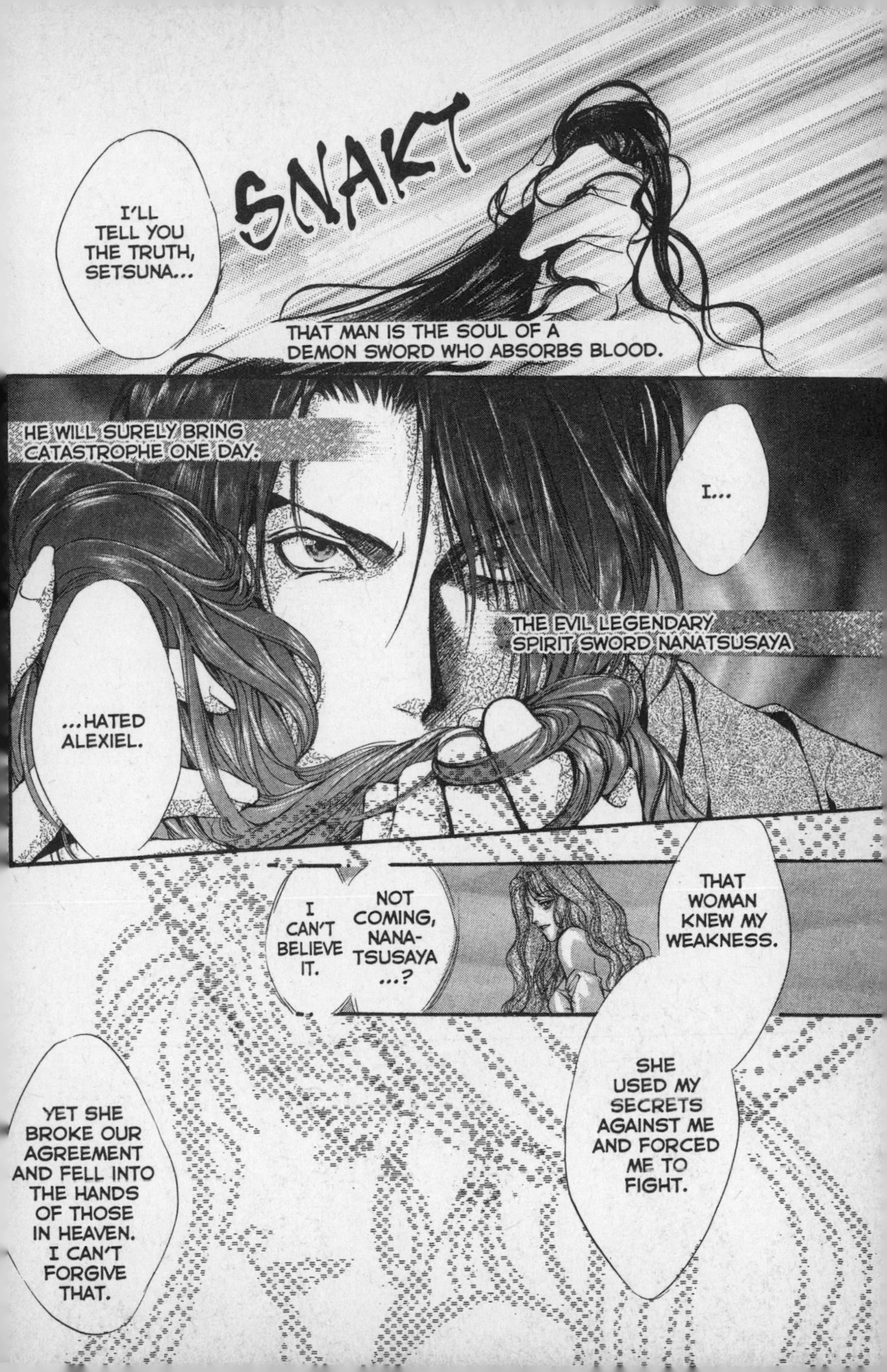
SNAKT
I'LL TELL YOU THE TRUTH, SETSUNA...
THAT MAN IS THE SOUL OF A DEMON SWORD WHO ABSORBS BLOOD.
I...
HE WILL SURELY BRING CATASTROPHE ONE DAY.
THE EVIL LEGENDARY SPIRIT SWORD NANATSUSAYA
...HATED ALEXIEL.
THAT WOMAN KNEW MY WEAKNESS.
NOT COMING, NANA-TSUSAYA ...?
I CAN'T BELIEVE IT.
SHE USED MY SECRETS AGAINST ME AND FORCED ME TO FIGHT.
YET SHE BROKE OUR AGREEMENT AND FELL INTO THE HANDS OF THOSE IN HEAVEN. I CAN'T FORGIVE THAT.

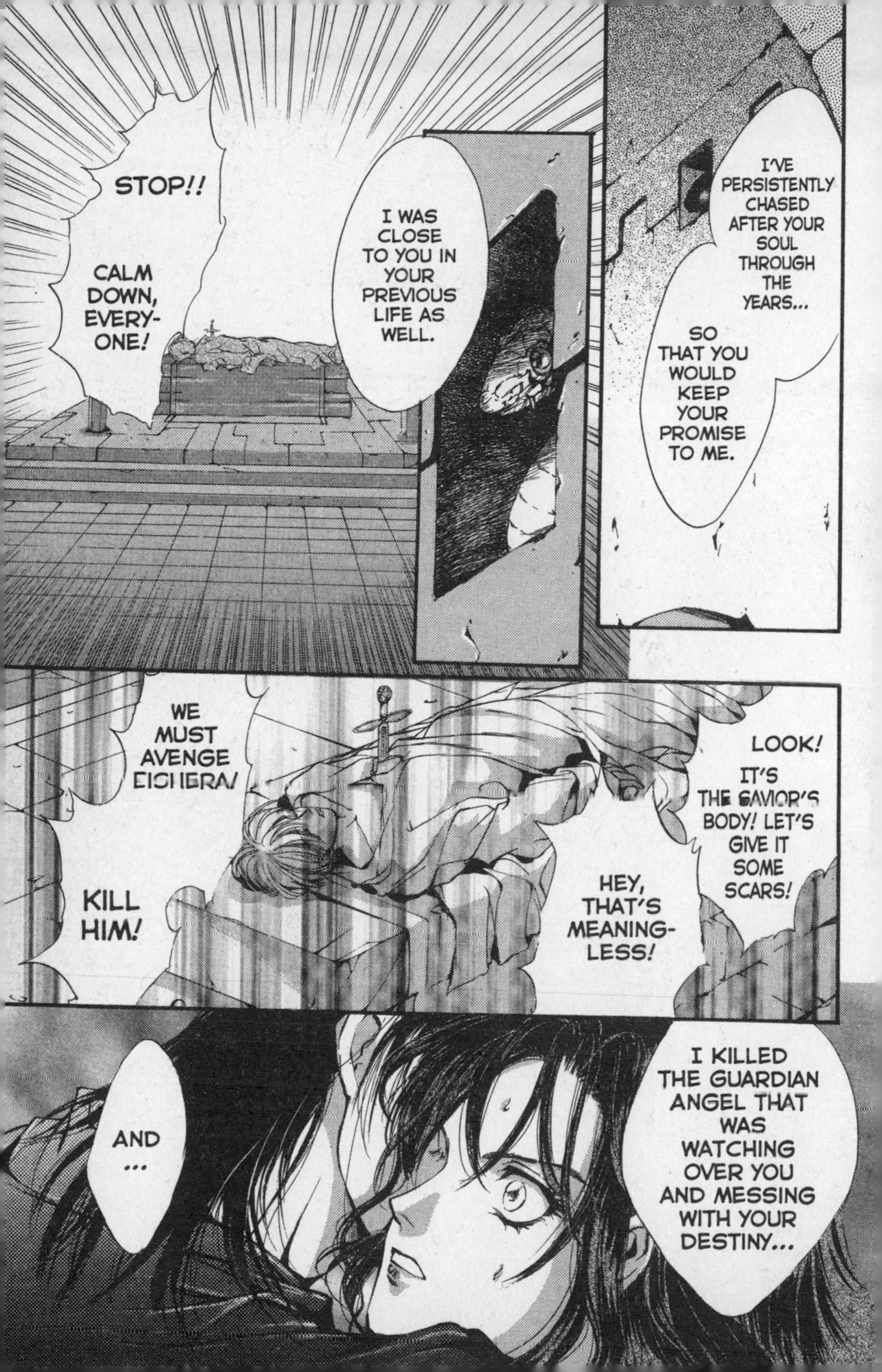
I'VE PERSISTENTLY CHASED AFTER YOUR SOUL THROUGH THE YEARS...
SO THAT YOU WOULD KEEP YOUR PROMISE TO ME.
I WAS CLOSE TO YOU IN YOUR PREVIOUS LIFE AS WELL.
STOP!!
CALM DOWN, EVERY-ONE!
LOOK!
IT'S THE SAVIOR'S BODY! LET'S GIVE IT SOME SCARS!
HEY, THAT'S MEANING-LESS!
WE MUST AVENGE EISHERA!
KILL HIM!
I KILLED THE GUARDIAN ANGEL THAT WAS WATCHING OVER YOU AND MESSING WITH YOUR DESTINY...
AND ...

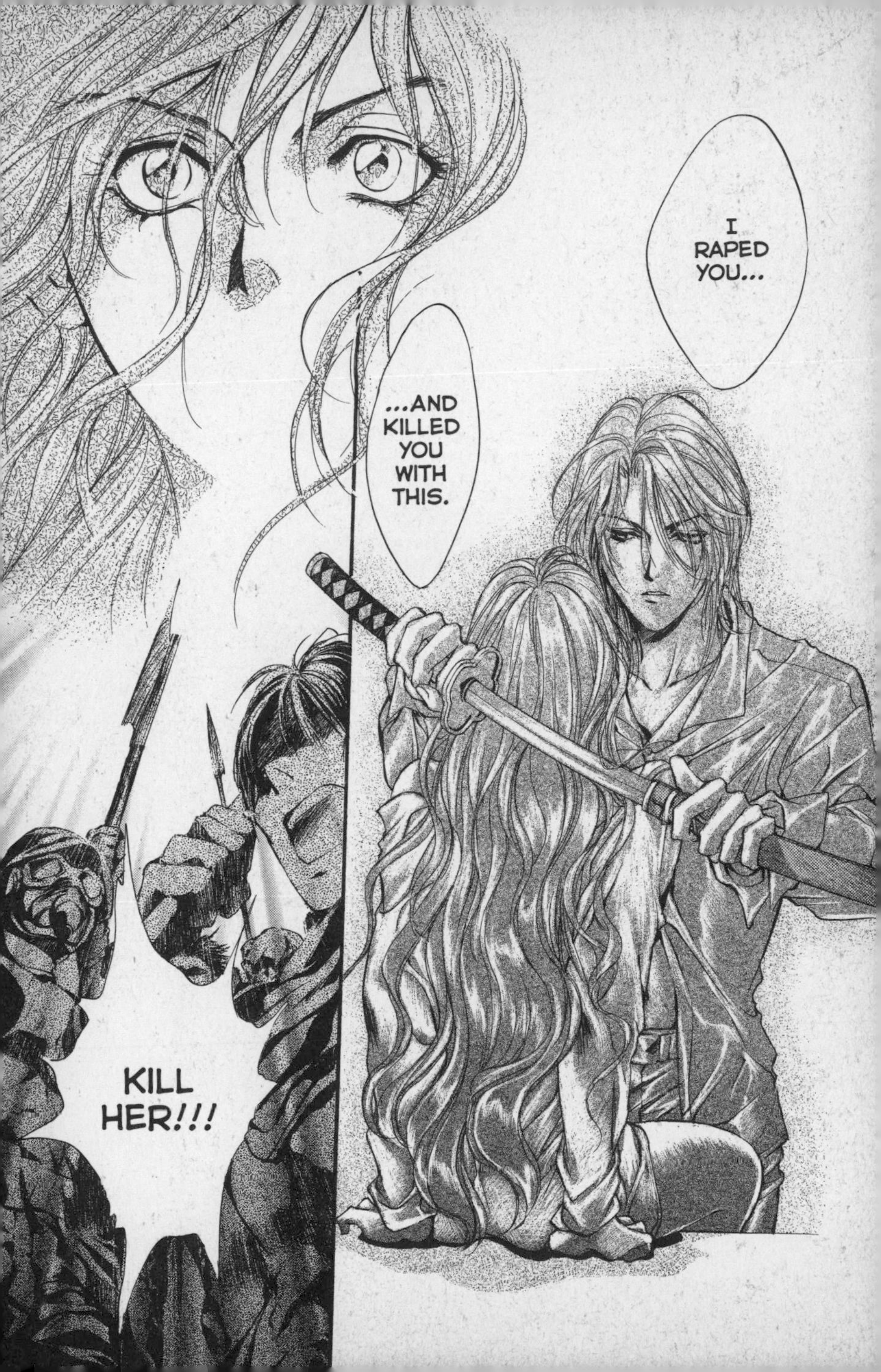
I RAPED YOU...
...AND KILLED YOU WITH THIS.
KILL HER!!!

YES, I DO COMMEND YOU FOR BRILLIANTLY SEEING THROUGH MY LIES AND NOT FALLING FOR MY TRICKERY. ***HOWEVER,*** THE DECEPTION AUTHORIZED AGAINST ME FROM THE HEAVENS NEITHER HARMS NOR BOTHERS ME AT ALL. BECAUSE...

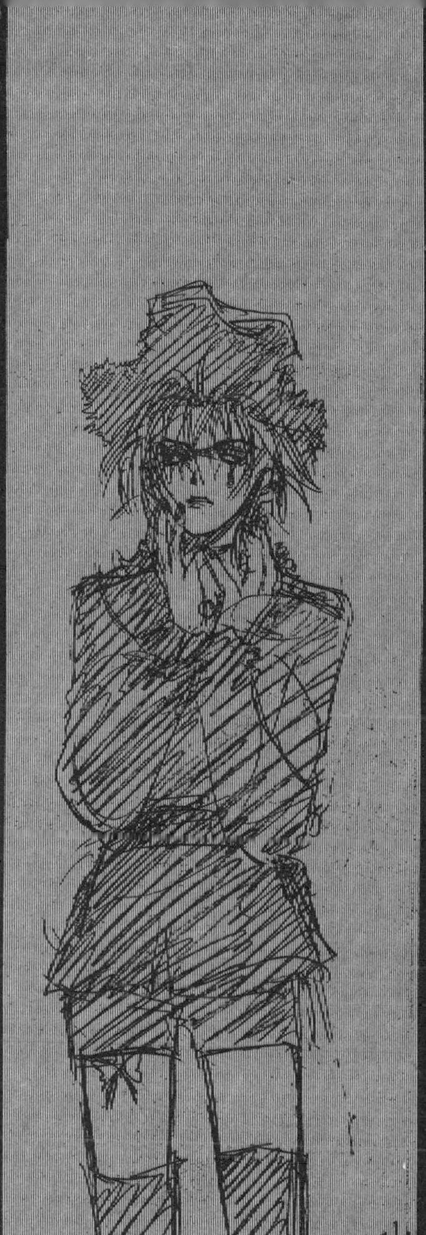
Belial

...MY ALMIGHTY LEADER HAS ACKNOWLEDGED THAT EVEN WITHIN THOSE ANGELS WHO HAVE FALLEN INTO A LIVING HELL FOR LOVING IMMORALITY, THERE IS NO ONE AS INSOLENT AND BAWDY AS I. YES, HE KNEW FROM THE BEGINNING, YET ACTED AS IF HE DID NOT. WHY ELSE WOULD HE HAVE CALLED ME ***BELIAL THE TRAITOR*** FROM THE MOMENT I WAS BORN?

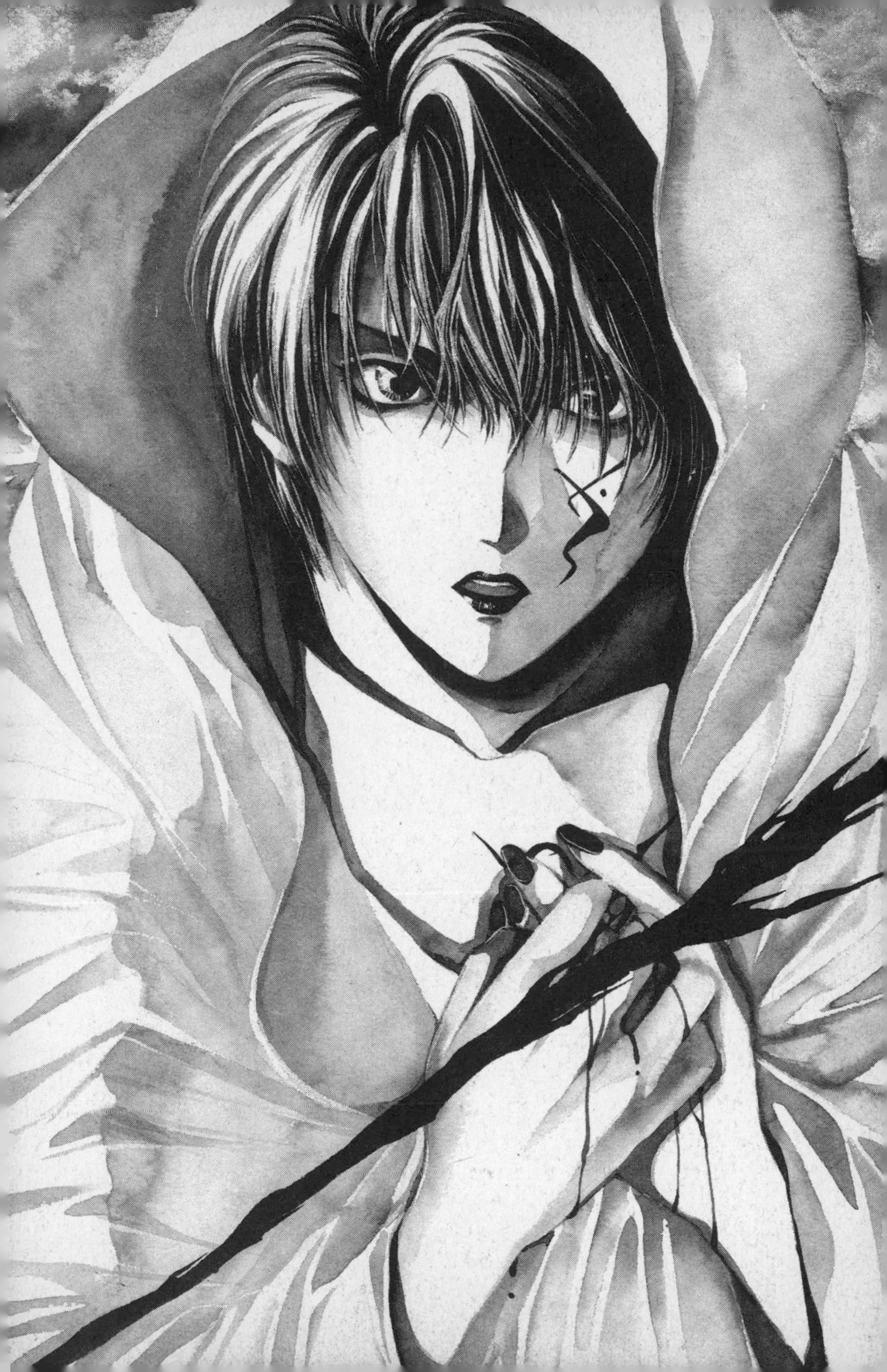

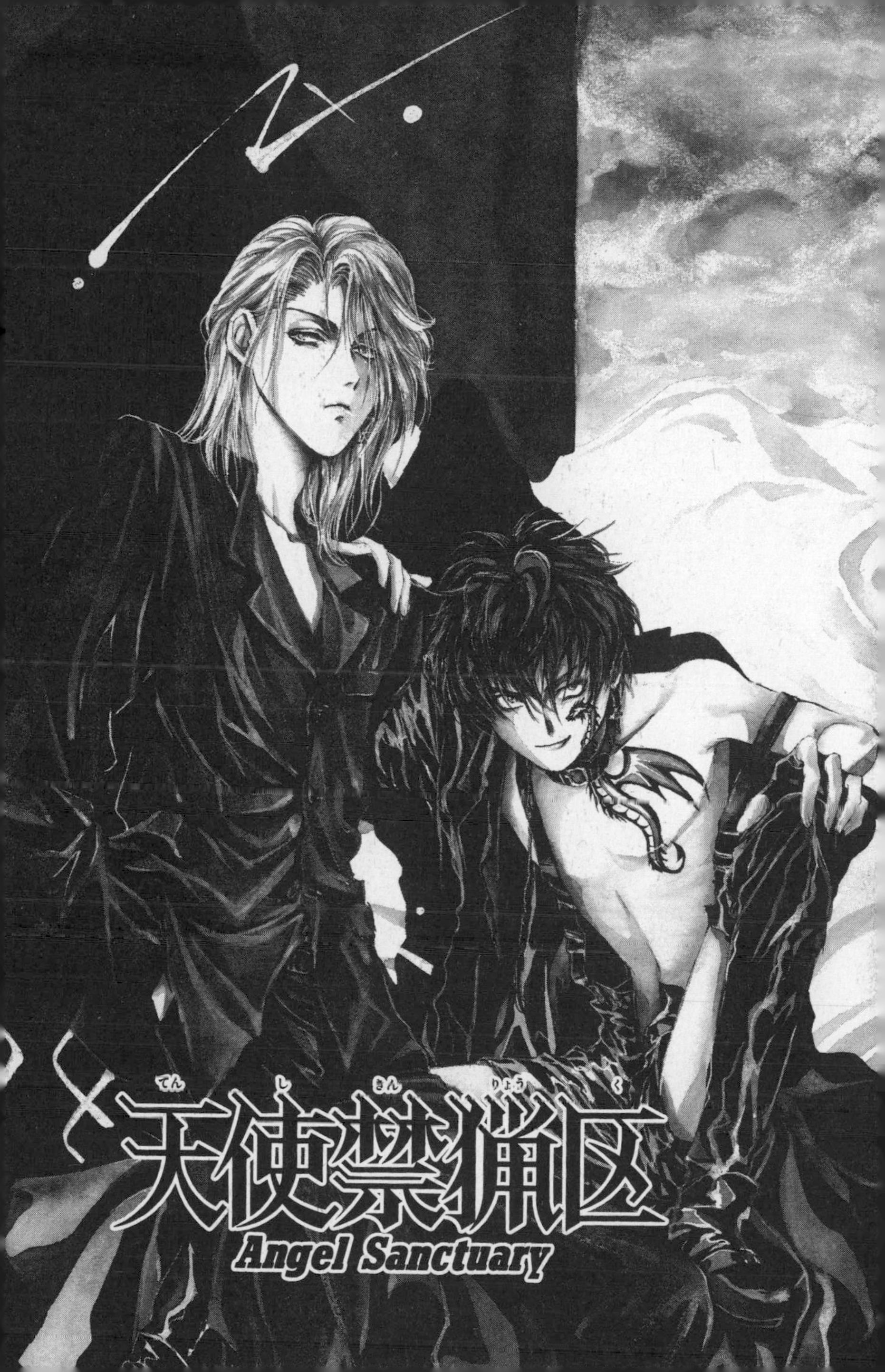
天使禁猟区
Angel Sanctuary

A  S

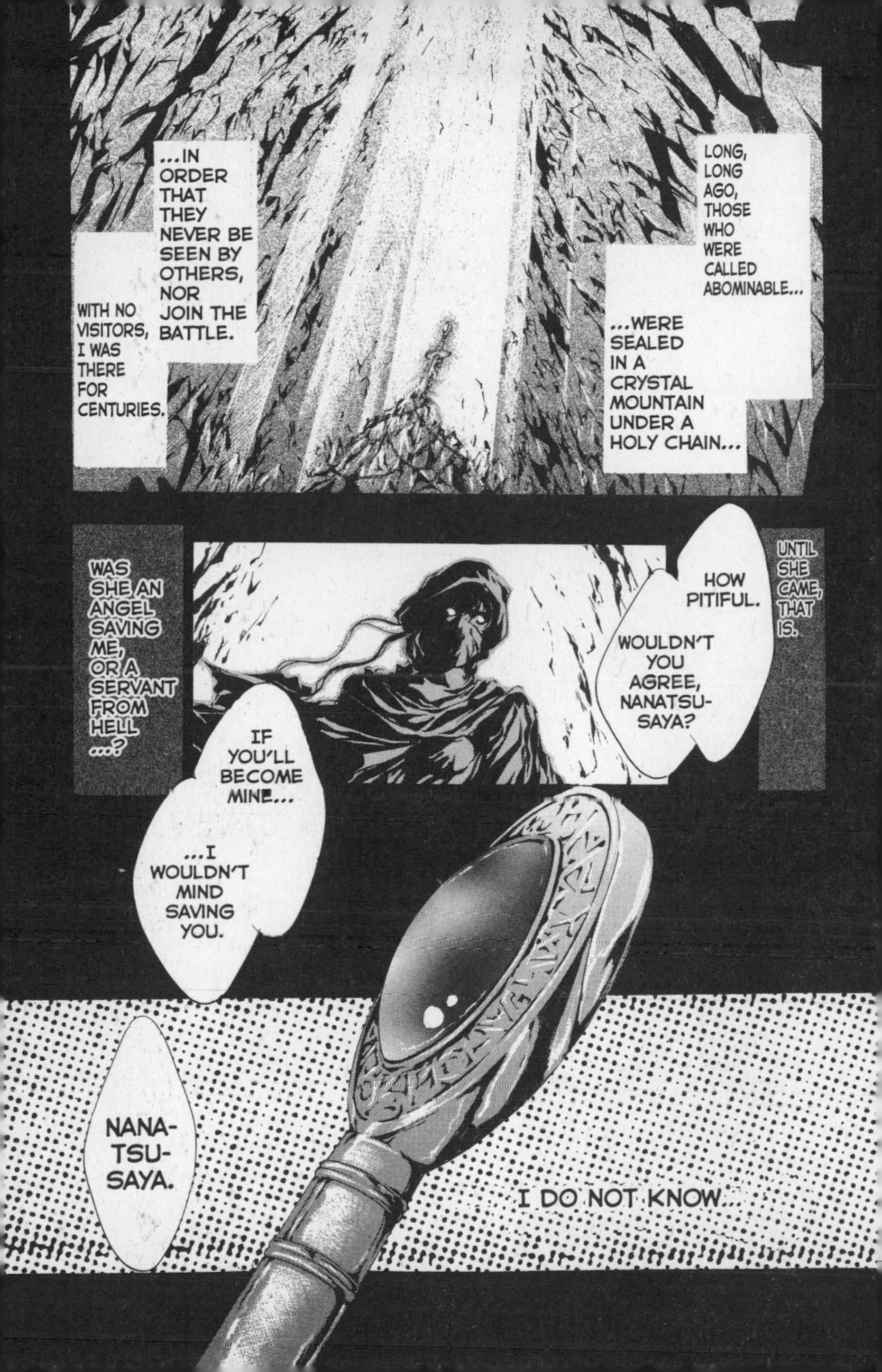
LONG, LONG AGO, THOSE WHO WERE CALLED ABOMINABLE...
...WERE SEALED IN A CRYSTAL MOUNTAIN UNDER A HOLY CHAIN...
...IN ORDER THAT THEY NEVER BE SEEN BY OTHERS, NOR JOIN THE BATTLE.
WITH NO VISITORS, I WAS THERE FOR CENTURIES.
UNTIL SHE CAME, THAT IS.
HOW PITIFUL.
WOULDN'T YOU AGREE, NANATSU-SAYA?
IF YOU'LL BECOME MINE...
...I WOULDN'T MIND SAVING YOU.
WAS SHE AN ANGEL SAVING ME, OR A SERVANT FROM HELL...?
I DO NOT KNOW...
NANA-TSU-SAYA.

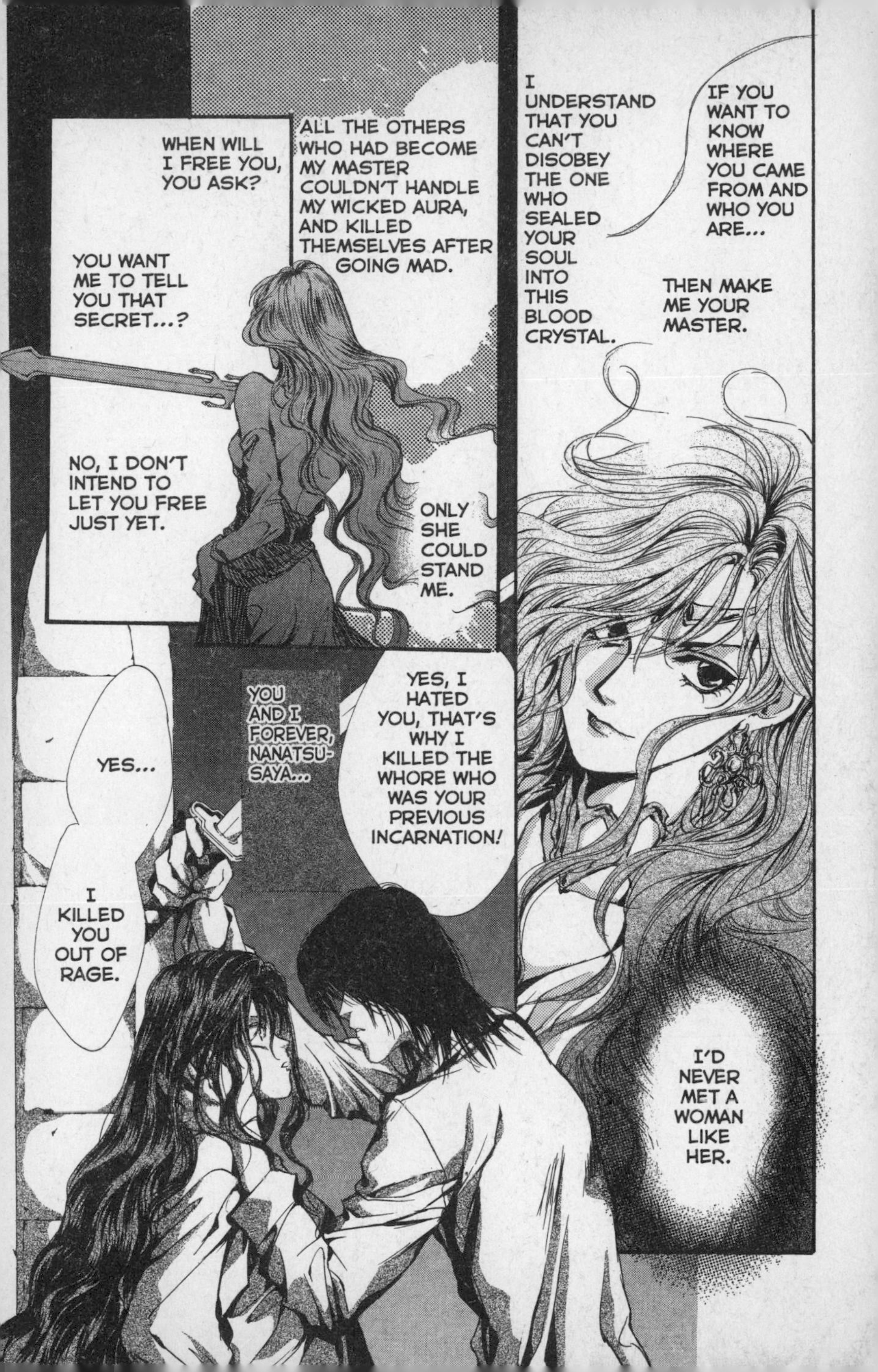
IF YOU WANT TO KNOW WHERE YOU CAME FROM AND WHO YOU ARE...
I UNDERSTAND THAT YOU CAN'T DISOBEY THE ONE WHO SEALED YOUR SOUL INTO THIS BLOOD CRYSTAL.
THEN MAKE ME YOUR MASTER.
I'D NEVER MET A WOMAN LIKE HER.
ALL THE OTHERS WHO HAD BECOME MY MASTER COULDN'T HANDLE MY WICKED AURA, AND KILLED THEMSELVES AFTER GOING MAD.
WHEN WILL I FREE YOU, YOU ASK?
YOU WANT ME TO TELL YOU THAT SECRET...?
NO, I DON'T INTEND TO LET YOU FREE JUST YET.
ONLY SHE COULD STAND ME.
YES, I HATED YOU, THAT'S WHY I KILLED THE WHORE WHO WAS YOUR PREVIOUS INCARNATION!
YOU AND I FOREVER, NANATSU-SAYA...
YES...
I KILLED YOU OUT OF RAGE.

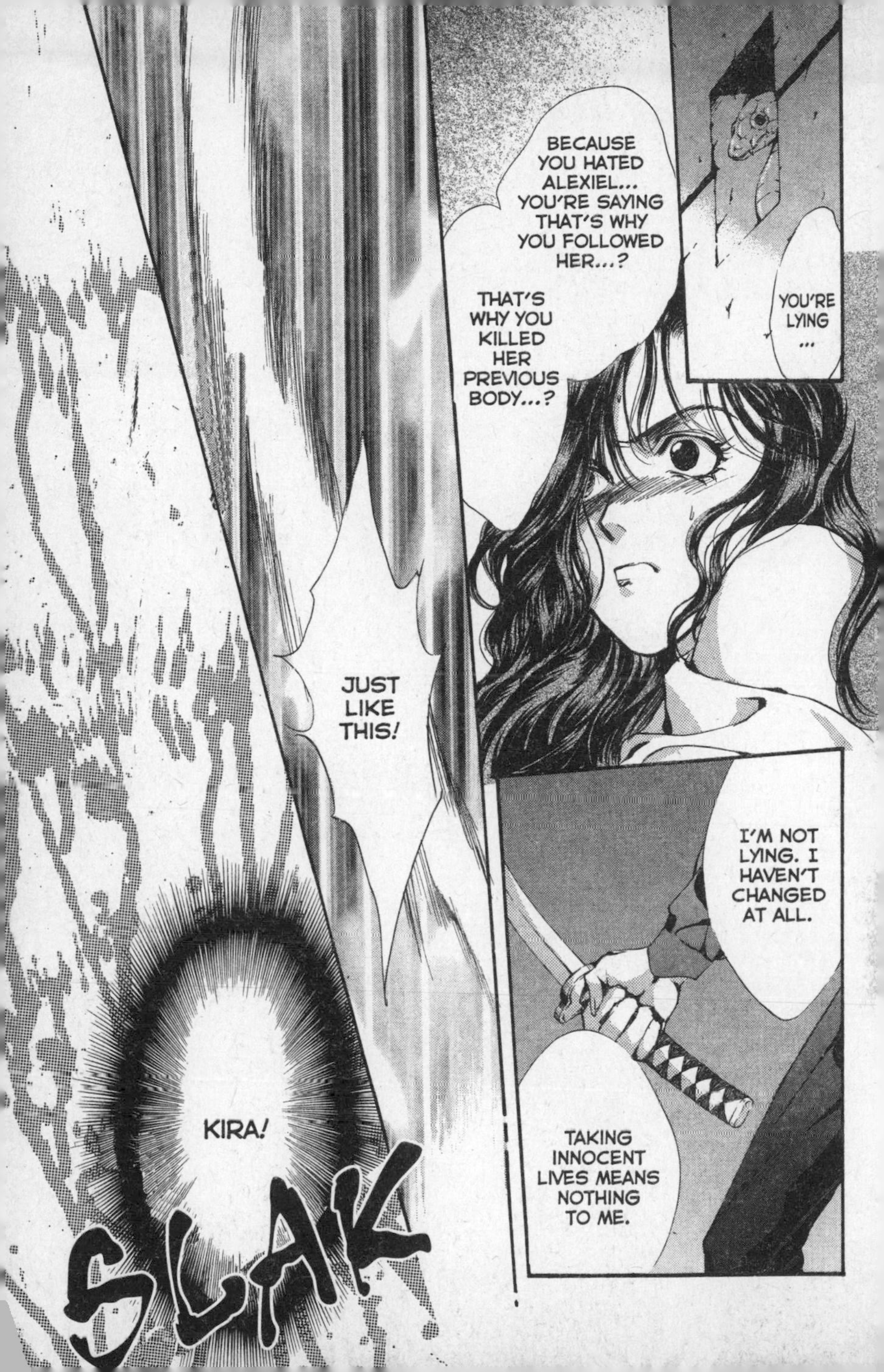
BECAUSE YOU HATED ALEXIEL... YOU'RE SAYING THAT'S WHY YOU FOLLOWED HER...?
THAT'S WHY YOU KILLED HER PREVIOUS BODY...?
YOU'RE LYING ...
I'M NOT LYING. I HAVEN'T CHANGED AT ALL.
TAKING INNOCENT LIVES MEANS NOTHING TO ME.
JUST LIKE THIS!
KIRA!
SLAK

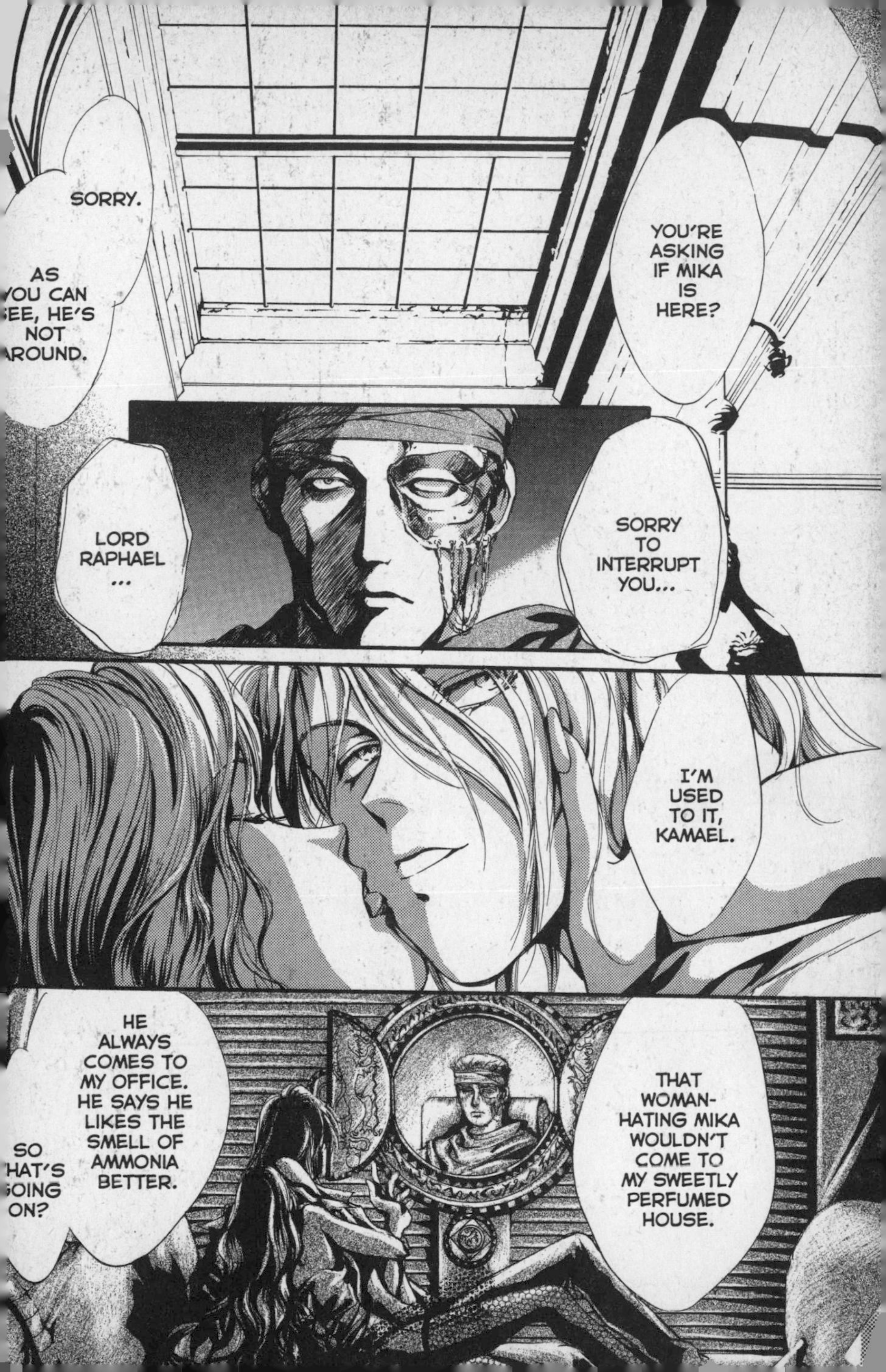
YOU'RE ASKING IF MIKA IS HERE?
SORRY.
AS YOU CAN SEE, HE'S NOT AROUND.
SORRY TO INTERRUPT YOU...
LORD RAPHAEL ...
I'M USED TO IT, KAMAEL.
THAT WOMAN-HATING MIKA WOULDN'T COME TO MY SWEETLY PERFUMED HOUSE.
HE ALWAYS COMES TO MY OFFICE. HE SAYS HE LIKES THE SMELL OF AMMONIA BETTER.
SO THAT'S GOING ON?

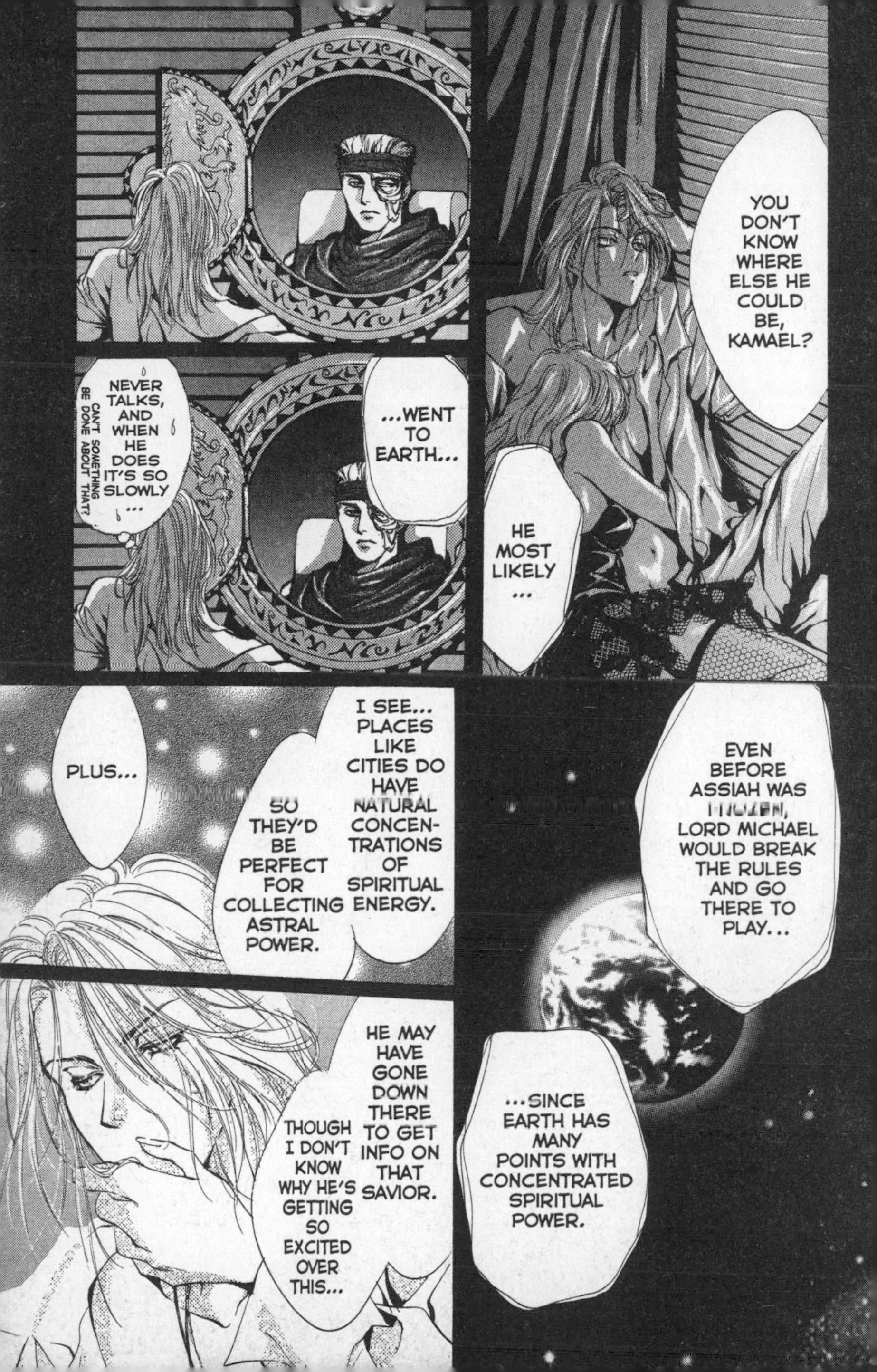
YOU DON'T KNOW WHERE ELSE HE COULD BE, KAMAEL?
HE MOST LIKELY...
...WENT TO EARTH...
NEVER TALKS, AND WHEN HE DOES IT'S SO SLOWLY...
CAN'T SOMETHING BE DONE ABOUT THAT?
EVEN BEFORE ASSIAH WAS , LORD MICHAEL WOULD BREAK THE RULES AND GO THERE TO PLAY...
...SINCE EARTH HAS MANY POINTS WITH CONCENTRATED SPIRITUAL POWER.
I SEE... PLACES LIKE CITIES DO HAVE NATURAL CONCENTRATIONS OF SPIRITUAL ENERGY.
SO THEY'D BE PERFECT FOR COLLECTING ASTRAL POWER.
PLUS...
HE MAY HAVE GONE DOWN THERE TO GET INFO ON THAT SAVIOR.
THOUGH I DON'T KNOW WHY HE'S GETTING SO EXCITED OVER THIS...

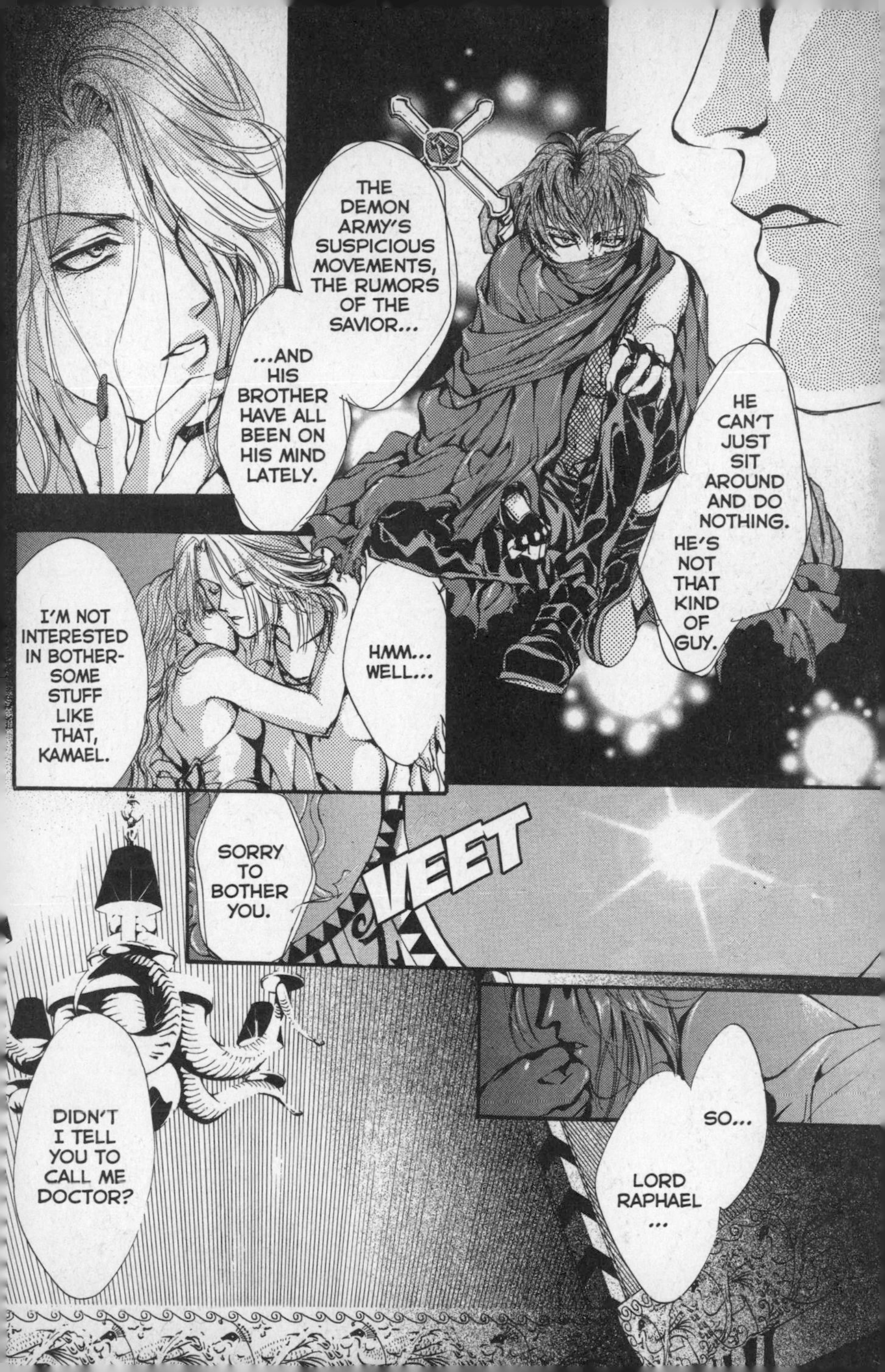
THE DEMON ARMY'S SUSPICIOUS MOVEMENTS, THE RUMORS OF THE SAVIOR...
...AND HIS BROTHER HAVE ALL BEEN ON HIS MIND LATELY.
HE CAN'T JUST SIT AROUND AND DO NOTHING. HE'S NOT THAT KIND OF GUY.
HMM... WELL...
I'M NOT INTERESTED IN BOTHER-SOME STUFF LIKE THAT, KAMAEL.
VEEET
SORRY TO BOTHER YOU.
SO...
LORD RAPHAEL ...
DIDN'T I TELL YOU TO CALL ME DOCTOR?

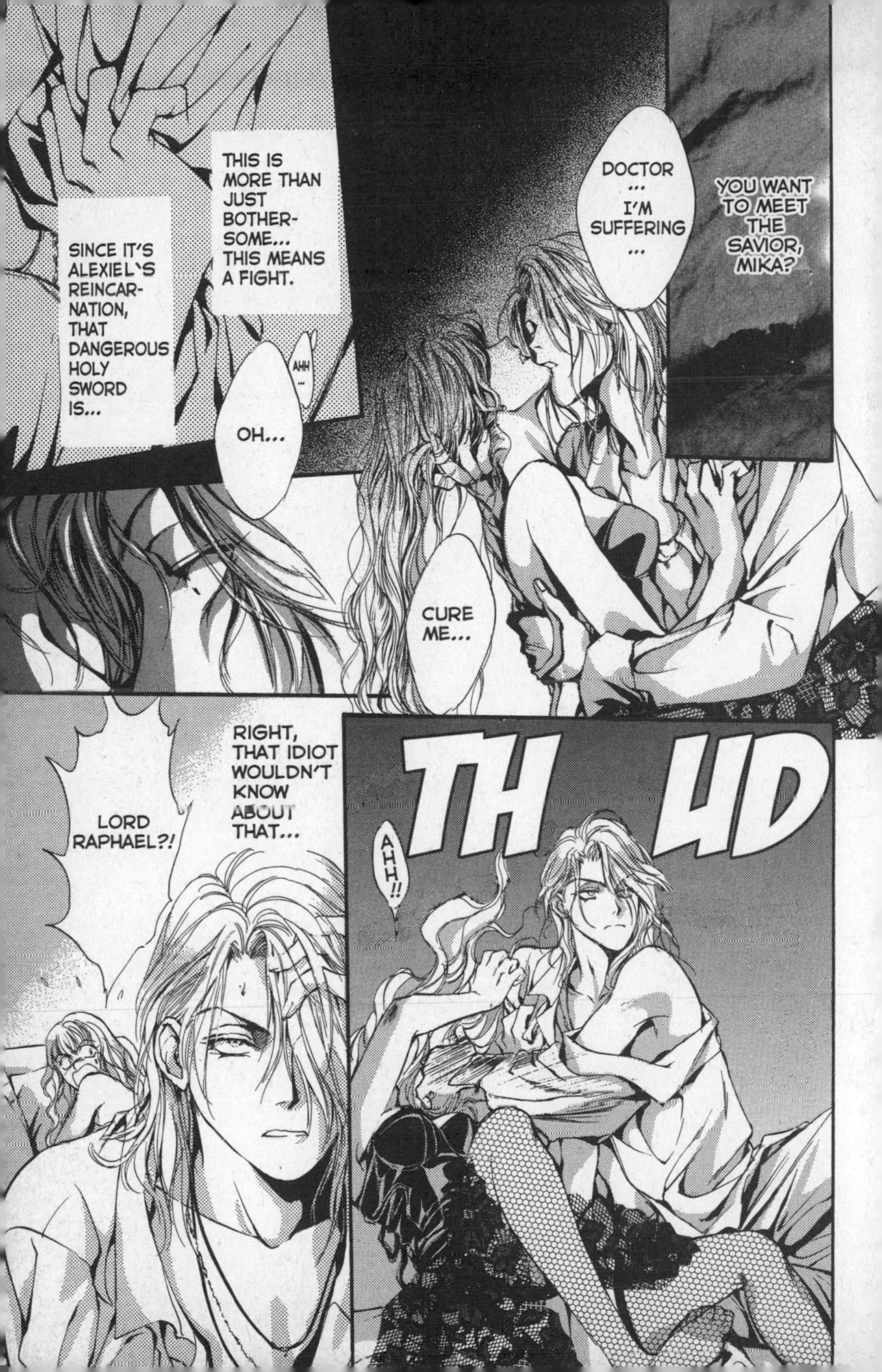
YOU WANT TO MEET THE SAVIOR, MIKA?
DOCTOR ... I'M SUFFERING ...
THIS IS MORE THAN JUST BOTHER-SOME... THIS MEANS A FIGHT.
SINCE IT'S ALEXIEL'S REINCAR-NATION, THAT DANGEROUS HOLY SWORD IS...
AHH ...
OH...
CURE ME...
THUD
AHH!!
RIGHT, THAT IDIOT WOULDN'T KNOW ABOUT THAT...
LORD RAPHAEL?!

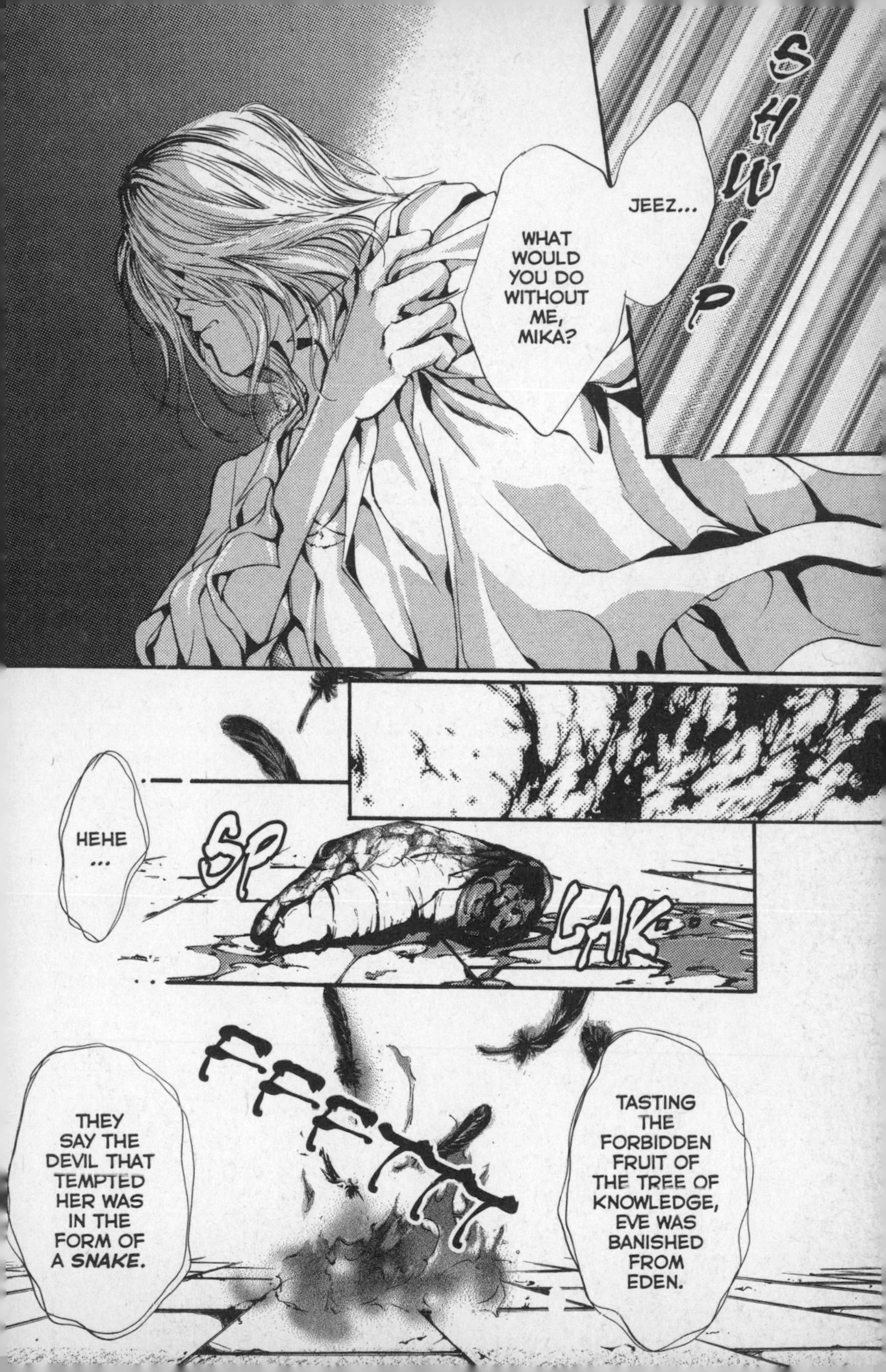
SHWIP
JEEZ...
WHAT WOULD YOU DO WITHOUT ME, MIKA?
SPLAK
HEHE...
TASTING THE FORBIDDEN FRUIT OF THE TREE OF KNOWLEDGE, EVE WAS BANISHED FROM EDEN.
FFFT
THEY SAY THE DEVIL THAT TEMPTED HER WAS IN THE FORM OF A *SNAKE*.

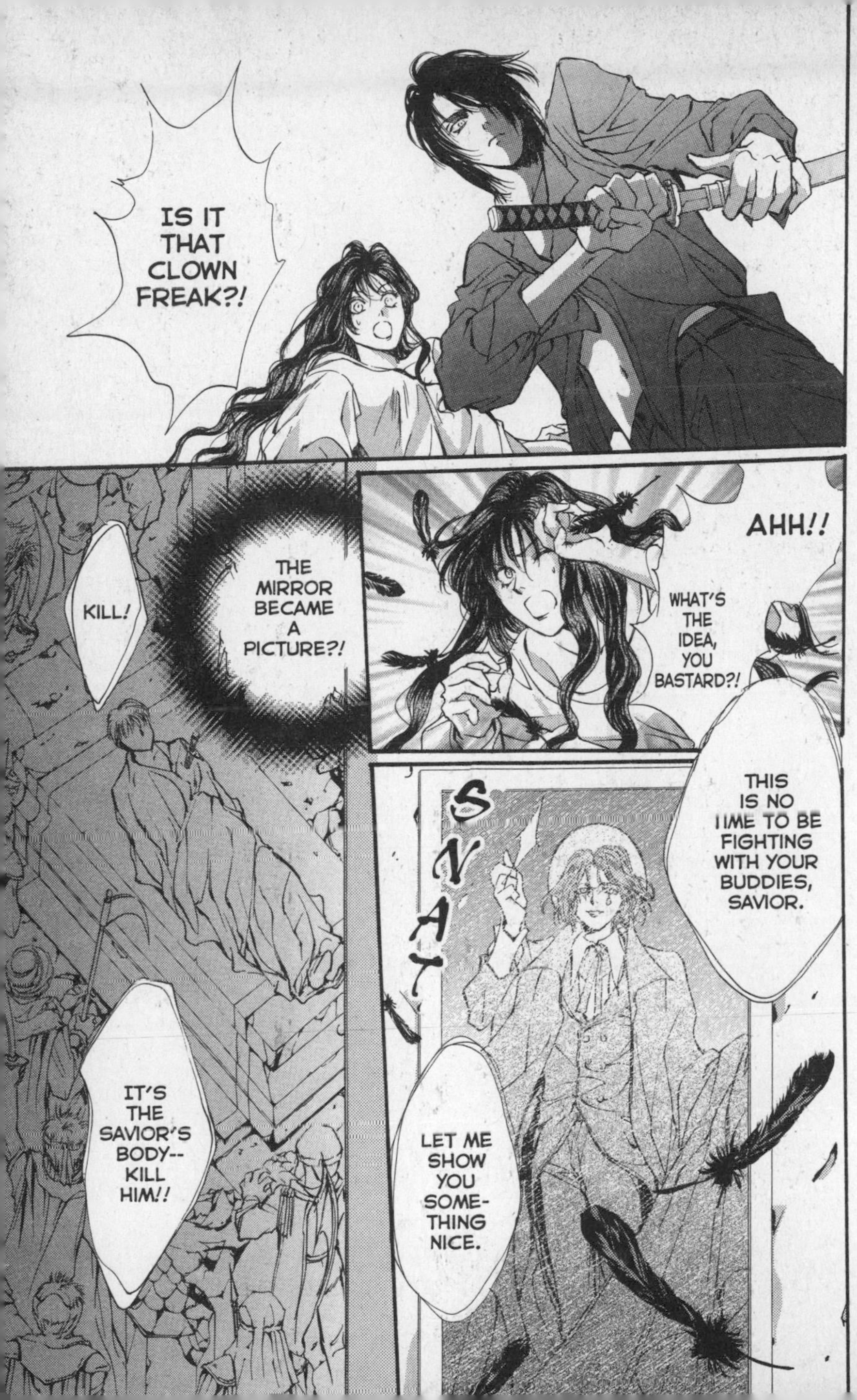
IS IT THAT CLOWN FREAK?!
AHH!!
WHAT'S THE IDEA, YOU BASTARD?!
SNAT
THIS IS NO TIME TO BE FIGHTING WITH YOUR BUDDIES, SAVIOR.
LET ME SHOW YOU SOME-THING NICE.
THE MIRROR BECAME A PICTURE?!
KILL!
IT'S THE SAVIOR'S BODY--KILL HIM!!

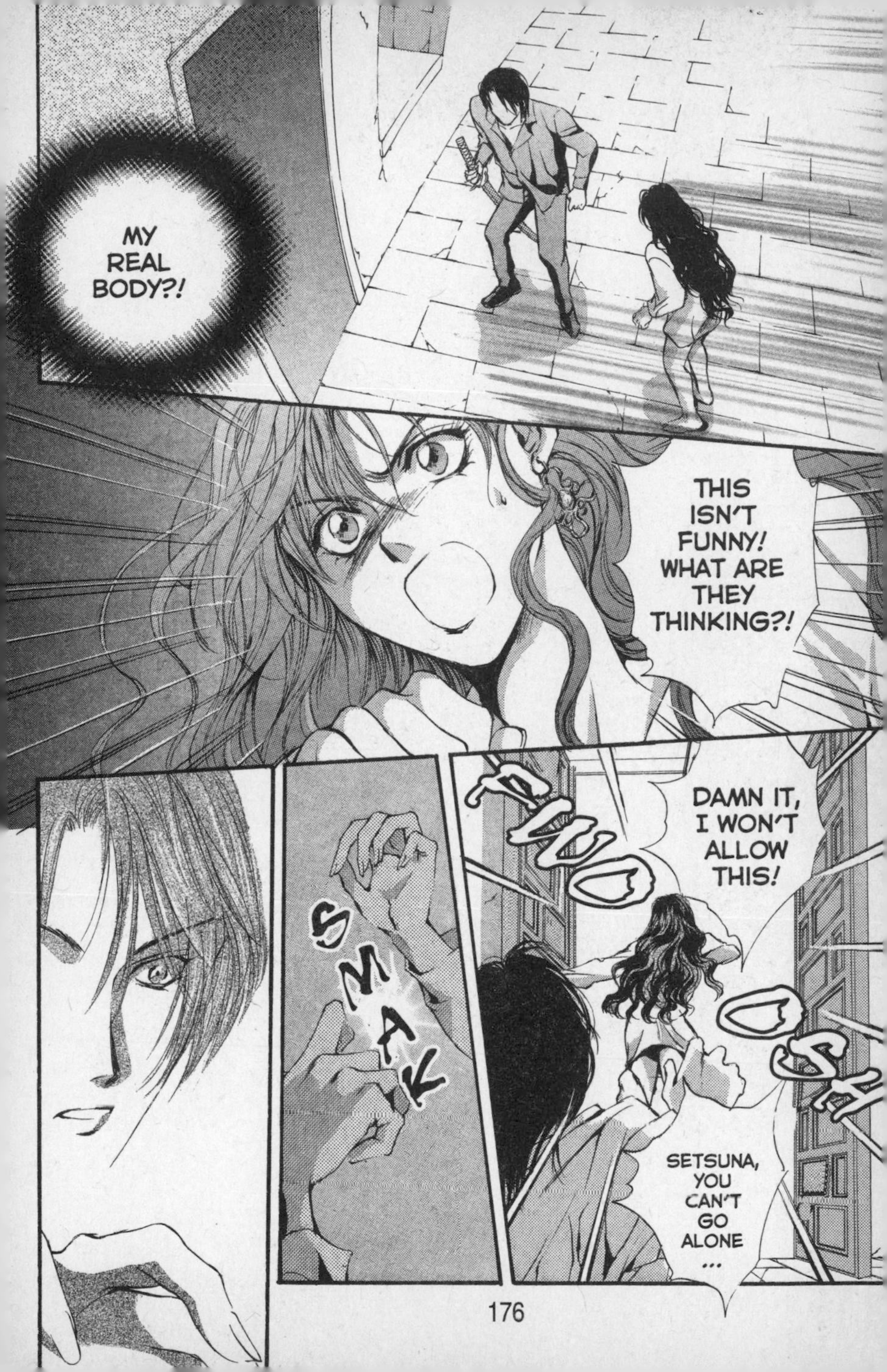
MY REAL BODY?!
THIS ISN'T FUNNY! WHAT ARE THEY THINKING?!
FWOOSH
DAMN IT, I WON'T ALLOW THIS!
SETSUNA, YOU CAN'T GO ALONE ...
SMAK

I drew Kamael to be a "Terminator-like silent character" but he did talk a bit in this chapter. His name kind of sounds funny (sorry) but he's actually supposed to be a big time angel. Well, who knows if he actually exists or not? We might have to wait till we die. I didn't plan for Noyz and Boyz to appear this much. You can totally tell that I never put that much work into creating them... And the whole idea around these worlds is really confusing, and I get letters saying "I don't get it..." And yet...these people are still fans, right? I don't get that.

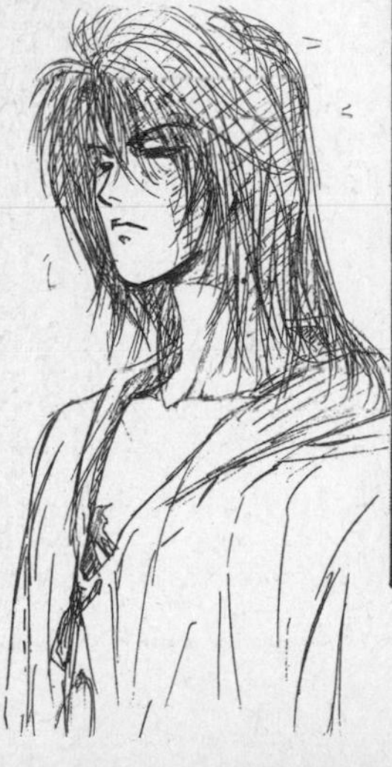

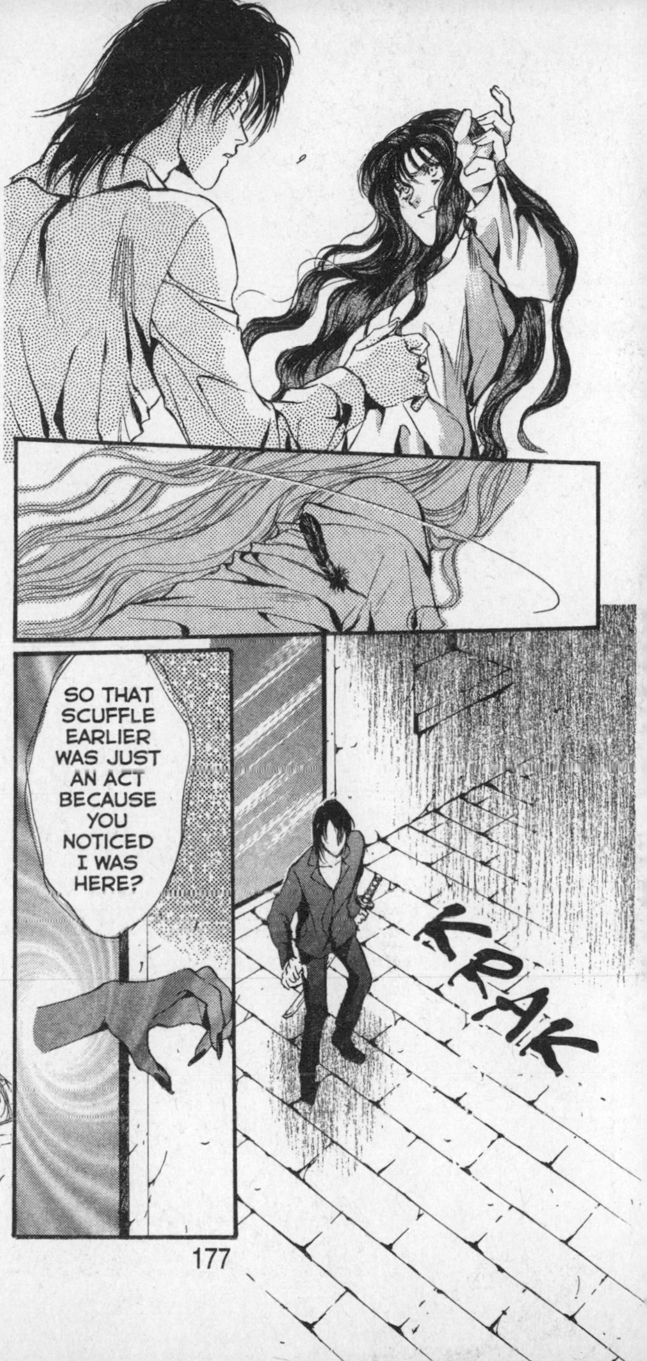
KRAK
SO THAT SCUFFLE EARLIER WAS JUST AN ACT BECAUSE YOU NOTICED I WAS HERE?

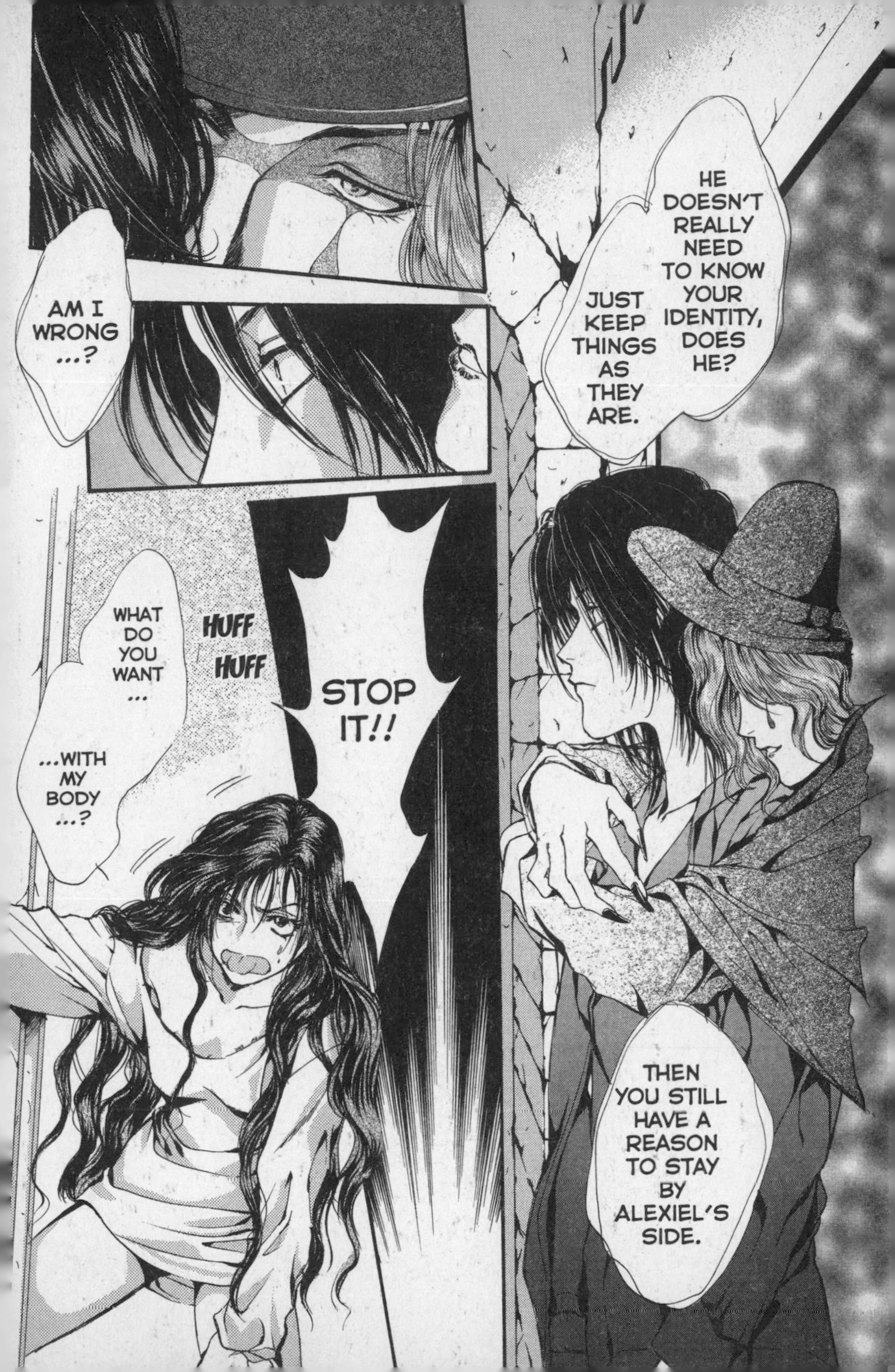
HE DOESN'T REALLY NEED TO KNOW YOUR IDENTITY, DOES HE?
JUST KEEP THINGS AS THEY ARE.
THEN YOU STILL HAVE A REASON TO STAY BY ALEXIEL'S SIDE.
AM I WRONG ...?
STOP IT!!
HUFF
HUFF
WHAT DO YOU WANT ...
...WITH MY BODY ...?

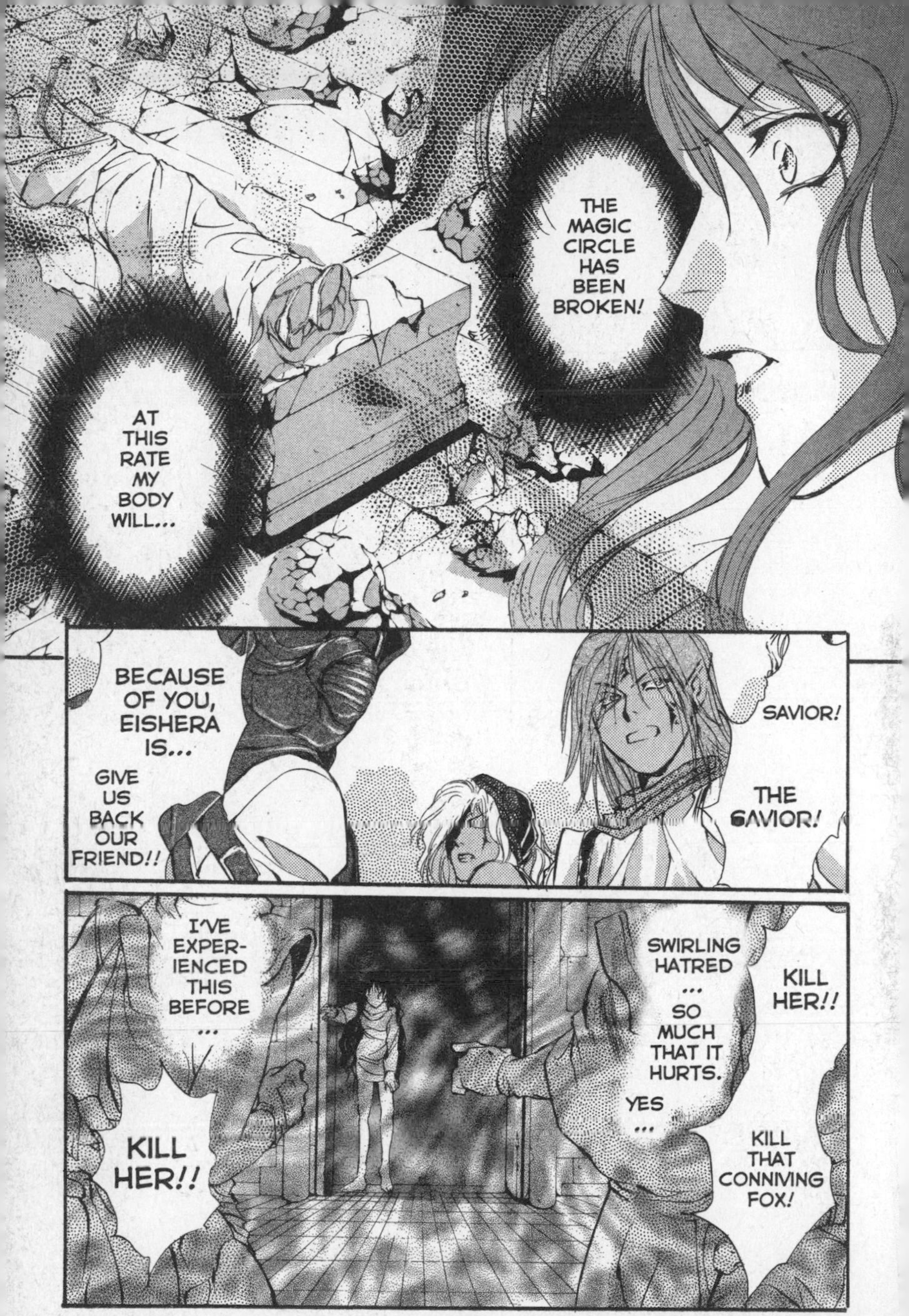
THE MAGIC CIRCLE HAS BEEN BROKEN!
AT THIS RATE MY BODY WILL...
SAVIOR!
THE SAVIOR!
BECAUSE OF YOU, EISHERA IS...
GIVE US BACK OUR FRIEND!!
KILL HER!!
SWIRLING HATRED ... SO MUCH THAT IT HURTS.
YES ...
KILL THAT CONNIVING FOX!
I'VE EXPERIENCED THIS BEFORE ...
KILL HER!!

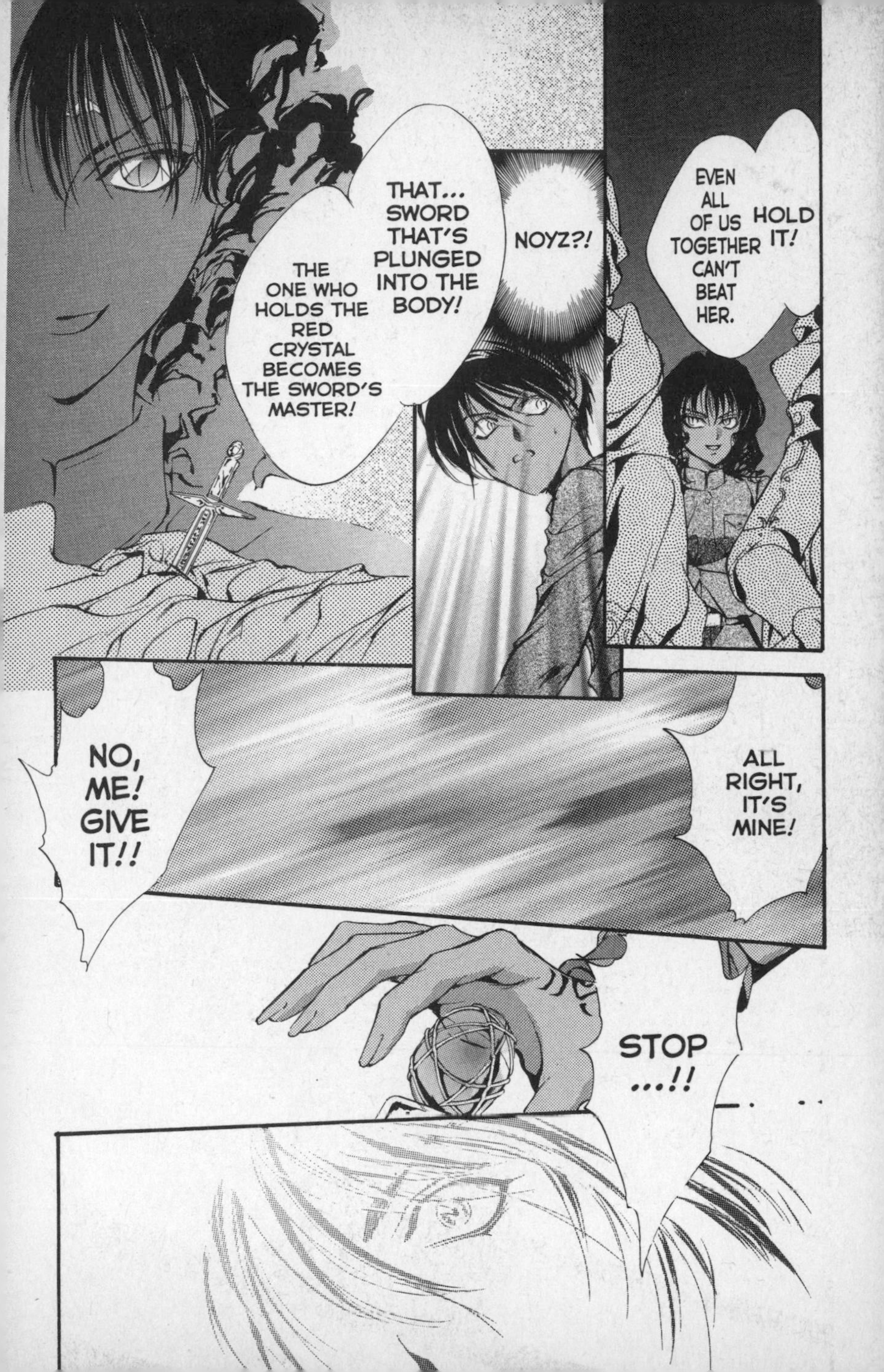
HOLD IT!
EVEN ALL OF US TOGETHER CAN'T BEAT HER.
NOYZ?!
THAT... SWORD THAT'S PLUNGED INTO THE BODY!
THE ONE WHO HOLDS THE RED CRYSTAL BECOMES THE SWORD'S MASTER!
ALL RIGHT, IT'S MINE!
NO, ME! GIVE IT!!
STOP ...!!

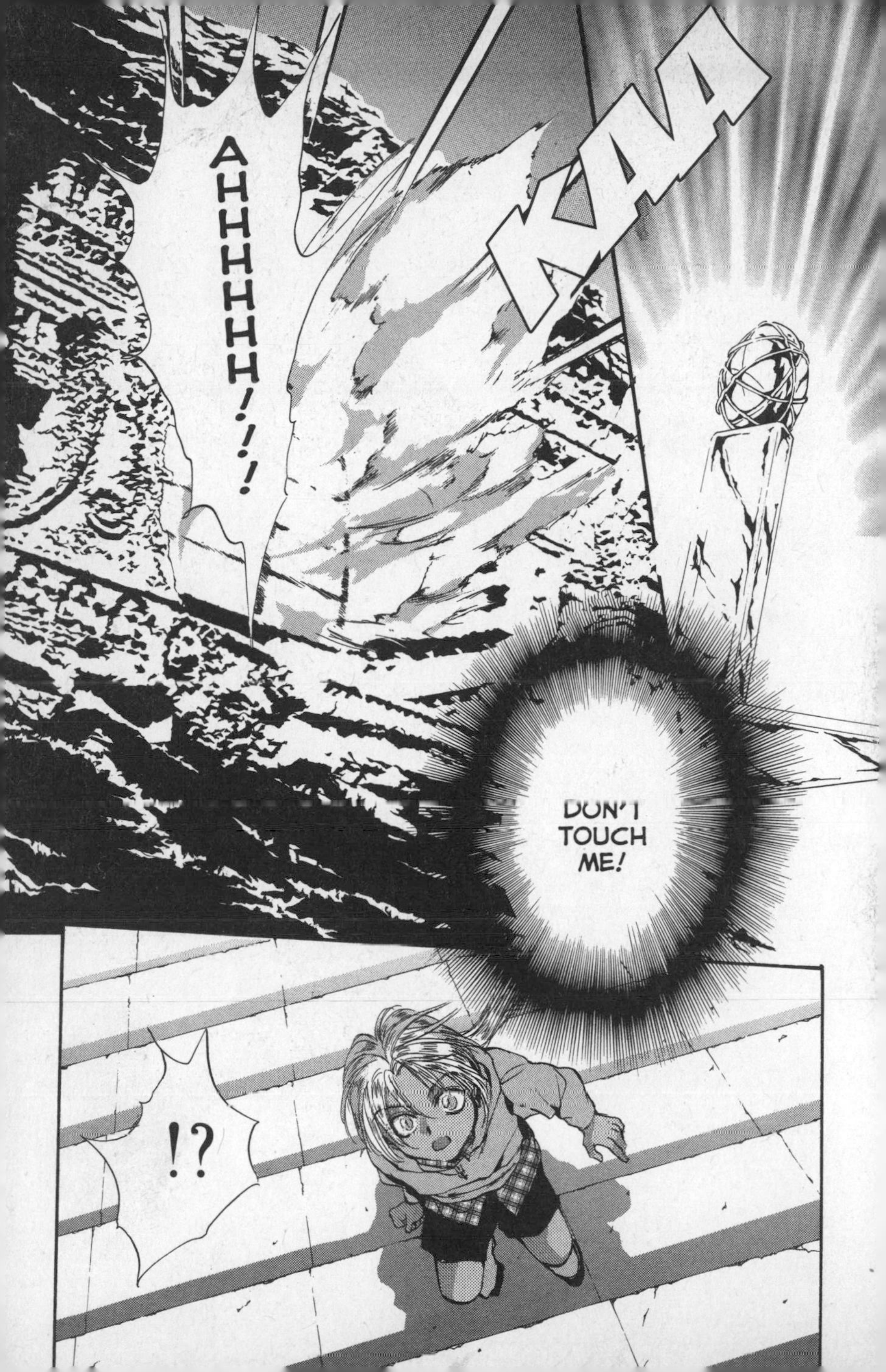
KAA
AHHHHHH!!!
DON'T TOUCH ME!
!?

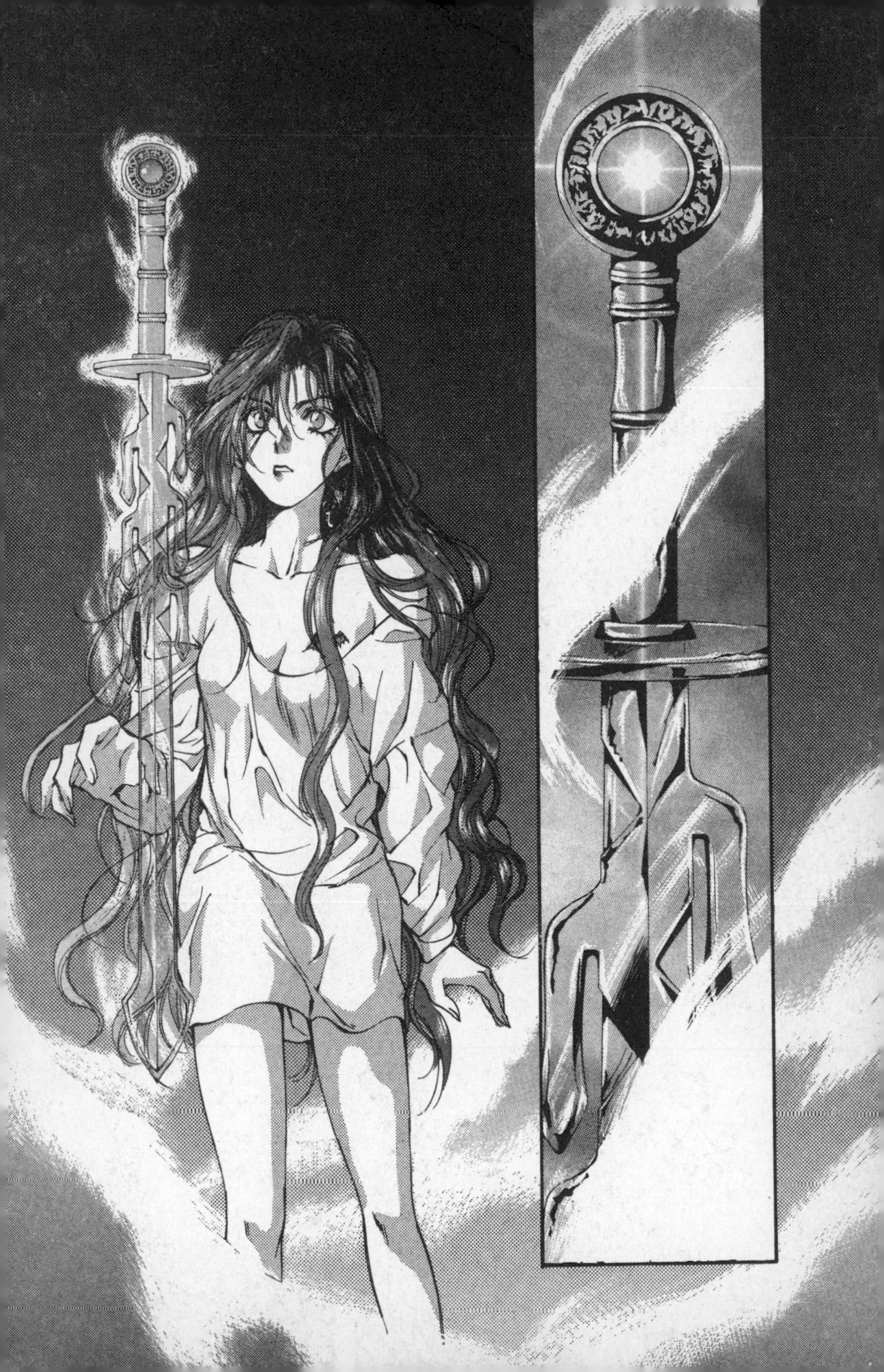

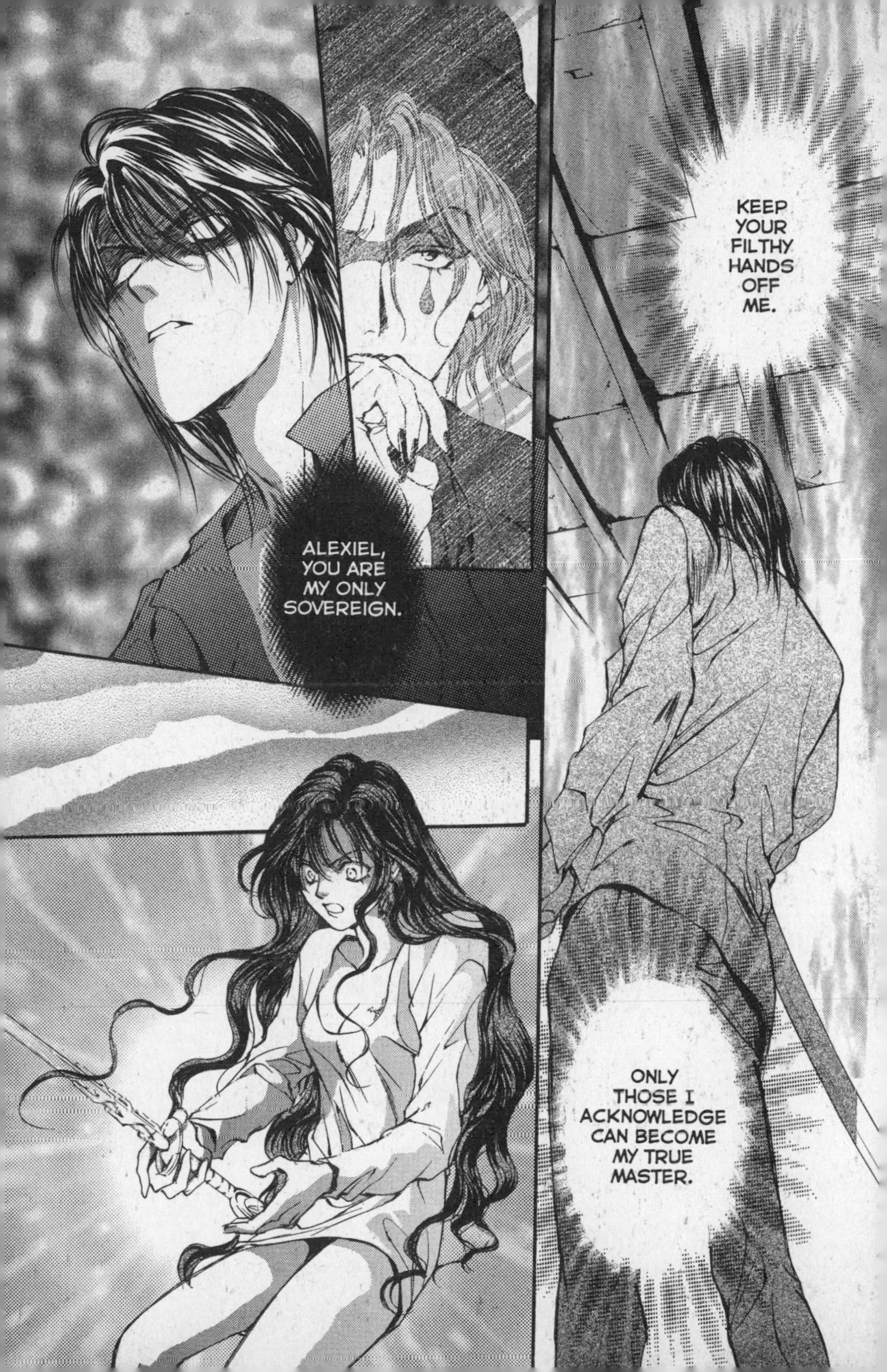
KEEP YOUR FILTHY HANDS OFF ME.
ONLY THOSE I ACKNOWLEDGE CAN BECOME MY TRUE MASTER.
ALEXIEL, YOU ARE MY ONLY SOVEREIGN.

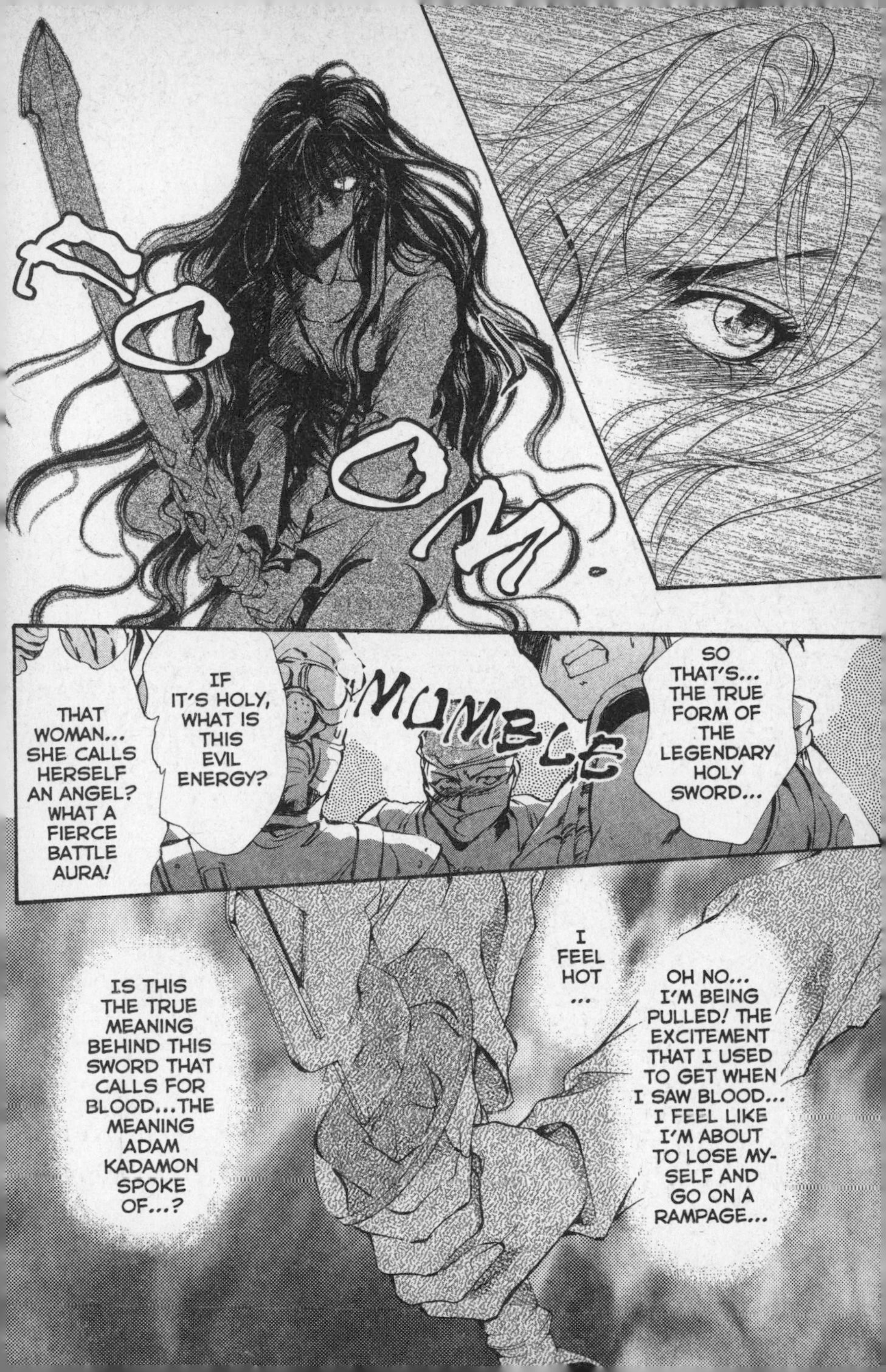
DOOM.
SO THAT'S... THE TRUE FORM OF THE LEGENDARY HOLY SWORD...
MUMBLE
IF IT'S HOLY, WHAT IS THIS EVIL ENERGY?
THAT WOMAN... SHE CALLS HERSELF AN ANGEL? WHAT A FIERCE BATTLE AURA!
OH NO... I'M BEING PULLED! THE EXCITEMENT THAT I USED TO GET WHEN I SAW BLOOD... I FEEL LIKE I'M ABOUT TO LOSE MY-SELF AND GO ON A RAMPAGE...
I FEEL HOT ...
IS THIS THE TRUE MEANING BEHIND THIS SWORD THAT CALLS FOR BLOOD...THE MEANING ADAM KADAMON SPOKE OF...?

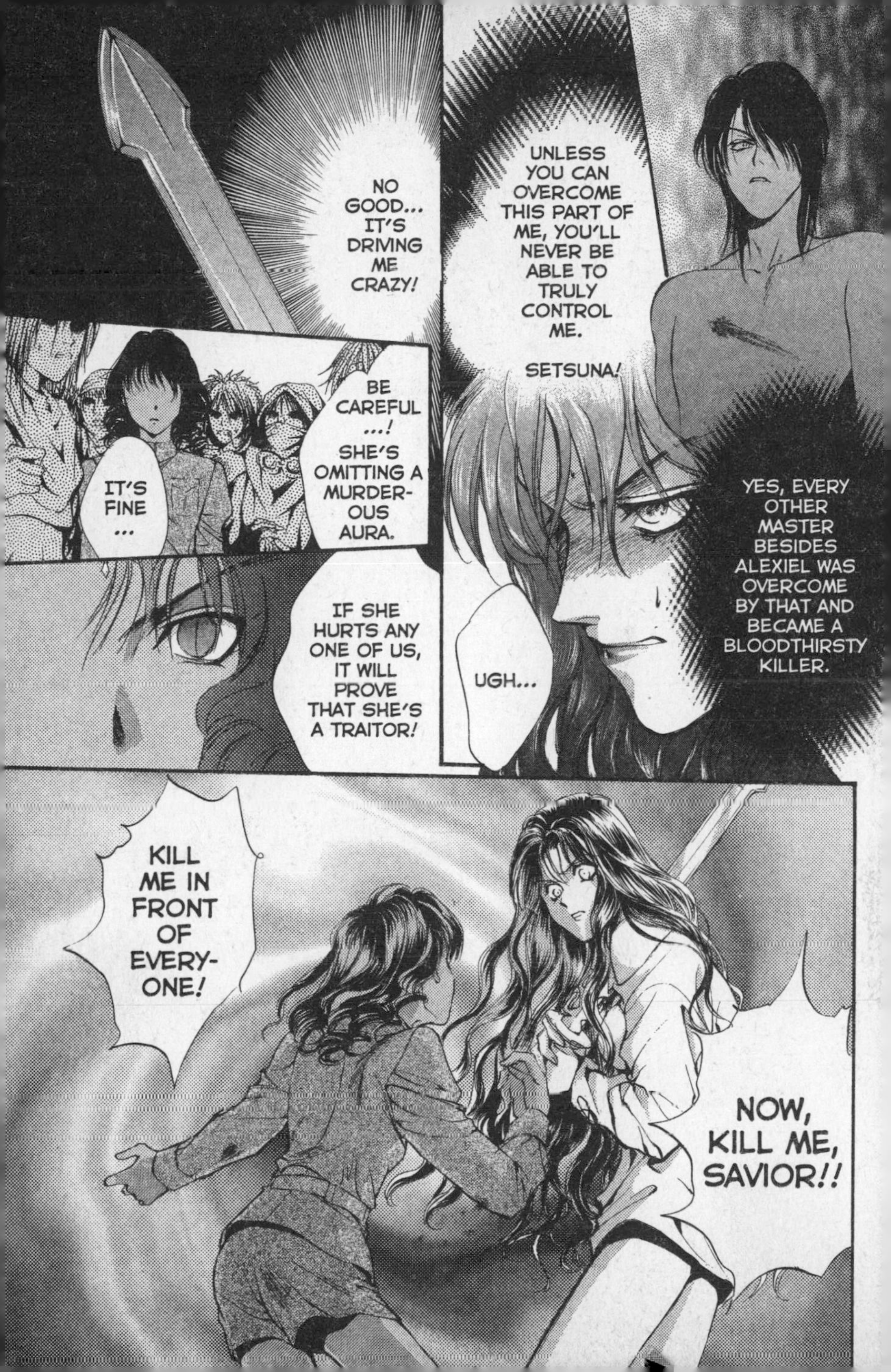
UNLESS YOU CAN OVERCOME THIS PART OF ME, YOU'LL NEVER BE ABLE TO TRULY CONTROL ME.
SETSUNA!
YES, EVERY OTHER MASTER BESIDES ALEXIEL WAS OVERCOME BY THAT AND BECAME A BLOODTHIRSTY KILLER.
UGH...
NO GOOD... IT'S DRIVING ME CRAZY!
BE CAREFUL ...! SHE'S OMITTING A MURDER-OUS AURA.
IT'S FINE ...
IF SHE HURTS ANY ONE OF US, IT WILL PROVE THAT SHE'S A TRAITOR!
KILL ME IN FRONT OF EVERY-ONE!
NOW, KILL ME, SAVIOR!!

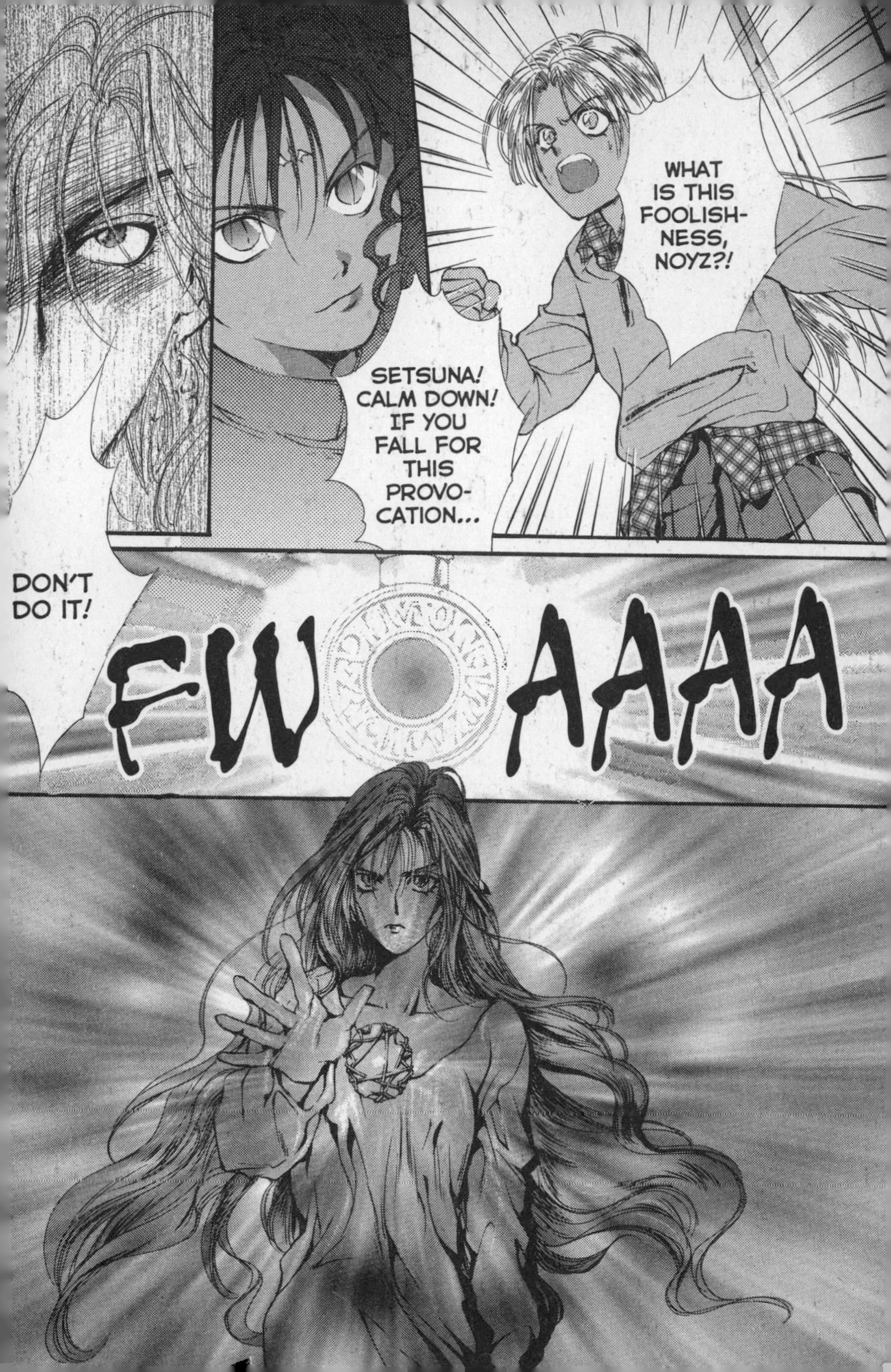
WHAT IS THIS FOOLISHNESS, NOYZ?!
SETSUNA! CALM DOWN! IF YOU FALL FOR THIS PROVOCATION...
DON'T DO IT!
FW AAAA

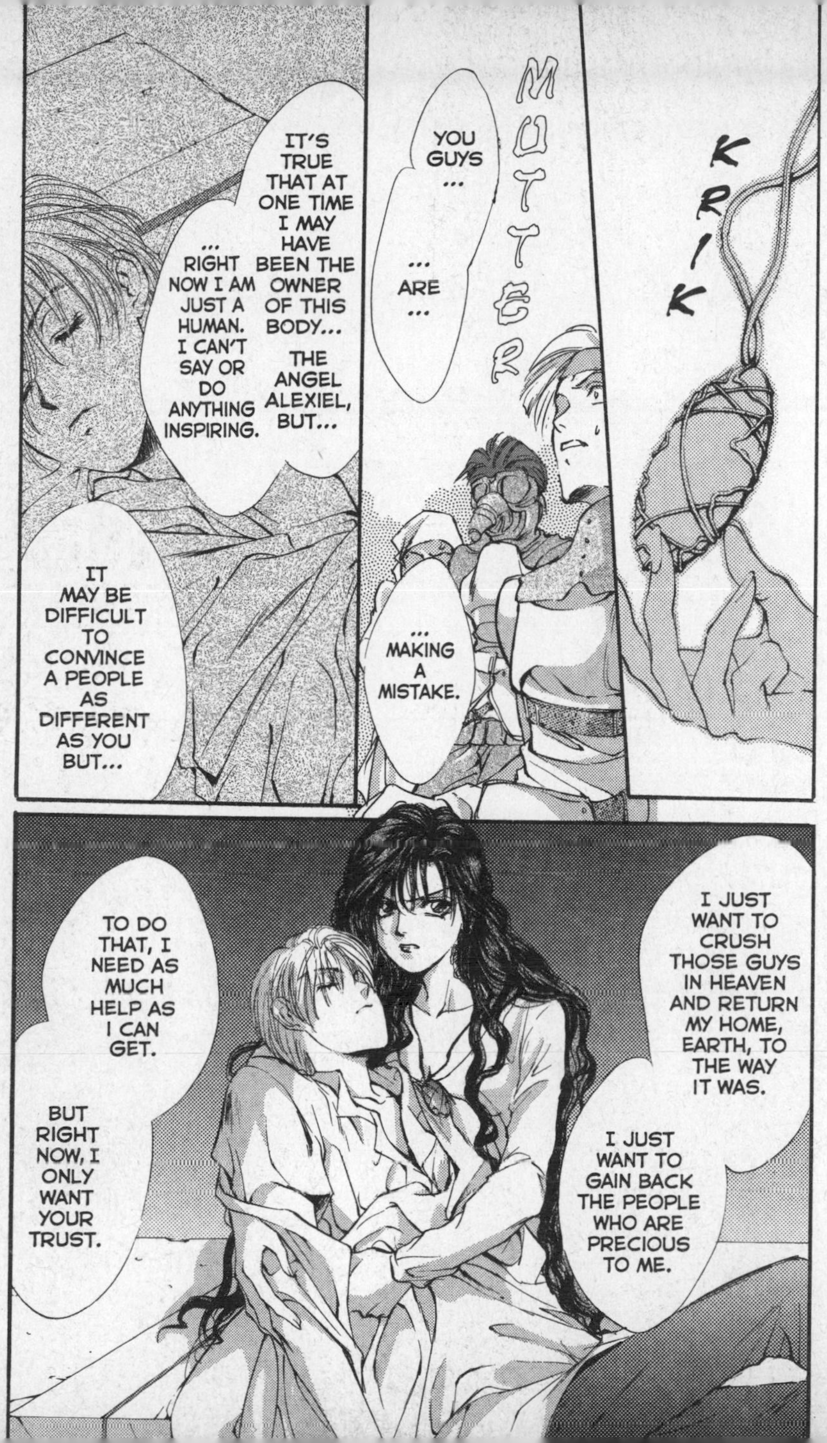
KRIK
MUTTER
YOU GUYS ...
... ARE ...
... MAKING A MISTAKE.
IT'S TRUE THAT AT ONE TIME I MAY HAVE BEEN THE OWNER OF THIS BODY... THE ANGEL ALEXIEL, BUT...
... RIGHT NOW I AM JUST A HUMAN. I CAN'T SAY OR DO ANYTHING INSPIRING.
IT MAY BE DIFFICULT TO CONVINCE A PEOPLE AS DIFFERENT AS YOU BUT...
I JUST WANT TO CRUSH THOSE GUYS IN HEAVEN AND RETURN MY HOME, EARTH, TO THE WAY IT WAS.
I JUST WANT TO GAIN BACK THE PEOPLE WHO ARE PRECIOUS TO ME.
TO DO THAT, I NEED AS MUCH HELP AS I CAN GET.
BUT RIGHT NOW, I ONLY WANT YOUR TRUST.

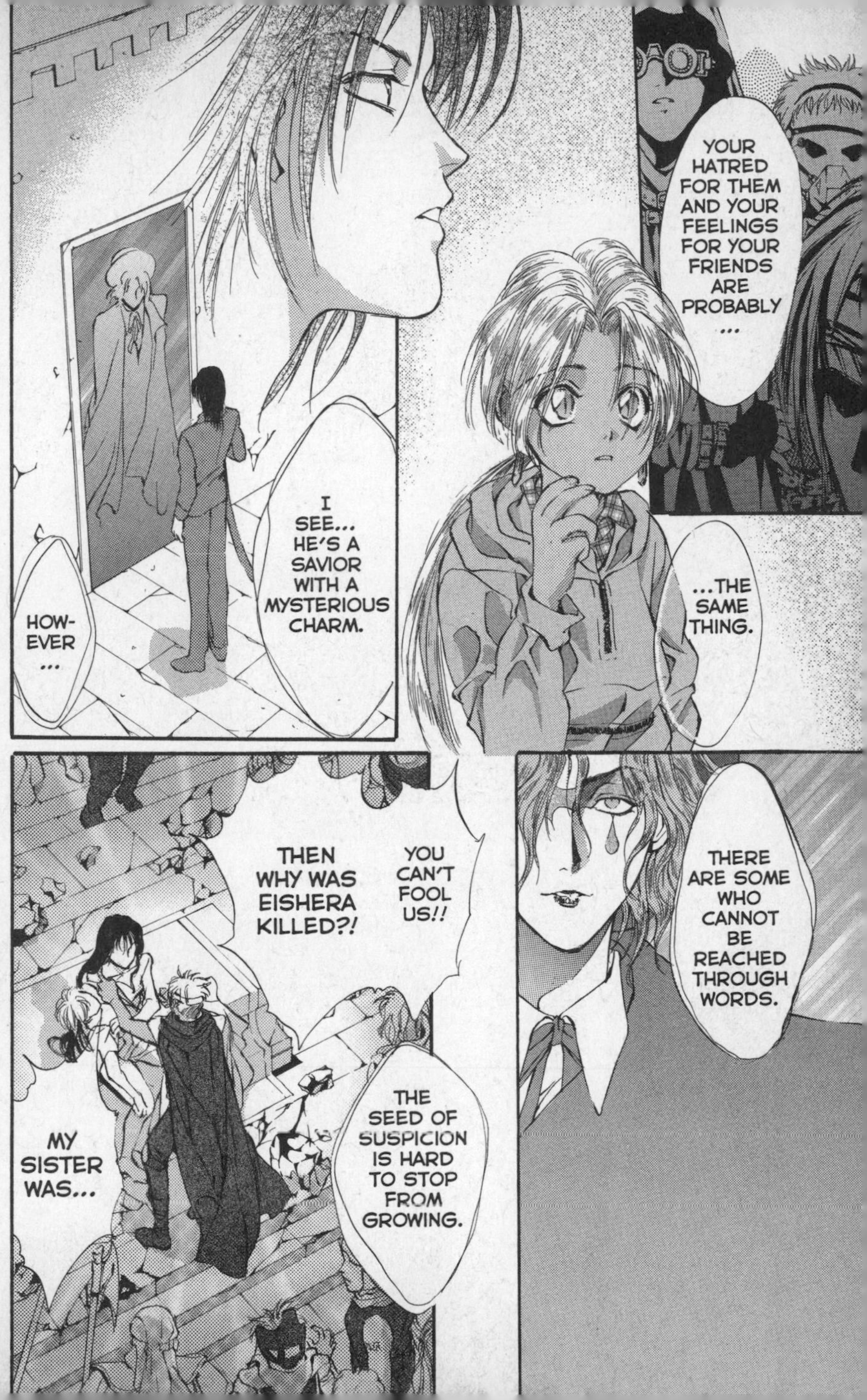
YOUR HATRED FOR THEM AND YOUR FEELINGS FOR YOUR FRIENDS ARE PROBABLY ...
...THE SAME THING.
I SEE... HE'S A SAVIOR WITH A MYSTERIOUS CHARM.
HOW-EVER ...
THERE ARE SOME WHO CANNOT BE REACHED THROUGH WORDS.
YOU CAN'T FOOL US!!
THEN WHY WAS EISHERA KILLED?!
THE SEED OF SUSPICION IS HARD TO STOP FROM GROWING.
MY SISTER WAS...

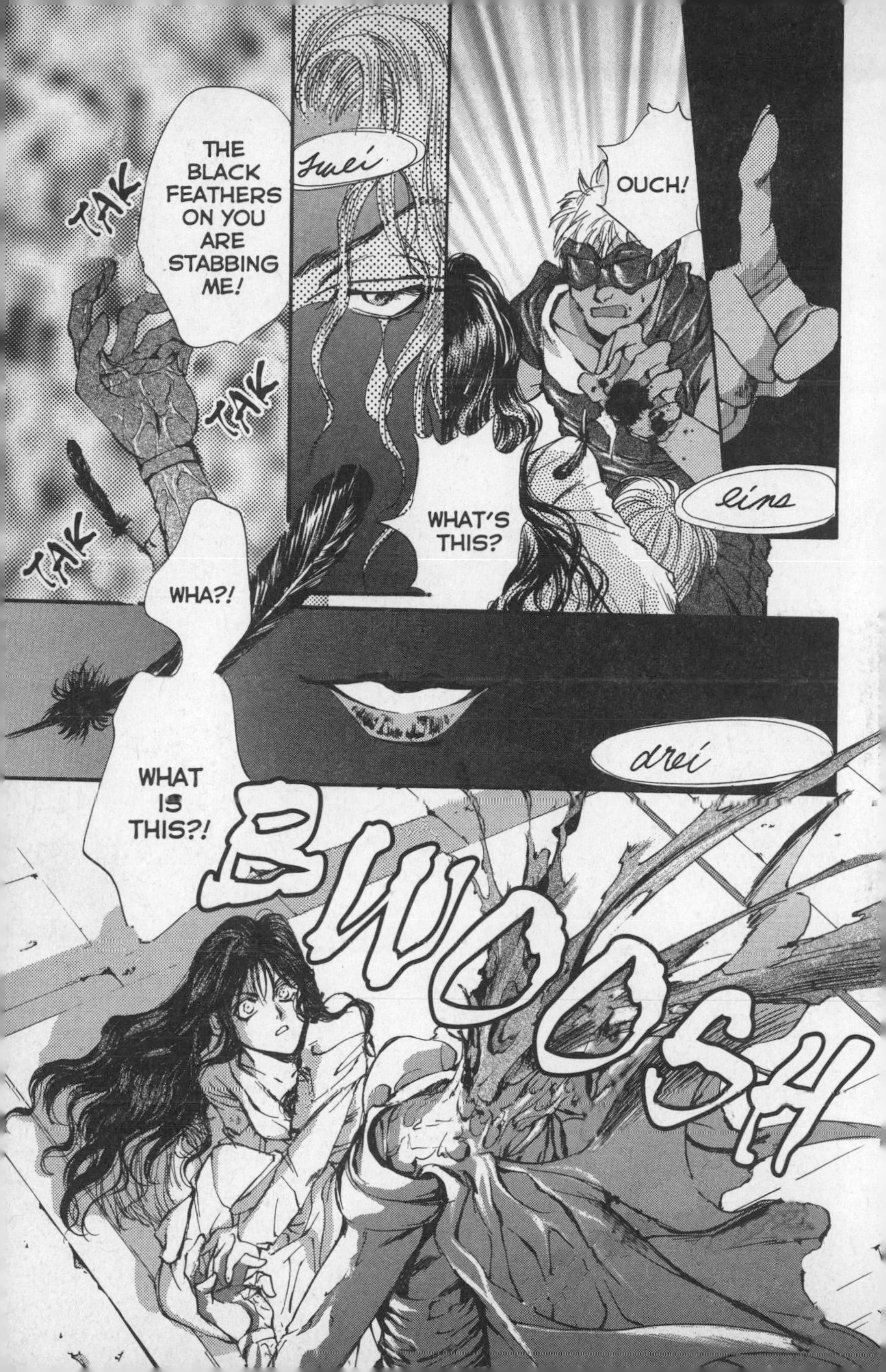
OUCH!
WHAT'S THIS?
eins
zwei
THE BLACK FEATHERS ON YOU ARE STABBING ME!
TAK
TAK
TAK
WHA?!
drei
WHAT IS THIS?!
BWOOSH

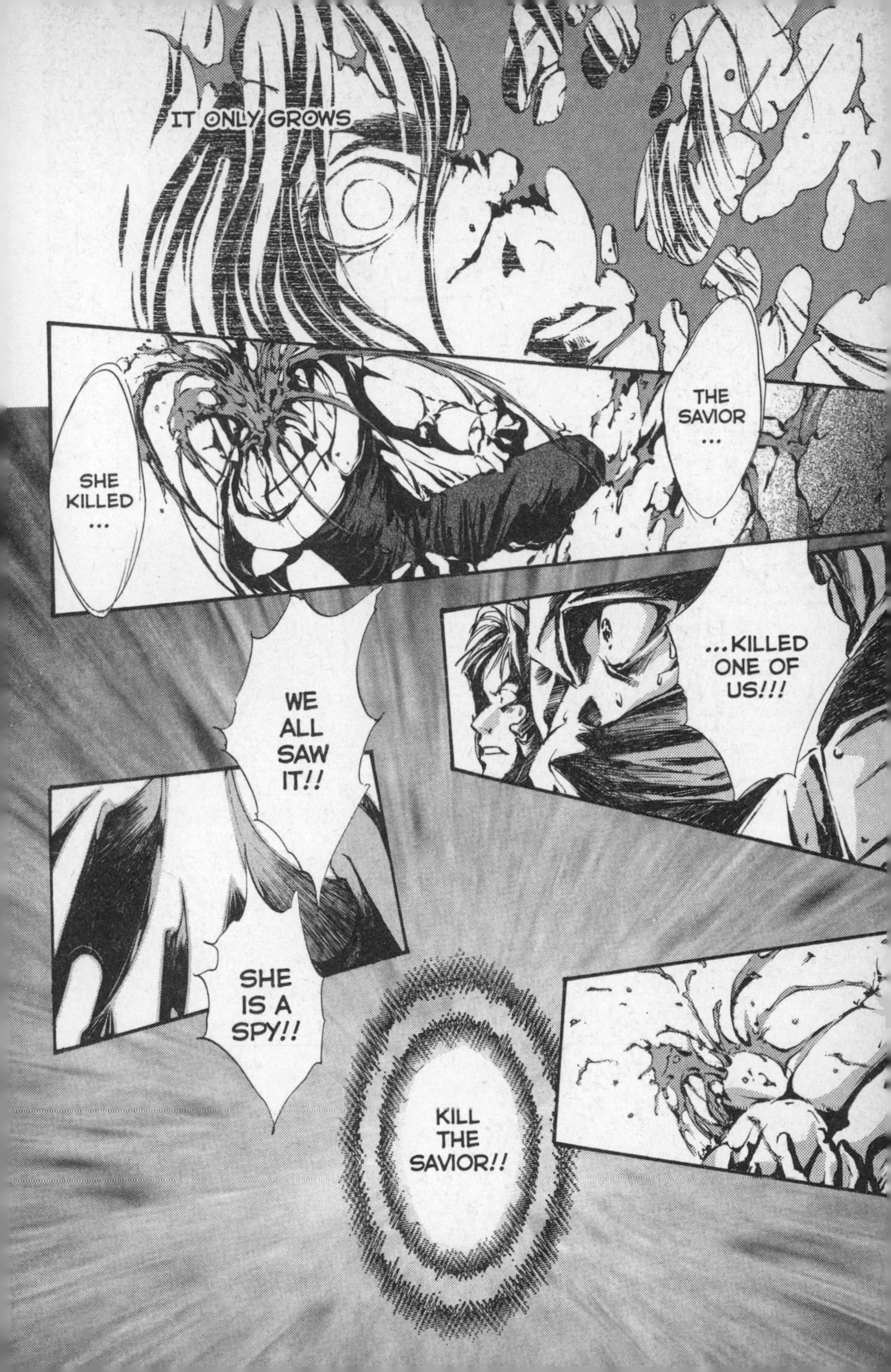
IT ONLY GROWS
THE SAVIOR ...
SHE KILLED ...
...KILLED ONE OF US!!!
WE ALL SAW IT!!
SHE IS A SPY!!
KILL THE SAVIOR!!

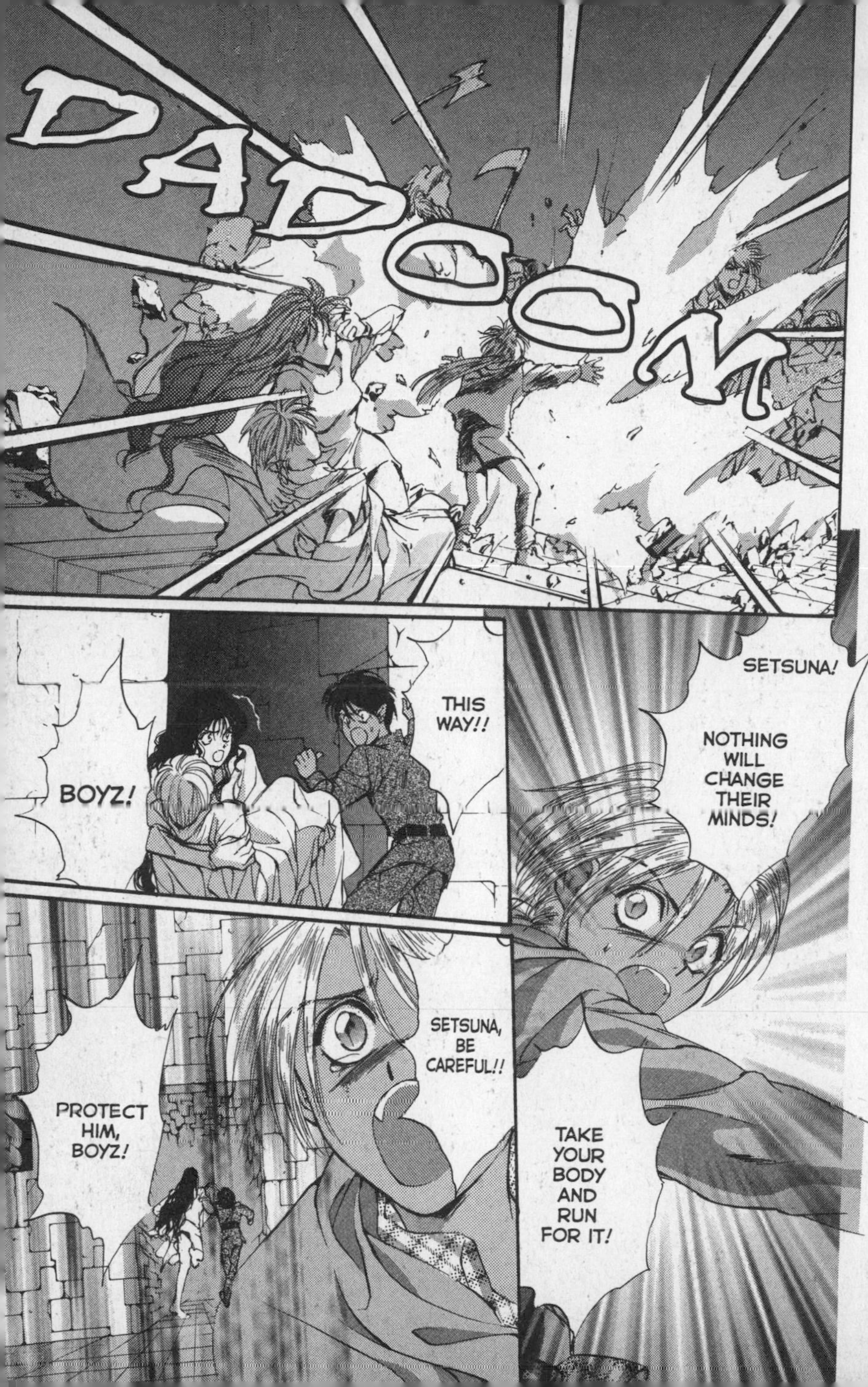
DADOOM
SETSUNA!
NOTHING WILL CHANGE THEIR MINDS!
TAKE YOUR BODY AND RUN FOR IT!
THIS WAY!!
BOYZ!
SETSUNA, BE CAREFUL!!
PROTECT HIM, BOYZ!

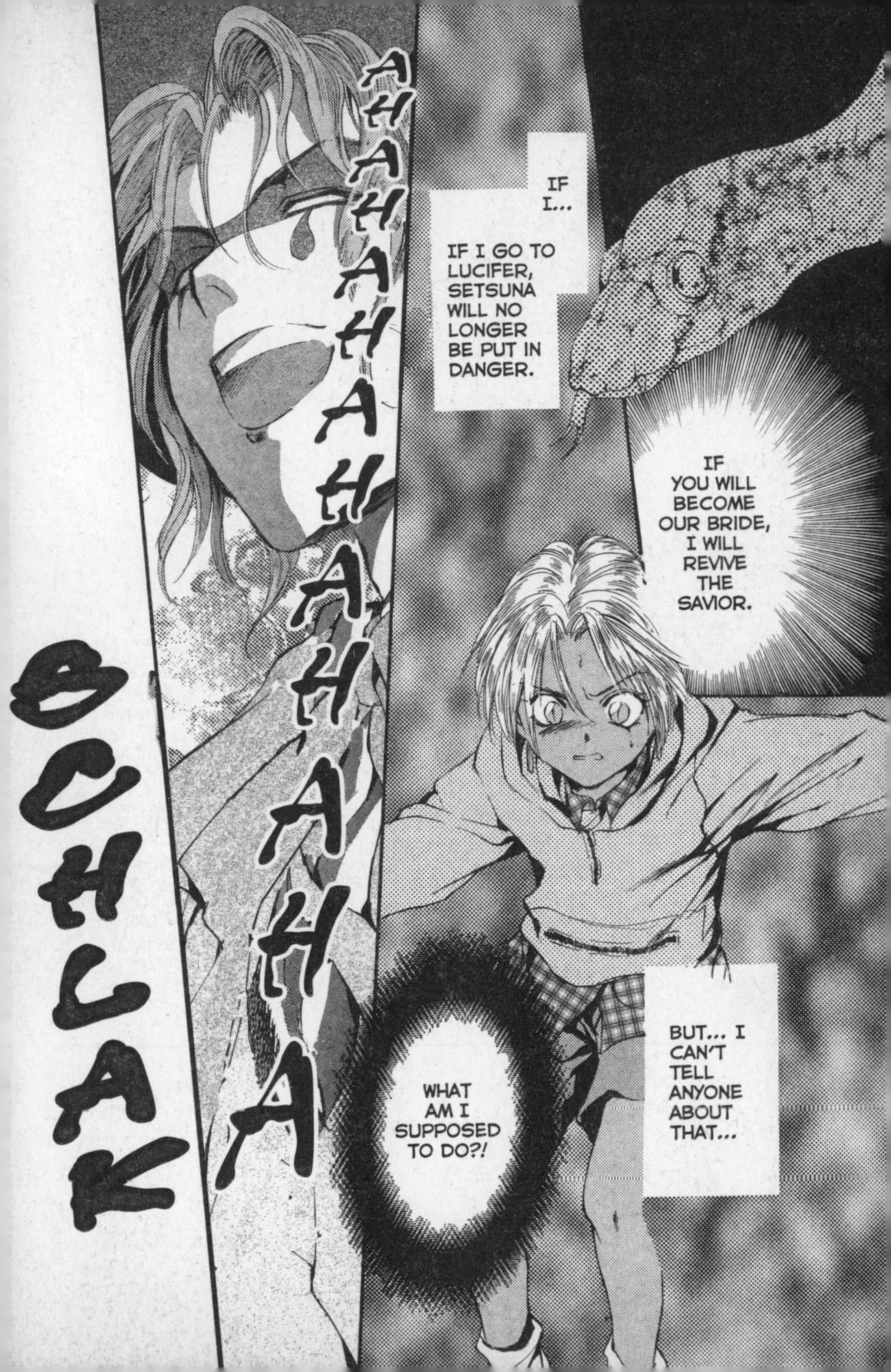
IF I...
IF I GO TO LUCIFER, SETSUNA WILL NO LONGER BE PUT IN DANGER.
IF YOU WILL BECOME OUR BRIDE, I WILL REVIVE THE SAVIOR.
BUT... I CAN'T TELL ANYONE ABOUT THAT...
WHAT AM I SUPPOSED TO DO?!
AHAHAHAHAHAHAHAHA
BCHLAK

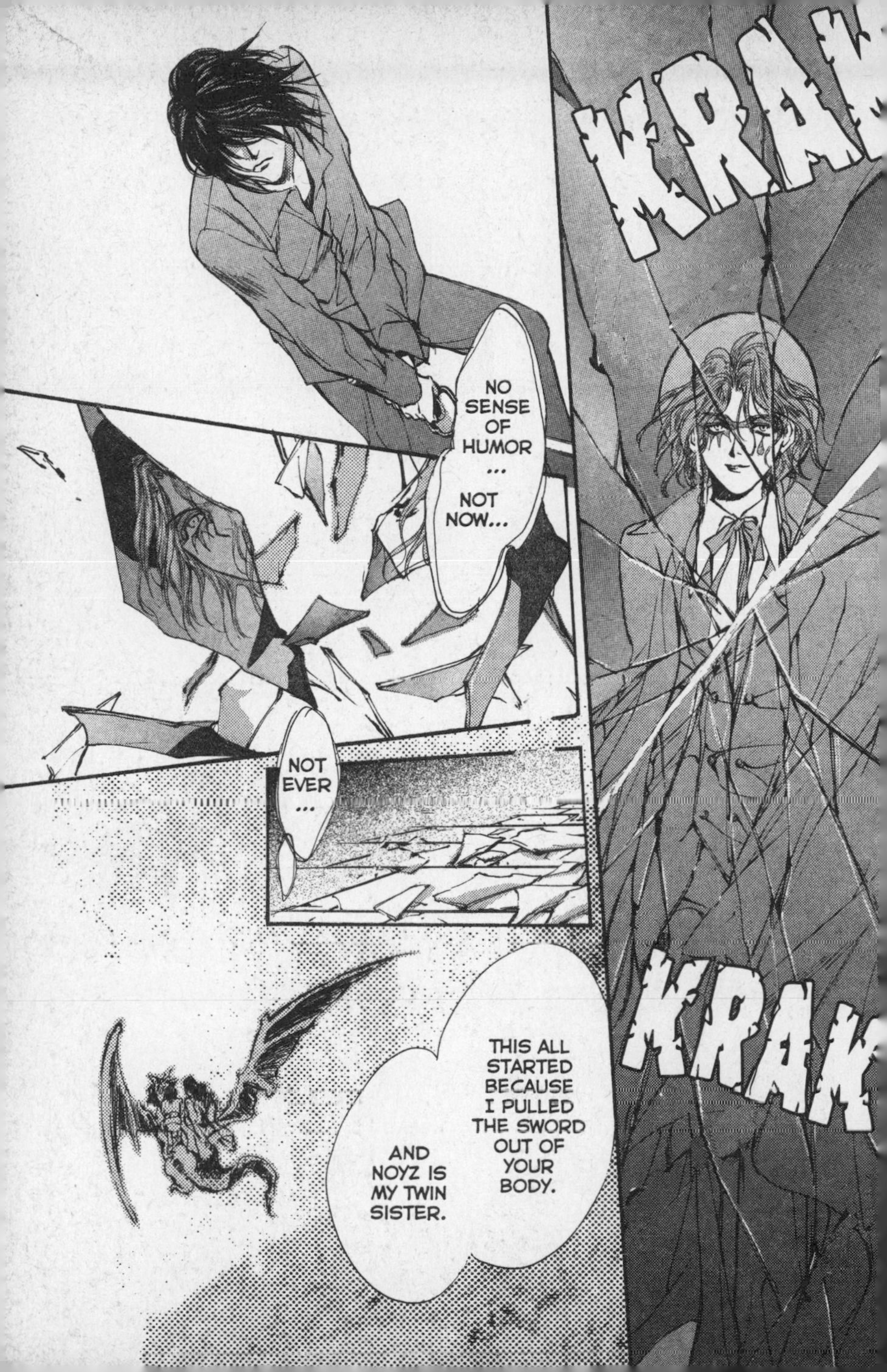
KRAK
KRAK
NO SENSE OF HUMOR ... NOT NOW...
NOT EVER ...
THIS ALL STARTED BECAUSE I PULLED THE SWORD OUT OF YOUR BODY.
AND NOYZ IS MY TWIN SISTER.

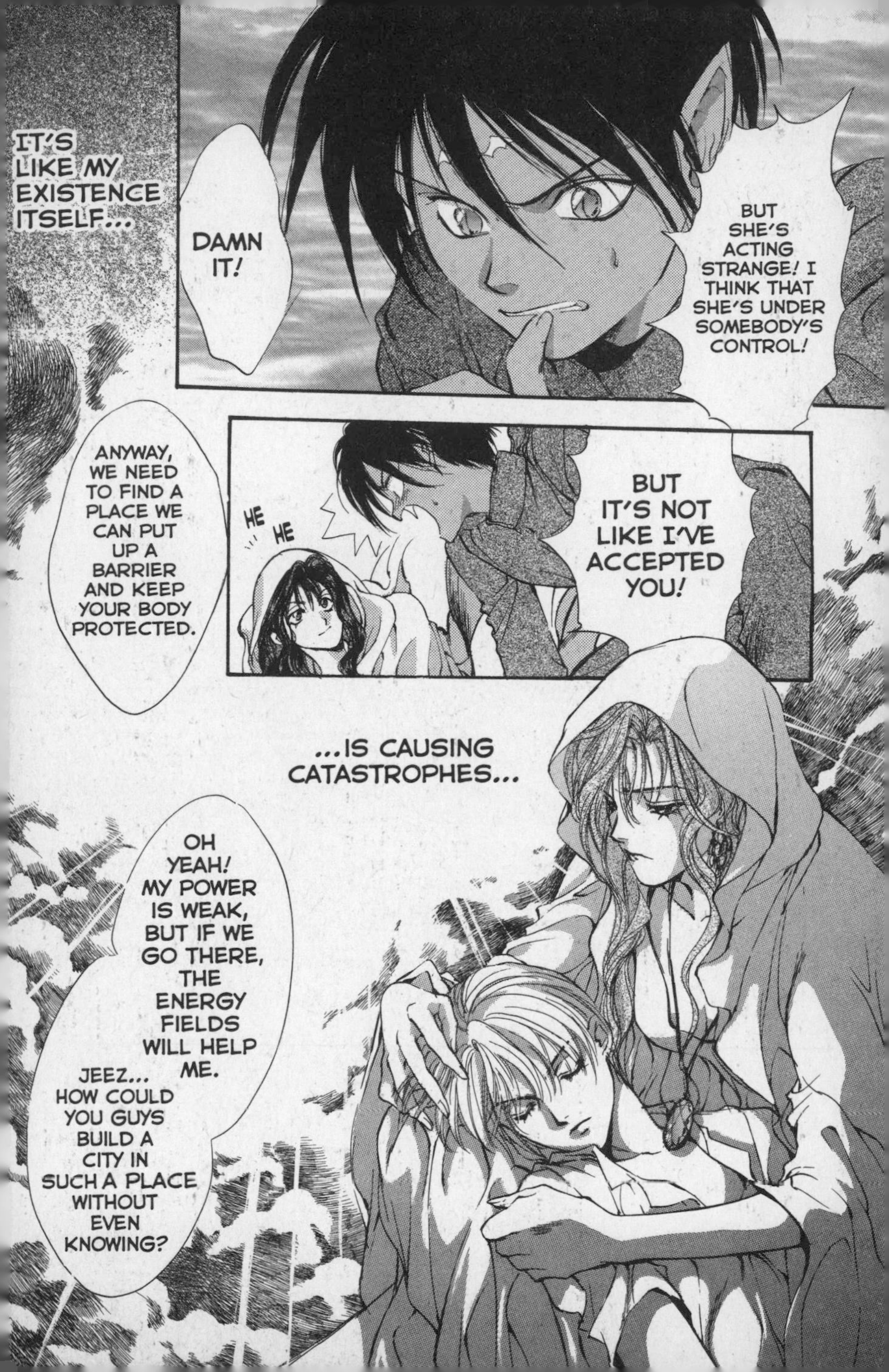
BUT SHE'S ACTING STRANGE! I THINK THAT SHE'S UNDER SOMEBODY'S CONTROL!
DAMN IT!
IT'S LIKE MY EXISTENCE ITSELF...
BUT IT'S NOT LIKE I'VE ACCEPTED YOU!
HE HE
ANYWAY, WE NEED TO FIND A PLACE WE CAN PUT UP A BARRIER AND KEEP YOUR BODY PROTECTED.
...IS CAUSING CATASTROPHES...
OH YEAH! MY POWER IS WEAK, BUT IF WE GO THERE, THE ENERGY FIELDS WILL HELP ME.
JEEZ... HOW COULD YOU GUYS BUILD A CITY IN SUCH A PLACE WITHOUT EVEN KNOWING?

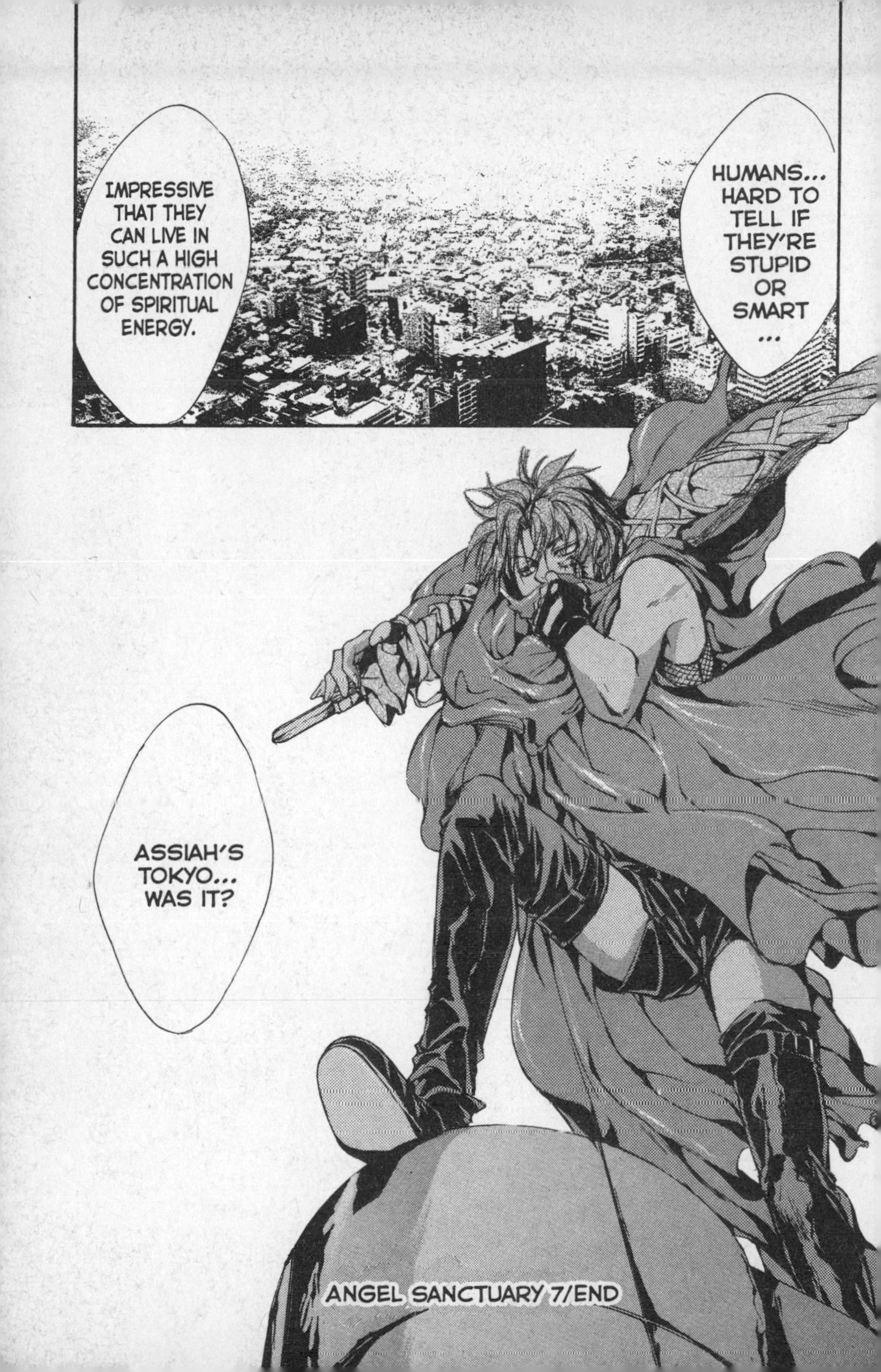
HUMANS... HARD TO TELL IF THEY'RE STUPID OR SMART ...
IMPRESSIVE THAT THEY CAN LIVE IN SUCH A HIGH CONCENTRATION OF SPIRITUAL ENERGY.
ASSIAH'S TOKYO... WAS IT?
ANGEL SANCTUARY 7/END

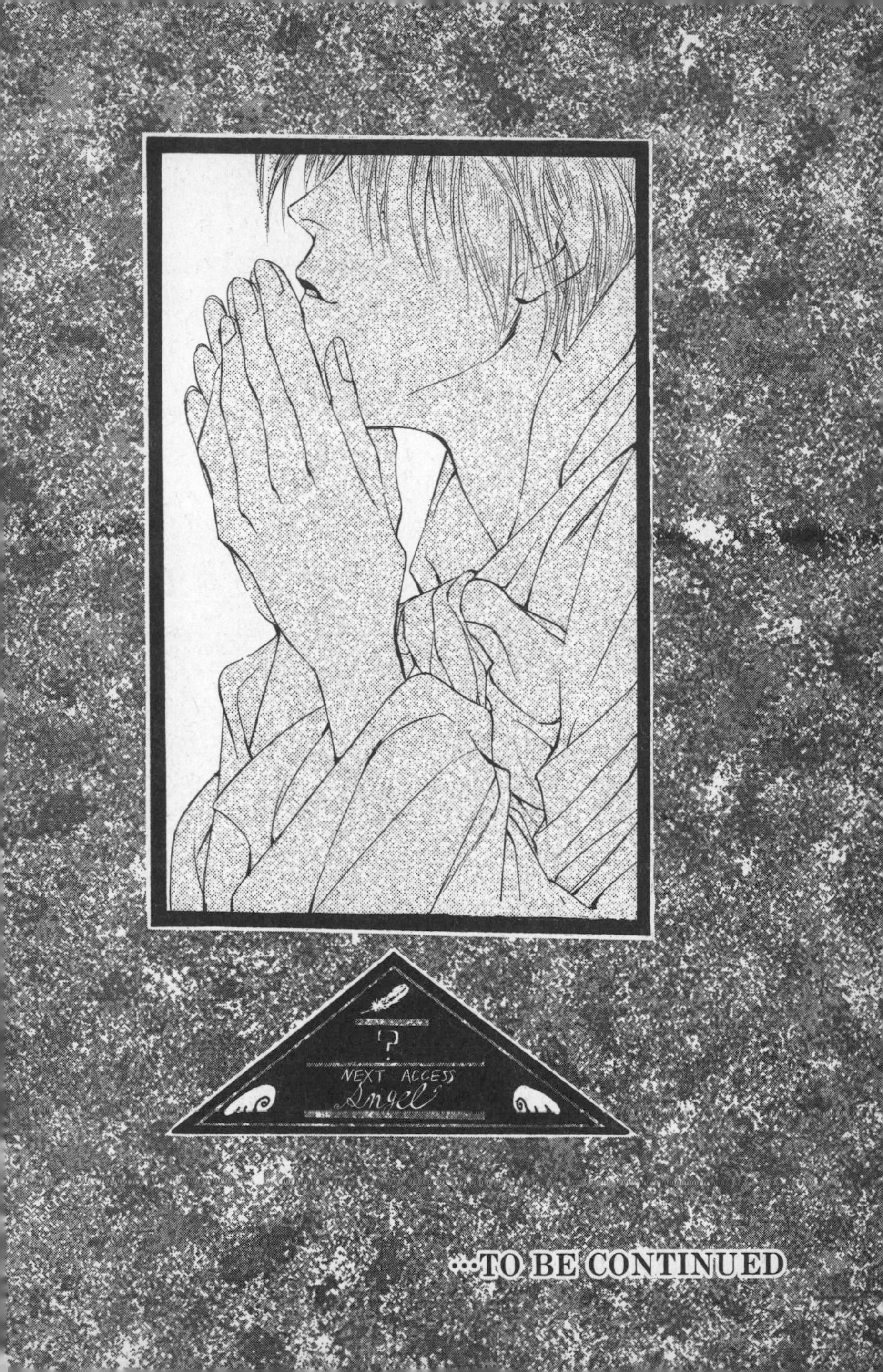
?
NEXT ACCESS
Angel
...TO BE CONTINUED

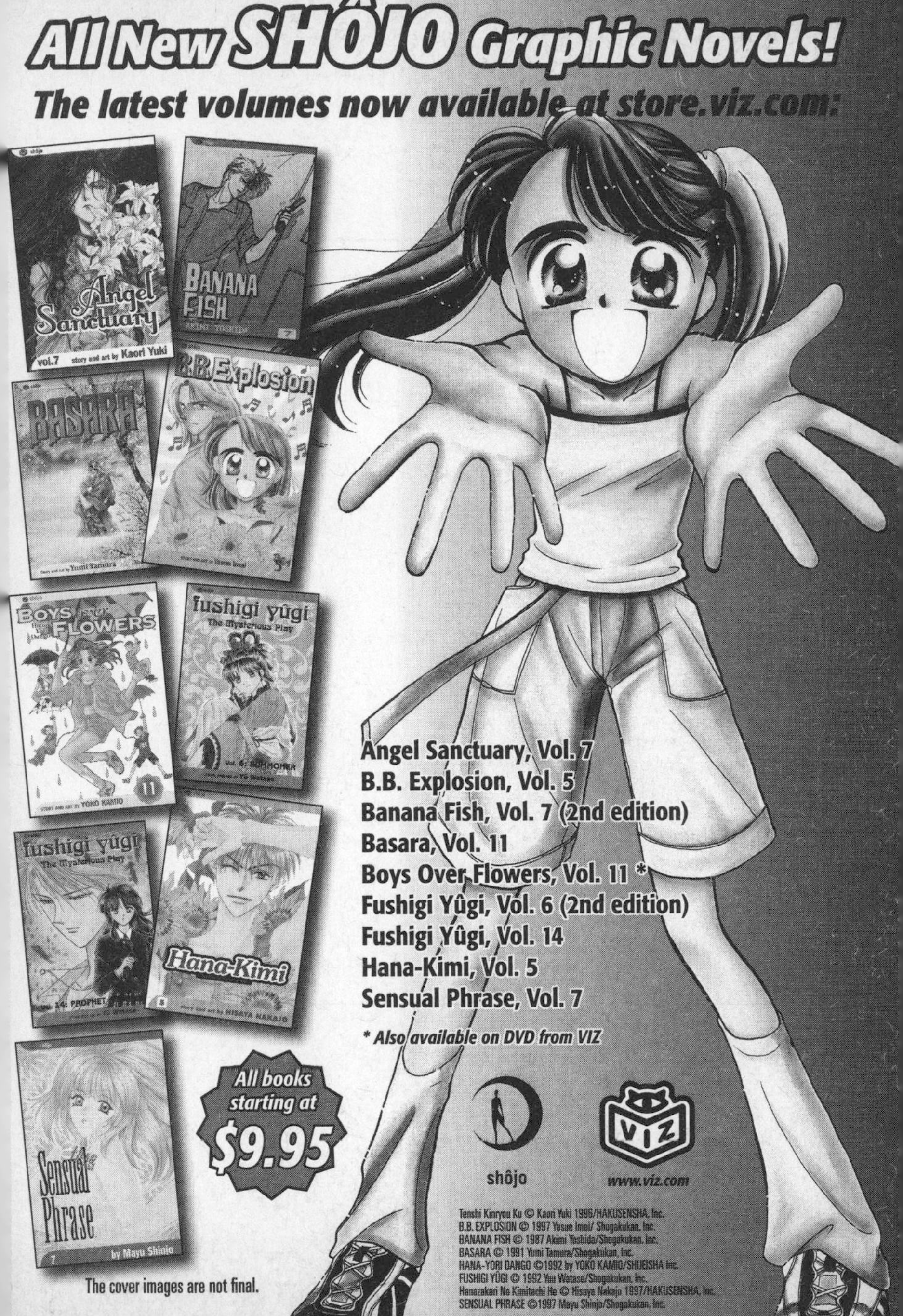
All New SHÔJO Graphic Novels!
The latest volumes now available at store.viz.com:
Angel Sanctuary, Vol. 7
B.B. Explosion, Vol. 5
Banana Fish, Vol. 7 (2nd edition)
Basara, Vol. 11
Boys Over Flowers, Vol. 11 *
Fushigi Yûgi, Vol. 6 (2nd edition)
Fushigi Yûgi, Vol. 14
Hana-Kimi, Vol. 5
Sensual Phrase, Vol. 7
* Also available on DVD from VIZ
All books starting at $9.95
shôjo
www.viz.com
Tenshi Kinryou Ku © Kaori Yuki 1996/HAKUSENSHA, Inc.
B.B. EXPLOSION © 1997 Yasue Imai/ Shogakukan, Inc.
BANANA FISH © 1987 Akimi Yoshida/Shogakukan, Inc.
BASARA © 1991 Yumi Tamura/Shogakukan, Inc.
HANA-YORI DANGO ©1992 by YOKO KAMIO/SHUEISHA Inc.
FUSHIGI YÛGI © 1992 Yuu Watase/Shogakukan, Inc.
Hanazakari No Kimitachi He © Hisaya Nakajo 1997/HAKUSENSHA, Inc.
SENSUAL PHRASE ©1997 Mayu Shinjo/Shogakukan, Inc.
The cover images are not final.

COMPLETE OUR SURVEY AND LET
US KNOW WHAT YOU THINK!

☐ Please do NOT send me information about VIZ products, news and events, special offers, or other information.

☐ Please do NOT send me information from VIZ's trusted business partners.

Name: _____

Address: _____

City: _____ **State:** _____ **Zip:** _____

E-mail: _____

☐ Male ☐ Female **Date of Birth** (mm/dd/yyyy): ___ / ___ / _____ (Under 13? Parental consent required)

What race/ethnicity do you consider yourself? (please check one)

☐ Asian/Pacific Islander ☐ Black/African American ☐ Hispanic/Latino

☐ Native American/Alaskan Native ☐ White/Caucasian ☐ Other: _____

What VIZ product did you purchase? (check all that apply and indicate title purchased)

☐ DVD/VHS _____

☐ Graphic Novel _____

☐ Magazines _____

☐ Merchandise _____

Reason for purchase: (check all that apply)

☐ Special offer ☐ Favorite title ☐ Gift

☐ Recommendation ☐ Other _____

Where did you make your purchase? (please check one)

☐ Comic store ☐ Bookstore ☐ Mass/Grocery Store

☐ Newsstand ☐ Video/Video Game Store ☐ Other: _____

☐ Online (site: _____)

What other VIZ properties have you purchased/own? _____

_____

How many anime and/or manga titles have you purchased in the last year? How many were VIZ titles? (please check one from each column)

ANIME	MANGA	VIZ
☐ None	☐ None	☐ None
☐ 1-4	☐ 1-4	☐ 1-4
☐ 5-10	☐ 5-10	☐ 5-10
☐ 11+	☐ 11+	☐ 11+

I find the pricing of VIZ products to be: (please check one)

☐ Cheap ☐ Reasonable ☐ Expensive

What genre of manga and anime would you like to see from VIZ? (please check two)

☐ Adventure ☐ Comic Strip ☐ Science Fiction ☐ Fighting

☐ Horror ☐ Romance ☐ Fantasy ☐ Sports

What do you think of VIZ's new look?

☐ Love It ☐ It's OK ☐ Hate It ☐ Didn't Notice ☐ No Opinion

Which do you prefer? (please check one)

☐ Reading right-to-left

☐ Reading left-to-right

Which do you prefer? (please check one)

☐ Sound effects in English

☐ Sound effects in Japanese with English captions

☐ Sound effects in Japanese only with a glossary at the back

THANK YOU! Please send the completed form to:

VIZ

NJW Research
42 Catharine St.
Poughkeepsie, NY 12601

All information provided will be used for internal purposes only. We promise not to sell or otherwise divulge your information.